THE RISE OF
THE CREATIVE CLASS,
REVISITED

THE RISE OF THE CREATIVE CLASS,

REVISITED

RICHARD FLORIDA

BASIC BOOKS

A Member of the Perseus Books Group
New York

Published in 2012 by Basic Books,
A Member of the Perseus Books Group

Previous edition published in 2002 by Basic Books

Books published by Basic Books are available at special discounts for bulk purchases in the
United States by corporations, institutions, and other organizations. For more information,
please contact the Special Markets Department at the Perseus Books Group, 2300 Chestnut
Street, Suite 200, Philadelphia, PA 19103, or call (800) 810-4145, ext. 5000, or e-mail
special.markets@perseusbooks.com.

Designed by Pauline Brown

Typeset in 12 point Minion Pro by the Perseus Books Group

Library of Congress Cataloging-in-Publication Data are available for this book.
LCCN 2012936719

ISBN (hardcover): 978-0-465-02993-8

ISBN (e-book): 978-0-465-02995-2

10 9 8 7 6 5 4 3 2 1

CONTENTS

PART FOUR: COMMUNITY

PART FIVE: CONTRADICTIONS

CONCLUSION

PREFACE TO
THE RISE OF THE CREATIVE CLASS, REVISITED

This book was—and is—my attempt to explain the key underlying forces that have been transforming our economy and culture over the past several decades. When I first started writing it in late 1999 and early 2000, I was struck by how much attention was being paid to surface-level changes; I wanted to focus on the long-lasting and truly tectonic forces that were altering the way we work and live. Our world, it seemed to me, was changing as dramatically as it had since the early days of the Industrial Revolution. It wasn't just the Internet, or the rise of new technologies, or even globalization that were upending our jobs, lives, and communities, though all those things were important. Beneath the surface, unnoticed by many, an even deeper force was at work—the rise of creativity as a fundamental economic driver, and the rise of a new social class, the Creative Class.

Spanning science and technology, arts, media, and culture, traditional knowledge workers, and the professions, this new class made up nearly one-third of the workforce across the United States and considerably more than that in many individual communities. The rise of this new class and of creativity as an economic force were the underlying factors powering so many of the seemingly unrelated and epiphenomenal trends we had been witnessing, from the ascent of new industries and businesses, to changes in the way we live and work, extending even into the rhythms, patterns, desires, and expectations that structure our daily lives.

In the decade since this book first appeared, a whole series of world-shattering events occurred—from the collapse of the tech bubble and 9/11, to the economic and financial meltdown of 2008—any one of which might have been sufficient to derail or reverse the trends it described. Instead, they have only become more deeply ensconced. By late 2011, the social media site LinkedIn reported[1] that the word most used by its members to describe themselves was—you guessed it—"creative." As *TechCrunch* put it: "In a time of high unemployment, when traditional skills can be outsourced or automated, creative skills remain highly sought after and highly valuable. We all want to be part of the Creative Class of programmers, designers, and information workers. The term used to mean artists and writers. Today, it means job stability."[2] At a time when the US unemployment rate topped 10 percent, the rate of unemployment for the Creative Class did not even hit 5 percent. The Creative Class has become truly global, numbering between one-third to nearly one-half of the workforce in the advanced nations of North America, Europe, Asia, and around the world.

I could go on. But so many of the things that seemed shockingly new and outlandish when I first wrote about them—and that sent my critics into such a lather—are now seen as the norm. My ideas that the talented were beginning to favor cities over suburbs, that urban centers were challenging suburban industrial park nerdistans as locations for talent and high-tech industry, that older cities were starting to regain some of the ground they'd lost to Sun Belt boomtowns—were widely derided as ludicrous when I first began to write about them. Ten years later, they aren't even controversial.

A decade ago, many critics dismissed as a precious affectation my notion that a vibrant music scene can be a signal that a location has the underlying preconditions associated with technological innovation and economic growth. What possible pertinence, they sniffed, could such rarified matters have for economic development?

I caught a lot of flak for proposing that diversity—an openness to all kinds of people, no matter their gender, race, nationality, sexual orientation, or just plain geekiness—was not a private virtue but an economic necessity. I earned a certain measure of notoriety for suggesting that a visible gay presence in a city can be seen as a leading indicator for rising housing values and high tech. Some were outraged at the very suggestion and accused me of everything from putting the proverbial cart before the horse to trying to undermine the conventional family, even Judeo-Christian civilization as we have come to know it. Popular opinion now favors gay marriage, and a growing body of research notes the connection between diversity, innovation, and economic growth.

Rereading all the pages I wrote back then about the disappearance of dress codes and the advent of flexible hours, the respect for diversity and the meritocratic values that creative people bring to the workplace and society, I find myself wondering what all of the fuss was about. All of those things are taken for granted, they're so much a part of the cultural moment that it's easy to forget how new and daring they once seemed—and how many pundits were ready to stake their reputations on the certainty that they were only passing trends, that after the next dip in the NASDAQ, people would get their suits out of mothballs and return to business as usual.

I was accused of confusing chickens and eggs when I said that the secret to building better, more vibrant locations was not just attracting companies with handouts and tax breaks, but rather building a "people climate" that could attract the diverse human talents that drive true prosperity. I was roundly derided when I critiqued the conventional menu of downtown renewal through stadium complexes and generic retail districts and malls and countered instead that a simpler, less expensive path to revival was to improve neighborhood conditions with smaller investments in everything from parks and bike paths to street-level culture that would make people's everyday lives better, improve the underlying quality of place, and signal a community that is open, energized, and diverse. The conventional wisdom insisted that such "frills and frivolities" come about as *products* of economic development, not that they are a way to spur it. Ten years later, forward-looking communities, large and small alike, are busily reclaiming their disused waterfronts and industrial areas and transforming them into parks and green spaces; at the same time, suburbs are seeking to remake themselves into better, more livable communities by adding transit, shoring up their arts and culture scenes, and developing pedestrian-friendly town centers that are filled with the best features of real cities.

Hand in hand with the revival of cities and the densification of suburbia, the dawning of the Creative Age has ushered in a newfound respect for livability and sustainability. This, too, is part and parcel of the deeper shift. The quest for clean and green is powered by the same underlying ethos that drives the Creative Economy. Where the green agenda is driven by the need to conserve natural assets, the Creative Economy is driven by the logic that seeks to fully harness—and no longer waste—human resources and talent. The old Fordist industrial system was premised on the exploitation of workers and nature. Workers performed the same boring, exhausting tasks until they burned out. The environment was treated as a source for resources that were scoured out of the ground and as a bottomless receptacle for waste. As human capabilities and potential became greater factors of production in the knowledge-based industries that began to emerge in the 1960s, manufacturing also evolved along a parallel continuum, from zero inventory to zero defects and, ultimately, to zero emissions. Waste became the enemy. The creative ethos demands that we cultivate and utilize all of our natural and human resources.

Whereas some have dubbed the very concept of the Creative Class as elitist and accused me of privileging it over other classes, or derided me as a "neo-liberal" with a naively optimistic faith in the power of markets, I assure you that neither is the case. The key thesis of my argument is as simple as it is basic: every human being is creative. That the Creative Class enjoys vast privileges is true, but to acknowledge that fact is not to endorse it. The essential task before us is to unleash the creative energies, talent, and potential of everyone—to build a society that acknowledges and nurtures the creativity of each and every human being. Creativity is truly a limitless resource; it is something we all share. Scientists like to say that they "stand on the shoulders of giants." So do we all. As a species, we build on the collective creativity not just of those in our own time but of those who have come before us. Marx long ago said that what made the proletariat a universal class was the collaborative nature of physical labor. But what sets us apart from all other species is our collective creativity, something that is innate in each of us and shared by every one of us.

From that underlying point of view, it's not just that diversity and inclusion are moral imperatives, which of course they are. They are economic necessities. Creativity *requires* diversity: it is the great leveler, annihilating the social categories we have imposed on ourselves, from gender to race and sexual orientation. This is why the places that are the most open-minded gain the deepest economic advantages. The key is not to limit or reverse the gains that the Creative Class has made but to extend them across the board, to build a more open, more diverse, more inclusive Creative Society that can more fully harness its members'—*all* of its members'—capacities.

Yet as I write these words, all is far from well: the great promise of the Creative Age is not being met.

Just six or so years after the original edition of this book was published, the economy came crashing down. The economic meltdown of 2008 was not just a crisis of Wall Street, of risk-taking by banks, of wanton financial speculation, and of an economy that had been debt-bingeing on housing and consumer goods, though all of those things were implicated. It was a deeper crisis that ran to the roots of the old Fordist order and the very way of life it engendered. At bottom, the crisis signaled the end of the old order and the beginnings of the new. Here's how the Nobel Prize–winning economist Joseph Stiglitz put it in 2011:

> The trauma we're experiencing right now resembles the trauma we experienced 80 years ago, during the Great Depression, and it has been brought on by an analogous set of circumstances. Then, as now, we faced a breakdown of the banking system. But then, as now, the breakdown of the banking system was in part a consequence of deeper problems. Even if we correctly respond to the trauma—the failures of the financial sector— it will take a decade or more to achieve full recovery. Under the best of conditions, we will endure a Long Slump. If we respond incorrectly, as we have been, the Long Slump will last even longer, and the parallel with the Depression will take on a tragic new dimension.[3]

We are in that strange interregnum when the old order has collapsed and the new order is not yet born. As steep as the levies that the economic crisis exacts, as unfairly incommensurate as the returns to mental as compared to physical labor may be, we can't turn back the clock. The old order has failed. Attempts to bail it out, to breathe new life into it or to somehow prop it back up are doomed to history's dustbin. A new global economic order is taking shape, but it is still confined within the brittle carapace of the old, with all of the outmoded, wasteful, oil-dependent, sprawling, unsustainable ways of life that went along with it.

Like other such epochal transformations, this one is fraught with challenges and difficulties, with winners and losers. In fact, it has intensified and magnified the economic, social, cultural, and geographic cleavages that already divide the classes—between nations, across regions, and within our cities and metro areas.

Such large-scale transformations occur across long time scales, at least a decade or more, as the economists Kenneth Rogoff and Carmen Reinhart noted in their book *This Time Is Different: Eight Centuries of Financial Folly*. My assessment is that the crisis we are living through is fully comparable to the Panic and Long Depression of the 1870s and the Great Depression of the 1930s, which took the better part of a generation to fully resolve.[4]

If such economic resets are generational events, building more robust, fully articulated social and economic systems takes even longer. Although many focus on the social compact that emerged after the New Deal and World War II, they forget that it was more than a century in the making—and the product of sustained struggle. It can take on the order of seventy, eighty, even a hundred years before social change catches up to economic change and new and more robust institutions are built to undergird more widely shared prosperity. Viewed in retrospect, history always seems like a more linear process than it really was. We forget the detours and false starts and dead ends—the collapse of the Paris Commune in 1871; how Weimar Germany was upended by Hitler's rise; how Trotsky's revolutionary state devolved to Stalin's gulags.

The rise of a new economic and social order is a double-edged sword. It unleashes incredible energies, pointing the way toward new paths for unprecedented growth and prosperity, but it also causes tremendous hardships and inequality along the way. We are in the midst of a painful and dangerous process, and one that is full of unknowns. We tend to forget what a fraught and dangerous business childbirth is. My hope is that by understanding this new order, we can speed the transformation this time around.

Still, that new order will not simply or automatically assert itself into existence. It will require new institutions, a new social compact, and a new way of life to bring it into being. We must turn our attention from housing starts, automobile sales, energy consumption, and other crass material measures to new measurements that reflect a shared and sustainable prosperity that improves human well-being and happiness and restores meaning and purpose to life. We must shift from a way of life that valorizes consumption, in which we take our identities from the branded characteristics of the goods we purchase, to one that enables us to develop our talents and our individuality, to realize our truest selves through our work and other activities. Our fledgling Creative Economy needs to give way to a fully Creative Society, one that is more just, more equitable, more sustainable, and more prosperous: our economic future depends on it.

This time, perhaps for the first time in human history, economic logic is on our side. Prosperity in the Creative Age turns on human potential. It can only be fully realized when each and every worker is recognized and empowered as a source of creativity—when their talents are nurtured, their passions harnessed, and they are appropriately rewarded for their contributions.

A great stumbling block in the United States has been the huge rise in inequality, the bifurcation of the labor market between higher-skilled, higher-wage Creative Class jobs and lower-skilled, lower-pay Service Class jobs in fields like food preparation, home health care, and retail sales, where more than 60 million Americans work, 45 percent of the labor force. This stark divide in economic prospects has been exacerbated by the demise of so many once high-paying Working Class jobs. The only way forward is to make all jobs creative jobs, infusing service work, manufacturing work, farming, and every other form of human endeavor with creativity and human potential. We forget that manufacturing jobs weren't always good jobs. William Blake dubbed England's factories "satanic mills" and Marx bemoaned the tremendous exploitation of the

Working Class. We made them the good jobs that they became through collective effort and by building new institutions, notably the postwar social compacts that afforded workers better pay and established social safety nets for the less fortunate—efforts that were roundly resisted at the time by entrenched interests.

As these pages will show, the United States (along with a few other nations) is actually an outlier when it comes to inequality. Across most of the advanced nations, greater innovation and creativity tend to go hand in hand with *less* inequality. This book's last chapter will argue that a new social compact—a *Creative Compact*—is needed to turn our Creative Economy into a just and Creative Society, in which prosperity is widely shared.

While driven and molded by economic logic, the key institutions and initiatives of the future will be shaped, as they always have, by human agency. They will be the products of political choices, which turn on political power. And the mobilizing force today—the leading force at the beachhead of social, cultural, and economic change—is the Creative Class. The problem until now, as I noted in the original edition, had been that the Creative Class was lacking in class consciousness. In contrast to the industrial Working Class, which was forged around strong ties and hoarded into factories and dense city neighborhoods, the Creative Class is a highly individualized and even atomized social stratum. Thus far, its members have been content with personal betterment, staying fit, developing themselves, renovating their houses and apartments, questing after new experiences. Although Creative Class people are generally liberal-minded, solidarity has not been their strong suit.

Still, the Creative Class stands at the forefront of what the political scientist Ronald Inglehart has termed the transition to a post-materialist politics—a shift from values that accord priority to meeting immediate material needs to ones that stress belonging, self-expression, opportunity, environmental quality, diversity, community, and quality of life.[5] Although there are certainly divisions within this new class and its members do not fit neatly into the old left–right spectrum, its values are staunchly meritocratic. Many are offended by inequality of opportunity and repelled by a system that is rigged against so many—and that is so wasteful of natural and human resources. These attitudes and inclinations are political veins that can—and are—being tapped.

The protracted economic crisis and outrageous inequality of our time has stirred up some of these dormant political energies, as witnessed by the uprisings across the Arab world in the spring and summer of 2011 and the incredible resonance of the global Occupy Movement. It's ironic to remember how "transgressive" some proponents of the New Economy once considered themselves to be. If their grandiose pronouncements about remaking capitalism were mostly fantasies, the insurrectionary forces that the rise of the Creative Class are unleashing are potentially volcanic. As the distinguished historian Eric Hobsbawm noted, those uprisings have more to do with the Creative Class than they do with traditional Working Class movements. "The traditional left was geared to a kind of society that is no longer in existence or is going out of business," he remarked. "It believed very largely in the mass labour movement as the carrier of the future. Well, we've been de-industrialised, so that's no longer possible. The most effective mass mobilisations today are those which start from a new modernised middle class, and particularly the enormously swollen body of students."[6]

Of course, traditional Working Class movements still have considerable life in them and must be part of any more general movement for social change. But the driving force of change is the Creative Class—artists and cultural creatives, students, professionals. Although these movements have been propelled by the Internet, by Facebook, Twitter, and other forms of social media, it's important to note that they take shape in space—in real physical places—from Tahir Square to Zucotti Park.

In the original edition of this book, I argued that place would continue to become a more central factor in our economy and our identity, and that it would likely supplant the factory and industrial organizations as the rallying point of class struggle, forming the key axis of cleavage and mobilization in our time. What I could not have predicted is how far-flung and synchronous this new age of mobilization would become. Whether these specific movements ultimately succeed or fail is not the real question. The consortia of place, social media, and the Creative Class will be the fulcrums for future social movements that can provide the energy and force needed for economic and social transformation.

Our time, like all periods of great change and transition, is one that is fraught with difficulty, disruption, and challenge. But ultimately, I am optimistic. Not to be overly deterministic, but the basic logic of economic and social progress is on our side. Human creativity is the most spectacularly transformative force ever unleashed, and it is something that all of us can draw on to one degree or another. If the rise of this new order and new social class poses tremendous challenges, it carries the seeds of their resolution as well.

Overview of the Revised Edition

With all this in mind and a ten-year anniversary looming, Basic Books asked me to revisit the original edition of *The Rise of the Creative Class* and bring it up to date. *The Rise of the Creative Class, Revisited* is not a tweak, but a wholesale revision. My team and I went through every chapter thoroughly and rewrote virtually every word. I have pored over the dozens of academic studies we conducted and the three major books I've written over the intervening decade —*The Flight of the Creative Class, Who's Your City?* and *The*

Great Reset—and incorporated their most important insights. I've added citations to countless colleagues whose work complements mine, and I've sought to answer my critics.

With the help of Kevin Stolarick, Charlotta Mellander, and other members of my research team, I have updated all data on the Creative Class and the other classes in Chapter 3, bringing these data forward to 2010 and extending the historical time series back to 1800. Chapter 3 also summarizes a range of new research on the demography of the Creative Class, on specific Creative Class occupations, and other new research that has occurred since the original edition. I have updated all the data on the Creative Class and 3T's of economic development—technology, talent, and tolerance—for all US metros. This material is found in Chapters 11 and 12, which also report a whole range of findings from new empirical studies.

All of the original chapters have been revised and updated, and several have been combined. The original edition's Chapters 2 and 3—The Creative Ethos and The Creative Economy—have been combined into a single Chapter 2; and the original edition's Chapters 7 and 8—The No-Collar Workplace and Managing Creativity— have also been combined into a single chapter, titled simply No-Collar. Several other chapters have new titles.

Five chapters are completely new. Chapter 13, Global Reach, summarizes my own and others' research on the spread of the Creative Class around the world. It provides data on the Creative Class and the 3T's for eighty-two nations and examines the global effects of the Creative Class on innovation, economic competitiveness, inequality, and happiness. The experience of nations, notably those in Scandinavia and Northern Europe, that combine high levels of the Creative Class with low levels of inequality show that a high-road path to prosperity is indeed possible. Chapter 14 draws on a major survey I undertook with Gallup, as well as other qualitative information from case studies and ethnographic research, to deepen our understanding of the key features and factors that shape "quality of place."

I devote two new chapters to the persistent and deepening economic, social, and geographic divides that continue to vex our society. Chapter 16 examines The Geography of Inequality across US cities and metros, clarifying the roles technology, class, race, and poverty play in shaping it. Chapter 17, The Inclining Significance of Class, shows that despite predictions of a more fluid and classless society, class continues to constitute an undeniably powerful force, shaping everything from our economic opportunities and political choices to our health, fitness, and happiness.

Chapter 18, which concludes this book, is new as well. I title it Every Single Human Being Is Creative to signal the fundamental importance I place on this core construct. It argues that new institutions are required to rebuild our economy and society, outlining six key principles of a new social compact for our time. If the logic of economic development—which seeks out creativity in its many and varied forms—is on our side, the ongoing social and political mobilization of the Creative Class and other segments of society provides the pragmatic impetus for it.

When all is said and done, a new era of broadly shared prosperity turns on stoking the creative furnaces that lies deep within each and every one of us. Only when we unleash that great reservoir of overlooked and underutilized human potential, will we truly enjoy not just sustained economic progress but a better, more meaningful, and more fulfilling way of life.

PREFACE TO
THE ORIGINAL EDITION

This book describes the emergence of a new social class. If you are a scientist or engineer, an architect or designer, a writer, artist, or musician, or if your creativity is a key factor in your work in business, education, health care, law, or some other profession, you are a member. With 38 million members, more than 30 percent of the nation's workforce, the Creative Class has shaped and will continue to shape deep and profound shifts in the ways we work, in our values and desires, and in the very fabric of our everyday lives.

As with other classes, the defining basis of this new class is economic. Just as the feudal aristocracy derived its power and identity from its hereditary control of land and people, and the bourgeoisie from its members' roles as merchants and factory owners, the Creative Class derives its identity from its members' roles as purveyors of creativity. Because creativity is the driving force of economic growth, the Creative Class has become the dominant class in society in terms of its influence. Only by understanding the rise of this new class and its values can we begin to understand the sweeping and seemingly disjointed changes in our society and begin to shape our future more intelligently.

Like most books, this one did not spring to life fully formed. Rather, my ideas evolved gradually from things I saw and heard that seemed to be at odds with conventional wisdom. In my work on regional economic development, I try to identify the factors that make some cities and regions grow and prosper, while others lag behind. One of the oldest pieces of conventional wisdom in this field says the key to economic growth is attracting and retaining companies—the bigger the company, the better—because companies create jobs and people go where the jobs are. During the 1980s and 1990s, many cities in the United States and around the world tried to turn themselves into the next "Silicon Somewhere" by building high-tech office parks or starting up venture capital funds. The game plan was to nourish high-tech start-up companies or, in its cruder variants, to lure them from other cities. But it quickly became clear that this wasn't working.

I saw this firsthand in the mid-1990s with Lycos, a Carnegie Mellon spin-off company. Lycos's Internet search technology was developed in Pittsburgh. But the company eventually moved its operations to Boston to gain access to a deep pool of skilled managers, technologists, and businesspeople. These departures were happening repeatedly, in Pittsburgh and elsewhere. All too often the technologies, the companies, and even the venture capital dollars flowed out of town to places that had bigger and better stocks of talented and creative people. In a curious reversal, instead of people moving to jobs, I was finding that companies were moving to or forming in places that had the skilled *people*.

Why was this happening? This was the basic puzzle that ultimately led to this book. Frustrated by the limits of the conventional wisdom and even more by how economic development was actually being practiced, I began asking people how they chose where to live and work. It quickly became clear to me that people were not slavishly following jobs to places. Their location choices were based to a large degree on their lifestyle interests and these, I found, went well beyond the standard quality-of-life amenities that most experts thought were important.

Then came the real stunner. In 1998 I met Gary Gates, then a doctoral student at Carnegie Mellon. While I had been studying the location decisions of high-tech industries and talented people, Gates had been exploring the location patterns of gay people. My list of the country's high-tech hotspots looked an awful lot like his list of the places with the highest concentrations of gay people. When we compared the two lists with greater statistical rigor, his Gay Index turned out to correlate very strongly with my measures of high-tech growth. Other measures I came up with, like the Bohemian Index—a measure of the density of artists, writers, and performers in a region—produced similar results. My conclusion was that rather than being driven exclusively by companies, economic growth was occurring in places that were tolerant, diverse, and open to creativity—because these were places where creative people of *all* types wanted to live. While some in academe were taken aback by my findings, I was amazed by how quickly city and regional leaders began to use my measures and indicators to shape their development strategies.

As I delved more deeply into the research, I came to realize that something even bigger was going on. Though most experts continued to point to technology as the driving force of broad social change, I became convinced that the truly fundamental changes of our time had to do with subtler alterations in the way we live and work—gradually accumulating shifts in our workplaces, leisure activities, communities, and everyday lives. Everything from the kinds of lifestyles we seek to the ways in which we schedule our time and relate to others was changing. And yes, there was a common thread: the role of creativity as the fundamental source of economic growth and the rise of the new Creative Class.

Despite the giddy economic euphoria so prevalent in the late 1990s, it became increasingly evident to me that the emerging Creative Economy was a dynamic and turbulent system—exciting and liberating in some ways, divisive and stressful in others. My thinking was reinforced by earth-shaking events that occurred while I was writing this book. First came the bursting of the stock-market bubble, the rapid fall of technology stocks, and the subsequent recession of 2000. This put an end to the naive optimism of the so-called New Economy and to the always unfounded notion that new technology is a magic elixir that will make us rich, eliminate our economic problems, and cure pressing social ills. The NASDAQ's plummet was an early signal that it was time for people to get serious.

Then came the tragic events of September 11, 2001. For me and for many others, the stunning attack on the United States was a potent wake-up call. In addition to showing us how vulnerable we are, it brought home the message that too many of us, particularly the members of the Creative Class, had been living in a world of our own concerns—selfishly pursuing narrow goals with little regard for others or for broader social issues. We had grown complacent, even aimless, but also discontent at having become so.

Here I found myself confronting a great paradox. Even as I was chronicling their rise and impact, it struck me that the members of the Creative Class do not see themselves as a *class*—a coherent group of people with common traits and concerns. Emerging classes in previous times of great transition had pulled together to forge new social mechanisms and steer their societies. But not this group. We thus find ourselves in the puzzling situation of having the dominant class in America—whose members occupy the power centers of industry, media, and government, as well as the arts and popular culture—virtually unaware of its own existence and thus unable to consciously influence the course of the society it largely leads.

The Creative Class has the power, talent, and numbers to play a big role in reshaping our world. Its members—in fact, all of society— now have the opportunity to turn their introspection and soul searching into real energy for broader renewal and transformation. History shows that enduring social change occurs not during economic boom times, like the 1920s or 1990s, but in periods of crisis and questioning such as the 1930s—and today. The task before us is to build new forms of social cohesion appropriate to the new Creative Age—the old forms don't work, because they no longer fit the people we've become—and from there, to pursue a collective vision of a better and more prosperous future for all.

This is easier said than done. To build true social cohesion, the members of the Creative Class will need to offer those in other classes a tangible vision of ways to improve their own lives, either by becoming part of the Creative Economy or, at the very least, by reaping some of its rewards. If the Creative Class does not commit itself to this effort, the growing social and economic divides in our society will only worsen, and I fear that we will find ourselves living perpetually uneasy lives at the top of an unhappy heap.

It's time for the Creative Class to grow up and take responsibility. But first, we must understand who we are.

INTRODUCTION

CHAPTER 1

The Transformation of Everyday Life

Something's happening here but you
don't know what it is, do you, Mr. Jones?
—*Bob Dylan*

Here's a thought experiment. Take a typical man on the street from the year 1900 and drop him into the 1950s. Then take someone from the 1950s and move him Austin Powers–style into the present day. Who would experience the greater change?

At first glance the answer seems obvious. Thrust forward into the 1950s, a person from the turn of the twentieth century would be awestruck by a world filled with baffling technological wonders. In place of horse-drawn carriages, he would see streets and highways jammed with cars, trucks, and buses. In the cities, immense skyscrapers would line the horizon, and mammoth bridges would span rivers and inlets where once only ferries could cross. Flying machines would soar overhead, carrying people across continents and oceans in a matter of hours rather than days or weeks. At home, our 1900-to-1950s time-traveler would grope his way through a strange new environment filled with appliances powered by electricity: radios and televisions emanating musical sounds and moving images, refrigerators to keep things cold, washing machines to clean his clothes automatically, and much more. A massive new supermarket would replace daily trips to foodmongers, offering an array of technologically enhanced foods, such as instant coffee and frozen vegetables that come overcooked and oversauced in a box. Life itself would be dramatically extended. Many once-fatal ailments could be prevented with an injection or cured with a pill. The newness of this time-traveler's physical surroundings—the speed and power of everyday machines—would be profoundly disorienting.

On the other hand, someone from the 1950s would have little trouble navigating the physical landscape of today. Although we like to think that ours is the age of boundless technological wonders, our second time-traveler would find himself in a world not all that different from the one he came from. He would still drive a car to work. If he took the train, it would likely be on the same line leaving from the same station. He could probably board an airplane at the same airport. He might still live in a suburban house, though a bigger one. Television would have more channels, color pictures, and bigger, flatter screens, but it would basically be the same, and he could still catch some of his favorite 1950s shows on reruns. He would know how, or quickly learn how, to operate most household appliances—even the personal computer, with its familiar QWERTY keyboard. In fact with just a few exceptions, such as the Internet, CD and DVD players, the cash machine, and wireless phones, computers, and entertainment systems that slip into his pocket, he would be familiar with almost all current-day technology. Perhaps disappointed by the pace of progress, he might ask: "Why haven't we conquered outer space?" or "Where are all the robots?"

On the basis of big, obvious technological changes alone, surely the 1900-to-1950s traveler would experience the greater shift, whereas the other might easily conclude that we'd spent the second half of the twentieth century doing little more than tweaking the great innovations that had so transformed its first half.[1]

But the longer they stayed in their new homes, the more each time-traveler would become aware of subtler dimensions of change. Once the glare of technology had dimmed, each would begin to notice their respective society's changed norms and values, the different ways in which everyday people live and work. And here the tables would be turned. In terms of adjusting to the social structures and the rhythms and patterns of daily life, our second time-traveler would be much more disoriented.

Someone from the early 1900s would find the social world of the 1950s remarkably similar to his own. If he worked in a factory, he might find much the same divisions of labor, the same hierarchical systems of control. If he worked in an office, he would be immersed in the same bureaucracy, the same climb up the corporate ladder. He would come to work at 8:00 or 9:00 AM and leave promptly at 5:00, his life neatly segmented into compartments of home and work. He would wear a suit and tie. Most of his business associates would be white and male. Their values and office politics would hardly have changed. He would seldom see women in the workplace except as secretaries, and almost never interact professionally with someone of another race. He would marry young, have children quickly thereafter, stay married to the same person and probably work for the same company for the rest of his life. In his leisure time, he'd find that movies and TV had largely superseded live stage shows, but otherwise his recreational activities would be much the same as they were in 1900: taking in a baseball game or a boxing match, maybe playing a round of golf. He would join the clubs and civic groups befitting his socioeconomic class, observe the same social distinctions, and fully expect his children to do likewise. The tempo of his life would be structured by the values and norms of organizations. He would find himself living the life of the "company man" so aptly chronicled by writers from Sinclair Lewis and John Kenneth Galbraith to William Whyte and C. Wright Mills.[2]

Our second time-traveler, however, would be quite unnerved by the dizzying social and cultural changes that had accumulated between the 1950s and today. At work he would find a new dress code, a new schedule, and new rules. He would see office workers dressed like folks relaxing on the weekend, in jeans and open-necked shirts, and be shocked to learn that some of them occupy positions of authority. People at the office would seemingly come and go as they pleased. The younger ones might sport bizarre piercings and tattoos. Women and even nonwhites would be managers. Individuality and self-expression would be valued over conformity to organizational norms—and yet these people would seem strangely puritanical to this time-traveler. His ethnic jokes would fall embarrassingly flat. His smoking would get him banished to the parking lot, and his two-martini lunches would raise genuine concern. Attitudes and expressions he had never thought about would cause repeated offense. He would continually suffer the painful feeling of not knowing how to behave.

Out on the street, this time-traveler would see different ethnic groups in greater numbers than he could ever have imagined— Asian, Indian, Afro and Latin Americans, and others—mingling in ways he found strange and perhaps inappropriate. There would be mixed-race couples, and same-sex couples carrying the upbeat-sounding moniker "gay." Although some of these people would be acting in familiar ways—a woman shopping while pushing a stroller, an office worker eating his lunch at a counter—others, such as grown men clad in form-fitting gear, whizzing by on high-tech bicycles, or women on strange new roller skates with their torsos covered only by "brassieres," would appear to be engaged in alien activities.

People would seem to be always working and yet never working when they were supposed to. They would strike him as lazy and yet obsessed with exercise. They would seem career conscious yet fickle—doesn't anybody stay with a company more than three years?—and caring yet antisocial: What happened to the ladies' clubs, Moose Lodges, and bowling leagues? Why doesn't everybody go to church? Even though the physical surroundings would be relatively familiar, the *feel* of the place would be bewilderingly different.

Although the first time-traveler had to adjust to some drastic technological changes, it is the second who experiences the deeper, more pervasive transformation. It is the second who has been thrust into a time when lifestyles and worldviews are most assuredly changing—a time when the old order has broken down, when flux and uncertainty themselves seem to be part of the everyday norm.

The Force Behind the Shift

What caused this transformation? What happened between the 1950s and today that did not happen in the earlier interval? Scholars and pundits have floated many theories, along with a range of opinions on whether the changes are good or bad. Some bemoan the passing of traditional social and cultural forms; others herald a rosy future based largely on new technology.

The real driving force is the rise of human creativity as the key factor in our economy and society. Both at work and in other spheres of our lives, we value creativity more highly and cultivate it more intensely than we ever have before. The creative impulse—the attribute that distinguishes us, as humans, from other species—is now being unleashed on an unprecedented scale. The purpose of this book is to examine how and why this is so, and to trace its effects as they ripple through our world.

Many say that we now live in an information economy or a knowledge economy. But what's more fundamentally true is that for the first time, our economy is powered by creativity. Creativity—"the ability to create meaningful new forms," as *Webster's* dictionary puts it—has become the decisive source of competitive advantage. In virtually every industry, from automobiles to fashion, food products, and information technology itself, the long-run winners are those who can create and keep creating. This has always been true, from the days of the Agricultural Revolution to the Industrial Revolution. But in the past few decades we've come to recognize it clearly and act upon it systematically.

Dean Keith Simonton, a leading scholar of the subject, describes creativity as the act of bringing something useful, that works, and is non-obvious into the world, or as he succinctly puts it, that is the "conjunction of novelty, utility and surprise."[3] It is a mistake to think, as many do, that creativity can be reduced to the creation of new blockbuster inventions, new products, and new firms. In today's economy, creativity is pervasive and ongoing: it drives the incremental improvements in products and processes that keep them viable just as much as it does their original invention. Moreover, technological and economic creativity are nurtured by and interact with artistic and cultural creativity. This kind of interplay is evident in the rise of whole new industries, from computer graphics to digital music and animation. Creativity also requires a social and economic environment that can nurture its many forms. Max Weber said long ago that the Protestant ethic provided the underlying spirit of thrift, hard work, and efficiency that motivated the rise of early capitalism. In a similar fashion, the shared commitment to the creative spirit in all its many manifestations is what underpins the new creative ethos that powers our age.

Thus, creativity has come to be the most highly prized commodity in our economy—and yet it is not a "commodity." Creativity comes from people. And it annihilates the social categories we have imposed on ourselves. A Creative Economy requires diversity because every human is creative—creativity cannot be contained by categories of gender, race, ethnicity, or sexual orientation. And though people can be hired and fired, their creative capacity cannot be bought and sold, or turned on and off at will. Thus, our workplaces have changed and continue to do so. Schedules, rules, and dress codes have become more flexible to cater to how the creative process works. Creativity must be motivated and nurtured in a multitude of ways, by employers, by creative people themselves, and by the places we live. Capitalism has expanded its reach to capture the talents of heretofore excluded groups of eccentrics and nonconformists. In doing so, it has pulled off yet another astonishing mutation: taking people who would once have been viewed as bizarre mavericks operating at the bohemian fringe and placing them at the very heart of the process of innovation and economic growth. These changes in the economy and in the workplace have in turn helped to propagate and legitimize similar changes in society at large. The creative individual is no longer viewed as an iconoclast. He—or she—is the new mainstream.

In tracing economic shifts, I often say that our economy is moving from an older corporate-centered system defined by large companies to a more people-driven one. This view should not be confused with the unfounded and silly notion that big companies are dying off. Nor do I buy into the fantasy that our economy is being reorganized around small enterprises and independent "free agents."[4] Companies, including very big ones, obviously still exist, are still influential, and almost certainly always will be. I simply mean to stress that as the fundamental source of creativity, people are the critical resource of the new age. This has far-reaching effects—for instance, on our economic and social geography and the nature of our communities.

It has often been said that in this age of globalization and modern communication technology, "geography is dead," "the world is flat," and place no longer matters.[5] Nothing could be further from the truth. Place has become the central organizing unit of our time, taking on many of the functions that used to be played by firms and other organizations. Access to talented and creative people is to modern business what access to coal and iron ore was to steel-making. It determines where companies will choose to locate and grow, and this in turn changes the ways that cities must compete. As I once heard Carly Fiorina tell this nation's governors when she was CEO of Hewlett-Packard: "Keep your tax incentives and high-way interchanges; we will go where the highly skilled people are."[6] In this environment, it is geographic place rather than the corpo-ration that provides the organizational matrix for matching people and jobs.

The New Class

The economic need for creativity has registered itself in the rise of a new class, which I call the Creative Class. More than 40 million Americans, roughly one-third of all employed people, belong to it. I define the core of the Creative Class to include people in science and engineering, architecture and design, education, arts, music, and entertainment whose economic function is to create new ideas, new technology, and new creative content. Around this core, the Creative Class also includes a broader group of *creative professionals* in business and finance, law, health care, and related fields. These people engage in complex problem solving that involves a great deal of independent judgment and requires high levels of education or human capital. In addition, all members of the Creative Class— whether they are artists or engineers, musicians or computer scientists, writers or entrepreneurs—share a common ethos that values creativity, individuality, difference, and merit.

The key difference between the Creative Class and other classes lies in what its members are primarily paid to do. Members of the Working Class and the Service Class are primarily paid to do routine, mostly physical work, whereas those in the Creative Class are paid to use their minds—the full scope of their cognitive and social skills. There are gray areas and boundary issues in my scheme of things, to be sure. And though some may quibble with my definition of the Creative Class and the numerical estimates that are based on it, I believe it has a good deal more precision than existing, more amorphous definitions of knowledge workers, symbolic analysts, or professional and technical workers.

The class structure of the United States and other advanced nations has been the subject of great debate for well over a century. For a host of writers in the 1800s and 1900s, the big story was the rise, and then the decline, of the Working Class, which peaked at roughly 40 percent of the US workforce before beginning its long slide to roughly one in five workers today.[7] For writers like Daniel Bell and others in the mid to later twentieth century, a second big story was the rise of a postindustrial society, in which many of us shifted from making goods to delivering services.[8] The Service Class, which includes such fields as personal care, food services, and clerical work, is the largest class today, with some 60 million members, more than 45 percent of the entire US workforce. The big story unfolding now—and it has been unfolding for some time—is the rise of the Creative Class, the great emerging class of our time.

Although the Creative Class remains somewhat smaller than the Service Class, its crucial economic role makes it the most influential. The Creative Class is dominant in terms of wealth and income, with its members earning nearly twice as much on average as members of the other two classes and as a whole accounting for more than half of all wages and salaries.

Creativity in the world of work is not limited to members of the Creative Class. Factory workers and even the lowest-end service workers have always been creative in valuable ways. Also, the creative content of many Working and Service Class jobs is growing—a prime example being the continuous-improvement programs on many factory floors, which call on line workers to contribute their ideas as well as their physical labor. On the basis of these trends, I expect that the Creative Class, which is still emergent, will continue to grow in coming decades, as more traditional economic functions are transformed into Creative Class occupations. And, as I will argue in the last chapter of this book, I strongly believe that the key to improving the lot of underpaid, underemployed, and disadvantaged people lies not in social welfare programs or low-end make-work jobs, nor in somehow bringing back the factory jobs of the past, but rather in tapping their innate creativity, paying them appropriately for it, and integrating them fully into the Creative Economy.

The Creative Class is the norm-setting class of our time. And the norms of the Creative Class are different from those of more traditional society. Individuality, self-expression, and openness to difference are favored over the homogeneity, conformity, and "fitting in" that defined the previous age of large-scale industry and organization. Our private lives are different than they once were. During the *Leave It to Beaver* era of the 1950s and early 1960s, roughly eight in ten Americans lived in married households, but by 2010, less than half did. In 1960, almost half of all Americans were part of a nuclear family, with a mom, a dad, and kids in the house; by 2010, that number had fallen to just one in five. These profound changes are not, as commonly portrayed, signs of the reckless self-indulgence of a spoiled people. They are undergirded by powerful economic forces that are reshaping our society and our lives.

The Creative Class is also the key force that is reshaping our geography, spearheading the movement back from outlying areas to
urban centers and close-in, walkable suburbs. A relatively mobile
class, it is much more concentrated in some cities and metros areas
than in others. As of 2010, the Creative Class composed more than
40 percent of the workforce in larger metro areas like San Jose, the
fabled Silicon Valley, greater Washington, DC, and Boston, as well
as smaller college towns such as Durham, North Carolina; Ithaca,
New York; and Boulder and Ann Arbor. These places are prospering, distinguished by a new model of economic development that
takes shape around the 3T's—technology, talent, and tolerance.
The most successful and prosperous metros excel at all three.

Not all is rosy in this emerging mainstream of the Creative Age.
People today bear much more personal risk than did the corporate
and working classes of the Organizational Age—as has become all
too obvious with the onset of the economic crisis. Stress levels, too,
are high. The technologies that were supposed to liberate us from
work have invaded our lives. Our increasingly unequal society has
become deeply divided, sorted, and segmented by level of education,
the kinds of work we do, and where we live, and this in turn shapes
ever more divisive culture wars and politics. One of the most significant fault lines of our age is the growing geographic segregation
of the Creative Class and the other classes.

Although the immediate occasion for the crash of 2008 was the
bursting of the real estate bubble, economic historians will see it
as the last crisis of the old Fordist industrial order—the tipping
point when an outmoded, exhausted set of social and institutional
structures could no longer contain or harness the productive power
of the new Creative Age. We have seen this happen before—in the
earth-shattering religious, political, intellectual, and social upheavals
that accompanied the shift from feudalism to capitalism; in the cat-
astrophic Panic and Long Depression of 1873, which coincided

with the rise of modern industry; and in the Great Depression of 1929, which followed the rise of mass-production capitalism.

These powerful economic and social shifts are altering the structure of everyday life. As witnessed by our two time-travelers, the deepest and most enduring changes of our age are not technological, but economic, cultural, and geographic. These changes have been building for decades and are only now coming to the fore, driven by the rise of the Creative Economy and of the Creative Class.

PART ONE

THE CREATIVE AGE

CHAPTER 2

The Creative Economy

P owering the great ongoing changes of our time is the rise of human creativity as the defining feature of economic life. Creativity has come to be valued—and systems have evolved to encourage and harness it—because it is increasingly recognized as the font from which new technologies, new industries, new wealth, and all other good economic things flow. As a result, our lives and society have begun to resonate with a creative ethos. An ethos is defined as the fundamental spirit or character of a culture, and it is our commitment to creativity in its varied dimensions that forms the underlying spirit of our age. To grasp the spirit and character of the emerging Creative Age, this chapter takes a closer look at creativity itself: what it is, and where it comes from. In order to structure the arguments that follow, I start with three basic points.

First, creativity is essential to the way we live and work today, and in many senses it always has been. As the economist Paul Romer has said, the biggest advances in standards of living—not to mention the biggest competitive advantages in the marketplace—have always come from "better recipes, not just more cooking."[1] Second, human creativity is not limited to technological innovation or new business models. It is multifaceted and multidimensional; it is not something that can be kept in a box and trotted out when one arrives at the office. Creativity involves distinct habits of mind and patterns of behavior that must be cultivated on both an individual basis and in the surrounding society. The creative ethos pervades everything from our workplace culture to our values and communities, reshapes the way we see ourselves as economic and social actors and molds the core of our very identities. It reflects norms and values that both nurture creativity and reinforce its role. Furthermore, it requires a supportive environment—a broad array of social, cultural, and economic stimuli. Creativity is thus associated with the rise of new work environments, lifestyles, associations, and neighborhoods, which in turn are conducive to creative work. Such a broadly creative environment is critical for generating technological creativity and the commercial innovations and wealth that flow from it.

The third, and perhaps the most critical, issue is the ongoing tension between creativity and organization. The creative process is social, not just individual; forms of organization are necessary. But organizations can and frequently do stifle creativity. A defining feature of life in the early to mid-twentieth century—a period referred to as the Organizational Age—was the dominance of large-scale and highly specialized bureaucracies. Writing in the 1940s, the economist Joseph Schumpeter deplored the stifling effect of large organizations on creativity. In his landmark book *Capitalism, Socialism and Democracy,* Schumpeter noted that capitalism's great strength had long been the "function of entrepreneurs" who "revolutionize the pattern of production." And then he gloomily predicted its demise. "Technological progress is increasingly becoming the business of teams of trained specialists who turn out what is required and make it work in predictable ways," he wrote. The perfectly bureaucratized giant industrial unit not only ousts the small or medium-sized firm and "expropriates" its owners, but in the end it also ousts the entrepreneur.[2] In an interview I conducted in 2000, a young woman described this chilling effect in stark and memorable terms: "Where I grew up, we were conditioned to play the roles that we were dealt. We were not encouraged to create and build our visions, but rather to fit into the visions of a select few. I like to say that we were 'institutionalized' individuals—because institutions defined our lives."[3]

The ascent of creativity as an economic force over the past few decades has brought new economic and social forms into existence that mitigate this tension to a certain degree, but they have not fully resolved it. Everything from the rise of the entrepreneurial start-up company and the formal venture capital system to the loosening of traditional cultural norms regarding work and life reflects attempts to elude the strictures of organizational conformity. But this doesn't mean that creativity has won the day or that large organizations are going the way of the dinosaurs. We still need large organizations to do many things; bureaucracies continue to play dominant roles in our society. Whereas one person can write brilliant software, it takes large organizations to consistently upgrade, produce, and distribute that software. Large organizations may be more nimble and flexible than they once were, but they are still evolving, still developing new ways to foster creativity while providing a structure in which to produce and manage work.

Our new creative economic system is far from fully formed. Furthermore, it is not a panacea for the myriad social and economic ills that confront modern society. The emerging Creative Economy will not magically alleviate poverty, eliminate unemployment, overcome the business cycle, and lead to greater happiness and harmony for all. In some respects, left unchecked and without appropriate forms of human intervention, this creativity-based system may well make some of our problems worse.

Creative Dimensions

Creativity is often viewed as a rather mystical affair. Over the past few decades, however, systematic studies have considerably enlarged our understanding of it. Researchers have observed and analyzed creativity in subjects ranging from eminent scientists and artists to preschoolers and chimpanzees. They have pored through the biographies, notebooks, and letters of great creators of the past; modeled the creative process by computer; and tried to get computers to *be* creative.[4] Occasionally but notably, they have studied its workings across entire human societies. From this body of literature I will abstract several main themes that surface repeatedly. As we trace these themes and begin to see what creativity really is, we will also begin to get a deeper sense of how and why the creative ethos has emerged with such force in our lives today.

Let's start with the basics. Creativity is not the same as "intelligence." One study summarized the difference this way: "Many studies recognize creativity as cognitive ability separate from other mental functions and particularly independent from the complex of abilities grouped under the word 'intelligence.' Although intelligence—the ability to deal with or process large amounts of data—favors creative potential, it is not synonymous with creativity."[5]

Creativity involves the ability to synthesize. Albert Einstein captured this nicely when he characterized his own work as "combinatory play." It is a matter of sifting through data, perceptions, and materials to come up with combinations that are new and useful. A creative synthesis might result in such different outcomes as a practical invention, a theory or insight that can be applied to solve a problem, or a work of art that can be appreciated aesthetically.[6]

Creativity requires self-assurance and the ability to take risks. In her book *The Creative Mind*, Margaret Boden noted that creativity requires the combination of passion and confidence. "A person needs a healthy self-respect to pursue novel ideas, and to make mistakes, despite criticism from others," she wrote. "Breaking generally accepted rules, or even stretching them, takes confidence. Continuing to do so, in the face of skepticism and scorn, takes even more."[7]

Small wonder that the creative ethos marks a strong departure from the conformist ethos of the past. Creative work in fact is often downright subversive, because it disrupts existing patterns of thought and life. It can feel unsettling even to its creator. One famous definition of creativity is "the process of destroying one's gestalt in favor of a better one." Schumpeter wrote about the "creative destruction" that transforms existing industries and creates entirely new ones. The economic historian Joel Mokyr notes: "Economists and historians alike realize that there is a deep difference between *homo economicus* and *homo creativus*. One makes the most of what nature permits him to have. The other rebels against nature's dictates. Technological creativity, like all creativity, is an act of rebellion."[8]

Yet creativity is not the province of just a few select geniuses who can get away with breaking the mold because they possess superhuman talents. It is a capacity inherent to varying degrees in virtually all of us. According to Boden, who sums up a wealth of research: "Creativity draws crucially on our ordinary abilities. Noticing, remembering, seeing, speaking, hearing, understanding language, and recognizing analogies: all these talents of Everyman are important."[9] And she explodes the idea of the lone "creative genius."

The romantic myth of "creative genius" rarely helps. Often it is insidiously self-destructive. It can buttress the self-confidence of those individuals who believe themselves to be among the chosen few (perhaps it helped Beethoven to face his many troubles). But it undermines the self-regard of those who do not. Someone who believes that creativity is a rare or special power cannot sensibly hope that perseverance, or education, will enable them to join the creative elite. Either one is already a member, or will never be. Monolithic notions of creativity, talent, or intelligence are discouraging in the same way. Either one has got "it" or one hasn't. Why bother to try if one's efforts can lead only to a slightly less dispiriting level of mediocrity? . . . A very different attitude is possible for someone who sees creativity as based in ordinary abilities we all share, and in practised expertise to which we can all aspire.[10]

Creativity is multidimensional and experiential. Simonton writes that "creativity is favored by an intellect that has been enriched with diverse experiences and perspectives," and that it is "associated with a mind that exhibits a variety of interests and knowledge."[11] The varied forms of creativity that we typically regard as different from one another—technological creativity (or invention), economic creativity (entrepreneurship), and artistic and cultural creativity, among others—are in fact deeply interrelated. Not only do they share a common thought process, they reinforce each other through cross-fertilization and mutual stimulation. This is one reason that historical and present practitioners of different forms of creativity have tended to congregate and feed off one another in teeming, multifaceted creative centers—Florence in the early Renaissance; Vienna in the late 1800s and early 1900s; the many fast-growing creative centers across the United States today.

Stimulating and glamorous as it may sometimes be, creativity is in fact hard work. Both Thomas Edison (a paragon of technological creativity) and George Bernard Shaw (a cultural creative) liked to say that genius is 90 percent perspiration and 10 percent inspiration.[12] Or as the journalist Red Smith once said of the demands of his craft: "There's nothing to writing. All you do is sit down at the typewriter and open a vein." Here we have an inventor, a playwright, and a sportswriter sounding a common theme: the creative ethos is built on discipline and focus, sweat and blood. As Boden put it: "A person needs time, and enormous effort, to amass mental structures and to explore their potential. It is not always easy (it was not easy for Beethoven). Even when it is, life has many other attractions. Only a strong commitment to the domain—music, maths, medicine—can prevent someone from dissipating their energies on other things."[13]

Creativity can take a long time before it bears fruit—there are many stories of great mathematicians and scientists mulling a problem for months or more, only to be finally "illuminated" while stepping onto a bus or staring into a fireplace—but even this apparent magic is the result of long preparation. Thus Louis Pasteur's famous dictum: "Chance favors only the prepared mind." Or as Wesley Cohen and Daniel Levinthal have put it in their studies of firm-based innovation: "Fortune favors the prepared firm."[14]

Because of the all-absorbing nature of creative work, many great thinkers of the past were people who "formed no close ties." They had lots of colleagues and acquaintances, but few close friends and often no spouse or children. In fact, muses the psychiatrist Anthony Storr, "if intense periods of concentration over long periods are required to attain fundamental insights, the family man is at a disadvantage." Quoting the famous bachelor Isaac Newton on his process of discovery—"I keep the subject constantly before me, and wait till the first dawnings open slowly by little and little into the full and clear light"—Storr notes that "If Newton had been subject to the demands of a wife for companionship or interrupted by the patter of tiny feet, it would certainly have been less easy for him."[15]

Surely some creative people are inspired by money, but studies find that truly creative individuals, from artists and writers to scientists and open-source software developers, are driven primarily by internal motivations, by the intrinsic rewards and satisfactions of their pursuits. Too much pressure from the outside might even inhibit them. In a study of motivation and reward, Harvard Business School psychologist Teresa Amabile observed, "Intrinsic motivation is conducive to creativity, but extrinsic motivation is detrimental. It appears that when people are primarily motivated to do some creative activity by their own interest and enjoyment of that activity, they may be more creative than when they are primarily motivated by some goal imposed upon them by others."[16]

Although creativity is often viewed as an individual phenomenon, it is an inescapably social process. Even the lone creator relies heavily on contributors and collaborators. Successful creators have often organized themselves and others into teams for systematic effort. When Edison opened his laboratory in Menlo Park, New Jersey, he called it an "invention factory" and announced his intention to produce "a minor invention every ten days and a big thing every six months or so."[17] The artist Andy Warhol similarly dubbed his Manhattan studio The Factory. Warhol liked to cultivate a public image of bemused indifference, but he was a prolific organizer and worker—mobilizing friends and colleagues to publish a magazine and produce films and music, pursuing his own art all the while.

Creativity flourishes best in a unique kind of social environment: one that is stable enough to allow for continuity of effort, yet diverse and broad-minded enough to nourish creativity in all its subversive forms. Simonton identifies four key characteristics of the times and places where creativity flourishes the most: "domain activity, intellectual receptiveness, ethnic diversity, [and] political openness." In a study of the history of Japanese culture—a culture that has been "highly variable in its openness to outside influences"—Simonton found that "those periods in which Japan was receptive to alien influx were soon followed by periods of augmented creative activity."[18]

One final cautionary note: Mokyr, a historian, notes that technological creativity has tended to rise and then fade dramatically at various times and places, when social and economic institutions turn rigid and act against it. Spectacular fade-outs occurred, for instance, in late medieval times in the Islamic world and in China. Both societies, which had been leaders in fields from mathematics to mechanical invention, then proceeded to fall far behind Western Europe economically. When one takes the long view of human history, Mokyr writes, one sees that "technological progress is like a fragile and vulnerable plant, whose flourishing is not only dependent on the appropriate surroundings and climate, but whose life is almost always short. It is highly sensitive to the social and economic environment and can easily be arrested."[19] A continual outpouring of creativity "cannot and should not be taken for granted," Mokyr warns—even today. Creativity doesn't automatically sustain itself over long periods, but requires constant attention to and investment in the economic and social forms that feed the creative impulse. This is all the more reason to study the institutions of the Creative Economy closely, so that we can understand their inner workings and nourish them appropriately.

The Ultimate Source of Creativity

Creativity is not only inherent in humans, it is literally what distinguishes us, economically speaking, from other species. "We produce goods by rearranging physical objects, but so do other animals, often with remarkable precision," notes the economist Paul Romer. "Where people excel as economic animals is in their ability to produce ideas, not just physical goods. An ant will go through its life without ever coming up with even a slightly different idea about how to gather food. But people are almost incapable of this kind of rote adherence to instruction. We are incurable experimenters and problem solvers."[20]

"We are not used to thinking of ideas as economic goods," he continues, "but they are surely the most significant ones that we produce. The only way for us to produce more economic value— and thereby generate economic growth—is to find ever more valuable ways to make use of the objects available to us." Ideas, he notes, are especially potent because they are not like other goods, such as mineral deposits and machines, which deplete or wear out with use.[21] A good idea, like the concept of the wheel, "can be used over and over again" and in fact grows in value the more it is used. It offers not diminishing returns, but *increasing returns.* Moreover, an idea can be built upon. As other people apply their own creativity to a new scientific theory or product design, they can tinker with it, improve it, and combine it with other ideas in growing proliferations of new forms. This is what has happened in recent centuries. The early 1900s were a time when waves of invention—the accumulated fruits of that creativity—were being harnessed, mass-produced, and widely promulgated through society as never before. What we are living through now is the next step. Now it is not just the fruits or artifacts of creativity, but creativity itself that is being harnessed on a truly massive scale and promulgated as never before.

Today we like to think that we clearly understand creativity as a source of economic value. Many commentators, for instance, trumpet the point that "intellectual property"—useful new knowledge embodied in computer programs, or patents, or formulas—has become more valuable than any kind of physical property. It's no surprise that we litigate over intellectual property and argue about the proper means of protecting it as fiercely as miners battled over claims during the California Gold Rush. But as Lawrence Lessig has powerfully argued, our penchant for overprotecting and overlitigating intellectual property may well serve to constrain and limit the creative impulse.[22] In the long run, we cannot forget what the fundamental cornerstone of our wealth is. Although useful knowledge may reside in programs or formulas, it does not originate in them, but in people. The ultimate intellectual property—the one that really replaces land, labor, and capital as the most valuable economic resource—is the human creative faculty.

Karl Marx had it more than partly right when he foresaw that workers would someday control the means of production. This is beginning to happen to a certain degree, although not as Marx thought it would, with the proletariat rising up and taking over factories. If workers control the means of production today that is because it is inside their own heads; they *are* the means of production. Thus, the ultimate "control" issue is not who owns the patents or whether the creative worker or the employer holds the balance of power in labor market negotiations. While those battles swing back and forth, the ultimate control issue—the one we have to stay focused on, individually and collectively—is how to keep the creative furnaces that burn inside each and every human being fully stoked.

Creativity Versus Organization

This brings us back to one of the core tensions or contradictions of our time—that between creativity and organization. Creative people come in many different forms. Some are mercurial and intuitive in their work habits, others methodical. Some prefer to channel their energies into big, radical ideas; others are tinkerers and improvers. Some like to move from job to job, whereas others prefer the security of a large organization. Some are at their best when they work in groups; others like nothing better than to be left alone. Moreover, many people don't fall at the extremes—and their work and lifestyle preferences may change as they mature.

What all of these people have in common is a need for organizations and environments that will allow them to be creative—that value their input, challenge them, have mechanisms for mobilizing resources around ideas, and that are receptive to both small changes and the occasional game changer. Companies and places that can provide this kind of environment, regardless of size, will have an edge in attracting, managing, and motivating creative talent. The same companies and places will also tend to enjoy a flow of innovation, reaping competitive advantage in the short run and evolutionary advantage in the long run.

Although certain environments promote creativity, others most certainly kill it. Adam Smith noted this as early as 1776, in *The Wealth of Nations*. In his famous description of the pin factory, Smith praised the division of labor, a concept that allowed pins to be made efficiently by splitting the process into eighteen distinct steps, with each worker or group of workers typically doing only one step. "The man whose whole life is spent in performing a few simple operations," he also noted, "has no occasion to exert his understanding or to exercise his invention," adding: "He naturally loses, therefore, the habit of such exertion, and generally becomes as stupid and ignorant as it is possible for a human creature to become. The torpor of his mind renders him, not only incapable of relishing or bearing a part in any rational conversation, but of conceiving any generous, noble, or tender sentiment."[23]

In their insightful book *The Social Life of Information*, John Seely Brown and Paul Duguid describe the inherent tug-of-war between the ways that organizations generate knowledge and creativity, and the means by which they translate those assets into actual products and services.[24] Creativity comes from individuals working in small groups, which Brown and Duguid refer to as "communities of practice." These communities emphasize exploration and discovery. Each develops distinctive habits, customs, priorities, and insights that are the secrets of its creativity and inventiveness. But process and structure are required to link these communities to one another, transfer knowledge, achieve scale, and generate growth. Practice without process becomes unmanageable, but process without practice damps out the creativity required for innovation; the two sides exist in perpetual tension. Only the most sophisticated and aware organizations are able to balance these countervailing forces in ways that lead to sustained creativity and long-run growth.

This fundamental tension between organization and creativity is reflected in a remarkable dialogue between two of the greatest chroniclers of everyday life in the mid-twentieth century, William Whyte and Jane Jacobs. Whyte's classic book, *The Organization Man,* published in 1956, documented the stifling effect of organization and bureaucracy on individuality and creativity.[25] A journalist at *Fortune* magazine, Whyte showed how the big corporations of the time selected and favored the type of person who goes along to get along, rather than someone who might go against the grain. The result, he wrote, was "a generation of bureaucrats." Even research and development, though lavishly funded, was becoming bureaucratized: "Money, money everywhere . . . but not a cent to think." Whyte's organization man had an average workweek of fifty to sixty hours, was more interested in work than in his spouse, and depended on the corporation for his very identity. He often lived in prepackaged suburban developments like Park Forest, Illinois, a place Whyte studied exhaustively. The new suburban communities were seen as more progressive and liberating than the old small towns. But as Whyte showed, they came to exert strong pressures of their own for social adaptation and conformity. In Park Forest, as in the corporations for whom many of its upwardly mobile residents worked, the idiosyncratic individual was quickly stigmatized.

In contrast, Jacobs's monumental work, *The Death and Life of Great American Cities,* published just five years later in 1961, celebrated the creativity and diversity of urban neighborhoods like her own Greenwich Village in New York City.[26] The creative community, Jacobs argued, required diversity, an appropriate physical environment, and a certain kind of person to generate ideas, spur innovation, and harness human creativity. In contrast to the conformity, homogeneity, and insularity that Whyte had deplored, Jacob's neighborhoods were veritable fountainheads of individuality, difference, and social interaction. The miracle of these places, she argued, was found in the hurly-burly life of the street, which provided the venue for a more or less continuous conversation, a source of both civility and creativity. People of all classes and educations, with all kinds of ideas, were constantly jostling against each other and striking intellectual sparks. Jacobs documented in painstaking detail the way this worked in and around Hudson Street, where she lived, a neighborhood of tenement apartments and town houses, shops, and bars, among them the famed White Horse Tavern, where workers, writers, musicians, and intellectuals gathered for relaxation, conversation, and the occasional new idea.

What made Hudson Street so fertile was its combination of physical and social environments. It had short blocks that generated the greatest variety in foot traffic. It had a wide diversity of people, from virtually every ethnic background and walk of life. It had broad sidewalks and a tremendous variety of types of buildings—apartments, stores, even small factories—which meant that there were always different kinds of people outside and on different schedules. There were lots of old, underutilized buildings, ideal for individualistic and creative enterprises ranging from artists' studios to small entrepreneurial businesses. Hudson Street also fostered and attracted exemplars of a certain type of person: Jacobs's all-important "public characters." These people—shopkeepers, merchants, and neighborhood leaders of various sorts—were the antitheses of Whyte's organization men. Utilizing their positions in social networks, they connected and catalyzed people and ideas, playing critical roles in resource mobilization.

Ironically but not surprisingly, Jacobs and Whyte were the closest of friends. When asked in March 2001, on the fortieth anniversary of the publication of *The Death and Life of Great American Cities*, to name her most admired contemporaries, Jacobs had this to say: "Holly Whyte, William H. Whyte. . . . He was an important person to me and he was somebody whose ideas, yes, were on the same wavelength. And it was through Holly that I met my . . . publisher. . . . I told him what I wanted and he agreed to publish it and gave me a contract."[27]

This bond is also evident in their work. Whyte lamented the rise of organizational society and the alienation, isolation, and conformity it engendered. Jacobs showed the possibility of an alternative, a setting where difference, nonconformity, and creativity could thrive. Who at the time could have guessed what verdict history would render? For much of the past half century, intelligent observers of modern life believed it was Whyte's world that had triumphed. But now it appears that Jacobs's world may well be carrying the day. Not only are urban neighborhoods similar to Hudson Street reviving across the country, but many of the principles that animated Hudson Street are diffusing throughout our economy and society. Personal lives and workplaces, whole industries and geographic regions are beginning to operate on the principles of constant, dynamic, creative interaction.

The Rise of the Creative Economy

I certainly agree with those who say that the advanced nations are shifting to information-based, knowledge-driven economies. The always-prescient Peter Drucker, who outlined the rise of the so-called knowledge economy, was one of the first and most noted exponents of this view: "The basic economic resources—'the means of production,' to use the economist's term, is no longer capital,

nor natural resources . . . nor 'labor.' It is and will be knowledge,"
he wrote.[28] Yet rather than knowledge, I see creativity—the faculty
that enables us to derive useful new forms from knowledge—as the
key driver of today's economy. In my formulation, knowledge and
information are merely the tools and the materials of creativity. Innovation, whether in the form of a new technological artifact or a
new business model or method, is its product.

None of this is totally new, of course; human beings have been
engaged in creative activities since antiquity, often with spectacular
results. But what we are doing now is mainstreaming these activities;
building an entire economic infrastructure around them. Scientific
and artistic endeavors, for instance, have become industries unto
themselves, and they have combined in new ways to create still
newer industries. The joint expansion of technological innovation
and creative content work has increasingly become the motor force
of economic growth.

As far as I can tell *BusinessWeek* was the first to introduce the
concept of the Creative Economy, in August 2000.[29] Not long afterward, John Howkins documented its global impact in his aptly
titled book *The Creative Economy*,[30] though he used the term in a
somewhat different sense than I do. Whereas I define the Creative
Economy in terms of occupations, Howkins defines it to include
fifteen creative industry sectors such as software, R&D and design,
and creative-content industries like film and music. These industries
produce intellectual property in the form of patents, copyrights,
trademarks, and proprietary designs.[31]

The Creative Factory

Not just the start-up company, the research laboratory, and the
artist's studio, but the factory itself can be and often is an arena for

creative work. In fact, my studies of high performance factories in the 1980s and 1990s served as the inspiration for my theory of the Creative Class. Given the chance factory workers are often the ones who come up with basic improvements in productivity and performance.[32] I saw this time and again in my studies of Japanese and US factories. Even in areas such as environmental quality, it was line workers doing little things—like putting in drip pans— who were the key to making factories greener and more productive at the same time.[33] Today more and more factory jobs require creativity as a condition of employment. In many advanced manufacturing plants, even candidates for entry-level assembly jobs must pass a battery of tests screening them for aptitudes such as problem solving and the ability to work in self-directed teams.[34] Increasing numbers of factory workers no longer touch the products they make but essentially monitor, control, and at times program the computers that run the production processes.[35] The manager of a fully automated steel mill in the American Midwest summed it up best when he told me: "The result is the rise of the creative factory, where factory workers contribute their ideas and intellectual talent as well as their physical labor."

I first came to understand the enormous power of creativity at work not from economic textbooks or from my research, but very early in life, from my father, Louis Florida. Born to Italian immigrant parents in Newark, New Jersey, he quit school at age fourteen and took a job in a factory that made eyeglass frames to help support his family during the Great Depression. After fighting in World War II—he was one of those who stormed the beaches at Normandy—he returned to his previous line of work at a place called Victory Optical. By the early 1960s, when I was a small boy, he had worked his way up from laborer to a supervisory post. On some Saturdays he had to put in a few hours at work; occasionally, he would give in to my pants-tugging pleas and let me tag along. My eyes ablaze with curiosity, we drove through Newark's sprawling, industrial Ironbound Section, so called because it was latticed with railroad lines, to the giant brick factory. Inside the plant, I would race on small legs to keep up with my father as he strode past the presses, the lathes, the vats of plating solutions, and huge bins of eyeglass frames of every kind. The energy was incredible; it was a phantasmagoria of rapidly moving people, set amid the sounds of whirring machines and foreign-accented English, and the smells of cutting fluids, melted plastic, and finely shaved metal chips.

My father and his colleague Karl, a German-born machinist, would talk about the latest machinery from Italy and Germany and the advanced production systems used by their European competitors. But my father would always remind me that the real productive power of the factory came not from its machines and presses but from the intelligence and creativity of its workers. "Richard," he would say, "the factory does not run itself. It is those incredibly skilled men who are the heart, soul, and mind of this factory."

My most vivid lesson on that score occurred when I was a Cub Scout and I entered my first Pinewood Derby, a racing event for small model cars. Each scout was given the same basic materials to work with: a rectangular block of wood, plastic wheels, and metal axles. The instructions were to fashion a car from the materials supplied, and not to add additional weight in excess of five ounces. The cars would race by rolling down a sloped track. The week before my first race, I worked on the car with my father. We basically fastened the wheels to the block of wood, added a coat of paint and showed up. Suffice it to say, we were badly beaten. Our primitive clunker literally fell apart, its wheels flying in all directions, as the sleek cars of the other scouts flew by. Those sharp-looking cars fascinated me, and I made my father promise to help me build one.

The next year we set to work early, designing a streamlined racer. We started by talking to the machinists and machine-tool designers at Victory Optical, taking the car to the factory on weekends to seek their advice. We honed that block of wood into an efficient aerodynamic design. We added a precise amount of lead weight, per the guidelines, to gain additional speed. We fashioned a little test track. In trial runs, the front axle began to crack under the strain of repeated impact with the stopping barrier at the bottom. With the help of the machinists, we developed an innovative solution, carving a bit of wood from the rear of the car and gluing it to its nose to protect the axle. We added a metallic paint job, decals, a roll bar, and the pièce de résistance—a little plastic driver. The finished car looked like a Formula One racer. With the collective ingenuity of Victory Optical in our corner, we went on to win every Pinewood Derby championship for the remainder of my Cub Scout career, at which point the dynasty passed along to my younger brother's racers. The creativity of the workers in the eyeglass-frame factory was multidimensional: it could be applied to my world, too.

My father's factory also taught me about the consequences of bad management—and the squelching of creativity—in the age of high Fordism. For years, the Victory Optical plant had been an exception to the Organizational Age rule: it was operated entirely by foremen and self-made managers like my father, who had worked their way up from the shop floor. These managers had tremendous respect for the ideas of the factory workers. I can remember the workers looking at samples of the latest designer eyeglass frames from overseas and coming up with their own designs to improve on the high-priced imports. Then, in the late 1960s and 1970s, the plant owners began to hire college-educated engineers and MBAs to oversee the factory's operations. With considerable book knowledge but little experience in the actual workings of the factory, these new recruits proposed complex new ideas and systems that inevitably failed and, at worst, brought production to a grinding halt. Their ideas not only were ineffective but created growing animosity among the workforce. The bitter standoff between workers and management finally became intolerable. One day in the late 1970s, when I was at college, my father called me on the phone and said, "Today, I quit."

At the time, I was a little skeptical about my father's version of events: could college-educated experts really have ruined his factory? I was a college student myself, after all, trying to use education to move up the socioeconomic ladder. But within a couple of years, I realized how right he had been. As the workforce grew more demoralized, problems mounted. Skilled people quit. Machinists left in droves. The foremen and supervisors who had come up from the floor quickly followed. Without their storehouse of knowledge and institutional memory, the factory could not operate. Less than three years after my father's departure, Victory Optical was bankrupt. The huge, vibrant factory that had captivated me in my youth was shuttered, vacant, abandoned. It was as heartbreaking as it was ironic. Just when the leading edge of the corporate world had begun moving toward the creative factory concept—the concept that Victory had been run by all along—Victory had moved in the opposite direction: back to the past, to the deadening paradigm that delegated creativity to the men at the top and denied it to the rank and file.

The image of the factory as an arena for rote physical labor alone has always been wrong. It never gave a complete picture of the economic activity that went on inside. Workers have always used their intellects and creative capabilities to get things done. And though they were stifled for long periods in many industries, factory workers today are coming to be valued more for their ideas about quality and continuous improvement than for their ability to perform routine manual tasks. Across the board, in a multitude of jobs, work has taken on an explicitly creative component.

CHAPTER 3

The Creative Class

The rise of the Creative Economy has had a profound effect on the sorting of people into social groups or classes, changing the composition of existing ones and creating new ones. I am far from the first to have raised the idea that the advanced industrial economies have given birth to new classes. During the 1960s, Peter Drucker and Fritz Machlup described the growing economic role played by "knowledge workers." Sometime later, Daniel Bell identified a meritocratic class structure of scientists, engineers, managers, and administrators that had been engendered by the shift from a manufacturing to a "postindustrial" economy. The sociologist Erik Olin Wright has written extensively about the rise of what he called a new "professional-managerial" class.[1] Robert Reich advanced the term "symbolic analysts" to describe members of the workforce who manipulate ideas and symbols.[2] All of these observers picked up on economic aspects of the emerging class structure that I describe here.

Others zeroed in on the wider repercussions of these changes on social norms and value systems. Near the end of his 1983 book *Class,* the University of Pennsylvania's Paul Fussell taxonomized many of the attributes that I now assign to the Creative Class. After a witty romp through status markers that delineate, say, the upper middle class from "high proles," Fussell noted the presence of a growing "X" group that seemed to defy existing categories.

> You are not born an X person. You earn X-personhood by a strenuous effort of discovery in which curiosity and originality are indispensable.
>
> The young flocking to the cities to devote themselves to "art," "writing," "creative work"—anything, virtually, that liberates them from the presence of a boss or superior—are aspirant X people.
>
> The middle-class person is "always somebody's man," the X person is nobody's.
>
> X people are independent-minded. They adore the work they do, and they do it until they are finally carried out, "retirement" being a concept meaningful only to hired personnel or wage slaves who despise their work.[3]

Others have charted the rise of knowledge workers. In 1996, Stephen Barley estimated that professional, technical, and managerial occupations increased from just 10 percent of the workforce in 1900 to 30 percent by 1991, while both blue-collar work and agricultural work had fallen precipitously.[4] In 2001, the sociologist Steven Brint estimated that the "scientific, professional and knowledge economy" accounted for 36 percent of all US employment in 1996. Brint's human-capital–based estimate included industries in which at least 5 percent of the workforce has graduate degrees, including agricultural services, mass media, chemicals, plastics, pharmaceuticals, computers and electric equipment, scientific instruments, banking, accounting, consulting and other business services, health services and hospitals, education, legal services, and nearly all religious and governmental organizations.[5]

In *Bobos in Paradise,* David Brooks described a new blending of bohemian and bourgeois values among upper-income professionals.[6] But Creative Class identity runs much deeper than a set of changing affections and affectations; it is rooted in our changed economic circumstances. What binds it together is not just its values and attitudes but the place it occupies in the economic structure.

Class membership follows from people's economic functions. Their social identities as well as their cultural preferences, values, lifestyles, and consumption and buying habits all flow from this. Whereas members of the Working Class work mainly with their physical bodies, members of the Creative Class work mainly with their minds. And for all those who believe this kind of mental or creative labor does not match up to physical work, listen to what the great chronicler of the Working Class, Karl Marx, had to say:

> Nature builds no machines, no locomotives, railways, electric telegraphs, self-acting mules, etc. These are products of human industry; natural material transformed into organs of the human will over nature, they are organs of the human brain, created by the human hand; the power of knowledge objectified. The development of [technology] indicates to what degree general social knowledge has become a direct force of production, and to what degree, hence, the conditions of the process of social life itself have come under the control of the general intellect and have been transformed in accordance with it.[7]

There are no shortages of social scientists who believe that class has declined as a social and economic category. I disagree with them fundamentally. Class, in particular the rise of the Creative Class, exerts an increasingly powerful influence over virtually every aspect of our lives. Throughout this book, and in its penultimate chapter, added especially for this revised edition, I will illustrate the effects class has on myriad aspects of our very existence, from the economic performance of our cities, regions, and nations to our political views and values, from the ways we work to our very health and well-being.

In this book's original edition, I noted that although my field research and interviews made it clear that members of the Creative Class did not yet see themselves as members of a unique social grouping, they actually did share many tastes, desires, and preferences. I added that this new class may not be as distinct in this regard as the industrial Working Class was in its heyday, but it does have an emerging coherence. Since that time, the Creative Class has become increasingly self-aware, not just within nations but globally.

This chapter updates all of the statistics on the Creative Class and the new class structure, based on the most current available data. It also summarizes a great deal of new research on the definition of the Creative Class that has appeared since this book was first published.

Defining the Creative Class

The distinguishing characteristic of the Creative Class is that its members engage in work whose function is to "create meaningful new forms." I define the Creative Class by the occupations that people have, and I divide it into two components. What I call the *Super-Creative Core* of the Creative Class includes scientists and engineers, university professors, poets and novelists, artists, entertainers, actors, designers, and architects, as well as the thought leadership of modern society: nonfiction writers, editors, cultural figures, think-tank researchers, analysts, and other opinion makers. I define the highest order of creative work as producing new forms or designs that are readily transferable and widely useful—such as designing a consumer product that can be manufactured and sold; coming up with a theorem or strategy that can be applied in many cases; or composing music that can be performed again and again. Whether they are software programmers or engineers, architects, or filmmakers, the people at the core of the Creative Class engage in this kind of work regularly; it's what they are paid to do. Along with problem solving, their work may entail problem *finding*: not just building a better mousetrap, but noticing that a better mousetrap would be a handy thing to have.

Beyond this core group, the Creative Class also includes "creative professionals" who work in a wide range of knowledge-intensive industries, such as high-tech, financial services, the legal and health care professions, and business management. These people engage in creative problem solving, drawing on complex bodies of knowledge to solve specific problems. Doing so typically requires a high degree of formal education and thus a high level of human capital. People who do this kind of work may sometimes come up with methods or products that turn out to be widely useful, but it's not part of their basic job description. What they *are* required to do regularly is to think on their own, apply or combine standard approaches in unique ways to fit different situations, exercise a great deal of judgment, and perhaps even try something radically new from time to time. Creative Class people such as physicians, lawyers, and managers may also be involved in testing and refining new treatment protocols, new legal interpretations or management techniques, and may even develop such things themselves. As they do more of this latter kind of work, perhaps through a career shift or promotion, they move up to the Super-Creative Core: producing transferable, widely usable new forms is now their primary function.

Much the same is true of the growing number of technicians who apply complex bodies of knowledge to their work with physical materials. They are sufficiently engaged in creative problem solving that I have included a large subset of them in the Creative Class. In an insightful study,[8] Stephen Barley of Stanford University emphasized the growing importance and influence of this group of workers, who are taking on increased responsibility to interpret their work and make decisions, blurring the old distinction between white-collar work (done by decision makers) and blue-collar work (done by those who follow orders).

There has been a robust debate over how to define the Creative Class since this book was originally published. One common misperception is that the Creative Class is just another way of counting people who have college degrees—the more conventional measure of human capital. In his review of the original edition of this book, the Harvard University urban economist Edward Glaeser wrote: "While Florida acts as if there is a difference between the human capital theory of city growth and the 'creative capital' theory of growth, that is news to me. I have always argued that human capital predicts urban success because 'high skilled people in high skilled industries may come up with new ideas.'"[9] Or as *Forbes* writer Mark Bergen tweeted about the Creative Class on October 7, 2011, "If you just called it the 'Bachelor's Degree or Higher Class,' it'd be a whole lot less confusing."

The reality is, while degree holders and the Creative Class overlap considerably, they're hardly the same.[10] Across the entire United States, nearly three-fourths (72.2 percent, to be exact) of adults with college degrees are members of the Creative Class. But less than 60 percent (59.3 percent) of the members of the Creative Class have college degrees, according to a detailed analysis by my colleagues Kevin Stolarick of the University of Toronto and Elizabeth Currid-Halkett of the University of Southern California. In other words, four in ten members of the Creative Class—16.6 million workers—do *not* have college degrees. As Stolarick and Currid-Halkett write: "Thus, while some correlation would be expected, our results indicate that human capital and the Creative Class do not necessarily capture the same people nor is a measure of each's respective presence in a regional economy indicative of similar trends."[11]

With data supplied by Stolarick, Glaeser ran a regression analysis of the relative economic effects of my Creative Class measures versus the conventional human capital measure (the share of adults with at least a college degree) and found that the conventional variable substantially outperformed mine. "Maybe there is more to creativity than just schooling," he writes, "but the regression doesn't show it." Maybe he should talk with Sir Ken Robinson, the education expert who shows that schooling often inhibits and retards creativity.[12] But that's beside the point. The metric that Glaeser used to capture performance was population growth, and population growth and economic growth are not the same thing at all. Many regions that grow population experience little or no economic growth. In fact, there is no correlation between the two.

The fact is, a significant body of research shows that the Creative Class measure operates in addition to and through other channels than the standard human capital variable. A large-scale study by Stolarick, Mellander, and myself shows that the Creative Class has a bigger effect on wages—a key element of regional productivity— whereas education tends to have a greater effect on income.[13] Independent research by economist Todd Gabe and others backs this up, showing that the Creative Class continues to have a substantial effect on regional economic growth when controlling for the effects of education and other factors.

More to the point, having a Creative Class job also brings economic benefits that extend beyond those of going to college. A college graduate working in the same occupation as a non-college graduate earns approximately 50 percent higher wages. But having a Creative Class job adds another 16 percent, about the same as another 1.5 years of additional education, according to Gabe's research.[14] Even more important, just counting years of education ignores a lot of people who do very creative work, including world-shaping entrepreneurs such as Steve Jobs and Bill Gates, or artists and others who did not complete college.

Others criticized my concept of the Creative Class as a "hodge-podge," saying it includes too broad a spectrum of occupations and types of work to be really meaningful. For example, businesspeople make a lot more money than artists. True, artists, designers, entertainers, and media workers earn about half ($52,290 per year in 2010) of what those in management occupations earn and considerably less than lawyers, engineers, and architects. Of the major Creative Class occupations, only education workers make less. But the pay differences within the Creative Class pale when you compare them to the differences between the classes (see Table 3.1). Other critics pointed out that artists, engineers, and businesspeople are very different kinds of people, with different interests and personalities. If you weren't likely to find them at the same cocktail party, how could you say they belonged to the same class? I could say that they missed the point, but there is a better

Table 3.1   Average Annual Wages and Salaries for the Classes, 2010

Class/Occupation	Salary
Creative Class	$70,714
Management	$105,440
Legal	$96,940
Computer and Mathematical	$77,230
Architecture and Engineering	$75,550
Health Care Practitioners and Technical	$71,280
Business and Financial Operations	$67,690
Life, Physical, and Social Science	$66,390
Sales (high-end)	$61,484
Arts, Design, Entertainment, Sports, and Media	$52,290
Education, Training, and Library	$50,440
Working Class	$36,991
Service Class	$29,188
Agriculture	$24,324
All Occupations	$44,410

Source: U.S. Department of Labor, Bureau of Labor Statistics, Occupational Employment Statistics (OES) Survey, 2010. Available online at http://www.bls.gov/oes/. Analysis by Kevin Stolarick.

answer. My original definition of the Creative Class was admittedly based upon my research teams' subjective assessments of the skill content of work. But objective new data have since become available. In a major 2007 study, David McGranahan and Timothy Wojan, two economists with the US Department of Agriculture, independently updated the definition of the Creative Class, using detailed data from the Bureau of Labor Statistics' Occupational Information Network (O*NET) to specify the skills for each of the occupations I included in my original definition.[15] For the most part, they found that my original definition held up, and that the correlation between my original and their updated definition was substantial.[16]

In his bestselling *Shop Class as Soulcraft: An Inquiry into the Value of Work,* Matthew Crawford, a philosophy-PhD'd think-tanker turned motorcycle repairman, charged me with trying to elevate the mind work of faux bohemians, information techies, and creative professionals over the old fashioned physical skills of shop floor workers (he dubs it the "cult of creativity"). He accused me of subscribing to the fashionable hippie nostrum that "Creativity is what happens when people are liberated from the constraints of conventionality." Chastizing me, he notes that "the truth, of course, is that creativity is a by-product of mastery of the sort that is cultivated through long practice."[17] First, it's simply not true that I elevate one kind of work over another. In the previous chapter, I showed how Creative Class theory is built off my own experiences as a young boy in my father's creative factory, and later from my studies of the advanced factories of Japan, which led a revolution in productivity by tapping into workers' knowledge and creative talents as well as their physical skills.

The empirical fact that the Creative and Service Class sectors are growing while blue-collar physical jobs are in dramatic decline cannot be avoided. Crawford makes an impassioned case for the kind of skilled trade work that he does in his motorcycle repair shop, as well he should—such work has been and continues to be the source of good livelihoods and much fulfillment to those fortunate enough to be able to do it. The unfortunate truth, however, is that the kind of work Crawford does is available to only a small minority of workers. There are 5.3 million installation, repair, and maintenance workers in the United States, less than one-tenth of the more than 60 million workers who toil in mainly low-skill, low-paid service jobs. Only 16,850 of them are motorcycle mechanics, a fraction of a percent of the total US workforce. Crawford's own job is particularly enviable. As the owner-operator of his own shop, he's not an immiserated proletarian by any means, but an entrepreneur. What makes Crawford's job a good job—a great one, really—is more than the physical skills he's honed. It's that he is one of a very small minority of workers who can use his full complement of talents and skills—cognitive, social, physical, and managerial. He has near-complete control over how his work is done, and the flexibility to do it how and when he likes—to be his own boss. For these reasons, his work is a source of great pride and obvious joy. What Crawford does in his shop, in fact, has much in common with Creative Class work. Most manufacturing and production work isn't like this. Much of it remains mind-numbing, de-skilled, and controlled by machines—a modern, high-tech version of Charlie Chaplin flailing away as he tries to keep up with the assembly line.

Tracking the Classes

Working with my colleague Kevin Stolarick, first at Carnegie Mellon University and now at the University of Toronto's Martin Prosperity Institute, I developed a detailed statistical portrait of the rise of the Creative Class and the changing class structure of the United States through history, based on detailed occupational data collected by the US Census. (The Appendix provides a complete explanation

Figure 3.1 The Class Structure, 1800–2010

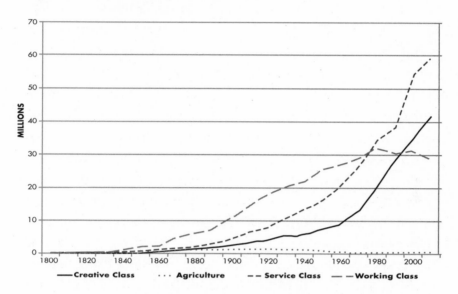

Source: Analysis by Kevin Stolarick. See the appendix for full detail on sources.

of all data and sources.) Our original time line covered the years 1900–1999; we have updated and expanded it to cover 1800 through 2010 (see Figures 3.1 and 3.2).

As of 2010, the Creative Class included some more than 41 million Americans, roughly one-third of the entire US workforce. This is up from the 38 million plus workers and 30 percent of the workforce in 1999 that I reported in the original edition. But consider how much it has expanded over the long sweep of history. In 1800, the Creative Class accounted for just 12 percent of the US workforce, and it hovered between that and 16 percent until 1960. It increased gradually to 19 percent in 1970, to 24 percent in 1980, and now stands at 32.6 percent as of 2010. In dollars-and-cents terms, Creative Class members make quite a lot more than those in other classes, averaging more than $70,000 per year. Taken as a whole, the Creative Class packs an even larger economic punch, accounting for roughly half of all US wages and salaries.

Figure 3.2   The Class Structure, 1800–2010 (Percent of Workforce)

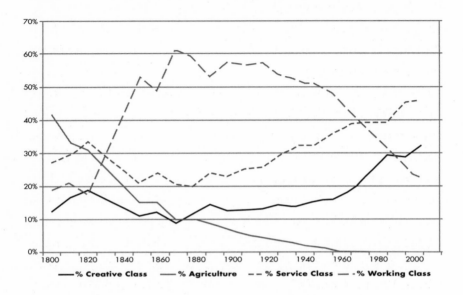

Source: Analysis by Kevin Stolarick. See the appendix for full detail on sources.

Growing alongside the Creative Class is the Service Class, which contains low-end, typically low-wage and low-autonomy occupations such as: food-service workers, janitors and groundskeepers, personal care attendants, secretaries and clerical workers, and security guards, among many others. In US Bureau of Labor Statistics (BLS) projections from the late 1990s and 2000, service jobs like "janitors and cleaners" and "waiters and waitresses" were some of the fastest-growing job categories alongside creative ones like "computer support specialists" and "systems analysts." A decade later, in 2012, the fastest-growing job categories the BLS predicted out to 2020 included "personal care aides" and "home health aides" ahead of Creative Class jobs for "biomedical engineers."[18]

The Service Class includes some 60 million workers, or 47 percent of the US workforce, making it the largest group of all. This is up from 55.2 million, or 43 percent of the workforce, when I wrote the original edition ten years ago. The Service Class grew from about one in five workers in the late nineteenth century to one-third of the workforce by 1950 before climbing to 45 percent with the new millennium.

The growth of this Service Class is in large measure a response to the demands of the Creative Economy. As the economy has become more specialized and the occupational division of labor has deepened, the Creative Class has increasingly outsourced functions that were previously provided within the family to the Service Class. Some Service Class members have high upward mobility and will eventually move into the Creative Class—college students working nights or summers as food servers or office cleaners, for example, or highly educated recent immigrants driving cabs in New York City or Washington, DC. A few entrepreneurially minded members may be successful enough to open their own restaurants, lawn and garden services, and the like. But many have no way out; they are stuck for life in menial jobs.

At its minimum-wage worst, life in the Service Class is a grueling struggle for subsistence amid the wealth of others. By going "undercover" as a service worker, Barbara Ehrenreich provided a moving chronicle of life on the bottom of the economic food chain in *Nickel and Dimed*,[19] a book that is even more relevant ten years after its first publication (it was rereleased in 2011 with a new afterword). The economic gap between the Creative Class and the Service Class underpins the widening economic inequalities in America and elsewhere. Members of the Service Class earn just slightly more than $30,000 annually, roughly 40 percent of what the Creative Class does.[20] And though they make up more than 45 percent of the workforce, they account for just one-third of all wages and salaries. More than this widening gap in income and economic security, this trend reflects a fundamental divide in what people are able to do with their lives, and how the economic positions and lifestyle choices of some people drive and perpetuate the choices available to others.

Finally, there is the traditional Working Class, which has about 26 million members, down roughly 20 percent from the 33 million I reported in the original edition of this book. It consists of workers in production operations, transportation and materials moving, repair and maintenance, and construction work.

The Working Class share of the workforce surpassed that of agriculture around 1830, and continued to climb steadily, reaching 60 percent of the workforce by 1870. America remained a majority Working Class nation until the 1950s and the Working Class share of the workforce remained above 40 percent into the 1970s. It has declined ever since, hitting 31 percent of the workforce in 1990 before declining to 21 percent by 2010. The share of the workforce engaged in direct production has declined even more, to just 6 percent. In 2010, the Working Class averaged $34,015 in annual wages, roughly half (52 percent) of the Creative Class.

Alongside the growth in Creative Class occupations, we are also seeing growth in creative content across other kinds of jobs. As this increases—as the relevant body of knowledge becomes more complex and workers are more valued for their ingenuity in applying it—some now in the Working Class or Service Class may move into the Creative Class. A prime example of this can be seen in the secretary in today's pared-down offices. In many cases this person not only takes on a host of tasks once performed by a large staff but becomes a true office manager—channeling the flow of information, devising and setting up new administrative systems, often making key decisions on the fly. This person contributes more than intelligence or computer skills. He or she adds creative value. My recent research with Charlotta Mellander shows not only that Working Class and Service Class members do engage in creative work but that when they do so, it results in higher productivity and higher wages (a crucial point I will return to in the final chapter of this book). Not all workers are on track to join the Creative Class, however. Since we cannot truly prosper with a system that harnesses the creativity of only one-third of its workforce, the key task of the future must be to fully engage the creative talents of the other two-thirds.

The Crisis and the Creative Class

Marx long ago showed how capitalist crises fuel the rise of new classes and the eclipse of older ones and the economic systems they are inextricably connected to. The Great Depression of the 1930s and the Panic and Long Depression of the 1870s, as I have written elsewhere, reset the economic and social order, accelerating the rise of new production systems and new classes that were attached to them. We are seeing this happen again. The crisis that began in 2008 has hit hardest at the Working Class and especially at blue-collar men, so hard, in fact, that some pundits dubbed its fallout the "mancession." Hanna Rosin's much-discussed *Atlantic* article, "The End of Men," argued that the age of male dominance might have come to its end. "What if," she asked, "the modern, postindustrial economy is simply more congenial to women than men?"[21]

As the Working Class shrank, the Creative Class expanded. Between 2001 and 2010, the Creative Class grew by 2.8 million workers, or 7.2 percent, expanding from 38.7 million to 41.4 million members. The Working Class lost some 6 million of its members—nearly one in five workers—over this same period, shrinking from 32.2 million to just 26 million. The shift can also be seen in the share of the workforce accounted for by each of these classes. The Creative Class share of the total workforce increased from 27.5 percent in

2001 to 32.6 percent in 2010, while the Working Class share fell from 22.9 percent to 20.5 percent. Creative Class employment did fall over the course of the crisis, declining by about 700,000 workers, or about 1.5 percent, between 2008 and 2010. But this pales in comparison to what the Working Class and Service Class endured. The Working Class lost more than 5 million jobs during that same period, and Service Class lost another 2 million jobs. Figure 3.2 shows the small blip in Creative Class growth caused by the crisis—a deficit that it will more than make up in short order. According to Bureau of Labor Statistics projections, the Creative Class is projected to add another 5.4 million jobs by 2020.

The effects of the crisis can also be seen in the very different ways that the various classes experienced unemployment. The overall US unemployment rate more than doubled, rising from less than 5 percent in November 2007 to 10.1 percent by October 2009. During the period of rapidly surging unemployment from January through June 2009, the unemployment rate for the Working Class rose to 15.2 percent, up from 6.2 percent before the onset of the crisis, while Service Class unemployment hit 9 percent. But the unemployment rate for the Creative Class, which was a negligible 1.8 percent in 2007, rose to just 4.4 percent at its apex in 2009—less than one-half the rate for the Service Class and less than one-third of that of the Working Class.

With Todd Gabe from the University of Maine and my Martin Prosperity Institute colleague Charlotta Mellander, I undertook a detailed statistical analysis to gauge the effects of a person's socioeconomic class on unemployment prior to and near the official end of the recession, controlling for the effects of gender, age, education, and other factors that might be expected to have an effect on unemployment.[22] Working Class members were more likely to be unemployed even before the crisis struck: belonging to the Working Class increased the probability of being unemployed by 1.8 percentage points as of March 2007. This probability more than doubled, to 4.1 percentage points, by March 2009. Creative Class members faced far less risk of unemployment over the course of the crisis. Having a Creative Class job actually lowered a person's probability of being unemployed by 2.8 percentage points—a very big impact. We also found that having a large Creative Class presence in a region lessened the impact of the crisis on members of the Working Class—mainly because, as Part 4 will show, such regions are more economically vibrant and resilient across the board.

A separate study by Stolarick and Currid-Halkett examined the relationship between the Creative Class and unemployment rates between July 2007 and February 2011 across more than 350 US metropolitan areas.[23] Overall, they found the Creative Class to be negatively associated with regional unemployment: the larger a region's creative workforce, the lower its unemployment rate. They note:

> At the peak, a 1% increase in the creative class and a 1% decrease in the working class, *ceteris paribus,* are associated with an unemployment rate that is 5.7% *lower*. Increasing the creative class by 1% and decreasing the service class by 1%, *ceteris paribus*, would reduce unemployment by 7.1%. Increasing the working class by 1% with a service class decrease of 1%, *ceteris paribus*, would increase unemployment by 1.4%. The overall impact indicates that a higher share of creative workers is associated with lower unemployment, from the expansion of the crisis through to the current day.

Just the class variables alone explained between 30 and 57 percent of the variation in regional unemployment rates. "Cities with a larger creative class experienced slower unemployment as the crisis started, and the rate was even slower as joblessness was expanding across the country," they write. "Cities with a creative workforce reached a lower peak unemployment rate and then recovered more quickly." They conclude, "In short, having a creative workforce going into the crisis helped mitigate its effects on the regional economy."

This pattern has been the case not just for the current crisis but going back more than four decades. Figure 3.3 tracks the unemployment rate for the three major classes from 1971 to 2009. The Working Class unemployment rate surged to 14.5 percent in the recession year of 1975, hit 16.8 percent in 1983, 12 percent in 1992, and then 15.2 percent in 2009. Service Class unemployment hit 9 percent in 1983 and again in 2009. Creative Class unemployment never topped 5 percent over this entire period, hitting highs of 3 percent in 1976, 3.7 percent in 1983, 3.1 percent in 1993 and again in 2003, and its modern-day high of 4.4 in 2009.

Figure 3.3 The Unemployment Rate by Class, 1971–2009

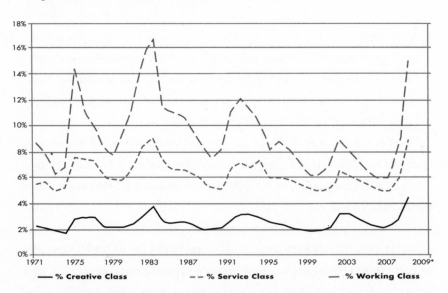

* Jan.–June 2009 seasonally adjusted, otherwise annual average

Source: U.S. Bureau of Labor Statistics and the Current Population Survey, various years. Analysis by the Martin Prosperity Institute.

Which isn't to say that the crisis hasn't been hard on some members of the Creative Class—it's been hard on everyone. On October 1, 2011, *Salon*'s Scott Timberg went so far as to declare that the Creative Class's very existence is in jeopardy in an article that bore the provocative title "The Creative Class Is a Lie."[24] Just as video purportedly killed the radio star, the Internet and the economic crisis is murdering the Creative Class, in Timberg's view. "This creative class was supposed to be the new engine of the United States economy, post-industrial age, and as the educated, laptop-wielding cohort grew, the U.S. was going to grow with it," he wrote. "But for those who deal with ideas, culture and creativity at street level— the working- or middle-classes within the creative class—things are less cheery. Book editors, journalists, video store clerks, musicians, novelists without tenure—they're among the many groups struggling through the dreary combination of economic slump and Internet reset. The creative class is melting, and the story is largely untold," he added.

To Timberg's point, the Creative Class did have its share of losers during the last decade. The biggest job losses occurred among "news analysts, reporters, and correspondents" (a category that lost 15,130 jobs, a substantial 22.9 percent decline), musicians and singers (8,830 jobs lost, down 16.9 percent), photographers (10,810 jobs lost, down 16.5 percent), and editors (5,050 jobs lost, down 4.9 percent). But as I pointed out when I responded to Timberg's *Salon* piece, other segments of the Creative Class experienced substantial job growth. Jobs for producers and directors went up by nearly 80 percent (36,770 new jobs); art director jobs grew by 45 percent; nearly 60,000 new jobs opened up for graphic designers (up 45 percent); and audio and video equipment technician jobs increased by roughly 40 percent. Overall, the Creative Class added nearly 3 million jobs between 2001 and 2010, growing jobs at a 7 percent clip. The subgroup of the Creative Class that spans arts and media grew at nearly double that rate (13.8 percent) over the same period. Average Creative Class wages increased by more than one-third (34.5 percent), from $52,707 to $70,890, over this decade—more than any other major occupational group—and wages for arts and media creatives rose by 31.5 percent.

The Creative Class's hard times hardly register in comparison to the outright decimation of the blue-collar Working Class, which lost a staggering 6.2 million jobs over the same decade. Not to mention that Creative Class workers, even in the hardest-hit fields, have the skills and education that allow them to switch jobs and even careers when required—an option that is largely unavailable to blue-collar and service workers. Although some parts of the Creative Class have fared better than others, people who work with their heads haven't suffered nearly as much as those who work with their hands.

Gender, Race, and the Creative Class

The original edition of this book tracked the Creative Class as a monolithic unit, but gender and race remain key fault lines in American society. To what extent do they register in and across the Creative Class and other classes? Utilizing detailed data from the American Community Survey, Charlotta Mellander and I took a close look at this issue.

Women make up the majority of the Creative Class, accounting for 52 percent of its members. A greater percentage of women hold Creative Class jobs (37.1 percent) than men (32.6 percent). But Mellander and I found that Creative Class men earn about 40 percent more than women—$82,009 versus $48,077—a gap of nearly $35,000.[25] Some of this can be explained by differences in work experience, skills, education, and longer work hours. But even when we control for these factors, Creative Class men still outearn Creative Class women by a substantial $23,700—nearly 50 percent of the average salary for Creative Class women.[26]

Men continue to dominate the Working Class, holding more than 80 percent of positions. Four in ten men are members of the Working Class, compared to just 6 percent of women. Women hold the lion's share of Service Class jobs—nearly two-thirds (62.2 percent). More than half of women (54 percent) hold Service Class jobs, compared to just 30 percent of men.

These statistics help explain the different ways that the crisis has affected women and men. Before the crisis struck, the unemployment rate was pretty similar for men and women—4.3 percent for men and 3.8 percent for women. By 2009, the differential had grown to more than two percentage points—9.5 percent for males and 7.1 percent for women. A large part of this difference comes from the concentration of men in the Working Class and women in the Creative and Service Classes.

Race is the source of even more substantial divides within the Creative Class. More than eight in ten (80.9 percent) of Creative Class jobs are held by whites, who make up just 74 percent of the nation's population. The rest are more or less evenly split among the three remaining racial groups—African Americans (6.8 percent), Hispanics (6.2 percent), and Asians (6.1 percent).

When we look within racial groups, we find an interesting racial division of labor, so to speak. Asians are by far the most heavily represented in Creative Class work. Nearly one-half (47 percent) of them work in Creative Class jobs, compared to roughly one-third (34 percent) of whites, 24 percent of African Americans, and 18 percent of Hispanics. The Service Class is more evenly split across the races. Roughly 40 percent of whites and Hispanics do Service Class work, compared to 48.2 percent of blacks and 37 percent of Asians. Four in ten Hispanics are members of the Working Class, compared to 28 percent of blacks, 25 percent of whites, but just 16 percent of Asians.

Creative Class Values

The rise of the Creative Class is reflected in powerful and significant shifts in values, norms, and attitudes. Although these changes are still in process, a number of key trends can be identified. Not all of these attitudes break with the past: most have long been associated with more highly educated and creative people; some represent a melding of traditional values with newer ones. On the basis of my own interviews and focus groups, along with a close reading of statistical surveys conducted by others, I cluster them along three basic lines.

Individuality.   Members of the Creative Class exhibit a strong preference for individuality and self-expression. They are reluctant to conform to organizational or institutional directives and resist traditional group-oriented norms. This has always been the case among creative people, from "quirky" artists to "eccentric" scientists. But it has become far more pervasive. In this sense, the increasing nonconformity with organizational norms may represent a paradoxically new mainstream value. Members of the Creative Class endeavor to create individualistic identities that reflect their creativity. This can entail a mixing of multiple creative identities.

Meritocracy.   Merit is very strongly valued by the Creative Class, a quality shared with Whyte's class of organization men. The Creative Class favors hard work, challenge, and stimulation. Its members have a propensity for goal setting and achievement. They want to get ahead because they are good at what they do. There are many reasons for this emphasis on merit. Creative Class people have always been motivated by the respect of their peers. They are ambitious and want to move up based on their abilities and effort. But meritocracy also has its dark side. Qualities that confer merit, such as technical knowledge and mental discipline, are socially acquired and cultivated. Yet those who have these qualities may easily begin to believe that they were born with them, or acquired them all on their own, or that others just "don't have it." By papering over the causes of cultural and educational advantage, meritocracy may subtly perpetuate the very prejudices it claims to renounce. Of course, meritocracy also ties into a host of values and beliefs we'd all agree are positive—from faith that virtue will be rewarded to valuing self-determination and mistrusting rigid caste systems. Researchers have found such values to be on the rise, not only among the Creative Class in the United States, but throughout our own and other societies.

Diversity and Openness.   Diversity has become a politically charged buzzword. To some it is an ideal that we should always be striving for; to others it is the Trojan-horse concept that introduced affirmative action and other liberal abominations to our society. The Creative Class people I study use the word a lot, but not to press any political hot buttons. Diversity is simply something they value, in all its manifestations. It is spoken of so often, and so matter-of-factly, that I take it to be a fundamental marker of Creative Class values. As my focus groups and interviews reveal, members of this class strongly favor organizations and environments in which they feel that anyone can fit in and get ahead.

Diversity is favored first of all out of self-interest; it can be a signal of meritocratic norms. A number of Creative Class people have told me that they always ask if a company offers same-sex partner benefits when they are interviewing for a job, even if they are not gay themselves. What they're seeking is an environment that is open to differences—of gender, sexual preference, race, or even personal idiosyncrasies. Many highly creative people, regardless of their ethnic background or sexual orientation, grew up feeling like outsiders, like they were different in some way from most of their schoolmates. They may have odd personal habits or extreme styles of dress. Also, Creative Class people are mobile and tend to move around to different parts of the country; they may not be "natives" of the places where they live, even if they are American-born. When they are sizing up a new company and community, acceptance of diversity is a sign that reads "nonstandard people welcome here." Diversity also registers itself in changed behaviors and organizational policies. For example, in some Creative Class centers like Silicon Valley in California and Austin, Texas, the traditional office Christmas party is giving way to more secular, inclusive celebrations. The big event at many firms is now the Halloween party: Just about anyone can relate to a holiday that involves dressing up in costume. Surveys show such openness to diversity has increased substantially over the past decade. The astounding celerity with which gay marriage has moved from the unthinkable to mainstream acceptance provides an indication of how widely Creative Class values have been disseminated—and how deeply they've penetrated the culture.

Although the Creative Class favors openness and diversity, to some degree it is a diversity of elites, with membership limited to highly educated, creative people. Speaking of a small software company that had the usual assortment of Indian, Chinese, Arabic, and other employees, an Indian technology professional said: "That's not diversity! They're all software engineers." Although the rise of the Creative Class has opened up new avenues of advancement for women and members of ethnic minorities, its existence has certainly failed to put an end to long-standing divisions of race and gender. Within high-tech industries in particular, these divisions still seem to hold. As we have seen, although women make up the majority of the Creative Class, a substantial gender gap persists in wages and salaries. Race remains an even more salient factor. The high-tech world doesn't include many African Americans. Several of my interviewees noted that a typical high-tech company "looks like the United Nations minus the black faces." On October 8, 2011, the scholar and tech entrepreneur Vivek Wadhwa sent out an apposite tweet on this subject: "More than 50% of Silicon Valley is foreign born. Less than 5% women, almost no blacks or Hispanics, sadly. A lot needs to be fixed."

This is unfortunate but not surprising. As we have seen, African Americans are underrepresented in Creative Class occupations and make nearly $10,000 less than their white peers, even when controlling for education, skill, and work effort—a substantial gap. And though my research for the original edition of this book found a strong association between centers of high-tech industry and communities that are more open toward immigrants and gays, it also found a troublingly strong negative correlation between high-tech concentrations and the percentage of the population that is nonwhite.

Global Values Shift

In more than three decades of careful research, Ronald Inglehart, a political science professor at the University of Michigan, has documented the powerful shift in values as these norms and attitudes took hold. Researchers participating in Inglehart's World Values Survey have administered detailed questionnaires to random samples of adults in countries around the world five times since 1981 (a sixth wave of surveys will conclude in 2012).[27] By 2007, the end of the last survey period, the number of nations studied had grown to ninety-seven, including some 88 percent of the world's population. Along with specific issues like divorce, abortion, and suicide, the survey has delved into matters such as deference to authority versus deciding for oneself, openness versus insularity ("can strangers be trusted?"), and what, ultimately, is most important in life. Inglehart and his colleagues have sifted the resulting data to look for internal correlations (which kinds of values tend to go together) and for correlations with economic and social factors, such as a nation's level of economic development, its form of government, and its religious heritage. The researchers compared nations to one another, mapping out various similarities and differences—and they also looked for changes over time.

Among other things, Inglehart has found a worldwide shift from economic growth issues to lifestyle values, which he sometimes refers to as a shift from "survival" to "self-expression" values. Moreover, where lifestyle values are rising or dominant, as in the United States and most European societies in the present day, people tend to be relatively tolerant of other groups and in favor of gender equality, which is very much in line with Creative Class values. In everything from sexual norms and gender roles to environmental values, Inglehart finds a continued movement away from traditional norms to more progressive ones. Furthermore, as economies grow, living standards improve and people grow less attached to large institutions; they become more open and tolerant in their views about personal relationships.

Inglehart believes this new value system reflects a "shift in what people want out of life, transforming basic norms governing politics, work, religion, family and sexual behavior." Research that my team and I have conducted on more than one hundred countries since the original edition of this book was published (which I will discuss in later chapters) finds that the Creative Class is strongly associated with Inglehart's "self-expression" and "secular-rational" values across nations.[28] And other studies I conducted with my colleagues (which I will also discuss in detail later) show a strong association between the Creative Class and openness toward gays and ethnic and racial minorities across nations.[29]

This shift in values and attitudes, as Inglehart notes, is driven by changes in our material conditions. In agricultural societies and even for much of the industrial age, people endured chronic conditions of scarcity. We had to work simply to survive. The rise of an affluent or "post-scarcity" economy means that we no longer have to devote all our energies just to staying alive, but have the wealth, time, and ability to enjoy other aspects of life. This in turn affords us choices we did not used to have. "Precisely because they attained high levels of economic security," writes Inglehart, "the Western societies that were the first to industrialize have gradually come to emphasize post-materialist values, giving higher priority to the quality of life than to economic growth. In this respect, the rise of post-materialist values reverses the rise of the Protestant ethic."[30] Elsewhere, Inglehart comments that "the overriding trend appears to be an intergenerational shift from emphasis on economic and physical security toward increasing emphasis on self-expression, subjective well-being, and quality of life. . . . This cultural shift is found throughout advanced industrial societies; it seems to emerge among birth cohorts that have grown up under conditions in which survival is taken for granted."[31]

Although conservative commentators frequently bemoan these shifts as hedonistic, narcissistic, and damaging to society, the Creative Class isn't subversive through and through—far from it. On the one hand, its members have taken what look to be alternative values and made them mainstream: by making nonconformity mandatory, they've instilled a new kind of conformity. On the other hand, many of its most strongly held values—such as the commitment to meritocracy and to hard work—are quite traditional and system reinforcing in and of themselves. In my interviews, members

of the Creative Class resist characterization as alternative or bohemian. Those labels carry the connotation of standing outside or
even against the prevailing culture, and they insist that they are
working and living within it. It is in this sense that they represent
not an alternative group but a new and increasingly norm-setting
mainstream of society. This has become even more pronounced
over the past decade as the Creative Class and its values have permeated society, in the United States and also around the world.
Perhaps we are indeed witnessing the rise of what economic historian Joel Mokyr has dubbed *homo creativus.* We live differently
and pursue new lifestyles because we see ourselves as new kinds of
people. We are more tolerant and more liberal because our material
conditions and way of life allow it.

When I first published this book, I argued that the rise of the Creative Class had already permanently transformed our economy and
society—and I predicted that there would be deeper changes to
come. The last decade has borne that out. Far from calling Creative
Class theory into question, the economic meltdown provided dramatic confirmation that our world has become a fundamentally
different place than most of us were born into. We are living in the
eye of the storm, a period of life-altering creative destruction as a
new economic order and a new way of life emerges from the old.

PART TWO

WORK

CHAPTER 4

The Machine Shop
and the Hair Salon

During the late 1990s, I served on the board of Team Pennsylvania, an economic development advisory group convened by then governor Tom Ridge. At one of our meetings, the state's secretary of labor and industry, a big burly man, banged his fist on the table in frustration when the topic turned to the shortage of welders and machine-tool operators. "Our workforce is out of balance," he steamed. "We're turning out too many hairdressers and cosmetologists, and not enough skilled factory workers. What's wrong?"

The problem was not limited to Pennsylvania. There were acute shortages of skilled factory workers across the United States at the time that many found perplexing. Machinists, for example, earn good wages and benefits. They do important work. For many years, a machinist's job was considered an elite career for anyone not college bound. It is the sort of good job that politicians and editorial writers fret that our economy is losing. Yet as older machinists retire, there are not enough young people to fill their positions. Trade schools that teach skills like machining and welding have had to cut back or close their programs for lack of interest. Meanwhile, young men and women flock to beauty academies.

At the Team Pennsylvania meeting, the diagnosis was that (1) guidance counselors at high schools have been steering the kids wrong, because (2) our job projections have been off. If we fixed the projections and worked with the high schools—and maybe did some public-image work—surely droves of young people would come back to those good, secure manufacturing jobs.

After the meeting, I laid out the problem to my first-year public policy students (I was teaching at Carnegie Mellon at the time). I asked them: if you had just two career choices open to you, where would you work—in a machine shop, with high pay and a job for life, or in a hair salon, with less pay and where you were subject to the whims of the economy?

Virtually every student chose the hair salon, and mainly for the same reasons. Even though the pay was not as good, they saw the work as more stimulating and more flexible. You're scheduled to meet your clients and are then left alone with them, instead of grinding away to meet quotas and schedules with your bosses looking over your shoulder. It's clean. You get to work with interesting people and you're always learning new things, the latest styles. You get to add your own touches and make creative decisions, because every customer is a new challenge, and you're the one in charge. When you do good work, you see the results right away: people look good; they're happy. If you're really talented, you can open your own salon. Maybe you could even become a hairdresser to the rich and famous and get written up in celebrity magazines—like Christophe or Vidal Sassoon. Even when I pressed the issue of pay, most said the pay differential really didn't matter. In almost every case, the content of the job and the nature of the work environment mattered much more than the compensation.

I don't think guidance counselors can change this. My students who chose the hair salon over the factory saw it as the more creative, exciting, and satisfying place to work. It offers intrinsic rewards—rewards inherent in the nature of the job. I suspect that similar motives drive many of the people who choose the hair salon in real life—as well as the growing numbers of young people who are good with their hands but choose to wrap their hands around a tattooing needle, a DJ turntable, a chef's knife, or landscaping tools rather than the controls of a turret lathe. Those same values and attitudes turned up time and time again in more structured interviews and focus groups that I conducted with Creative Class people and others across the United States.

My students were onto something I did not, and could not, fully understand at the time. Work in the hair salon is creative work—among the most creative work in the entire economy. When economist Todd Gabe mapped the twenty most creative industries in the United States based upon the share of workers in high-creativity jobs (using data that were unavailable to my team and me when I wrote the original edition of this book), he came to a startling conclusion. Guess what was the single most creative occupation of all, besting artists, computer scientists, designers, and scores of others? Work in beauty salons, where nearly eight in ten jobs—for hairdressers, stylists, and cosmetologists—require high levels of creativity. Compare this to 76 percent for specialized designers, 60 percent for computer system designers, and 58 percent for independent artists.[1]

Although just finding a job has become a bigger concern since 2008, I continue to hear the same kinds of things from younger college grads today, who are unwilling to sacrifice freedom, flexibility, and challenging work simply for security and pay. This is not suprising from an economic standpoint. Although college grads have not been unaffected by the crisis, they have seen much lower rates of unemployment and joblessness than their less-educated peers. Even though the job pickings are scarcer than they might have been for their older siblings, they still feel that they have some latitude, that they have the freedom to make their own choices. Although many young college grads are burdened with substantial student loan debt, they are much less likely to be saddled with large mortgages or have children to support. In fact, one consequence of the crisis has been that younger people are putting off home buying and marriage, continuing to room together with friends or moving back in with their parents.

In a much-talked-about story in *New York* magazine, "The Kids Are Actually Sort of All Right," Noreen Malone described the fallout from the recession that she and her twenty-something friends, most of them college graduates, were suffering. "This is not just a rotten moment to be young," she wrote. "It's a putrid, stinking, several-months-old-stringy-goat-meat moment to be young."[2] But the lifestyle she describes—a combination of slacking, travel, trying out new jobs and new personas—sounds almost alluring, a far cry from the bleak prospects faced by the unskilled and uneducated.

Why are people's desires so different than what the pundits and policy makers say they should be? The reason is basic and reflects the changing nature of work for the Creative Class. Conventional wisdom says people work for money, that they will go where the financial opportunities are best and the shot at financial security is surest. In the halcyon days of the so-called New Economy, this was widely assumed to be true even of high-tech workers, whose overriding goal, the story went, was to turn stock options into untold wealth. That assumption was wrong. "You cannot motivate the best people with money," says Eric Raymond, author of *The Cathedral and the Bazaar* and a leading authority on open-source software. "Money is just a way to keep score. The best people in any field are motivated by passion."[3] Writing at the apex of the dot-com boom in the 1990s, Peter Drucker had this to say:

> Bribing the knowledge workers on whom these industries depend will therefore simply not work. The key knowledge workers in these businesses will

surely continue to expect to share financially in the fruits of their labor. But the financial fruits are likely to take much longer to ripen, if they ripen at all. . . . Increasingly, performance in these new knowledge-based industries will come to depend on running the institution so as to attract, hold, and motivate knowledge workers. When this can no longer be done by satisfying knowledge workers' greed, as we are now trying to do, it will have to be done by satisfying their values, and by giving them social recognition and social power. It will have to be done by turning them from subordinates into fellow executives, and from employees, however well paid, into partners.[4]

Of course people work to make money: Money is necessary, but it's not sufficient in and of itself. I am hardly the first observer to notice that money isn't the only thing people want. Yet my research has convinced me that many firms, scholars, and business pundits still overrate money as a motivating factor, especially in the world of creative work. What I find generally is this: yes, people want enough money to live in the manner they prefer. But money alone will not suffice to make most workers happy, committed, or motivated. As this chapter will show, drawing on my own research and that of leading management theorists and organizational psychologists, creative workers are most motivated by their work's intrinsic rewards—which flow from its very creativity.

What Creatives Want at Work

For all the attention given to workplace motivation over the years, surprisingly little hard numerical research or analysis has been done on what motivates today's creative workers.[5] But back in the summer of 2001, I had a chance to address this issue by analyzing data from surveys conducted by the magazine *InformationWeek*, which I believe are among the largest and most comprehensive on the subject. Some 20,000 information technology (IT) workers completed these surveys in 2000 and 2001, answering detailed questions about their pay and benefits as well as a host of other questions about their job satisfaction and dissatisfaction and other work-related issues. Approximately 11,000 identified themselves as staff and 9,000 as management. The samples were not scientifically random, in that people self-selected by choosing to respond. But they were extremely large and reached far beyond the computer and software industries per se, including IT workers in virtually every sector of the economy.

IT workers provide an interesting vantage point from which to examine these issues. On the one hand, they are regarded as a fairly conventional sector of the Creative Class. They are certainly a good deal more mainstream than artists, musicians, or advertising copywriters. On the other hand, IT workers are said to care a great deal about money. They were a highly paid segment of the workforce to begin with, and during the late 1990s, companies went to great lengths to provide bonuses, stock options, six-figure salaries, and other financial incentives to lure them.

One key question in the survey asked: "What matters most to you about your job?" It then listed thirty-eight factors, from which respondents could check one or more. My colleague Kevin Stolarick and I combed through the raw data and repeatedly resifted it to seek a better understanding of what IT workers value. From our first glance at the data, one bottom line was clear: money was an important but insufficient motivator. Base pay ranked fourth as a key factor, selected by 38.5 percent of respondents. Nearly twice as many selected the top-ranked factor, "challenge of job/responsibility." Interestingly, the ability to share in the financial upside through stock options did not even make the top twenty: Fewer than 10 percent of all respondents selected it. When we sorted the thirty-eight individual job factors in the *InformationWeek* survey into eleven broad clusters, challenge was by far the top-ranked factor, followed by flexibility and job stability. Compensation was fourth again, followed by peer respect, technology, and location; further down the list were company orientation, organizational culture, career orientation, and benefits.

The things that matter to IT workers stayed fairly constant as economic conditions changed between 2000, when the tech boom was at its zenith, and 2001, after the NASDAQ crash. The same three general attributes—a challenging job, a flexible workplace, and job stability—topped the list in both years. Only a small percentage of people in each survey, the roughly 10 percent cited above, ranked stock options as being very important. Both before and after the NASDAQ crash, pay was generally important, but not nearly so much as intrinsic rewards.

Challenge and Responsibility

The primacy of intrinsic rewards wasn't something that particularly surprised me. Interview subjects and participants in the focus groups I conducted in the late 1990s and early 2000s persistently told me that they like to be on the front lines, doing work that makes a difference. They talked about wanting to work on "exciting projects," "great technology," and "important stuff." And it was very important for them to work on things that would see the light of day. One of the most frustrating events they reported was having their project dropped, pecked to death, or strangled in red tape. One person commented, "I would go crazy if I could not contribute. I would die if I had to deal with constant bureaucracy and could not contribute directly."[6] My respondents displayed a general disdain for the bureaucratic strictures and long career development paths of the past. I believe this was a key factor that drove people to small companies during the high-tech boom. In a small firm, everyone counts.

One young woman in Des Moines, Iowa, described the mind-numbing tedium of her first job after college. She worked for an insurance company in an entry-level post that was essentially that of a better-paid secretary. "They had me Xeroxing paper all day and answering phones," she said. "So I quit, even though the pay was great, I had normal hours, and a secure job." She left for a job in a smaller company. There, she said, "[I could] use my skills, make a contribution, and not be bored silly all day."[7]

The young chief technology officer of a Seattle software start-up offered still another take on the subject. A boyish thirty-something of Asian American descent, he had earned his PhD in computer science at Carnegie Mellon and taught at Harvard. He had given up a promising career at the pinnacle of academia for the high-risk world of a start-up because he wanted to see his ideas have an effect in the real world. "It's not enough to just publish papers and advance theory," he told me. "I did that. For me and for an increasing number of people of my generation, you have to show the impact of your work in the commercial market. You have to show that your technology can make a real difference in the market and in people's lives."[8] This desire has only increased over the past decade; it's become a literal precondition for creative work.

Flexibility

The people in the focus groups and interviews I conducted a decade ago blanched at the very idea of a nine-to-five schedule or a standard dress code. For them, how you use your time and how you dress and adorn yourself are intensely personal aspects of life; they would not compromise on those matters simply to get a job. Many spoke of wanting to be able to "bring themselves to work"—their real identities and selves—rather than have to create a separate, instrumental self to function in the workplace. This was nothing new—

creative people from artists to professors and even scientists in corporate R&D labs have always demanded flexibility of this sort. But now it had become part and parcel of all creative work.

Flexibility means more than the freedom to show up at the office at 10:00 AM wearing a nose ring. Creative people want the freedom and flexibility to pursue side projects and outside interests—some of which are directly related to their work, others perhaps less so, like being a musician or artist or being involved in community affairs. Regardless of whether they are directly work related, creative people see such activities as a necessary means for cultivating their creativity. In a detailed ethnographic study of high-tech design firms in Chicago, the sociologist Richard Lloyd quoted one person as saying: "The place where I'd want to work would support my creative endeavors and the kinds of creative things that I did on the side, and would recognize the fact that if I was continually building my skills with my own stuff, it would also benefit the company."[9]

Another key aspect of flexibility is having input into the design of your workspace—and your role in the organization. Scientists have always controlled their work environments, setting up their own labs and designing their own experiments. The people in my focus groups and interviews wanted the same kind of freedom. In her research on high-tech start-up firms, Laurie Levesque found that this process of role making is highly valued by creative employees and their employers alike. Levesque studied eight firms in depth, interviewing both top executives and employees on their roles in the organization.[10] The most salient attributes, cited as desirable by both executives and workers, were "flexibility," meaning adapting to different responsibilities, and "defining one's own role" in the organization. Many of the employers said a key criterion for hiring an individual was that person's penchant for "wearing many hats." This was important because employers were too busy to be constantly monitoring employees. The employees, meanwhile, thrived on "ambiguity" and the ability to "create" their own role in the enterprise, which they defined as being able to take on tasks and figure out what they needed to accomplish on their own. As one high-tech worker told Levesque: "My role is unclear, and that's how I like it." Much of this looseness is a function of size. Small, emergent companies have less structure or hierarchy by their nature. People can make it up as they go along. But as a company grows, division of labor develops and people get pigeonholed in particular roles: structure emerges inexorably.

Peer Recognition

Peer recognition has always been a strong motivator for thinkers and scientists. The sociologist Robert Merton pointed to its importance in the work life of scientists a long time ago, whom he found to be motivated more by reputation than by money.[11] Building on Merton's idea, the economists Partha Dasgupta and Paul David argued that peer recognition is the primary force in the "new economics of science" because it motivates scientists to be lauded as the first to discover something new.[12] The economist Scott Stern has calculated that academic scientists actually "pay" to engage in science, sacrificing roughly 25 percent of their potential private-sector earnings in order to pursue self-defined projects at prestigious universities.[13]

In one sense, these scientists are the polar opposite of the chief technology officer I interviewed, who had abandoned academia because he wanted his work to have a commercial impact. But in another sense, they are the same. Both chose jobs that let them do what they want to do. Neither was motivated primarily by money or security, whether in the form of academic tenure or a fat corporate pension plan.

Peer recognition and reputation provide powerful sources of motivation for open-source software developers, who have evolved a complex, self-organizing, self-governing system of peer review that works much like that in academic science.[14] Most are paid nothing for the time they devote to such work. They post their contributions for free so that their peers will recognize them as competent and successful developers.

The intrinsic nature of my work is what keeps me at my keyboard for hours, hardly noticing that it's long past bedtime and hardly caring that I've missed the chance to go to a party or have some other kind of fun. The work itself is the reward. The psychologist Mihaly Csikszentmihalyi dubs this feeling a state of "flow"[15] that is both productive and rewarding. Can this kind of passion for work and flow come dangerously close to workaholism? Of course it can. But for me and many others, it is far better than work that has you counting the minutes until it's time to stop.

Location and Community

For a long time, people have been arguing—wrongly, I believe—that globalization and technology are rendering community and location obsolete and irrelevant. Showing the limits of that kind of thinking and the ongoing role of place, community, and location in the economy and in our lives has been a key focus of my research over the past several decades. Virtually all of the creative workers I talked to when I was first writing this book, those I have interviewed since, and my empirical studies underline the fact that location and community are more important than ever. My interview subjects continually recounted their desire and *need* to live in places that offer stimulating, creative environments. Many would not even consider taking jobs in certain cities or regions—a stark contrast to the Organizational Age, when people gladly let firms shuttle them from one backwater to another as part of the price of climbing the corporate ladder. Some told me they used location as their primary criterion in a proactive sense: they picked the place they

wanted to live and then focused their job search there. Many subsequent studies have noted this tendency as well.

Almost one in five of the workers in the 2000 and 2001 *InformationWeek* surveys reported that the geographic location of their
workplace (18.7 percent) and the amount of time they had to commute to get there (18.8 percent) had been important factors in
their choice of jobs—more important than the potential for promotion, bonus opportunities, financial stability, company prestige,
stock options, on-site child care, telecommuting, and the ability
to work from home. Research proves that long commutes are truly
misery inducing. When the behavioral economist and Nobel laureate Daniel Kahneman and the economist Alan Krueger asked
900 women to rate their favorite activities, commuting came in
dead last.[16]

People not only want to live near their workplace; they want to
like living there. In the original edition of this book, I noted that
picking a location simply for economic reasons can and often does
backfire. My focus groups and interviews provided many examples
of people who moved strictly for a job and later quit in quest of a
location that was a better fit for their lifestyle. Back then I often
heard from former students who were looking to leave the high-
paying consulting jobs they'd landed for improved quality of life.
Economic conditions have become even more unequal since the
crash of 2008, making location more important still, both for access
to jobs and quality of life.

Numerous Creative Class people I interviewed noted their desire
to become actively engaged in the places they live—to contribute
to their communities and to have some latitude in their jobs to do
so. Of course, executives have long been enlisted to lead charitable
campaigns or to serve on the boards of nonprofit institutions. But
Creative Class people don't just dutifully add their names to blue-
ribbon committees; they seek direct involvement on their own

terms, in part because it is an expression of who they are, of their essential creative identity—a point I will return to later in this book.

The idea that young creatives might care as much about where they live as who they work for seemed a bit strange to some readers a decade ago. But more and more—and not just in the United States, but around the world—it has become the norm, so much so that I now teach a graduate course at the Rotman School of Management in which I challenge my students to develop locational strategies for selecting and being involved in their communities. The key point is that people use these extracurricular activities as a way of cultivating their interests, values, and identities, both in the workplace and in society more generally. In my view, they reflect a broader process of self-actualization and an attempt to use work as a platform for pushing forward an overall creative identity.

Money and More

Compensation, of course, still matters, and compensation involves more than base pay. The decade before this book was first published, the 1990s, saw a rapid run-up in the use of alternative forms of compensation, such as stock options and bonuses. Workers, it was understood, were trading job stability and security for bigger paydays. Although the kinds of outsized bonuses that executives in the financial industry paid themselves have fallen into justifiable disrepute, many commentators still believe that bonuses can provide an effective means of aligning company and individual interests.

So how do workers value these various forms of compensation? The 2000 and 2001 *Information Week* survey data offered a number of insights. Job stability was more highly valued than any form of direct compensation. More than 40 percent of workers chose it as a key factor. Base pay was slightly less important, with 38.5 percent saying it was a key factor. Vacation and time off ranked next highest, chosen by slightly more than one-third. Benefits (such as medical insurance and pension plans) mattered almost as much as vacation time. Surprisingly enough, bonuses were not critical. At the time the *InformationWeek* surveys were conducted, the American Compensation Association reported that 83 percent of companies offered bonuses to upper management, 80 percent to middle management, and 74 percent to technical staff. Despite (or perhaps because of) their extensive use, bonuses rated twentieth of thirty-eight factors in the surveys, with just 18 percent of workers identifying them as important. They ranked lower than location, commuting distance, casual attire, and job atmosphere.

Long offered to top management, stock options became popular for other employees as well during the tech boom, because they allegedly enabled employees to share in company growth. Stock options are said to serve three interrelated functions: to lure top job candidates, to provide additional incentives for senior management, and to act as "golden handcuffs" to keep key people on the job until they become fully vested. Yet for all that, stock options ranked thirtieth in the *InformationWeek* surveys, with less than 10 percent of workers rating them as important.

Not surprisingly, job stability and security have increased in importance since the onset of the economic crisis. I'll have more to say about the crisis in a moment, but first, let's take a look at how pay and compensation interact with other factors to shape overall job satisfaction. Back in 2000 and 2001, more than half of all IT workers were satisfied with their compensation and nearly two-thirds were satisfied with their jobs overall. Roughly nine in ten of those who were satisfied with their compensation were also satisfied with their jobs.

But that only tells part of the story. The most satisfied workers were also the ones who made the most money; overall job satisfaction climbed in tandem with compensation. Perhaps the best-paid workers felt they could "afford" to focus on the other intrinsic aspects of their work. Or perhaps those workers had been performing better than their peers for a long time and so earned raises, management approval, and greater control over their jobs.

For whatever reasons, dissatisfied workers rate pay as one of the principal factors of their dissatisfaction. Furthermore, people looking for new jobs are frequently seeking higher pay. More than three-fourths of the IT workers who were looking for work in 2000 and 2001 said "higher compensation" was the main reason, followed by dissatisfaction with management (42.4 percent), the desire for "more interesting work" (39.5 percent), and "more responsibility" (31.1 percent). Job stability (18.5 percent), stock options (13.4 percent), and the chance to join a start-up company (2.9 percent) were among the lowest-rated answers. Pay clearly has much more to do with job *dissatisfaction* than satisfaction.

So what can we say about the almighty dollar? Creative people want challenging work and the ability to do their jobs flexibly, and, as with anyone else, those who receive low pay are more likely to be unhappy. But though money is important, it is not all-important. According to a series of surveys that Gallup conducted over the past decade and incorporated into its *Wellbeing*[17] books and programs, two factors—employee engagement and good, ethical management—are the real keys to job satisfaction. The more engaged employees are in their work, the more satisfied they are. On the flip side, nothing contributes to employee dissatisfaction more than meddling, incompetent management.

Herding Squirrels

Unlike the traditional Working Class, Creative Class workers expect to be treated as distinct individuals. But working from the raw data

in the *Information Week* salary surveys, Stolarick and I were able
to sort the respondents into six broad preference groups. (Our percentages add up to more than 100, as many people fell into more
than one category, and people in every group desired challenge in
their work.)

- About one-third of the IT workforce sample (34.5 percent) valued flexibility over other factors. Important job factors for these
  people included a flexible work schedule and the ability to work
  from home when they like.
- Another one-third (34 percent) were compensation driven, favoring base pay, benefits, and vacation time.
- One in five were technologists, motivated principally by the
  opportunity to work with leading-edge technology and highly
  talented peers.
- Roughly 15 percent were professionals, desiring skill development, effective supervision, and recognition for work well done.
- Company men and women (14 percent) tended to align their
  interests with the overall success of the company.
- About one in ten (11 percent) were entrepreneurs who preferred to work in start-up companies and rated stock options
  as important.

Employers seeking to align such workers' needs with their own
requirements must consider two additional points. The first is that
while motivations have always varied, these variations can no longer
be ignored. The nature of both the work and the workers has
changed. Second, employees' preferences are frequently mixed and
subject to change over time. For a long stretch of his life, our ex-
Harvard Seattle software CTO believed that academic research
suited him. But then he began to feel he had been there, done that,
so he moved on to fulfill another yearning. Most creative workers

are already on the upper rungs of the ladder of Abraham Maslow's classic hierarchy of needs, in which physiological and social needs have been largely met and intrinsic rewards, such as a sense of accomplishment, are sought. Having satisfied their basic needs for safety and security, they can and do move laterally, trying out first one form of esteem and self-actualization and then another.

Coping with the Crisis

So how have things changed a decade later—especially in the wake of the devastating economic and jobs crisis? Many commentators have noted that workers have become more hunkered down and fearful, more oriented to the basics. They've let go of their dreams of challenge and flexibility and are happy to have a job, any job, so long as it pays. At best, that's only partly true. Yes, the economic crisis has made people more cautious. But the biggest trade-offs they're making are not in the realm of pay but in job security. And that is not so much of a difference after all. Recall that we found that "job stability was more highly valued than any form of direct compensation." When we analyzed the 2000–2001 *Information Week* surveys, "More than 40 percent of workers chose it as a key factor." It has become even more highly valued since.

Looking at the published results of *InformationWeek*'s 2010 Salary Survey for Insurance IT Professionals (a much narrower sample than those we worked with in 2000 and 2001), a few trends pop out. Crisis or not, two-thirds overall and nearly three-fourths (72 percent) of managers said they were "satisfied" or "very satisfied" with their jobs. Although the crisis clearly had a big impact on their thinking at first, their attitudes were beginning to rebound by 2010.

Base pay shot up in importance at the outset of the crisis—56 percent of IT managers cited it as mattering most to their job in

2008, besting "challenge of job/responsibility" (52 percent); only one-third (33 percent) cited "my opinion and knowledge are valued" as their most important consideration. But by 2010, that had turned around with less than one-half (47 percent) citing base pay, compared to more than one-half (51 percent) citing "challenge of job/responsibility," and 50 percent citing "my opinion and knowledge are valued." "Job/Company stability" also became more important, understandably, rising from one-third in 2008 (33 percent) to 50 percent in 2010.

But the very same job dimensions that I described as important in 2000–2001 rebounded between 2008 and 2010. "Recognition for job well done" rose from a low of 25 percent in 2008 to 35 percent in 2010. "Job atmosphere" rose from 25 percent in 2008 to 30 percent in 2010. "Working with highly talented peers" climbed from 18 percent in 2008 to 27 percent in 2010. "Corporate culture and values" rose from 27 percent in 2008 to 33 percent in 2010.

IT workers in the 2010 salary survey felt much more secure than other workers. A large majority felt their jobs were at least somewhat secure, and most felt their jobs were much more secure than other workers', so much so that more than one-third of both managers and staff were actively looking for better work prospects. Pay was clearly important (66 percent of staff and 58 percent of management cited "higher compensation" as key reasons), but many were looking for "more interesting work" (55 percent of staff and 47 percent of management), "seeking more personal fulfillment" (49 percent of management and 40 percent of staff), "didn't like the present company's management/culture" (41 percent of staff and 43 percent of management), or wanted more responsibility (35 percent of staff, 40 percent of management). Only 6 percent of staff and 13 percent of managers cited stock options as a reason for looking for a new job.

Just one in ten (11 percent) cited the geographic location of the job as something that mattered most in 2008, but that rebounded to nearly one in five (18 percent) in 2010. Commuting distance sank to 11 percent in 2008 but rebounded to 19 percent in 2010. Job atmosphere fell to 25 percent in 2008 but rebounded to 30 percent in 2010.[18]

In his book *The Fourth Great Awakening*, Robert Fogel notes that in the advanced industrial nations, growing segments of the population work for challenge or enjoyment, to do good, to make a contribution, and to learn.[19] Such motivations, he suggests, will eventually eclipse compensation as the most important motivators for work. Within the Creative Class, this has already happened—and high unemployment and economic insecurity have not reversed the trend.

CHAPTER 5

Brave New Workplace

Hayes Clement did not seem like the type of person who would someday be stuffing and delivering gift baskets for a living. Born into an upper-middle-class family in suburban Atlanta, he grew up tall and athletic, with razor-sharp intelligence and Brooks Brothers good looks. After earning his undergraduate degree at Duke University and an MBA at the University of Virginia's Darden School, he was aggressively recruited and took a prime offer from PricewaterhouseCoopers in New York City. His significant other from Darden had also landed a job in New York with the pharmaceutical firm Pfizer, so they made the move together. For about ten years, life in most respects was beautiful. With two healthy salaries, the pair was able to move from a cozy but cramped apartment in Greenwich Village to a large, stylishly redone place on a much-sought-after block. Clement was on the glamour side of PWC—consulting, not accounting—and he worked in a glamour division as well, media and entertainment. His job offered plenty of variety and challenge, and he was good at it. But he came to see consulting as a treadmill: the constant new assignments, the unrelenting travel, the lurching from project to project, never seeing the end result of his labors. He wanted to build something.

Along came the perfect opportunity. One of his clients was a high-tech start-up called MediaSite that had developed a technology for searching video and still images—a revolutionary and much-needed development that an MIT survey had lauded as one of the top-ten emerging technologies that would change the world. MediaSite was not just an R&D project masquerading as a company: it had a real market, real customers, and a bright, energetic staff. In early 2000, at the peak of the New Economy boom, Clement left PWC to become MediaSite's vice president of business development. The firm was in Pittsburgh, but that was only four hundred miles from New York; he would commute between his work life and his social circle. The pay was much less than at PWC, but there were stock options, and the real upside was the chance to be part of a long-running success story.

Clement's honeymoon didn't last for long. A new CEO was brought in from Silicon Valley to ready the firm for an IPO. As the NASDAQ began to track downward, things got frantic, and management, in Clement's view, lost focus. Changes of direction became so frequent that he stopped asking himself, "Do we have an executable strategy?" and began asking, "Do we have a strategy?" One day, barely six months into the job, Clement walked into the CEO's office and said: "I don't want to be here. You don't want me to be here. So let's make it easy and get an amicable divorce."

Back in New York, Clement received frequent calls from headhunters. But why rush the next step? He was about to turn forty and, thinking back, he realized he'd never taken more than a week or so off at a time. His partner—the only member of their old Darden School gang who'd stayed with the same firm since graduation—was by now a senior executive at Pfizer; money was not an issue. So Clement decided to just hang for a while, do some reading, and catch up with friends. One of those friends had a small gift-basket company. As the weeks passed and holiday orders began to stream

in, the man asked Clement if he might enjoy a little workplace slum-
ming, taking orders and getting the baskets out. Clement said,
"What the heck, I'll do it."

He found he enjoyed coming to work. The people were friendly;
the place had energy; it seemed to fit. Before long, Clement was having ideas on how to grow the business: they could cultivate elite corporate accounts; they could put gourmet foods and digital goodies
into fancy containers like leather-bound chests; they could expand
into markets outside New York City. He had the contacts from his
consulting days, he had the skills, and better yet, for the first time
in years, he was having fun. Clement invested in the business, threw
himself into the work, and gradually the firm took off.[1] A happy
ending? No, more like a happy restart. Clement has since moved on
to other ventures. As I was revising this book, in fact, in the summer
of 2011, he was making a name for himself in local politics, running
for mayor of Kingston, New York! Clement's story illustrates how
people have been charting new paths for themselves in the Creative
Economy—and sometimes reinventing themselves altogether.

As the tech bubble swelled and burst more than a decade ago,
the stereotype of the New Economy career path went something
like this: someone leaves a boring, humdrum job at a big company
for a high-tech start-up because it's exciting and cool and free-floating
and promises instant wealth. Then the start-up folds and the chas-
tened Icarus slinks back to the traditional job market, looking for
a job with more security. But Clement had already been in a "cool,"
exciting industry. What he wanted—and what I consistently find
that most people want—was to exercise his creativity in building
something, to experience the whole cycle of having ideas, putting
them into action, and seeing them bear fruit.

MediaSite hadn't come close to folding: in fact, it was acquired
by a successful, publicly traded company in late 2001—some of
Clement's ex-colleagues did in fact cash in. What bugged him,

and what drove him to leave, was the chaos and confusion—it wasn't shaping up as a place where he could enjoy that whole cycle of creativity. Once Clement recognized this, he didn't say, "I'll give it two more years," or even one. He left and he found an environment where he could be himself and feel at home and do what he really wanted to do. But even then, after he had scratched that itch for a while, other opportunities beckoned and he moved on again.

Both time and the economic crisis have provided perspective from which to view the kinds of work and the kinds of jobs that arose with the Creative Class and the Creative Economy more than a decade ago. Looking back, I was perhaps too optimistic about the potential for worker mobility, flexibility, and freedom. I have tried to temper that view in this revision. That said, the main facets of Creative Class work remain pretty much as they were then. But the level of uncertainty and risk that goes along with them—especially in the form of unportable benefits—is unacceptable. A new social compact is required, one I will detail in the next chapter.

More than two decades ago, in our book *The Breakthrough Illusion,* Martin Kenney and I were already pointing to what we dubbed the "hypermobility" of labor in high-tech clusters like Silicon Valley and Boston's Route 128 area, where workers changed jobs with astonishing frequency.[2] Soon that would become the norm across the whole economy. In 2001, when I wrote the original edition of this book, Americans were changing jobs every 3.5 years; workers in their twenties were doing so on average every 1.1 years. One-fourth of workers in the 2000–2001 *InformationWeek* salary surveys said that they had been in their current job for two years or less and expected to change jobs within a year.

Economic mobility took a big hit with the economic crisis, with rates of residential mobility hitting record lows, according to US

Census data. The housing crisis exacerbated this, trapping many people in homes whose mortgages were underwater or for which buyers simply couldn't be found because of the glut on the market. By 2010, Americans' rate of job changing had slowed to a median tenure of 4.4 years, almost a year more than in 2001 but still well short of a gold watch. Interestingly enough but perhaps not surprisingly, professional, technology-oriented, and creative workers were now staying in their jobs the longest—perhaps because of their skills and relative job security—with a median tenure of 5.2 years, compared to 3.1 years for service workers and just 2.3 years for food service workers.[3] As Chapter 3 has shown, creative workers were spared the worst of the crisis, with unemployment rates less than half those of blue-collar workers. But by 2010, according to many sources, some high-flying Silicon Valley companies were resuming their war for talent, offering bonuses to attract new workers and retain existing talent. The churn—at least at the higher levels of the high-tech world—was beginning again.

The shift is epoch making. Under the old industrial or Fordist order, companies provided their employees not just with economic security but with social identities as well. And this was backed up with the New Deal social compact among capital, labor, and government. Many towns—even big cities like Detroit and Pittsburgh—were literally company towns, with just a few big corporations providing most of the employment, and a whole social and economic infrastructure. You were a company man, identifying with the company and often moving largely in the circles created or dictated by it. Since the rise of the Creative Economy, Creative Class workers have increasingly assumed the risks that companies and the government, to a certain extent, used to absorb. This downloading of risk is onerous enough for well-paid creative workers; it has been even more problematic for Working Class and Service Class workers who make a fraction of Creative Class salaries, whose jobs are at substantial risk, and who have many fewer options for reemployment when they are laid off.

Free-Agent Nation or the End of the Job?

As with many issues, the debate over the new labor market often tends to polarize into two extreme camps. On one side are those utopian optimists who behold a free-agent paradise, a way to cut loose from the corporate system for a more lucrative independent existence. On the other side are pessimists, who believe the change in the market is just another sign of growing corporate oppression, social fragmentation, and the end of work. As far back as 1994, a cover story in *Fortune* proclaimed "The End of the Job."[4] In 1999, Alan Burton-Jones predicted that in two generations people would be asking their grandparents, "What was it like being employed?"[5] Although both sides in this debate make some valid points, they overstate their cases and miss the deeper and more fundamental factors that are reshaping the world of work.

Daniel Pink is among the most astute observers of the new world of work.[6] He introduced the concept of free-agent liberation in his 2001 book, *Free Agent Nation,* in which he identified a revolutionary new class of workers that he claimed was already 33 million strong. "One-fourth of the American workforce," he wrote, "has declared its independence from traditional work." The real numbers, however, did not add up so neatly. Back in 2001, in the original edition of this book, I noted that the Bureau of Labor statistics placed the number of self-employed people at 12.9 million, roughly one-third of Pink's estimate. According to *InformationWeek*'s 2000–2001 salary survey, just 1.1 percent of IT workers considered themselves to be "freelance or self-employed" (another 2.3 percent considered themselves "contract workers"), while an overwhelming 95 percent of

IT workers classified themselves as full-time employees. The majority of them worked for big companies—more than one-half for companies with more than 1,000 employees, and more than one-fourth for companies with more than 10,000 employees. I concluded then that most creative workers are *not* free agents. No matter how their respective human resources departments might have classified them, they worked for companies or institutions and their fundamental condition was that of employees.

But that was then. The trend has accelerated over the ensuing decade, especially in the wake of the 2008 crisis, as companies have shifted more and more to temps and contingent workers to bolster their bottom lines—improving their profits and worsening the prospects for permanent or at least stable employment, especially for older workers. Writing in *The Atlantic* online on September 1, 2011, Sara Horowitz, the founder of the Freelancers Union, dubbed the "freelance surge" the "Industrial Revolution of our time." Like most revolutions, she wrote, it has brought a plethora of both good things and bad.

> We haven't seen a shift in the workforce this significant in almost 100 years when we transitioned from an agricultural to an industrial economy. Now, employees are leaving the traditional workplace and opting to piece together a professional life on their own. As of 2005, one-third of our workforce participated in this "freelance economy." Data show that number has only increased over the past six years. Entrepreneurial activity in 2009 was at its highest level in 14 years, online freelance job postings skyrocketed in 2010, and companies are increasingly outsourcing work. While the economy has unwillingly pushed some people into independent work, many have chosen it because of greater flexibility that lets them skip the dreary office environment and focus on more personally fulfilling projects.[7]

But for those who work this way, conditions can be trying and at times no less disheartening than the prospect from cubicle-land.

The rosy view is that free agents work from the comfort of their homes, perhaps commuting virtually and doing only the kinds of work that interest them, picking the hours and conditions they want. In reality, freelancing carries considerable risks. The kinds of work you want might not be widely available, especially in a deep recession, and the assignments may not always pay well. Assuming you're in demand, you have a choice: be selective about what you do and settle for less money; or do a lot of things you don't really like, much as employees often have to do, and make more. One thing you haven't escaped is competition—if you turn down an onerous rush job because you've got a nice weekend planned, the client will call another freelancer deemed more "responsive" and perhaps they'll stick with that person in the future. Moreover, once you are on a project, guess what? You have to meet deadlines. You have to please the people in charge. You have to make it to meetings. You might work late into the night, doing it not your way but the client's way. As one commentator aptly put it, "It takes more than a home office and temporary badge to build a workers' paradise."[8] And then there are the issues raised by working at home—the pressures it puts on family life, the complications that ensue for child care and gender roles.[9]

About a million and a half young, educated workers are experiencing a new kind of contingent employment—one for which they receive little or no compensation. Ross Perlin's book *Intern Nation: How to Earn Nothing and Learn Little in the Brave New Economy* describes how companies big and little save billions in labor costs by luring ambitious young college graduates to toil for them for free in the hope of learning a profession—or getting an inside track to a real job.[10]

New ways of working have been underpinned with a new kind of employment contract. The old contract was group oriented and emphasized job security. The new one is tailored to the needs and desires of the individual. The old Organizational Age system was truly a package deal, literally a comprehensive social contract, in which people traded their working lives for money, security, and the sense of identity that came from belonging to the firm. They took their places in the hierarchy, followed bureaucratic rules, and worked their way up the ladder. In the words of William Whyte, an "ultimate harmony" developed between the managerial class and the large companies it worked for, allowing its members to give themselves over more completely to the organization.[11] The new employment contract turns this on its head. Instead of a broad social contract, a key feature of today's employment relationship is that employees are seeking out and getting what Carnegie Mellon professor Denise Rousseau dubbed more individualized, or "idiosyncratic deals."[12]

Of course idiosyncratic individualism and flexibility has its downsides and costs. Back in 2001, a detailed study of new media professionals by Rosemary Batt and Susan Christopherson of Cornell University and two colleagues found a huge gap between the benefits received by full-time workers and free agents.[13] Whereas roughly three-fourths of full-time employees enjoyed comprehensive health insurance (itself an alarmingly low rate), only 11 percent of free agents received health coverage from their primary employers or clients, and just one-fourth received any sort of benefits at all. Even with new federal health care legislation under Obama, the situation ten years later has, for the most part, gotten even worse.

The free-agent world would be unthinkable without big companies. Even when creative workers are not employed full-time and work on a project basis, it's still mainly companies one way or another that dictate the terms of work available to free agents—many of whom survive by latching onto one or a handful of big clients that can provide them with a steady flow of well-paid work. It's hard to make a living catching nickel-and-dime projects from all over. And though companies may think this is a good deal, they don't always come out ahead themselves. As Stanford management expert Jeffrey Pfeffer has found, when companies rely heavily on freelance and contract workers, they implicitly accept high turnover, huge training costs, considerable productivity losses, and significant leakage of intellectual property. In some cases they virtually hand over key knowledge and ideas to competitors through turnover and defection.[14]

Such sweeping changes in the nature of work and jobs have inspired more than one jeremiad over the years. For Stanley Aronowitz and Jeremy Rifkin, the combination of advanced technology and globalization has systematically eliminated the prospect of secure, meaningful work for most of us, including creatives, taking a toll on social cohesion.[15] Corporate downsizing, they contend, has essentially turned high-paying "primary" sector jobs into lower-paying and less secure work in the "secondary" labor market, allowing companies to use people as needed and then spit them out.

The office has been transformed into a white-collar sweatshop,[16] others contend. Office workers put in longer hours, bring more of their work home, and suffer from mounting economic insecurity and stress. A new style of management uses layoffs and downsizing to instill fear in the white-collar world, squeezing the pay and benefits of those who still have full-time jobs and imposing ever-larger workloads on them. There's no denying that some white-collar workers have been permanently marginalized; many do toil under Dickensian circumstances. But as brutal as the economy has been and as devastating as some of its structural changes have been for whole classes of mostly blue-collar workers, most people today know intuitively that they enjoy better working conditions than their parents did, not to mention their grandparents, who might have endured long days of backbreaking, dangerous labor in the grisliest of factories.

The sociologist Richard Sennett warns that the dissolution of long-term attachments to large corporations leads to a corrosion of character and ultimately to the breakdown of society.[17] This view,

I confess, leaves me reeling. In a day and age when we finally accept that children can flourish in nontraditional families, are we really supposed to believe that long-term employment in a large organization is a necessary condition for the psychological stability of grown-ups? Long-term jobs and reasonably stable careers with firms are relatively recent phenomena, associated with the Industrial Revolution and the rise of modern unions and management. Before that, people established well-defined identities through their occupations and their families—as farmers, craftsmen, blacksmiths, and midwives; as children, siblings, parents, spouses, friends, and citizens. This is exactly the situation to which many are reverting today: finding their identities elsewhere than in a firm. I personally think it is healthier and more fitting for us to attach our strongest allegiances to our families and friends, our communities, and the things that truly interest and matter to us. Our own personal development is much more important than whatever company we happen to be working for.

Where the New Work Comes From

Gideon Kunda, Stephen Barley, and James Evans, leading ethnographers of the workplace, exhaustively studied engineers and other IT professionals who left jobs with established companies to go out on their own.[18] Their paper, titled "Why Do Contractors Contract?" tested a series of hypotheses regarding the shift in the way people work. First off, they looked at the theory of the contingent workforce. At its most extreme, this is the company-as-oppressor view, the one that says that people turn to freelance work only after big corporations throw them out. Then they tested the counterclaims associated with the free-agent perspective. "Advocates of free agency," they wrote, "promote a post-industrial vision of economic individualism in which entrepreneurial workers regain independence and recapture a portion of the surplus value that employers formerly appropriated for themselves." What they found is similar to what I have reported.

The "company-as-oppressor" view, Kunda, Barley, and Evans concluded, is dead wrong. The reasons most people struck out on their own had little to do with being thrown out of work. They did it to take control. Their decisions were in many respects liberating; certainly, they felt liberated from the constant fear of being thrown out. The study identified three major types of complaints that precipitated workers' leaving. Many were sick and tired of office politics. "You have to listen to a lot of people's agendas," noted one engineer in the study, "spend time in a lot of unnecessary meetings, trying to keep everybody happy, trying to play their game. It's not strictly work-related, it's very unproductive, and it can be very tense." Others left due to the Dilbert syndrome—the perception that higher-ups were incompetent or worse. "I was at the naval shipyard for a couple of years, and they were going nowhere," another engineer related. "I theoretically reported to the chief financial officer and they brought in a couple, how do we say, 'yo-yos.' We caught one of the CFOs funneling stuff into his condo in Florida."

Still others left because of a sense of inequity. Skilled creative workers get upset when they perceive that merit is not the coin of the realm or that things are done for the wrong reasons. "I was getting the project done not for the goals of the project but for the goals of the people above," noted one participant in the study. And again, while striking out on your own does not guarantee complete freedom, at least you become the person setting the goals and deciding how to play the cards. As one software developer put it, "I don't work for free anymore." Or as another high-tech worker posted on Fast Company's website in 2001: "Just after my daughter was born, I decided that I wanted to be home for dinner on more than just

weekends. I wanted to be a Dad, not a wallet. I wanted my daughter
to know who I am, not just what I was able to provide for her."

People I interviewed and encountered in focus groups cited the
same kinds of things. They got fed up with the politics and bureaucracy of corporate life, or if they'd worked in smaller, entrepreneurial companies, of the stress of management-by-chaos. They
told me they left their jobs because of the inconsistent, incompetent,
petty tyrannies that they labored under, because of a daily death
by 1,000 cuts and the constant fear of being fired. And though no
person can achieve total control, many chose this route to take
more control in the areas that mattered the most to them.

Although these changes may appear at first to be the product
of worker choices, at a deeper level they are inevitable concomi-
tants of profound, structural changes in the workplace. As Barley
observed in his 1996 study, *The New World of Work*, the economy
is moving toward "a more horizontal division of labor."[19] In the
old days, bosses were people who knew their business better than
their subordinates did, so both the typical organizational structure
and the typical career path were vertical. As you stuck around
and learned more about the business, you moved up. But with
growing specialization today, this no longer holds: "Those in authority," Barley writes, "no longer comprehend the work of their
subordinates." Even the eminent research scientist can't boss the
lab technicians around: they have knowledge and skills that he
doesn't. Thus, what we used to think of as jobs or occupations,
Barley argues, devolve into "clusters of domain-specific knowledge." These clusters must interact on an equal footing for things
to go well in any organization. This is why the vertical hierarchy
and traditional career ladder have been replaced by sideways career moves between companies and a horizontal labor market.
What conservatives criticize as self-indulgence and liberals deplore
as the consequence of new tactics of corporate oppression is in

fact the result of the rational evolution of economic forces. Workers not only identify more with their occupations or professions than with a company, focus groups and interviews show that they increasingly define themselves by both the creative content of their work and by their lifestyle interests: biker, climber, musician.

The Unraveling of the Social Contract

If the changing labor market is a product of evolutionary forces, there is no denying that shrinking corporate loyalty to workers and the demise of the old social contract have exacerbated things. For companies, it's become more efficient to be able to exercise greater flexibility in staffing decisions. Some companies have reduced costs by terminating employees and then promptly hiring them back as independent contractors. The company no longer has to provide benefits, and it doesn't have to promise continued employment once a project is done. Workers are responding in kind. As Joanne Ciulla writes,

> The downsizings of the 1990s were a wake-up call. The social compact—You do your job well and you stay employed—is dead, at least for the time being. Jobs were destroyed and lives were ruined, but one message came through loud and clear: Employment insecurity is the new way of life, even during times of low unemployment. Many workers have begun to rethink their commitment to employers, because their employers have changed their commitment to them. The extra sacrifice of missed family birthdays because of long hours at the office no longer makes sense, and maybe never did. As the old saying goes, people on their deathbeds never wish they had spent more time at the office.[20]

Or as Stanford's Pfeffer likes to say: Loyalty isn't dead. Companies have driven it away.

If the social contract was already fraying back in the 1990s, the crisis of 2008 annihilated what little was left. Individual workers have assumed most risks, corporate and government shock absorbers have been removed, and workers today bear more responsibility—perhaps I should say all responsibility—for their careers and lives. We not only take on all the risks of our job moves, we assume the task of taking care of our creativity—of investing in it, supporting it, and nurturing it. Creative workers invest tremendous amounts of time and money on their educations. They go through basic port-of-entry education, education for a career-track change, and on-going learning and upgrading of skills. People in my interviews and focus groups report that they, not their employers, are respon-sible for keeping their skills up to date. This is particularly true for workers in rapidly changing high-technology fields. According to that study of new media professionals by Batt and Christopherson, workers in New York City spent an average of 13.5 unpaid hours per week obtaining new skills,[21] one-third of a forty-hour workweek. The report concludes that skill acquisition has become an individual responsibility, "both because the interactive nature of computer tools allows new media workers to learn new skills at their own pace and within their own learning styles and because formal learning programs have not kept pace with skill needs in this fast-changing industry." Moreover, in the new labor market it no longer pays for companies to invest significantly in developing their people's skills and capabilities when they frequently leave for better opportunities and greater challenge. Just 30 percent of 262 network professionals in a Lucent Technologies survey of job satisfaction said that their company's formal training programs met their needs, even though nearly three-fourths (73 percent) said their careers required them to learn and grow.[22]

Perhaps the biggest change is that people now expect to manage their working lives in these ways, as impossible as it might be to do so. For her investigative book *Bait and Switch,* Barbara Ehrenreich joined the ranks of laid-off white-collar workers. She noted how our system encouraged them—the people who "did everything right," earning higher degrees, deferring gratification, working long hours at jobs that bored them—to blame themselves for their disappointments and traumas, marshaling battalions of outplacement counselors and career coaches to teach them how to adopt a more winning attitude.[23]

Increasingly, workers have come to accept that they are completely on their own—that the traditional sources of security and entitlement no longer exist, or even matter. This is a sea change, and in many ways, a disquieting one, with implications that go well beyond the workplace. The three downsized executives whose stories are told in the 2010 Ben Affleck movie *The Company Men* all internalized their anger and frustration. This is a sad commentary on how thoroughly we have capitulated to these new conditions— conditions that in themselves militate against the kind of solidarity that once animated the labor movement. Freelancers have difficulty finding each other, working alone as they mostly do. And they are conditioned to think of each other as competitors rather than colleagues. More and more, we simply accept our lot as the way things are and go about our busy lives.

CHAPTER 6

No-Collar

One spring day back in 2000, I was running late for a meeting and called ahead to say so. The meeting was with a securities lawyer and an accountant, so I asked the woman who answered the phone if I should take a few extra minutes to change from my usual jeans, black T-shirt, and boots into more professional attire. "That's unnecessary here," she said, "just come as you are." My heart sank as I parked my car and approached the grand stone building, a stunning exemplar of nineteenth-century corporate elegance in the heart of Pittsburgh's downtown business district. I walked sheepishly through the door, absolutely certain I was underdressed. To my surprise, the people I saw inside were dressed more casually than I was, in khakis and polo shirts, with sneakers and even sandals on their feet. Some of them were carrying gym bags. Was I in the wrong place, maybe a high-tech company, or the lobby of a new clothing store? No, the receptionist assured me. I was where I was supposed to be—at the oldest and most prestigious corporate law firm in town.

The environments in which we work are changing, and it isn't just the clothes. Many features of the workplace seem to be more open and user friendly: open-office layouts and other new office designs, flexible schedules, new work rules and management methods. Trends can be time-bound, of course, but the emergence of this new kind of workspace is no passing phase: it is an evolutionary adaptation to the changing nature of creative work, and its staying power is a tribute to its greater efficiencies. In the original edition of this book, I dubbed those changes the "no-collar workplace." As I argued then, it was no coincidence that their rise was concurrent with the rise of the Internet and dot-com businesses. The no-collar workplace integrates elements of the flexible, open, interactive model of the scientist's lab or artist's studio into the machine model of the factory or the traditional corporate office. It did not erupt on the scene overnight: many of its features had been evolving for decades and are continuing to do so. Some of the changes that seemed startling and even revolutionary as recently as a decade ago are so ensconced today that there's little more to say about them except to underline the fact that they are part and parcel of the emerging Creative Economy. The original edition also included an entire chapter about the unique challenges of managing creativity—and about the underside of this brave new workplace, in which workers internalized an insidious set of norms I dubbed "soft control." I combine those two chapters here.

New Codes

When I wrote the original edition of this book, few workplace trends were drawing more attention than the loosening of dress codes. Roughly one-fourth of information-technology workers in the 2000–2001 edition of the *InformationWeek* salary survey reported that the ability to wear "casual attire" was among the things that mattered most to them on their jobs. I told the story of my visit to the Seattle branch of Barney's, a high-end clothing store. The store was jammed with young professionals sipping mineral water and chilled white wine as they browsed the racks. The manager was a woman in her thirties, dressed in black, who had worked at the store since its inception. Over the last few years, she told me, she had noticed a significant change in the buying patterns of Seattle's Creative Class—particularly those who worked at Microsoft, long a haven for nerds. Sales of traditional suits had declined every year since the store opened, and sales of classic geek wear such as khakis, crewnecks, and blue blazers had declined as well. But the store was doing well with New York–style fashion wear: black pants, Helmut Lang T-shirts, Prada outerwear and shoes, leather jackets, and fashionable carry-all bags. Noting the preference for Prada and other cutting-edge designers among some Microsoft executives, a September 2000 story in the *Wall Street Journal* had dubbed the new look "geek chic."[1] A decade later, the tech geek look has given way to the even more artsy hipster look—sneakers, hoodies, skinny jeans, and V-neck tees.

For decades before office dress codes changed, dress outside the office had been becoming more and more casual. In the early decades of the twentieth century, men wore suits and ties to baseball games, and women wore long dresses and fancy hats to picnics. By the mid-1960s, around the same time that dress gloves ceased to be de rigueur for ladies and men stopped wearing hats, the suit came to be thought of as primarily a business uniform, with less and less utility outside the office. Casual dress crept into offices during the 1980s, partly for the simple reason that it's more comfortable, but also because creative work came to be more highly valued. Loosened dress codes aren't just about the way people look—they signal an acceptance of difference and diversity in the workplace, which is squarely in line with the desire to work flexibly and express one's identity. Status no longer accrues from being an officer, or, at the lower ranks, a good soldier. It accrues from being

a member of the creative elite—and creative people don't wear uni-
forms. They dress to express themselves, as artists do; they dress
simply and practically as professors and scientists do, so they can
focus on the serious creative work at hand. They dress as they please.

When they were first instituted, the new dress codes drew a storm
of reaction and criticism from more established quarters. During the
late 1990s, the *Wall Street Journal* ran numerous stories on women
who dressed in clothes perceived to be "too risqué" for the office.[2]
USA Today criticized casual dress as a recipe for slacking, deploring
"the casualization of America."[3] I experienced some of this back-
and-forth myself. Back in the 1980s, when I was first starting out,
I wore business suits and ties to meetings and speeches. But when I
started to give talks about the subject of this book in the late 1990s
and early 2000s, some requested that I wear casual clothes to reinforce
my message, while others—sometimes at the same organizations—
leaned the other way. In winter 2001, a flurry of e-mails came across
my desktop from the organizers of an event, asking about my dress
as well as the contents of my speech. Some thought I should wear a
suit and tie and not mention "controversial" subjects like gays. One
of the principals responded to his worried corporate partners: "I
spoke with Dr. Florida and he assured me that there is no cause for
concern. He will be giving his talk completely in ebonics, wearing a
pink tutu, with a large sombrero. At the conclusion, he will stomp
on a light bulb inside a white napkin. His only request is that everything in the ballroom be situated properly for positive feng shui."[4]

Nothing like that has happened for a long time—though not too
long ago, when I was speaking in the Middle East, I was asked not
to talk about my findings regarding tolerance toward gays. I did
not restrict my remarks, but that's another story.

The Creative Economy doesn't have one monolithic dress code;
it has a diversity of them. This was brought home to me one day in
2000 when I looked around at the participants in a meeting room

at a large Washington, DC, law firm. One person was wearing a business suit; another had on a blazer and khakis. A young woman in a short skirt and funky blouse sported a tongue ring. The talk at that moment had in fact turned to dress codes, and when someone pointed out the range of attire in the room, it suddenly dawned on us that up to that point we'd hardly even noticed it. Just telling that story dates me—the change is that complete.

Working Flexibly . . . and Longer

Office workers not only dress differently than they did just a decade or so ago, they have a different attitude toward the clock. Instead of following the Organizational Age core menu of Monday through Friday, nine to five, growing numbers of workers in all industries are now able to vary both the hours and the days they work. In the original edition, I cited 1997 Bureau of Labor Statistics (BLS) figures that showed that more than 25 million workers—27.6 percent of all full-time wage and salary workers—had varied their schedules to some degree, either formally or through informal arrangements with their employers.[5] More than two-thirds (68 percent) of workers were able to periodically change their starting and quitting times, according to a survey by the Families and Work Institute; more than half (55 percent) occasionally worked at home. By May 2004, this had grown to 36.4 million workers, about 30 percent of the total workforce. Flexible work schedules were much more likely to be found among Creative Class workers. In 2004, the BLS reported that more than 50 percent of all computer scientists and mathematicians; 49.7 percent of life, physical, and social scientists; 46.7 percent of managers; 44.5 percent of architects and engineers; and 41.9 percent of arts, design media, and entertainment workers had flexible schedules, compared to just 13.8 percent of production workers.[6]

The flexible schedule is partly a response to the realities of our lives today—in households with two working parents, for instance, someone might have to bail out early to see the children home from school. But it is also tied to the very nature of creative work. A lot of creative work is project work, and projects tend to run in cycles, with periods of crunch time followed by slower periods. Creative work requires enormous concentration; it also requires periods of downtime, even during the day. Many people tell me they like to work hard through lunch hour, then take a long run or bicycle ride in the afternoon to recharge themselves for the remaining part of their workday, which might extend well into the evening, amounting to almost a "second workday." Also, creative thinking is hard to turn on and off at will. It is an odd sort of activity: one often finds oneself percolating an idea, or hammering away desperately in search of a solution to a problem, only to see the answer begin clicking into place at unusual times.

Flexibility does not mean the end of long hours—not by any means. The long trajectory of modern capitalism has involved the relentless extension of the working day across time and space—first through electricity and the electric light and now via the personal computer, the mobile phone, and the Internet. According to BLS estimates, professional, technical, and managerial workers were the most likely to put in long workweeks of more than forty-nine hours[7]—and Creative Class people tend to put in the longest hours of all.

New Work/Space

Offices look different than they did not so long ago, and not just because most of the workers are dressed in shirtsleeves and slacks. Newly built or renovated offices often feature exposed pipes and unfinished-looking walls and floors; instead of acres of cubicles, there are more common spaces. As Ben Watson, the executive creative director of the office furniture giant Herman Miller told Alison Arieff in 2011: "Ten years ago, 80 to 90 percent of an organization's budget would be spent on individual workspaces. Now, it's 65 to 70 percent and is scaling down to 50 percent real fast. . . . Today, 70 percent of work in North America happens with two or more people. It's no longer about the individual worker. So we need to understand the way collaborative work happens, we need to create microenvironments—a mix of them, in fact, so you want to be at your office more than you want to be at home or at Starbucks."[8]

Silicon Valley's style of free-spirited, laid-back, blurred-boundaries, around-the-clock work is reflected in its campus-like workplaces. When Google opened its New York office in Chelsea in 2006 the *New York Times* took note of the culture clash:

The campus-like workspace is antithetical to the office culture of most New York businesses. It is a vision of a workplace utopia as conceived by rich, young, single engineers in Silicon Valley, transplanted to Manhattan. The New York tradition of leaving the office to network over lunch or an evening cocktail party has no place at Google, where employees are encouraged to socialize among themselves. There are groups of Gayglers, Newglers and Bikeglers (who bike to work together) . . . For a Thank God It's Almost Friday gathering on Dec. 14, Laura Garrett, a sales operations specialist, organized an art show. "Being a Googler and being part of Chelsea, I wanted to do something that was more downtownish than a typical Google event," said Ms. Garrett, a blonde wearing Marc Jacobs heels. Williamsburg artists created the work on display, for prices from $225 to $8,000 . . . The Empire State Building glowed red and green in the background as if color-coordinated to the Googleplex's interiors rather than Christmas. By 6:30 P.M., Steve Saviano, 22, a software engineer, was hanging out with his fellow Googlers at a table littered with empty beer and wine bottles. "This is academic life all over again," Mr. Saviano said. "But I'm getting paid. This is a 100 percent better option than graduate school."[9]

Scanning the photos that went with the story, I was struck by the similarity between Google's and other no-collar workplaces and college dorm rooms, or for that matter, the play spaces of privileged teenagers. You can't pump work out of creative people, assembly-line style. Motivating this kind of mental work requires a new kind of workplace—one that at the very least appears to be nurturing, attuned to individuality, and "fun."

The traditional vertical corporation, with its top-down hierarchy, was based on a factory model of information flow and work flow. There were bosses who required separate areas for privileged communication, and workers who followed routines and were put into standardized spaces to discourage deviation. Bosses and subordinates alike were literally required to think *inside* the box. The Creative Economy is premised on the rapid generation and transmission of ideas across the enterprise. This world of tight deadlines, uncertainty, and discovery—of knowledge creation, teamwork, and building off each other's ideas—requires the interactive space heretofore found only in the design studio or scientific lab.

Although there are infinite variations on the theme, creative work spaces generally come in two major types, each with its own ways of delivering symbolic and functional value. In the suburbs and sprawling high-tech office parks of places like Silicon Valley and North Carolina's Research Triangle, one typically finds new architecture. Big firms that require a lot of space—electronics design-and-assembly firms, for instance—often build expansive campuses in such locales. Exteriors may feature bold or unusual design elements. Inside the newer suburban buildings, open arrangements for high traffic flow are mostly the rule. Occasional design touches that disrupt the slick newness of the interiors (such as ragged surfaces or exposed infrastructure) help take the edge off the sterility of new space, making it feel livable. Overall, the suburban campus may have virtually everything a worker would want or need—from espresso bars and free food to on-site day care, state-of-the-art health facilities, outdoor Frisbee fields, and concierge services. The message and function are clear: no need to go wandering off; stay right here at work.

The other type is renovated space in older buildings found in downtowns and urban neighborhoods. Jane Jacobs anticipated this trend decades ago, when she wrote, "Old ideas can sometimes use new buildings. New ideas must use old buildings."[10] This kind of setting is also popular with smaller companies that require less space and perhaps want to establish their own identities. Older space, of course, has some obvious practical advantages. As long as extensive renovation isn't required, it can be had for cheap— ideal for a small firm bursting with ideas but not money. Open loft space is flexible and easy to equip. If located in a bustling urban area, the company can rely on the surrounding neighborhood to provide services such as cafés, shops, and health facilities that big suburban companies provide on their campuses (a point I will return to later).

Form Follows Function

Thomas Allen of MIT is an expert on the organization of innovation. In a ten-year study of engineers in R&D labs, he found that proximity matters: people interact most with those located close to them; people seated more than seventy-five feet apart rarely interact at all.[11] In the 1990s, I worked with Steelcase, which had been a leading maker of the much-maligned cubicles of the corporate age. Familiar with Allen's work and other studies, Steelcase wanted new designs to help its clients take advantage of proximity without sacrificing privacy. One result was the new line of work modules called "Personal Harbors," private work spaces mounted on wheels that could be rolled into groups around common areas as needed, to facilitate collaborative work, then rolled apart as people needed to work alone.[12]

In a thoughtful *New Yorker* essay, Malcolm Gladwell connected the layout of the new open-plan workspace to the urban-vitality theories of Jane Jacobs—and to the rise of the Creative Class. In the 1960s, Jacobs had been vehemently opposed to urban renewal schemes that destroyed the organic nature of neighborhoods, re-placing their bustling sidewalk life and diverse traffic flows with a planned order that deadened creative interaction. While city plan-ners largely ignored her, Gladwell suggests that her ideas informed the basic principles of the new office design. "Who, after all, has a direct interest in creating diverse, vital spaces that foster creativity and empathy? Employers do. Offices need the sort of social milieu that Jane Jacobs found on the sidewalks of the West Village," he wrote. And the new work space, like Jacobs's West Village, stimu-lates creative interaction by being conducive to "the casual, non-threatening encounter."

> When employees sit chained to their desks, quietly and industriously going about their business, an office is not functioning as it should. That's because innovation . . . is fundamentally social. Ideas arise as much out of casual conversations as they do out of formal meetings. More precisely, as one study after another has demonstrated, the best ideas in any workplace arise out of casual contacts among different groups within the same company.

Ideal interactions occur among people whose roles are different enough to give them different perspectives, but who have enough common knowledge and common interest to know what would be mutually useful. Old-style workspaces don't foster such serendip-itous sharing. They are like the suburbs, where functions and people are sequestered and important people occupy exclusive enclaves similar to gated communities. These workspaces are often found in high-rise towers, where, as Gladwell noted:

> The center part of every floor is given over to the guts of the building: elevators, bathrooms, electrical and plumbing systems. Around the core are cubicles and interior offices, for support staff and lower management. And around the edges of the floor, against the windows, are rows of offices for senior staff. . . . The best research about office communication tells us that there is almost no worse way to lay out an office. The executive in one corner office will seldom bump into any other. . . . To maximize the amount of contact among employees, you really ought to put the most valuable staff members in the center of the room, where the highest number of people can be within their orbit. Or, even better, put all places where people tend to congregate—the public areas—in the center. . . . Is it any wonder that creative firms often prefer loft-style buildings, which have usable centers?[13]

The no-collar workplace is the newest stage in the ongoing evolution toward more efficient ways of harnessing ideas and creativity. It aims to accomplish what John Seely Brown, the former director of Xerox PARC, called "the ability to leverage the community mind" by providing the physical and social context required for creativity.[14] Artists have long worked in open studio environments but they tended to work alone. Architects and designers extended the studio environment to creative group work, with open-plan offices to encourage collaboration, peer review, and feedback. Andy Warhol's original Factory was a raw, open space, entirely covered in silver foil, including the exposed pipes, to provide a space age look. Filling it out was a mélange of equipment for silk-screening, filmmaking, and other art forms—and a constant parade of friends and associates trooping in and out at all hours. Floating through it all was Warhol himself, the archetypal creative director: sometimes coddling or nudging, sometimes merely observing or recording what was going on, sometimes retreating into his own work.

Laboratories were also developed on the open-plan model, where scientists could come and go as they pleased, engaging their students and colleagues, where work could be done on a collaborative basis and ideas could flow. Even the large megacorporations of the mid-1900s created special places for the scientists and engineers who provided them with valuable innovations. R&D laboratories were often sited at college-like campuses that were far removed from the factory or the downtown headquarters, both to encourage flexibility and openness and to ensure that the eccentric ways of scientists and engineers would not infect the executives and managers or, worse, be seen by customers. A casual dress code was accepted at the R&D labs, too. Yet even there, bureaucracy and micromanagement often crept in. In *The Organization Man,* as earlier noted, Whyte noted that the truly creative R&D lab was an exception that proved a rule:

> In the great slough of mediocrity that is most corporation research, what two laboratories are conspicuous exceptions in the rate of discovery? They are General Electric's research department and Bell Labs: exactly the two laboratories most famous for their encouragement of individualism—the most tolerant of individual differences, the most patient with off-tangent ideas, the least given to the immediate, closely supervised team project. By all accounts, the scientists in them get along quite well, but they do not make a business of it, and neither do the people who run the labs. They care not a whit if scientists' eyes fail to grow moist at company anthems; it is enough that the scientists do superbly well what they want to do, for though the consequences of profit for The Organization are secondary to the scientist, eventually there are these consequences, and as long as the interests of the group and the individual touch at this vital point, such questions as belongingness are irrelevant.[15]

What motivated corporate leaders to create such labs in the first place? Simply put, they wanted to attract top scientific talent away

from leading academic centers. To get such people, they had to establish environments and procedures similar to those in academic
settings—allowing scientists to pursue their own lines of interest,
to host visitors in their labs, and freely publish their research in scientific journals.[16] It was the culture of these R&D centers, born at
laboratories like GE, Bell, and many others, that later companies
like Fairchild Semiconductor, Digital Equipment, Hewlett-Packard,
and even Apple and Microsoft, sought to emulate and build upon.
Gradually, their norms and practices began to seep into the technical divisions of other large companies. Before long they would
penetrate larger and larger segments of the economy.

These practices offered one great efficiency to firms—and one
incredible advantage to capitalism—which ultimately assured their
further diffusion. They enabled firms and the economy as a whole
to capture the creative talents of people who would have been considered oddballs, eccentrics, or worse during the high period of the
Organizational Age. In the emerging Creative Age, these people
are no longer hidden away—they're actively recruited and proudly
displayed. In a study that explored the sociology of new media enterprises, the sociologist Richard Lloyd quoted the founder of a
Chicago high-tech firm, "Lots of people who fell between the cracks
in another generation and who were more marginalized are [now]
highly employable and catered to by businesses that tend to be flexible with their lifestyles and lifecycles."[17]

Soft Control

When the first edition of this book was published, sociologists, culture
critics, and management gurus couldn't decide whether the big problem with the workplace was that it was becoming too stressful or too
comfortable. Some maintained that our offices were high-tech sweat-

shops, presided over by corporate Simon Legrees. Others, like the sociologist Arlie Russell Hochschild,[18] took the opposite stance, arguing that if anything, management coddles us; our offices have become so comfortable that we retreat to them to avoid the demands of private life. Both arguments presented an exaggerated, caricatured point of view, but they each captured a part of the truth: that in the quest to elicit creativity, the typical workplace tends to become both more stressful *and* more caring. The result could be called a "caring sweatshop," but as oxymoronic as it sounds, there's not really any contradiction. It's just the reality of a workplace in the Creative Economy.

Stress increases because the Creative Economy is predicated on change and speed. If a firm is to survive, it must always top what it did yesterday. Employees must be constantly coming up with new ideas; perpetually devising faster, cheaper, and better ways to do things—and that's brutally stressful. Back in 1999, more than four in ten American workers described themselves as workaholics in a Gallup poll.[19] And yet for all that frantic dedication, fewer than half of all professionals, according to a 2001 Towers Perrin study, responded that "my company inspires me to do my best work."[20] Ten years later, we still have far to go in both the knowledge and the practice of managing creative workers.

There is a vast literature on effective creative organization and management. Although there's an awful lot of academic jargon to cut through, most of it basically boils down to the idea that creative people and knowledge workers respond well to organizations that provide solid values, clear rules, open communication, good working conditions, and fair treatment. People don't want to be abandoned, and they don't want to be micromanaged. They don't want to take orders, but they do want direction. Creative work cannot be regimented, like rote work in the old factory or office. Because a lot of it goes on inside people's heads, you literally cannot see it happening—and you can't Taylorize what you can't see.

Peter Drucker famously said that knowledge workers do not respond to financial incentives, orders, or negative sanctions the way
blue-collar workers are expected to. I particularly like his observation that the key to motivating creative people is to treat them
as "de facto volunteers," tied to the firm by a commitment to its
aims and purposes, and often expecting to participate in its administration and its governance. "Volunteers," he wrote, "have to
get more satisfaction from their work than paid employees precisely
because they do not get a paycheck."[21] The commitments of creative
people are also highly contingent, and their motivation comes
largely from within.

But volunteerism isn't an entirely apt analogy for the no-collar
workplace. Although it appeals to employees' intrinsic motivations,
it runs on very subtle models of control. Rather than boss or bribe
us, it basically seduces us to work harder—and we are putty in management's hands when it comes to the so-called challenge of the
job and respect of our peers, as we saw in Chapter 4. As *Business-
Week* bluntly put it, "The smartest companies know this. Instead
of ensnaring employees with more signing bonuses and huge
salaries, they are trying to hook them emotionally."[22] It's an insidious internalization of work norms I call "soft control."

The practices and structures of creativity would eventually have
permeated corporate life on their own, but the meteoric rise of the
so-called New Economy of the late 1990s and early 2000 accelerated their diffusion. Like the early days of Silicon Valley before
it, the New Economy unleashed a powerful cultural force for business change, but in an even more pervasive way. The New Economy
uprooted the age-old distinction between appropriate business
norms and alternative culture. In those heady days, joining a new
dot-com became a form of self-expression and self-actualization.
Many companies actively embraced this by wedding their commercial zeal to a mission to transform business culture.[23] A clear

distinction was drawn between the outmoded, staid, and constrict-ing practices of the "old" economy and the open, progressive, lib-erating practice of the "new."

As the culture critic Andrew Ross noted at the time, "A lot of these companies presented themselves as alternatives to corporate America and took on all things bohemian." In propagating the myth of the New Economy as social force, this period raised people's expectations about what they wanted in a company and a job, which, as Ross put it, "meant that a lot of activism, or socially pro-ductive work that they otherwise might have done, was redirected into a kind of infatuation with changing the shape of corporate America. That could only have happened, of course, because of the particularly bohemian cast—the sort of counterculture cast—of the companies that recruited these employees, for better or worse."[24]

A lot of it was worse, in my view—amounting to little more than a well-choreographed charade. Many companies merely presented a cheap facade of the alternative—a ping-pong table, perhaps an espresso machine. And many otherwise sensible people bought into it because they were starved for something different. It wasn't about the money after all. As countless people in my focus groups and interviews told me, they wanted to be a part of a different, more inclusive, more progressive culture. Most of them, however, were quickly disappointed. A great migration turned into a great exodus, captured in this telling epitaph: "I'd rather work at Starbucks."[25]

In summer 2000, I was invited to address the top management of a major regional bank on how to attract and retain creative and talented workers. We selected an edgy high-tech company as the venue for our workshop and invited two of its top executives to join in the discussion. The bank managers wanted to know what creative people care about and seemed particularly interested in younger employees. They asked questions about the role of dress codes, work-space design, perks, compensation, location, and the like. It was very clear to me that they were genuinely concerned with managing and motivating their employees—if truth be told, with treating them like human beings.

As we got further into it, the two high-tech executives began to chime in with their views, which essentially amounted to "management by stress"—working people as long and as hard as they could stand it. It was painfully apparent that they didn't have the foggiest idea about how to treat, never mind motivate, creative people, let alone build an effective and enduring organizational culture. As the end of the workshop drew near and the clock edged toward 6:00 PM, the high-tech pair, seemingly unaware of the time, began an extended harangue. As the rest of us sat uncomfortably in our seats, one of the bank managers interrupted: "At our company," he said, "we respect the flexibility and the right of our people to go home, if need be, to their spouses, significant others and families, so I think we should draw this meeting to a close."

Too many of these sorts of companies became not workplace utopias but what Stanford management expert Jeffrey Pfeffer has aptly dubbed the "toxic workplace." The toxic workplace operates on the principle that "we own you." Or as Pfeffer puts it: "We're going to put you in a situation where you have to work in a style and on a pace that is not sustainable. We want you to come in here and burn yourself out—and then you can leave."[26]

The NASDAQ crash and 9/11 were wake-up calls, as I pointed out in the original edition of this book. No longer so beguiled by the myth of striking it big, people became much savvier about the kinds of places where they really wanted to work—companies that combined the flexibility and openness of the no-collar workplace with job stability, that had reasonable expectations about working hours, and that offered talented peers and responsible management. The real legacy of the rise and fall of the New Economy is that it brought people back down to earth, recalibrating their expectations about their jobs. For this alone, it was an invaluable collective learning experience.

And then the economic crisis of 2008 hammered it home. The old order really has entered a terminal crisis; the new order has yet to fully emerge. Still, the management of many if not most big companies only partially gets it. In 2011, the Harvard Business School's Teresa Amabile and the independent researcher Steven Kramer noted that nearly one-third of American workers are unhappy and unmotivated in their jobs, and no wonder. "When we asked 669 managers from companies around the world to rank five employee motivators in terms of importance," they wrote, "they ranked 'supporting progress' dead last. Fully 95 percent of these managers failed to recognize that progress in meaningful work is the primary motivator, well ahead of traditional incentives like raises and bonuses."[27]

Managing Creativity at SAS

The software giant SAS Institute has enjoyed substantial revenue growth every year since its founding in 1976. Its employee turnover rate is less than 5 percent (compared to an industry average of 20 percent), and it has scored in the top twenty of *Fortune*'s "Best Companies to Work For" lists every year since they've been published. SAS's Fortune 500 customers are happy, too—they renew their subscriptions to its products at an astounding 98 percent rate. What are the keys to its success?

In 2005, I had the privilege of collaborating with SAS's cofounder and CEO Jim Goodnight on a study of the social and management contexts in which SAS has most effectively nurtured, harnessed, and mobilized creativity. We summarized our findings in an article entitled "Managing for Creativity," which was published in the July–August 2005 issue of the *Harvard Business Review*.

Through trial and error, as well as organic evolution, SAS has learned how to tap the creative energies of *all* of its stakeholders—customers, software developers, managers, and support staff alike. Beyond that, it has developed a unique framework for managing creativity that rests on three guiding principles: 1) help employees do their best work by keeping them intellectually engaged and by removing distractions and impediments to their productivity; 2) make managers responsible for sparking creativity, not enforcing rules; and 3) engage the customers as creative partners to be sure that the product always meets their needs.

A management framework like SAS's produces a corporate ecosystem in which creativity and productivity flourish, where profitability and flexibility go hand in hand, and where hard work and work-life balance aren't mutually exclusive.

Help Workers Be Great

SAS operates on the belief that invigorating mental work leads to superior performance and, ultimately, to better products. It doesn't bribe workers with stock options; it has never offered them. At SAS, the most fitting thanks for a job well done is an even more challenging project. SAS sends its developers to industry and technology conferences, where they can hone their skills and build relationships within the larger software community, and it encourages employees to publish papers and books.

SAS provides services and amenities like on-site day care and medical facilities; a pool, fitness room, and basketball courts; subsidized meals; haircuts; dry cleaning; and more. Flexible workday guidelines encourage people to strike a balance between work and family; the company takes its thirty-five-hour workweek seriously (and knows that employees will put in extra time when it's required). Creative people can be trusted to manage their own workloads;

their inner drive to achieve, not to mention accountability among their colleagues and peers, compels a high level of productivity. Employees who don't perform are swiftly winnowed. "Hire hard, manage open, fire hard," are SAS's watchwords.

We're All Creatives

Everyone at SAS is a creative, suits and workers alike. All of SAS's managers roll up their shirtsleeves from time to time, including its CEO, who still sometimes writes code. The willingness—even eagerness—of managers to delve into the "real" work of the organization sends an important message: we are all on the same team, working toward the same goal, the creation of a superior product. An egalitarian culture fosters mutual respect—and encourages openness and constructive criticism in both directions. Experimentation necessarily involves failures and dead ends; SAS's management recognizes that safety and stasis don't lead to new insights and encourages its employees to take risks. Fully 26 percent of its budget is dedicated to R&D (more than twice the norm for a high-tech company).

Focus on Customers and End-Users

SAS aggressively solicits customer feedback—and acts on it. It tracks complaints and makes sure they are addressed in product revisions; it treats its users' conferences as occasions to elicit criticism and ideas from its customers rather than simply to market to them. SAS resolves more than three-fourths of its customers' problems within twenty-four hours; the wait time on its tech support lines averages thirty-four seconds. Most important of all, the company strives to release bug-free products. Testing teams run through a product from a developer's standpoint, a salesperson's standpoint, and a customer's standpoint. Any glitches and it goes back to the drawing board.

The key elements of the SAS approach to managing creativity include:

- leveraging the intrinsic motivation of creative workers by stimulating their minds and minimizing their hassles;
- minimizing the barriers between managers and workers by ensuring that managers are creatives, too;
- tapping into the creative talents of customers as well as workers; and
- nurturing long-term relationships with users and employees alike.

As SAS has learned, a company's most important asset isn't raw materials, real estate, machinery, transportation systems, or political influence. It is its creative capital—its arsenal of creative thinkers whose ideas can be turned into valuable products and services. Successful companies recognize that their most valuable assets walk out the door every evening; they dedicate their best efforts to ensuring that they come back and give their very best every morning.

Although creative people take their jobs less for granted today than they did in flusher times, they still want to work for companies like SAS that value them, provide them with challenging yet stable work environments, nurture and support their creativity, and allow them to realize their full potential. They desire flexibility on matters such as hours, dress, and personal work habits. They seek a workplace that incorporates both the freedom and flexibility of a smaller start-up and the stability and direction of a larger firm. But the trajectory is not backward to the boredom and drudgery of a traditional corporate bureaucracy.

Even the most conservative companies are adopting aspects of the no-collar workplace in order to recruit and retain the best employees.

And when they start down this road, there's no turning back—improvements in workplace conditions tend to be sticky; once instituted, they are not easily reversed or rescinded. Companies of all types are converging on a new style of managing creative work. If we find this new style more suited to our needs than the old, so much the better.

PART THREE

LIFE

CHAPTER 7

Time Warp

I f the very word "time" elicits a tight, edgy feeling in your chest and makes your temples throb, you are not alone. Growing numbers of Americans feel increasingly pressed for time. Creative Class people do tend to work long hours, but the biggest news about time goes deeper than how long our workdays are. The key change is that our use of time has intensified. We now try to pack every moment full of activities and experiences—at work, at home, and at leisure. In the process, the ways in which we think about time as well as use it are being warped into new configurations.

This intensification of the experience of time began with the advent of the clock, which created a more finely divided day, changing the nature of work and subsequently the rest of life, as the British historian E. P. Thompson has noted.[1] In agricultural societies, people lived and worked by the sun and the seasons. With the Industrial Revolution, distinct compartments of work time and off time were formally demarcated. In the second half of the nineteenth century, new technologies like Edison's incandescent bulb facilitated the extension of the workday. Then at the turn of the twentieth century, Frederick Taylor's scientific management timed each movement in the performance of tasks, extending the division of labor into the division of time itself. The Organizational Age led to a further ordering and intensification of time and also helped promote the idea that a steady chronological climb up the corporate and status ladders was the normal life course. Today our sense of time is changing again, and the story is more insidious than you might think.

It is not so much that we suffer from overwork, but rather from a severe shortage of time. Between 1965 and 1995, researchers John Robinson and Geoffrey Godbey tracked detailed time diaries of thousands of Americans for the Americans' Use of Time Project and reported the results in their book *Time for Life*. Their main conclusion: Americans suffer from a "time famine." "Time has become the most precious commodity," they wrote, "and the ultimate scarcity for millions of Americans."[2] Their research found an across-the-board increase in people saying they felt "hurried" or "rushed" in their daily activities. The number reporting they "always feel rushed" increased from 24 percent of working-age (eighteen to sixty-four years old) respondents in 1965 to 38 percent by 1992.[3] High levels of time-related stress were most prevalent among the college educated and affluent. As Robert Putnam noted in the book's foreword, "The most worrisome social trend in America over the last several decades has been the widening gap in wealth and income between the social classes. Robinson and Godbey report a less noticed counterpart trend: less well-educated Americans appear to be enjoying more free time, whereas their college-educated counterparts, for the most part, are not. Paradoxically, as the authors put it, the 'working class' is spending fewer hours at work, while the erstwhile 'leisure class' has less leisure."[4]

A 2010 Gallup survey found that roughly one-third of Americans suffered from high levels of time-related stress. Most stressed were parents with young children and working women; people with higher levels of skills and income tended to suffer the most.[5] Paul Romer makes the intriguing argument that even when we are not actually pressed for time, we may perceive that we are because our time is worth more than it used to be. In advanced nations, Romer explains, the long-term trend is for average real income to increase. There are fluctuations, to be sure—real wages may stagnate or fall at times for various sectors of the workforce—but overall, adjusting for inflation, the dominant trend is for most of us to earn more per hour than our counterparts of previous years. This ought to make us feel pretty good about the returns we're getting on our time. But our minds don't work that way. Instead, we assign an ever-increasing cost to every minute that we spend *outside* work—and thus worry constantly about the minutes slipping away. It is, says Romer, an unavoidable side effect of our economy: "Our children will have more of almost everything, with one glaring exception: They won't have more time in the day. As income and wages increase, the cost of time will continue to grow and so will the sense that time is scarce and that life proceeds at a faster pace than in the past."[6]

Technology has contributed to the time famine. The past several decades have seen a relentless march of technologies that extend the workday. Many observers have noted how, thanks to smart phones and laptops, our work tends to follow us wherever we are. It follows us *whenever* we are, too. But creative work tends to follow you around regardless of technology, in the sense that it inhabits your head. At the end of each workday, there are usually problems remaining to be solved or decisions waiting to be made. These things may not occupy the foreground of your time off, but they linger in the background. If you mulled over these problems while riding your bike or eating dinner, would you bill the time to a client? Would you record it as work in a time diary? Creative workers may actually "work" more than statistics show.

This is compounded, of course, by the demands of home and family. Households with two working parents or a working single parent are increasingly numerous, and the absence of a support spouse crunches time tremendously. The Americans' Use of Time Project found that in 1995 the average (nonemployed) housewife was spending some forty-two hours per week on family care, household chores, and commuting duties—the equivalent of a full-time job (though this was down from fifty-four hours in 1965). It also found that women continued to provide more than two-thirds of all family care. When the housewife vanishes, paid caretakers such as maids and child-care workers can pick up some but not all of the slack. And though the flexible life of creative workers helps to create a demand for a 24/7 corps of service workers, it's not a zero-sum transaction. The all-night restaurant might be wonderful for the code writer who wants a hamburger at 3:00 AM, but it might not be so wonderful for the waitress. She isn't on a flexible schedule after all, just the night shift.

To cope, many people arrive at a complex interweaving of work and personal life: working to meet the demands of the job, certainly, but in patterns attuned to their own creative rhythms. From morning to night and from workplace to home, they intersperse bursts of work with chunks of personal time for exercise, errands, socializing, family time, or just plain downtime. The folks sitting in the coffee shop with their laptops—are they working or are they socializing? Well, both, sort of. Working now, but ready to shift quickly into social mode, they very much resemble the old craftsman in his shop on the village main street—busy, but always ready to share a pot of tea if somebody interesting walks in. Indeed, many people see interweaving as a natural way of operating, a sort of throwback to the cottage-industry days when life was integrated and whole. It seems a healthy reaction to the Organizational Age system, which split work and life into compartments and required you to be one person here, another there.

Unfortunately, the flexible, interwoven life can be more hectic than idyllic. The traditional nine-to-five workday required only a few transitions of mindset and location. You show up at work and stay there, then you switch off your work brain and go home. Maybe you run a few errands on the way. An interwoven day—with midday run or bike ride, late-night work, and meals and errands scattered across different times and places—requires many transitions. Although some of these are easy, many are taxing. They take *time*. You need to shift focus, remember where you put your papers and materials, be sure you've got everything—and be sure you're dressed properly. Moreover, there are times in the interwoven day when parallel worlds collide. It can happen in the coffee shop or at home with the children: you want to work, but someone is standing before you demanding something else. Do you get that tight, edgy feeling in your chest? That's the pang of the time famine.

And though your personal allocation of time may be flexible, scheduled events are not. A good bit of time stress comes from trying to meet someone else's schedule: the meeting is at 4:00 PM, the soccer game is at 6:00, the plane leaves without you if you're not on it. I think the stress is exacerbated if, like many creative workers, you spend much of the day working at a self-dictated pace and then suddenly have to switch to a mode dictated by the clock. This may be the most jarring transition of all. It reflects, in the realm of time, the ongoing tension between creativity and organization.

Front-Loading

In many Creative Class fields, people manage their careers by "front-loading"—working excruciatingly long and hard at the outset of their professional lives in the hope that it will pay off in greater income, marketability, and mobility later. Granted, young people have often worked hard in the past. Young executive-track hopefuls in the Organizational Age were certainly expected to be diligent, but in those days the responsibilities and the time demands grew as they climbed the ladder. Besides, you wanted to start a family early because it showed the company that you were a stable person and a belonger. Today that has all been turned upside down. Indicative of the trend, both men and women on average are getting married five years later in 2010 than they were in 1970.[7] In 2008, 41.4 out of 1,000 American adults had gotten married within the last twelve months; in 2012, that number dropped to 37.4. Just 9 percent of Americans age eighteen to twenty-four had a spouse in 2010, about one-fifth of the share for this age group in 1960, according to a December 2011 report from the Pew Research Center.[8]

The growing number of women in the professions—along with the fact that a lot of employers still don't care to see their young professional women on the mommy track—has been one factor driving the trend to front-load work and defer the rest of life, but there are many others. In the universities, postdocs and assistant professors have long been notorious for working fiendishly at their research. Often they forgo family aspirations and other nice things in life through their twenties because they are aiming for the tenure track. Academic tenure provides more than a secure lifetime position. It puts you in the ranks of the privileged. You get choice teaching assignments, a higher salary, a nicer office. As you build your reputation, it becomes easier to secure research funds, to generate novel findings, and to publish. Other universities bid for your talent. Something similar has always been the case with artists. Musicians, painters, writers, and actors may not aim for academic tenure at a university, but it makes a big difference if they come barreling out of their youth tagged as stars or at least comers. They still have to keep working hard, but the returns on their early investment are high. Now that they have been noticed, they can get the choice commissions, the savvy agents, the nice gigs. I would submit that a similar phenomenon is taking hold today in the private sector. It is particularly true in the so-called up-or-out professions such as law or consulting, where great advantages accrue to those who make partner status, whereas those who do not are essentially out of luck. But it is also becoming true more generally.

There are several reasons for this. Young recent graduates are the workhorses of many sectors of the Creative Economy. They have the most up-to-date skills in highly specialized fields like computing, consulting, or turbo-finance, and being young and un-attached, they are able to work ridiculous hours. Rather than being groomed slowly for advancement, they are thrown quickly to the front lines to see what they can do. And they set to it with a vengeance. They do so partly because they relish the challenge but also because, in a fluid market, this is the time to make your mark. You are hot now. If you want to be hot later—if you want to be call-ing the shots rather than waiting for calls, and have people bidding for you rather than screening your résumé—you need to be on the star track. If you acquire a reputation as just another hacker, you may spend the rest of your days on the hack track.

With so many people feeling chronically pressed for time, a new strategy of sorts has emerged: "time deepening." Robinson and Godbey describe it this way:

> Time-deepening fools people into thinking they can avoid sacrificing one activity for another. We instead seek to do it all, and see it all, and to do it and see it now. In effect, time has become a commodity, and time viewed as a commodity seems to have made people's lives shorter and less tranquil. The experience of life is increasingly catalogued in terms of a patternless checklist of "been there, done that."[9]

They note its four key elements:

- *Speeding up* of activities.
- *Substituting* a leisure activity that can be done more quickly for one that takes longer, such as getting take-out or home delivery

rather than cooking, playing racquetball rather than a slower game like tennis—or, in my case, an hour of spinning in the gym as opposed to a two- or three-hour bike ride with friends.

- *Multitasking,* or doing more than one thing at once: watching TV while reading the paper, eating dinner while editing a chapter, tweeting while on a conference call.
- *Detailed time planning and budgeting*—especially for leisure or recreational activities; compartmentalizing time so as to get a handle on it. Astoundingly, my students are never without their smart phones, which parcel their days into half-hour chunks. I certainly did not need to schedule my time like that when I was a student. I didn't even keep a calendar until I became an assistant professor.

Quite a trick, actually: to me, time deepening seems even more insidious than long hours. Robinson and Godbey also see it as part of a bigger shift from the "consumption of goods" to the "consumption of experiences." This is a theme that takes us from the sphere of work to the sphere of life as a whole. In the next chapter, I describe a key facet of the Creative Class lifestyle: the quest for rich and multidimensional experiences. In this classic creative view, time is truly deep not when it is rushed or crammed, but when it fully engages every faculty of one's being in every waking moment.

CHAPTER 8

The Experiential Life

At the dawn of the new millennium, on the morning of January 1, 2000, 10 million computer users logged into the domain DotComGuy.com and watched via webcam as a bland-looking twenty-six-year-old former systems analyst, who'd legally changed his name to DotComGuy, moved into a bland suburban house in North Dallas, Texas. There he would remain for the rest of the year, living entirely on goods and services ordered over the Internet: groceries from Food.com, housecleaning by TheMaids.com, and more.

He was as unlikely a media sensation as could be imagined. The secret of DotComGuy's appeal could not have been his daily routine, which often resembled that of an elderly shut-in waiting for Meals on Wheels to arrive. Nothing kinky here: no webcam sex or moody personal revelations. He spent much of his time playing with his dog, DotComDog, watching TV, or surfing the Web. Yet he drew a devoted online following for a while, including a chat room frequented by young girls commenting on his cuteness. News reporters and eager visitors came to call. What made DotComGuy so fascinating was that he perfectly embodied all the myths of *homo new economicus* in the Internet age. Here was the quintessential maverick, using the Internet to turn the system on its ear. He was a free agent and entrepreneur, out on his own, doing it his way. He had lined up corporate sponsors to provide everything he needed in exchange for publicity and banner ads on his website, and not just start-ups and gimmicks like online pizza deliverers but such long-established giants as UPS, Gateway, and 3Com. Rather than holding a faceless job in corporate America, DotComGuy had the big companies beating a path to *his* door. Rather than traveling for what he wanted, he had the world brought to him. He was a virtual Horatio Alger, a housebound king of infinite cyberspace. When DotComGuy left his house at the end of the year, he announced that he planned to marry a woman he had "met" in his website chat room.

Although some dubbed him an avatar of the Internet age, *Salon* called him the "Poster Child for Internet Idiocy."[1] In either case, his fifteen minutes didn't outlast the NASDAQ crash. Not long after he returned to the real world, DotComGuy changed his name back to the one his parents gave him and auctioned off his domain, which is now the trademark of a business that provides IT services. As it turned out, he wasn't such a bellwether after all. His entrepreneurial spirit and his flair for self-promotion might have anticipated the reality TV boom to come, but his virtual lifestyle was not at all what members of the Creative Class wanted. Although e-commerce has grown bigger than most would have imagined and social media like Twitter and Facebook have penetrated our lives to an extent that would have boggled even DotComGuy's imagination, the flip side of these trends has been an even more relentless quest for real community, real experiences, and, yes, real life.

On many fronts, the Creative Class lifestyle comes down to a passionate quest for experience. The ideal is to live a more creative life, packed with more intense, high-quality, multidimensional experiences. The interviews and focus groups I conducted in the late 1990s and early 2000s indicated that creative people favor active, participatory recreation over passive spectator sports. They like indigenous street-level culture—a teeming blend of cafés, sidewalk musicians, and small galleries and bistros, where it's hard to draw the line between participant and observer, creativity and its creators. They crave creative stimulation but not escape. As one young man told me, explaining why he and his friends favored nonalcoholic hangouts, "We can't afford the recovery time." In their book *The Experience Economy,* Joseph Pine and James Gilmore explain the shift from consumption of material goods to consumption of experiences as "a fourth economic offering, as distinct from services as services are from goods," noting:

> Experiences have always been around but consumers, businesses, and economists lumped them into the service sector along with such uneventful activities as dry cleaning, auto repair, wholesale distribution, and telephone access. When a person buys a service he purchases a set of intangible activities carried out on his behalf. But when he buys an experience, he pays to spend time enjoying a series of memorable events that a company stages—as in a theatrical play—to engage him in a personal way. . . . The newly identified offering of experiences occurs whenever a company intentionally uses services as the stage and goods as props to engage an individual. While commodities are fungible, goods tangible, and services intangible, experiences are *memorable.*[2]

The Creative Class is experience driven. My interviews and focus groups reveal a considerable orientation to active and authentic experiences that participants can structure themselves. In practical everyday terms, this means running, rock climbing, or cycling rather than watching a game on TV; it means travel to interesting, remote, and even risky locations that engage one physically or intellectually; it means the purchase of unique antique pieces or original midcentury modern furniture, as opposed to just buying something to sit on. In the 1950s, the psychologist Carl Rogers noted the connection between creativity and experiences, writing, "It has been found that when the individual is 'open' to all his experience then his behavior will be creative, and his creativity may be trusted to be essentially constructive."[3] He defined openness to experience as consisting of the following attributes: "lack of rigidity and permeability of boundaries in concepts, beliefs, perceptions, and hypotheses," "a tolerance for ambiguity," and an "ability to receive much conflicting information without forcing closure upon the situation." He found that in people who are open to experience, "each stimulus is freely relayed without being distorted by any process of defensiveness," whether it "originates in the environment, in the impact of form, color, or sound on the sensory nerves, or whether it originates in the viscera." Based on this, he concluded, "This complete openness of awareness to what exists at this moment is, I believe, an important condition of constructive creativity." The experiential lifestyle is about much more than fun. It complements the way members of the Creative Class work and is a fundamental component of their lives.

The Active Life

"In the early 1960s, there was no such thing as a middle-aged man jogging on the street," the journalist Andy Sheehan wrote in *Chasing the Hawk*, a book about his late father, Dr. George Sheehan, the well-known "running guru" of the 1960s and 1970s.[4] A successful doctor in Red Bank, New Jersey, George Sheehan began running in 1963 at the age of forty-five. At the time, grown men simply did not exercise in public; doing so entailed the risk of appearing frivolous or even "subversive." So Sheehan ran in his backyard. "It was with no small amount of wonder," his son writes, "that I stood on my back porch one day . . . and watched my father running the perimeter of our backyard. The backyard covered two acres, and I watched as he ran the length of the house, trotted down a small slope, turned right at a neighbor's fence." When his father eventually took to the streets, he did so "despite the honking horns and the sounds of laughter from the cars that passed him." The jibes were sometimes directed at the younger Sheehan and his siblings: "'Why does your father run around town in his underwear?' we children were asked." But through it all, according to his son, running helped establish George Sheehan as a creative person. "My father attributed a whole host of astonishing personal transformations to running. It made him stop drinking, freed him from anger, got him in touch with himself, and made him a creative being." Around the same time that Sheehan was discovering running on the Jersey shore, human potential pioneers at the Esalen Institute in Big Sur, California, were treating jogging and even golf as a spiritual practice.

Few of us, of course, achieve such a radical makeover from running or any other single activity. But we are engaging in many new behaviors that add up to a radical makeover of leisure in our society. And though Sheehan claimed that his pastime made him creative, I would suggest that for us, the causality runs the other way as well. Because we relate to the economy through our creativity and thus identify ourselves as "creative beings," we pursue pastimes and cultural forms that express and nurture our creativity.

The ensuing decades have witnessed a virtual revolution in active recreation. In 1964, when George Sheehan entered his first Boston Marathon, he was one of just 225 runners. Today the event is limited to 18,000. According to a 2000 Roper Starch survey, 67 percent of all Americans participated in active outdoor recreation on a monthly basis in 1999, up from 50 percent in 1994. The study also noted that an increasing number of people, some 30 percent, participate in more than five different active recreational activities per year.[5] By 2010, according to the US Bureau of Economic Analysis, Americans were spending $918.3 billion on recreation.[6]

Buried in this staggering statistic is the extent to which people—particularly Creative Class people—have thrown themselves into active sports and physical exercise. It is increasingly normal and even expected that Creative Class people, well into middle age and beyond, will engage in these activities that were once deemed juvenile or deviant. Health-club memberships in the United States grew from virtually nothing in the early 1960s to more than 15 million by the mid-1980s. By 2000, they'd reached 32.8 million; by 2009, the number had risen by almost another one-third, to 45.3 million.[7] An article in the *Wall Street Journal* on September 7, 2011, noted that "health clubs and gyms accounted for 8.8% of new leases signed so far this year by retail chains in the U.S., compared with 7.9% at the same point last year. . . . The rush into shopping centers has helped fuel a 57% increase in square footage occupied by U.S. health clubs since 2007, to more than 70 million square feet."[8] Many larger companies provide on-site physical exercise facilities. Some subsidize gym memberships or even reduce the employee contribution for health-care benefits for those who engage in regular exercise. Although much has been made of our increased television viewing (which ballooned from 10.4 hours a week in 1965 to 16 hours in 1995, climbing to 19 hours by 2010), active sports and exercise registered the largest percentage increase of all free-time activities, *tripling* between 1965 and 1995.[9]

In the original edition of this book I used data on American consumer behavior from Equifax to illustrate the experiential consumption preferences of higher income, more well-educated people.[10] According to these data, eighteen- to thirty-four-year-olds earning more than $75,000 a year were more than twice as likely to scuba dive, snow ski, travel, play tennis, fly frequently, or jog than their lower-paid peers, whereas those with incomes of $30,000 or less were more likely to play home video games, horseback ride, fiddle with electronics, camp, ride a motorcycle, or do automotive work. Looking at slightly older people, ages thirty-five to forty-four, higher-income people were more than twice as likely to travel, ski, or scuba dive, and one and one-half times more likely to play tennis, golf, jog, and enjoy wines. Lower-income people were more likely to horseback ride, play video games, collect stamps, ride motorcycles, camp, and do automotive work. Equifax stopped conducting this particular survey in the mid-2000s, but a 2008 Bureau of Labor Statistics Time Use Survey noted that "people with higher levels of education were more likely to participate in sports and exercise. Among people aged 25 years and older, those with a bachelor's degree or higher were more than twice as likely to participate in sports and exercise activities on an average day during the 2003–06 period as those with a high school diploma or less."[11]

My focus groups and interviews with Creative Class people revealed that they value active outdoor recreation very highly. They are drawn to places and communities where many outdoor activities are prevalent—both because they enjoy those activities, and because their presence is seen as a signal that the place is amenable to the broader creative lifestyle. The Creative Class people in my studies are into a variety of active sports, from traditional ones like bicycling, jogging, and kayaking to newer, more extreme ones like trail running and snowboarding.

Some of these class preferences reflect the nature of work itself. Members of the traditional Working Class spend the day engaged in physical labor and are thus inclined to relax during their time off. But if you spend your workday in front of a computer screen or an artist's canvas, you are probably not eager to spend your leisure time in front of a TV screen. You are much more likely to want to get out and be active. As one person I interviewed put it, "Recreation is stress relief away from everyday work."[12] Time and again, when people in my interviews and focus groups spoke of active sports, they used the word "release." Climbing a rock face or pedaling a bike releases the physical energy pent up through long hours of sitting, and it is also a form of mental release. As the wife of a high-powered executive put it, "He is compelled to engage in these kinds of activities simply to release the incredible energy he has."[13]

My Creative Class subjects were not especially interested in conventional spectator sports; they preferred to participate directly. On the infrequent occasions that they did take in a game, the sports they appeared to favor featured continuous action, like basketball and hockey, rather than football or baseball. Part of the reason is that continuous-action sports are more packed with experience. But beyond this, an even broader reason—highlighted in a fair number of my interviews—is that basketball and hockey games are played in the evening during times of year when the weather is cold and daylight ends early. My interview subjects said that they simply could not afford to "sacrifice" a warm summer evening to watch baseball, or an entire Sunday afternoon to attend a football game.

As noted earlier, Paul Fussell's book *Class* is full of barbed but often perceptive comments on everyone from "proles" to the "out-of-sight" wealthy. An obsession with spectator sports tends to be a marker of Working Class status for two reasons, he observes. One is the need "to identify with winners, the need to dance and scream, We're number one! while holding an index finger erect." And two, he adds that sports are also popular because they "sanction a flux of pedantry, dogmatism, record-keeping, wise secret knowledge, and pseudo-scholarship of the sort usually associated with the 'decision-making' or 'executive' or 'opinion-molding' classes," adding that "the World Series and the Super Bowl give every man his opportunity to play for the moment the impressive barroom pedant, to imitate for a brief season the superior classes identified by their practice of weighty utterance and informed opinion."[14]

There are other reasons that traditional spectator sports are less popular among the Creative Class. When people move frequently to pursue careers and lifestyle interests, it becomes harder for them to sustain the home-team allegiances built in youth. Also, as we have seen, more and more of the Creative Class are immigrants, people who grew up with cricket or field hockey or soccer. Still more are globally minded. The unprecedented US interest in the 2010 World Cup was perhaps a harbinger of some of these deeper cultural shifts.

When I undertook this revision, I asked my colleague Daniel Silver for his comments. In an email, he suggested that I had over-simplified some of these issues, writing:

> In my view even the generalities are more mixed than you make them out. Personal story: I am a big football fan, and I often do "waste" my Sundays to watch the 49ers. Just last weekend, I left my wife and kids in the middle of a neighborhood outdoor block party to go find a sports bar showing the game. I'm also relatively unconvinced by the argument that highly structured activities are unattractive to creative types. Martial Arts would be my prime example. In fact, they are near unique among most amenities in that they are associated with BOTH college grads and substantial and often rising levels of blacks and hispanics. But martial arts clubs are highly structured, and training your way up the belts requires that you learn all sorts of rigid rules. It is only at the most advanced levels that you are allowed to fully freelance and flow. For many, it is that very structure that is so attractive.

I could not agree more. Some Working Class people have no interest in spectator sports or motor sports. Some wealthy Creative Class people love them: think of Jay Leno or Jerry Seinfeld and their automobile collections, or Spike Lee in his courtside seat at New York Knicks games. I, too, am a big sports fan and follow not just the Knicks, but the Jets, Giants, and Yankees with the ardor of the most die-hard fanatic. The sociology of sport and class clearly contains many nuances and subtleties. That said, the Creative Class does have a special penchant, both comparatively and historically, for more active and participative pursuits.

Noting the toned bodies on so many young members of the Creative Class, my brother Robert, himself a fellow who likes to stay fit, says that "college students today look like they major in staying in shape." Much the same is true of another Creative Class subgroup, performing artists. Some musicians have bigger biceps than pro athletes did forty years ago. A number of middle-aged rock stars, such as Bruce Springsteen, Sting, and Madonna, appear fitter now than when they started out. If Bob Dylan were to come along today, his agent would probably send him to the weight room.

Every year since 2008, the American College of Sports Medicine has ranked America's fifty largest metros on its American Fitness Index, which takes into account both personal health indicators (statistics on specific diseases, obesity, smoking levels, and so on) and community and environmental factors (health-care access, community resources that promote fitness, and the like).[15] In 2011, its top fifteen metros were Minneapolis; Washington, DC; Boston; Portland, Oregon; Denver; San Francisco; Hartford; Seattle; Virginia Beach; Sacramento; San Jose; Richmond; San Diego; Cincinnati; and Salt Lake City. When Charlotta Mellander and I analyzed the data we found that fitter metros also had higher average wages and income, higher shares of residents with college degrees, greater levels of innovation, more high-tech companies, and a higher percentage of Creative Class workers than their less-fit counterparts.

This Creative Class obsession with fitness goes beyond a concern with health. And it is much more than a mere shifting of the aesthetic standard to favor, say, bigger biceps. With marriage often deferred and divorce more common, Creative Class people spend a lot of time on the mating market. Physical display is a key aspect of mating: you are more marketable if you look your best. Being economically mobile and entrepreneurial, members of the Creative Class also spend a lot of time advertising themselves to prospective employers, partners, and clients. And though it might be a pernicious stereotype, studies show that in-shape people are perceived to be not just more presentable but more reliable than their less-toned counterparts. Staying in shape creates more energy, more endurance, and more physical flexibility—it helps optimize the body for the long haul of a life of creative work.

Leisure as Work

And that might be what it's all about—not just leisure, but work masquerading as leisure. That's the point made by two thoughtful sociologists, Richard Lloyd and Mark Banks, who in their separate writings note that what at first glance might appear to be leisure activities—engagement in art, participation in active sports and recreation, even bohemian rejection of the status quo—may at a deeper level be a less-obvious form of work. In a 2009 essay, Banks criticized me on this score, writing that the "traditional notion of leisure as an autonomous, work-antithetical practice may be disappearing." And he added:

> What seems most apparent amongst Florida's emergent "creative class" is
> not simply that work and nonwork have become somehow "imbalanced,"
> or even "reversed" in meaning, but that work has come to colonize life to

such an extent that it has pervasively absorbed leisure into its own logic, entirely effacing the work-leisure distinction and, what is more, now appears to have achieved this with the express support and enthusiasm of labour."[16]

Again, I could not agree more, and I believe I said as much in the original edition. Leisure is undertaken not for its own sake but to enhance the creative experience—which for the Creative Class, *is* work. The boundaries between leisure and work have become so blurry that the two have effectively blended into one another.

The norms of work have likewise inserted themselves into leisure. As I noted in the original edition, when asked why he and his peers favor highly active forms of recreation, one young member of the Creative Class gave a succinct reply: "You get more entertainment value per unit of time." The young man went on to explain that in his view, even a relatively tame pastime like hiking or simply going for a walk is more continuously engaging, and on more levels, than watching baseball or playing a sport like golf. You are in motion every minute. The scenery is varied and changing; the world is unfolding around you. You can stop to sightsee or window-shop or talk with people along the way, get deep into conversation with a walking companion, or just walk solo and let your mind range.

An article in the *Wall Street Journal* in August 2011 noted the research of Marc Berman, a postdoctoral fellow at the Rotman School of Management at the University of Toronto, where I teach, whose experiments make a strong case for the proposition that the proverbial walk in the woods (or in this case, an arboretum) can boost performance on cognitive tests by as much as 20 percent. According to his research, a walk down a busy city street produced no such benefits. "In a follow-up study," the *Wall Street Journal* noted, "the researchers had participants take a break for 10 minutes in a quiet room to look at pictures of a nature scene or city street. Again, they found that cognitive performance improved after the nature break, even though it was only on paper. Although the boost wasn't as great as when participants actually took the walk among the trees, it was more effective than the city walk."[17]

Extreme sports like rock climbing provide mental benefits as well, albeit in a much more concentrated and demanding form. Climbing provides continuous engagement on both the physical and mental planes. You get variety and novelty, and the possibilities expand as you grow more skilled, because you can try new and more difficult climbs. The mental engagement of climbing, intense as it may be, is a profound release from work. One cannot think about tomorrow's meeting while grasping for a piton a hundred feet in the air, yet once you reach a secure perch, you can indulge in sightseeing and reverie. All told, it packs a lot of experience into each unit of time. The essence of climbing, hiking, and a host of similar sports that the Creative Class favors is to enter some other world, away from the workaday world, and explore it and experience it while performing a task that is challenging in and of itself. In short, the idea is to have an adventure. Game sports like baseball are fundamentally different. The world that it invites its spectators and participants into is highly structured: four bases at ninety feet apart, three strikes and you're out. And though rock climbing has its own rules and limits—you can't, for instance, violate the law of gravity—there are thousands of ways to apply the basic skills in picking your way up any given rock face; it's more of a freelance thing. Game sports are competitive: it's you against the opponent. Adventure sports are you against the task; against nature; against your own physical and mental limits.

"Riding a bike through a city," the musician and artist David Byrne wrote in his book *Bicycle Diaries*, "is like navigating the collective neural pathways of some vast global mind." Biking, he added, "facilitates a state of mind that allows some but not too much of the unconscious to bubble up. As someone who believes that much of the source of his work and creativity is to be gleaned from those bubbles, it's a reliable place to find that connection."[18]

I agree. My sport of choice is bicycling, too, more specifically, touring on a skinny-tired road bike. Summer evenings are a delight, because they give me a couple of hours' daylight after work to put on my helmet, head for the hills, and ride until dusk. Bicycling is multidimensional. A long ride combines physical exertion and challenge, release, exploration, and communion with nature. As you focus on pedaling you get into a rhythm and flow, losing track of whatever was on your mind, dumping the garbage. The mind's shelves are cleared for restocking while the body, the crucial infrastructure that sustains the mind, is reinvigorated. Sensory inputs are exquisite, for without the speed and roar of a motorized vehicle, you can really see and hear the world. Because you're breathing deeply, you can smell the world—damp earth in the countryside, fresh leaves and grass. There is also the "I'm doing it" factor: the joy of moving as fast as it is possible for a human to move under his or her own power, upward of 30 mph on level ground, 50-plus downhill; the satisfaction when you conquer a hill. Think, too, of the nature of the act of powering a bicycle. The up-and-down pumping of the legs, translated into the smooth rotation of the wheels, is very similar to the mesmerizing, almost mystical mechanism by which our beloved internal-combustion engine works: the explosive, up-and-down motion of the pistons flowing out through the crankshaft as rotary power. Except on a bicycle, it's *you* making it and feeling it happen. Certainly, motorcycles offer thrills of their own. To sit astride a motorcycle and control the powerful engine between your legs can be gratifying, I'm sure. But to climb onto a bicycle and be the engine is a fundamentally transforming experience—a creative experience.

The fact that the demographics of my sport are almost obscenely skewed has not escaped me. Nearly every rider I meet on my journeys is a graduate student, professor, transplant surgeon, corporate lawyer, engineer, entrepreneur, or something similar. Why is the sport so Creative Class? It can't be the expense. Although some bikes, like my titanium model, are undoubtedly pricey, an adequate machine can be had for much less. Bicycles cost little to maintain and nothing to ride. They are far less expensive than motorcycles. When my team at the Martin Prosperity Institute ran the numbers on the metros that had the highest shares of bike commuters in 2010, Creative Class communities came out on top. The top five were Eugene, Oregon; Fort Collins, Colorado; Missoula, Boulder, and Santa Barbara. College towns like Gainesville, Florida; State College, Pennsylvania; Santa Cruz, Madison, Champaign-Urbana, and Iowa City all ranked high as well. Our statistical analysis showed that metros with more bike commuters were more affluent, more educated, and more diverse than most communities, with higher shares of the Creative Class.

Taking It to the Street

For more than a century, the mark of a cultured city in the United States has been the presence of a major art museum plus an "SOB"—the high-art triumvirate of symphony orchestra, opera company, and ballet company. In many cities recently, museums and the SOB have fallen on hard times. Attendance figures have declined, donations have dried up, and audiences are aging: too many gray heads, not enough purple ones. Consultants have descended to identify the problems and offer solutions. One problem is static repertoire. In a museum, for instance, the permanent collection is, well, permanent: it just hangs there. A typical solution is to bring in more packaged traveling exhibits, preferably interactive multimedia exhibits, with lots of bells and whistles. Premiers serve

the same function in the SOB, but there aren't a lot of new sym-
phonies, operas, and ballets being composed, and fewer still are
being performed, because it is so expensive to stage them. One solution is to augment the experience. Instead of a night at the symphony, have a Singles Night at the Symphony. Sometimes orchestras
bring in offbeat guest performers—a jazz or pop soloist, say, or a
comedian for the kids. Or musicians are sent out to play in exotic
locales—the symphony in the park, a chamber group at an art gallery,
the symphony playing Tchaikovsky's 1812 Overture at the Fourth
of July fireworks. All this is reminiscent of the efforts of old-line
churches to fill seats by augmenting the experience—how about a
guitar and drum set with the organ?—or what many professional
sports teams do to attract fans to their stadiums: bring in cute mas-
cots, sexy cheerleaders, and exploding scoreboards.

Most of these efforts are wasted on the Creative Class, whose
members are more drawn to organic and indigenous street-level
culture,[19] which is typically found not in large venues like New York
City's Lincoln Center or in designated cultural districts like the
museum district in Washington, DC, but in multiuse urban neighborhoods. The neighborhood can be upscale like DC's Georgetown
or Boston's Back Bay, or reviving-downscale, like DC's U and H
Street Corridors, Brooklyn's Williamsburg, Toronto's West Queen
West neighborhood, or Pittsburgh's Lawrenceville. Either way, it
grows organically from its surroundings, and a sizable number of
the creators and patrons of the culture live close by. This is what
makes it indigenous. Much of it is native and of-the-moment, rather
than art imported from another century for audiences imported
from the suburbs. Certainly, people may come from outside the
neighborhood to partake of the culture, and they will undoubtedly
find things that are foreign in origin or influence, such as German
films or Senegalese music. But they come with a sense that they are
entering a cultural community, not just attending an event. I think

this is a key part of the form's creative appeal. You might not paint, write, or play music yourself, but if you are at an art-show opening or in a nightspot where you can mingle and talk with artists and aficionados, you might be more creatively stimulated than if you merely walked into a museum or concert hall, were handed a program, and proceeded to spectate. The people in my focus groups and interviews said they prefer street-level culture partly because it gives them a chance to experience the creators along with their creations.

The culture is called street level because it tends to cluster along certain streets lined with a multitude of small venues. These may include coffee shops, restaurants, and bars, some of which offer performances or exhibits along with food and drink; art galleries; bookstores and other stores; small to mid-sized theaters for film or live performance, or both; and various hybrid spaces—like a bookstore-tearoom-little theater or gallery-studio-live music space—often in storefronts or old buildings converted from other purposes. The scene may spill out onto the sidewalks, with dining tables, musicians, vendors, panhandlers, performers, and plenty of passersby at all hours of the day and night. This kind of "scene of scenes" where music, art, film, and nightlife scenes interact and overlap provides a key source of visual and aural energy.

In his book *Clubbing*, Ben Malbon provides a vivid description of the late-night street scene in London's Soho, drawn directly from his research diary:

> We stumble out of the club at around 3-ish—Soho is packed with people, crowding pavements and roads, looking and laughing—everyone appears happy. Some are in groups, bustling their way along noisily—others are alone, silent and walking purposefully on their way. . . . Cars crawl down narrow streets which are already impossibly full of cars, Vespas, people, thronging crowds. This wasn't "late night" for Soho—the night had hardly started.[20]

It is not just *a* scene but many. For the young people Malbon studied, the actual visit to a dance club was only a part of the experience. He describes, in detail, the lengthy and intricate processes of clubbers debating where and when to go, laying out clothes for the event, and discussing and creating histories of their experiences afterward. Malbon admits that he spent "150 nights out" researching the book, and as he puts it, "many of these were the best nights out I have had."

Which is not to say that members of the Creative Class avoid the high arts. Many also visit the big-ticket, high-art cultural venues, at least occasionally, as well as consume mass-market culture like Hollywood movies and rock or pop concerts. But street-level culture is a must. Consider just the practical reasons for this. Big-ticket, high-art events are strictly scheduled on a limited number of evenings, whereas the street-level scene is fluid and ongoing. As a large number of my interview subjects have told me, this is a big benefit for creative types who may work late and not be free until 9:00 or 10:00 PM, or work through the weekend and want to go out Monday night. Moreover, creative workers with busy schedules want to use their cultural time efficiently. Attending a large-venue event, be it a symphony concert or a professional basketball game, is a single, one-dimensional experience that consumes a lot of recreational resources: it is expensive and takes a big chunk of time. Visiting a street-level scene puts you in the middle of a smorgasbord; you can easily do several things in one excursion. The street scene also allows you to modulate the level and intensity of your experience. You can do active, high-energy things—immerse yourself in the bustle of the sidewalks or head into an energized club and dance until dawn—or find a cozy café to drink some espresso, a bar where you can listen to live jazz while sipping a brandy, or retreat into a bookstore where it is quiet.

Consider, too, the nature of the street-level smorgasbord's offerings. In culture as in business, the most radical and interesting stuff tends to start in garages and small rooms. Smaller independent venues offer a dense spectrum of musical genres from blues, R&B, country, rockabilly, world music, and their various hybrids to electronic music—techno and deep house, trance and drum and bass. Nor is everything new. The street-level scene is often the best place to find seldom-performed or little-known works of the past. On one block you might find a little theater showing a new production of an Elizabethan revenge drama; a gallery specializing in historic photography; a local folk-rock group performing old American political songs; and a street musician who plays violin repertoire that you won't hear on the classical radio programs that endlessly recycle the symphonic equivalent of the Top Forty.

The street scene is eclectic. This is another part of its appeal. Consider that eclecticism is also a strong theme within many of today's art forms. Think of DJs in Harlem nightclubs of the 1970s who started the technique known as sampling—or GirlTalk today, whose songs are mash ups and remixes of other people's songs, sometimes as many as a dozen at a time. Think of the proliferation of hyphenated music genres like Afro-Celtic, Balkan-Jazz, and Hip-Hop-Klezmer. Think of Warhol and Robert Rauschenberg decades ago and Shepard Fairey of the Obama "Hope" poster fame today, whose works appropriate images from news photos, comic strips, food packages, wherever. Eclectic scavenging for creativity is not new. Picasso borrowed from African art as well as Greco-Roman classical forms; rock-and-roll pioneers melded blues and R&B and country; and one could argue that the literary DJ who really pioneered sampling was T. S. Eliot in *The Waste Land,* a poem built largely by stringing together quotations and allusions from every corner of the world's literature. Today, however, eclecticism is rampant and spreading to a degree that seems unprecedented— and a taste for it is a social marker that can usually be counted on to distinguish a Creative Class person. Cultural intermixing, when done right, can be a powerful creative stimulus.

Street-level culture is social and interactive. In addition to the music or art that is on offer, one can meet people, hang out and talk, or just sit back to watch tonight's episodes of the human comedy. To many, the social milieu is the street's main attraction. If that sounds a bit vapid and superficial, sometimes it is. This is not high art; it admits amateurs. You don't hang out in a sidewalk café to experience the rarified, exquisitely crafted intensity of Beethoven's late string quartets. For some people, hitting the street-level cultural scene devolves into little more than cruising the singles scene. But even if experiencing culture is truly your goal, you are inevitably going to pick up a lot of chaff along with it. You run the risk of becoming chaff yourself: a dilettante, a poseur, a gallery gadfly, a coffee-shop talker.

Then again, people watching can be stimulating. As Andy Warhol liked to say, he didn't go to restaurants just to eat. Take the experience of strolling through a good street scene in, say, New York, or the city of your choice. The first thing that strikes you is the sheer visual variety of the people. Many ethnic groups are present, of course, in various ages, conditions, and sizes, and this alone is thought provoking. You might find yourself meditating on the history of our species—the many so-called races of humans, and how they came to grow apart as they spread across the globe, and how they endlessly intermix. You may find yourself brooding about your own history—how you were once as young as that one, and may someday be as old as that one, and are liable to look like that one if you don't mend your wicked ways. And then, if it is a proper street scene, there will be many people of exotic appearance: foreigners in long skirts and bright robes; young people with hair in colors and configurations that bend the laws of physics, at least Newtonian physics; people dressed as cowboys, Goths, Victorians, hippies—you get the picture. For many people, the experience of this picture is exhilarating, liberating, similar to the thrill of a costume party or carnival, when people literally put on new identities—

including masks that obliterate or alter the social masks they normally wear—and there is a delicious sense of adventure in the air. One has an awareness of the possibilities of life.

I would go so far as to say that this kind of experience is essential to the creative process. We humans are not godlike; we cannot create out of nothing. Creativity for us is an act of synthesis, and in order to create and synthesize, we need the stimuli of new experiences— bits and pieces to put together in new and unfamiliar ways, existing frameworks to deconstruct and transcend. I also feel it is inherent to the creative mind-set to want to maximize choices and options, to be always on the lookout for new ones, because in the game that Einstein called combinatory play, this increases your chances of coming up with novel combinations. As more people earn their keep by creating, the more these aspects of experience are likely to be highly valued and just plain necessary.

And finally there's this: the very eclecticism of scenes provides a means of both attracting and bridging diverse communities. A fascinating paper by Joseph Yi and Daniel Silver, entitled "God, Yoga, and Karate: Local Pathways to Diversity," draws on zip-code-level research across 40,000 localities to show how scenes and amenities can provide "spaces where people from across societal cleavages can find common pleasures and opportunities to take into account the other as more than an abstraction or stereotype."[21] A karate dojo, for example, as Silver noted in his personal communication to me, can bridge black and white, New Age and Christian communities; attending sporting events or shopping at discount superstores can have similar, though cruder and more superficial, effects as well.

Pitfalls of the Experiential World

There is much that seems good about the constant quest for experience. It is an energetic and productive way to live. It can even be a more humane and benevolent way to live. The emphasis on active, participatory recreation seems healthy physically and psychologically, as well as more satisfying than the thin diet of the TV junkie. Done properly, it should lead to good experiences all around. So where are the pitfalls? Where exactly does the insidiousness come in?

First, experiences can be packaged and sold. Commodified experience is often perceived to be—and often is—inauthentic. As Thomas Frank and others have noted, the commercialization of experience can empty it of its original creative content.[22] Retailers from H&M and AllSaints Spitalfields to Prada do this with clothes. They try to create brand recognition around experience and, in doing so, sell you experience as brand: just wearing the clothes supposedly makes you cool and with it. Or, to paraphrase what numerous Creative Class people have told me: "You can't just enjoy a ballgame; you have to go to a 'state-of-the-art' $500 million stadium for a multimedia circus that distracts you from the very game you paid to see." Many Creative Class people thus tend to shun the heavily packaged commercial venues they call "generica"—the chain restaurants and nightclubs, the stadiums with bells and whistles—or they patronize them but with a conscious sense of irony and camp, as in the obligatory trip to a business conference in Las Vegas. They prefer more authentic, indigenous, or organic venues that offer a wide range of options, places where they can have a hand in creating them.

But it can be a struggle to find such venues, because generica has a way of creeping in everywhere. Music clubs that used to be dynamic, street-level places to enjoy real music are more and more being replaced by late-night versions of those multimedia circuses. Not only do you immerse yourself in booming music, but you get digital lighting, smoke machines, and water sprinklers activated in concert with peaks in the music—everything you need to be hot and cool. Some such clubs have even become chains. What began as an organic development from the street has become a Disneyland facsimile of itself—safe, secure, and predictable—trafficking not in a series of unique experiences but in the same generic experience night after night. There are deeper concerns as well. "Clubbers distinguish themselves from others through their tastes in clothing, music, dancing techniques, clubbing genre and so on," notes Malbon. "These tastes are trained and refined, and constantly monitored not only in order to distinguish oneself from another, but also in identifying with those that share one's distinctive styles and preferences."[23] In all of these ways they are, he says, constructing identities. Not to be too judgmental here, but one could well say that Malbon's clubbers sound like little more than trendy sheep. Others have made much the same point about the uniform look of the hipster. If the goal is to construct an identity or discover an identity, there are other, better ways to do it. Neighborhoods do it, too. In many ways, when people select a neighborhood they are selecting a way of life and reinforcing their own identify.

Using the market to try to satisfy the craving for experience can turn weirdly self-contradictory in many ways. Writing in the *Wall Street Journal*, columnist Kara Swisher chronicled the thousands of dollars she spent outfitting her "fantasy kitchen," the equivalent of "about 1,000 takeout meals or at least 600 outings at pretty good restaurants."[24] The point is that all those pricey appliances and cookware are no longer appliances and cookware in the traditional utilitarian sense. They are there to provide experiences— the visual experience of looking at them, the status experience of owning them, and the active experience of cooking "like a professional" on those infrequent occasions when we actually do use them to whip up a dinner that mixes Pan-Asian, Italian, and homegrown influences.

In short, if we crave experiences, we will be sold experiences, and in the process we may find ourselves buying a bill of goods. The final pitfall is that in the attempt to avoid packaged-and-sold experiences, we may pack our lives so full that we overdo it. While we scorn the couch potatoes hooked on TV, the desire for constant stimulation and experiences can come close to an addiction itself. But no way of life is perfect, and the trend is inexorable. And when all is said and done, the experiential life is much more than a pastiche of recreational fads and marketing gimmicks. As I've shown, it is a product of the rising creative ethos—which, as I will argue in the next chapter, was born from a deep cultural fusion.

CHAPTER 9

The Big Morph

One blustery winter day in 2001, I boarded a plane in Pittsburgh and emerged a couple of hours later into warm southwestern air. I was in Austin, Texas, one of the country's leading creative centers, where, I would soon learn, more than the weather was different. I was there to speak about economic development at the Austin 360 Summit, an annual conference of local business and civic leaders. I had been to many such meetings in other cities, not to mention countless professional conventions and meetings of US mayors and governors. But the Austin 360 Summit was not like any of them.

Typically, this sort of meeting is held at the city's most lavish hotel or perhaps amid the classic Greek columns and Beaux Arts splendor of an important civic landmark. Here we gathered at the funky, folksy Austin Music Hall. Usually at such a conference, you check the agenda for the keynote speakers if you want to hear someone important. Here, Michael Dell, founder and chair of Dell Computers, was just one of many participants in a panel discussion. Of course, he didn't wear a tie, nor did anyone else. If you wanted to interrupt him with a question or comment in midspeech you went right ahead. All the trappings of status and privilege had been left at home.

The usual drill at a convention is to endure a long day of stuffy presentations and working-group sessions, then head out to the local nightspots and cut loose. At the Austin 360 Summit work and play went together all day long. When we filed into the noisy main meeting room in the morning, we were issued plastic Wiffle balls. If you didn't like what a speaker was saying, you could pelt him with one. The lunchtime keynote speech on the first day—typically delivered by a gray-headed pillar of the community—was a satiric monologue by the performance artist Steve Tomlinson, who appeared only because Sandra Bullock, originally scheduled, was on location making a film. A rock band performed during the interludes between conference sessions, and this wasn't the kind of watered-down, easy-listening rock band you sometimes hear at business functions. This was an excellent, hard-driving band, guys with real chops. Austin, after all, is the music capital of the Southwest.

After a half-day of this, it was my turn. I was the moderator of a panel of CEOs and venture-capital types, and the question I wanted them to address was one that I believed to be central to the region's future economic development: "Is Austin losing its soul?" I had gotten the idea from my cab driver on the way in from the airport, who worried that the crush of high-tech industry and people were threatening to drive out the ethnic and cultural diversity that had fueled Austin's creativity to begin with. After some predictable back-and-forth among the panelists about their investments in the music and cultural scene, I used the moderator's prerogative to interject. "Creativity is multidimensional," I boomed. "It's not something you can keep in a box and trot out at work. You can't have high-tech innovation without art and music. All forms of creativity feed off each other"—and so on. Then a sudden inspiration struck me. "If you really want to know how important this is," I said, "don't ask your fellow high-tech CEOs or the mayor or the head of the Chamber of Commerce. Ask the guys in the band!" I gestured grandly to the musicians seated at the edge of the stage, who looked like the members of Conan O'Brien's late-night ensemble. Then one of the panelists clued me in. The guys in the band, now grinning broadly at me, were not local grungers. All of them were high-tech CEOs and venture capitalists themselves. It was as if Jack Welch, George Soros, and Warren Buffett had gotten down and jammed for the crowd at Davos.

When the old markers that distinguish one type of person from another begin to fade and blur, it is a clear sign that profound social change is afoot. Although the blending of bourgeois and bohemian, highbrow and lowbrow, alternative and mainstream, work and play cuts across many aspects of our life and culture, the change hasn't been dramatic or sudden enough to be labeled a revolution. It is not a Big Bang but a *Big Morph,* an evolutionary process that flowered first and strongest in certain enclaves and is now gradually filtering through the rest of society. It is also a dialectical process, with major elements of society either fighting the shifts or at least passively resisting them. The Big Morph is not merely cultural and recreational. It originates from work and the workplace and moves outward from them to inform new cultural forms and lifestyles. This is what makes it so powerful. Changes in taste and lifestyle that at first glance seem superficial and unrelated are in fact rooted in a deeper economic change.

At the heart of the Big Morph is a new resolution of the centuries-old tension between two value systems: the Protestant work ethic and the bohemian ethic. Many observers have noted the clashing of these two systems, and some, most notably David Brooks, have commented on their blending.

The Protestant work ethic supposes that meaning is to be found in hard work. We are put here to serve others and we serve them by making ourselves productive and useful. It is our duty to work. And it is from this—inexorably, but almost incidentally, as a side effect—that flow the personal rewards that mark us as worthy. Writing at the turn of the twentieth century, the great German sociologist Max Weber called this ethic the very "spirit of capitalism."[1] The Protestant work ethic demanded a great deal of conscious structuring and budgeting—managing one's time, practicing thrift, deferring gratifications, and so forth. It was traditionally pursued within the structure of institutions, like the large corporations that grew economically and socially dominant in the late 1800s and that continued to dominate until the late twentieth century. Thus this ethic became an organizational and social ideology. One is productive and efficient so that the organization can be productive and efficient. As such, this ethic is essentially mainstream and conformist. One accepts the existing social structure as the way things are. As Paul admonished the early Christians, one obeys the secular authorities and observes the laws of the land—one does one's duty.[2]

The bohemian ethic is more hedonistic. It says that value is to be found in pleasure and happiness—not necessarily in gross indulgence or gluttonous excess, but in experiencing and appreciating what life has to offer. The bohemian ethic has its own form of discipline, which is largely aesthetic. In his classic but too-little-read book *Bohemian Versus Bourgeois,* the cultural historian Cesar Graña notes that Charles Baudelaire "gave his praises to cats because they appeared to him as the very embodiment of well-managed voluptuousness."[3] The bohemian ethic has its spiritual and sociopolitical dimensions, too. On these fronts, it tends to be intuitive rather than logical, and individualistic rather than conformist. In the cosmology of the English poet William Blake, the "dark Satanic mills" of the early Industrial Revolution were not just England's smoke-belching factories. They also evoked the mills of cold logic and clockwork materialism—the mental grindstones that ground men's souls to dust. In Blake's eyes they could only be countered by unleashing the "Poetic Genius" that lay divinely planted in every human breast. Over time, as writers and artists since Blake carried this theme forward, the bohemian ethic came to signify everything that the Protestant work ethic was not.

Conservative scholars worried long and loud about the experiential, bohemian culture that washed across America in the 1960s. Some feared that the Protestant work ethic had undermined itself by succeeding too well—bathing us in such a flood of material goods and leisure that we were turning soft. Salvos were fired from the bohemian side as well. In the patois of Rastafarian reggae musicians, the Satanic world of offices and factories was "Babylon"—the great whore that must someday fall.

The so-called culture wars did not begin in the twentieth century, however. Almost since the time of its emergence, industrial society has been a house divided.

The Great Divide

In Karl Marx's seminal analysis, capitalist society was the battleground for a war between two great classes, the bourgeoisie and the proletariat. The bourgeoisie were the true, literal capitalists who owned and controlled the means of production. The proletarians were the mostly poorer majority, who lived by selling their labor. Marx's sympathies, of course, lay with the proletariat, but his salient point for our purpose is this: The mainspring driving the course of modern history and shaping modern society was the ongoing tension between these two classes—and that tension was almost entirely caused by economic matters. Later cultural and social theorists believed that Marx had neglected the cultural dimensions of the struggle. Some of his disciples, from Georg Lukács and Antonio Gramsci to the members of the Frankfurt School, tried to construct a theory that dealt sufficiently with culture.[4]

Others, meanwhile, identified a second divide coinciding with the rise of capitalism—the divide between the bourgeoisie and the bohemians. Graña argues that this conflict came to life after the French Revolution. The toppling of the aristocracy frightened writers, artists, and intellectuals, who had, after all, depended on the aristocrats as their patrons. The new capitalist bourgeoisie were more concerned with amassing wealth than with advancing the arts or becoming culturally literate. They had brought to power with them the businesslike grinding of the Protestant ethic, combined with the gross materialistic tastes of what Thorstein Veblen would later dub "conspicuous consumption." In response, according to Graña, the self-styled bohemians of France in the early to mid-1800s created an ideology that valorized the aesthetic, challenged traditional social values, and espoused a distaste for material things. It was a powerful and enduring brew—and a direct assault on the bourgeois weltanschauung. Graña, who, by the way, was quite critical of bohemianism, noted, "The industrious man who shouldered his way into the leadership of modern society threatened all three ideals of intellectual aristocracy—the heroic, the formal, and the introspective." And he added, "By making new and unexpected demands on human vitality, modern pragmatism was also likely to undermine man's total sensitivity, his emotional free play, and that capacity for physical pleasure which in the past had represented a means both of biological and of aesthetic fulfillment."[5]

In the bohemian subculture of Paris—and in its later American counterpart, the café society of Greenwich Village that sprang up in the early 1900s—Marxists, anarchists, and labor radicals rubbed shoulders with artists and writers.[6] All of them had a common adversary, the bourgeois juggernaut. But in Graña's view, the essence of bohemianism was apolitical. The real enemy was not the oppressive capitalist economic order but the prevailing culture's suppression of key elements of the human spirit. Near the end of his book, Graña notes that the twentieth-century poet and novelist D. H. Lawrence was equally disenchanted with Western-style capitalism and Russian-style communism: "Lawrence," he writes, "said that all of modern society was 'a steady sort of Bolshevism; just killing the human thing and worshiping the mechanical thing.'"[7]

The bohemians not only valued creativity but were responsible for a vast and substantial outpouring of it: paintings in a succession of new styles, which saw the world in radically different ways, and a flood tide of novels and poetry depicting the struggles of modern men and women in their search for identity, love, and meaning—from Madame Bovary to J. Alfred Prufrock, Lady Chatterley, and Dean Moriarty.

Bewailers of Bohemianism

A far-seeing thinker who influenced my own thinking in powerful ways, Daniel Bell liked to describe himself as a social conservative and an economic liberal. His book *The Coming of Post-Industrial Society* put a label on our times that has stuck to the present day.[8] He wrote in another of his books, *The Cultural Contradictions of Capitalism*, "Modern culture is defined by this extraordinary freedom to ransack the world storehouse and to engorge any and every style it comes upon. Such freedom comes from the fact that the axial principle of modern culture is the expression and remaking of the 'self' in order to achieve self-realization and self-fulfillment."[9] Note that he put the word "self" in ironic quotation marks. Not only were our modern-day bohemians narcissistic,[10] according to Bell, they were also childish and unoriginal; he dubbed their lifestyle "pop hedonism" and said the counterculture amounted to little more than a "children's crusade." Worse yet, he added, capitalism had brought this upon itself. "In brief not work but the 'life style' became the source of satisfaction and the criterion for desirable behavior," he wrote. "What has happened in society in the last fifty years—as a result of the erosion of the religious ethic and the increase in discretionary income—*is that culture has taken the initiative in promoting change,* and the economy has been geared to meeting these new wants."[11]

But is that necessarily a bad thing? Isn't a free-market economy supposed to be geared to meeting our wants? It's bad, says Bell, because the economy is what supports all the other activity, and the economy will not work well if its ethical bedrock is undermined: "When the Protestant ethic was sundered from bourgeois society, only the hedonism remained, and the capitalist system lost its transcendental ethic," he noted. "The cultural, if not moral, justification of capitalism has become hedonism, the idea of pleasure as a way of life."[12]

The great error in this line of thinking is that it persists in seeing work and life, or the economy and the culture, as separate spheres with distinct value systems that should be allowed to interact only in certain prescribed ways. David Brooks recognized the emerging synthesis between these two spheres and chronicled their melding into a distinct new class. In his book *Bobos in Paradise*, he even gave its avatars a catchy handle—Bobos—short for bourgeoisie-bohemians.[13] "It used to be pretty easy to distinguish between the bourgeois world of capitalism and the bohemian counterculture," he wrote. "The bourgeois worked for corporations, wore gray and went to church. The bohemians were artists and intellectuals. Bohemians championed the values of the liberated 1960s; the bourgeois were the enterprising yuppies of the 1980s. But now the bohemian and the bourgeois are all mixed up. It is hard to tell an espresso-sipping professor from a cappuccino-gulping banker."[14]

Brooks traces the rise of the meritocratic ethic and diversity in the new Bobo world and describes how student populations on Ivy League campuses changed after World War II, from predominately upper-class WASPs to a mix of ethnicities and economic back-grounds. Much of the book, however, is not sociology so much as it is satire. Brooks takes us on a detailed tour of the lifestyles and consumption habits of this curious new class. Bobos buy food at upscale grocery stores like Whole Foods, furnish their homes at Pottery Barn and Restoration Hardware, and wear clothing from Banana Republic and J. Crew, or if they are a little edgier or a little more affluent, perhaps Gucci or Helmut Lang.

Although his observations of their visible quirks and affectations are acute and witty, Brooks neglects the deep economic shifts that shaped his Bobos and made them possible. In his portrayal, they are mostly aging baby boomers—bourgeoisie in bohemian clothing. When he does follow them to work, he fastens mostly on the trap-pings of the new workplace, missing the ways in which the content and meaning of work has become fundamentally different to the people at the heart of this synthesis. But even if he fails to recognize it himself, he has put his finger on something that runs far deeper than the lifestyle trends he so adeptly lampoons.

In "The Organization Kid,"[15] an April 2001 article in *The Atlantic,* Brooks added a grim coda to *Bobos in Paradise.* To see what kinds of children the Bobos had been rearing, he visited students at Princeton and found them to be grimly workaholic, obsessively ca-reer conscious, and deferential to any authority that will help them get ahead—a reversion to Whyte's organization man of the 1950s. His message is subtle but unmistakeable: the crazy 1960s are over; it's back to business as usual. The only difference is that these kids are deader inside than their businessmen grandparents ever were. Not only don't they have much fun, they have no uplifting sense of purpose or higher calling; they are driven by personal achieve-ment merely for its own sake—or more precisely, for *their* own sake. These kids, writes Brooks, are "missing [the] conceptions of character and virtue"; they've been reared in "a country that has lost, in its frenetic seeking after happiness and success, the language of sin and character-building."[16] The sole legacy of the 1960s was not only transitory and skin deep, but profoundly destructive.

I can't imagine how Brooks came to such conclusions. Perhaps he didn't stay up late enough to see what Princeton students do after people their parents' ages have gone to bed. He should have looked at my students. They work hard, but they also play hard. And they do not see any conflict between organization, discipline, and pleasure—all of which reflect one element or another of the creative ethos. Or perhaps the problem is that Brooks, in the same fusty spirit as Daniel Bell before him, is intent on drilling home the saw that the bohemianism of the 1960s was an adopted child that never amounted to much—and one that we should never have taken into our house.[17]

Co-Opting Cool

Critics at the liberal end of the spectrum, ironically, have also found the bohemian-bourgeois synthesis to be soul destroying, but in a different way. "Hip is how business understands itself," writes the political and cultural critic Thomas Frank, suggesting that the rise of new alternative cultures is just another feature of capitalism. There is no counterculture anymore—if there ever really was.[18]

In Frank's baleful view, the word *counterculture* is itself a misnomer. The counterculture was—and is—just popular culture, and popular culture is a ticket to sell things. In his best-selling books *One Market Under God* and *The Commodification of Cool,* Frank dolefully chronicled capitalism's co-optation of counterculture symbols in an onslaught of hip new products and advertising themes that target consumers who want to associate themselves with youth and alternative culture.[19]

The trends Frank described have continued apace over the past decade. The music of Nick Drake, for example, an underground jazz-rock cult hero, has been co-opted to sell Volkswagens. Generations of edgy new musicians, from 1960s bands to punks to reggae and hip-hop artists, have had their creative integrity compromised and their hard-edged political messages blunted by major labels that turned them into mass-market commodities—a new kind of Muzak that's played in workplaces to make people feel alternative and even subversive, when all that they're really doing is grinding away at a desk in Babylon.

But the liberal scolds are just as off-key as the conservatives. Millions of people would never have gotten to hear any number of fine musicians, either recorded or in concert, had they not been mass marketed. And let's not forget that many of these musicians *want* to be mass-marketed. The hip-hop artists who wear dollar signs on gold chains around their necks and chant lyrics about money and fine cars aren't indulging in poetic irony. They really do want a little of your cash.

Mass marketing doesn't necessarily compromise artistic integrity, either. Bob Dylan first hit it big as a folk and Southern-style blues balladeer in the traditional vein, armed only with an acoustic guitar and harmonica. Then came the infamous 1966 concert in Manchester, England, when he took to the stage with an electric guitar and rock-style backup band. People in the audience were outraged. One man memorably screamed "Judas!" at the top of his lungs. But Dylan wasn't selling out. On the contrary: he had already built a lucrative global brand on the basis of the traditional style. Not only was he taking an artistic risk, he was taking a bit of a commercial risk in departing from a proven and still viable formula. Indeed, the Manchester concert is now regarded as a seminal event in contemporary music. One critic claims that the torrent of sound that Dylan and his mates unleashed that night amounted to a proto-version of punk rock—"ten years before Johnny Rotten" and "rather better played."[20]

Dylan, of course, went on to experiment again and again, with forays into the Nashville-style country sound, Christian rock, and numerous other subgenres. Artistic integrity doesn't mean doing only the things you've done before. The security that comes from hitting it big can make it easier for artists to conduct experiments, to take greater artistic risks. Consider The Beatles and *Sergeant Pepper;* Peter Gabriel's excursions into Third World music; Sting's forays into the exotic: none of them would have been widely heard had they not already been wildly successful.

As for the fear that mass marketing kills the artist's political message: reports of that death have been greatly exaggerated. Although there are exceptions, of course, most cultural products have little political content to begin with. Many cultural theorists like to frame cultural forms such as graffiti and rap as political movements, expressing the voices of the oppressed. This does a disservice to both politics and art. True political movements, from the civil rights movement to the grassroots organizing of the right wing, are serious enterprises, laboriously put together and self-consciously directed to specific political ends. These movements sometimes adopt art forms, but they are not generated by them. Meanwhile, most good graffiti artists and rappers are like good artists of any kind. They mainly want to hone their skills and express themselves. They spend a lot of time practicing, as you may know if you live near any of them. If they can make money in the process, that's wonderful.

A final argument, heard from both the right and the left, is that the mass marketing of alternative culture produces an undesirable leveling effect, dragging high art down to the gutter and elevating low or gross art to a stature it doesn't deserve. This complaint relies on the always questionable assumption that art comes in "high" and "low" varieties to begin with. As the writer John Seabrook argued a decade ago, it is all really just "NoBrow."[21] In reality, the rise of the Creative Economy is drawing the spheres of innovation (technological creativity), business (economic creativity), and culture (artistic and cultural creativity) into one another, in more intimate and more powerful combinations than ever.

The Real Legacy of the 1960s

Conservative scholars exulted and liberal scholars lamented when the fruits of the so-called 1960s revolution seemed to be withering during the 1980s. Not only were many of the landmark legislative measures of the era rolled back by the Reagan and Bush administrations, but its bohemian cultural leaders were fading into obscurity. Timothy Leary had become a sideshow attraction on the lecture circuit. His former colleague Baba Ram Dass (né Richard Alpert) was off somewhere chanting at an ashram. Abbie Hoffman and Richard Brautigan died; Jimi Hendrix, Jim Morrison, Janis Joplin, and many others were long in their graves. For a brief while, the old corporate system based on the Protestant work ethic seemed to be firmly back in the driver's seat, with the surviving bohemians of the Woodstock generation relegated to cranking out tribute albums. The barbarians having been beaten back from the gates, we could all resume business as usual.

It didn't turn out that way. What happened instead was neither 1960s nor 1980s, neither bourgeois nor bohemian, but the opening of a path to something new. The great cultural watershed of the 1960s, as it turned out, was not Woodstock, but something that had evolved at the other end of the continent. It was Silicon Valley. This place in the very heart of the San Francisco Bay area became the proving ground for the new ethos of creativity. If work could be made more aesthetic and experiential; if it could be spiritual and useful in the poetic sense rather than in the duty-bound sense; if the organizational strictures and rigidities of the old system could be transcended; and if bohemian values like individuality—which also happens to be a tried-and-true all-American value—could be brought to the workplace, then we could move beyond the old categories. And though the Valley itself has now mushroomed into something quite different than it was, the ethos that it pioneered has spread and endured, and continues to permeate our society. It does so because, unlike Woodstock or Haight-Ashbury—and equally unlike the Beat subculture of the 1950s or the bohemian café society of Paris, from Baudelaire to Gertrude Stein—it has a wide and sustainable economic base. It engages the world of work and the world of life and weaves them together, profoundly changing both.

The 1960s are too easily stereotyped. They were not simple times, nor was what happened then merely a generational phenomenon. Many diverse movements and schools of thought—some of which had been building for decades and were spearheaded by people a lot older than the baby boomers, such as Martin Luther King Jr. and Betty Friedan—came to the fore during a period of social ferment that actually stretched from the mid-1950s, with the launching of a serious civil rights movement in the South, well into the 1970s. One common thread, however, is that few of these movements sought to fundamentally transform the world of work and economics. The civil rights movement and the women's movement affected the world of work mainly by crusading for equal workplace rights and treatment for certain groups of people. Ringing speeches often called for a fundamental transformation of the economic system, but this never quite made it to the top of the practical agenda. Similarly, the peace movement assailed the "military–industrial complex" that former president Dwight Eisenhower had famously warned of, but mainly aimed to lessen its influence, not to change the system fundamentally. Pure socialism never gained much of a foothold in the United States, even in the years of the Great Depression. And though it eventually proved quite successful in pushing its agenda, organized labor concerned itself mostly with the balance of power in the workplace. Largely through union efforts over many decades, rank-and-file working people gained higher pay, shorter hours, better benefits and working conditions, and such rights as collective bargaining and the power to contest an individual firing. But these powers and rights were all *within* the framework of the existing economic system.

The bohemian counterculture of the San Francisco Bay Area— which embraced phenomena as diverse as the Beat poets of the 1950s, the Free Speech Movement at Berkeley in the early 1960s, and the Summer of Love in 1966—included a wide spectrum of views on work and economics. Some in the hippie milieu preferred to opt out of the world of work altogether, perhaps living by their wits or the generosity of friends or parents. Some sought to rob "the system," as described how-to style in Abbie Hoffman's *Steal This Book*. For many, the strategy was to grudgingly coexist with the system. Get a job, even a haircut if you must; earn the money you need and do what you have to do, but no more.

There were various attempts to create alternative economic systems: farm-based communes, often in remote rural areas; urban experiments like that of the Diggers in San Francisco. Drawing their name from a seventeenth-century communal experiment in England, the Diggers promoted the building of a system within the system, based on a literally "free" market. Money was not to be used, nor were any barter accounts to be kept. If you worked at the free clinic, you would give your services without charge, but you could also take any goods you wanted at the free stores, or have your car repaired for free, and so forth. With both the need and the incentive to make money removed, ideally people would do what they were truly moved to do—whether by the calling of their own muses or by a sense of service. The Diggers actually put parts of their system into effect but never achieved the critical mass to sustain it in the midst of a larger system running by quite different rules.

And so it was with many other economic experiments of the time. As interesting as some of them were, they were small and highly localized. Most folded after a few years; they became footnotes to the history of the period. Still, some common bohemian themes that fired the experiments persisted, including a general dislike of large organizations and bureaucracy. Many so-called 1960s radicals, like earlier bohemians before them, found the existing capitalist system to be oppressive and dehumanizing, regardless of how the balance of power played out. The increase of human happiness and well-being, they believed, should be the explicit goal of both work itself and its products—not the incidental side effects of an invisible hand.

The Bay Area in the late 1960s and 1970s was full of eccentric technology types from Berkeley and Stanford. The broad valley south of San Francisco, midway between Haight-Ashbury and hippie havens like Monterey and Big Sur, was a natural gathering point for many of them. There were already a fair number of firms there that would hire you without worrying much about your long hair and jeans, or your weird personal habits and beliefs. The older engineers who populated companies like Hewlett-Packard, Fairchild Semiconductor, and Intel found it relatively easy to tolerate this new counterculture breed. Certainly, they were more open to idiosyncrasies of personal style than their East Coast corporate counterparts. The engineering culture tends to be meritocratic—you are what you produce—and this was, after all, the West Coast, where previous generations had come to escape the traditional norms of more established society. And it so happened that just as the younger counterculture computer people were infiltrating the Valley, a new dream was emerging. Computers were becoming both more powerful and more compact and affordable. By the late 1960s, the massive mainframes had been joined by a new generation of refrigerator-sized or smaller minicomputers built by companies like DEC. The next step, said the dream, would be computers that anyone could own and create with. Most people still considered this a radical idea, even a silly or pointless one: who would buy such a thing?

The entrepreneurs who pioneered the personal computer were farther outside the corporate and cultural mainstream than is commonly known. Lee Felsenstein, a prolific inventor and the moderator of the Valley's legendary Homebrew Club, where early personal-computer buffs met, had been a writer for the radical paper *The Berkeley Barb*.[22] The club's first meeting occurred in March 1975, when an anarchic cadre of thirty-two engineers, inventors, tinkerers, and programmers met in the Palo Alto garage of Frederick Moore—but only after Moore had spent the earlier part of the evening tacking up peace-activist notices on local bulletin boards and telephone poles. Homebrew Club members, many with their own tenuously financed garage firms, traded ideas and designs without worrying overly much about competitive considerations—a "hacker ethic" that would persist in the open-source software community and elsewhere. Many were associated with counterculture ventures like the People's Computer Company, a users' collective that published a newspaper. IMSAI, one of the first personal-computer makers in the Valley, was run by graduates of Werner Erhard's est training, a San Francisco–based consciousness-raising and personal-improvement program.

When Steven Dompier, a hobbyist hacker, played a rendition of the Beatles' "Fool on the Hill" on an Altair computer he had laboriously programmed, the members of the Homebrew Club gave him a rousing ovation. Early members Paul Allen and Bill Gates had done some mischief hacking in their teens, exploiting their ability to find bugs in mainframe systems. Others were phone hackers who tapped into the inner workings of the telephone system in the 1960s and 1970s. John Draper had earned his nickname "Captain Crunch" after he discovered that the tone produced by the whistle prize in the cereal box could unlock AT&T's long-distance system. In the old photos reproduced in Paul Freiberger and Michael Swaine's book *Fire in the Valley: The Making of the Personal Computer,* Steve Jobs and Steven Wozniak look like a couple of 1960s hippie-boppers who had refused to straighten up—which is exactly what they were. With their jeans and long scraggly hair, they wouldn't have made it past the receptionist if they had tried to raise investment capital in New York, Chicago, or Pittsburgh. Yet in Silicon Valley, they and others like them found a warm reception. As Donald Valentine, one of the original venture capitalists behind Apple Computer, told me some years ago, he didn't care what Steve Jobs looked like; the guy had an idea worth backing.[23] When Wozniak eventually left Apple "to pursue other interests," he really did just that—he launched not another high-tech company but the Woz Music Festival.

What set Silicon Valley apart was not just Stanford University or the warm climate. It was open to and supportive of the creative, the different, and the downright weird. The Valley integrated those who were offbeat; it didn't ostracize or discourage them. And its growth can only be understood in relation to the place that was a focal point of the Sixties Revolution—San Francisco. The same basic pattern can be found in almost every other high-growth technology region. Before these regions were high-tech hotspots, they were places where creativity and eccentricity were accepted and celebrated. Boston has always had Cambridge. Seattle was the home of Jimi Hendrix and later Nirvana and Pearl Jam as well as Microsoft and Amazon. Austin was home to Willie Nelson and its fabulous Sixth Street music scene long before Michael Dell ever set foot in his University of Texas fraternity house. Before Silicon Alley erupted, New York had Christopher Street, SoHo, and the East Village. All of these places were open, diverse, and culturally creative first. *Then* they became technologically creative, birthing high-tech firms and industries.

The tone of the Creative Economy was set. Bohemian values met the Protestant work ethic head-on, and the two more than survived the collision. They morphed into a new work ethic—the creative ethos—steeped in the cultivation of creativity. Everyone from software developers to circuit designers could now work as creative people, coming and going virtually as they pleased, taking breaks to exercise, working to blaring rock music if they so desired. Employees at Apple wore T-shirts that read "90 Hours a Week and Loving It," and why not? Their work was fun to them, and besides, they were changing the world.

Not everything stayed as it was in those early days—nothing ever does. Big firms like IBM and the Valley's own Hewlett-Packard belatedly entered the personal-computer market, of course, and soon made their presence strongly felt. Silicon Valley turned into a massively congested and high-priced suburban megalopolis. Nevertheless, the synthesis pioneered in those early days took root and spread through many elements of our economy and society. It even gave us a new cultural role model.

Microsoft and Jimi Hendrix

American society has romanticized some of the most unlikely occupations over the years. In the mid-1800s young men read *Two Years Before the Mast* and dreamed of becoming lowly merchant seamen. Well into the 1900s, the heroes of thousands upon thousands of books, plays, films, and cigarette ads were those miserable wage slaves of the Western plains, the cowboys. Other occupations traditionally have not fared so well. Through long centuries, from Shylock to Scrooge and Willy Loman, drama and literature have portrayed the businessman as either hardhearted or heartsick. And tell me this: how many well-known novels, films, or plays that appeared before, say, 1980, can you think of in which the hero was an engineer? Even in works of science fiction, the hero typically was the pilot who flew the spaceship, not the engineer who designed it. The engineer was kept in the background because he was a geek. Engineers were useful people, of course, but they were not cool. In fact, they were the opposite of cool, the very definition of the absence of cool. They had thick glasses and no sex lives. They told bad jokes, wore bad clothes, and toted slide rules in holsters. They worked for businessmen, for heaven's sake.

Now the picture has been reversed. Jobs, Wozniak, Gates, and others have inserted the idea of the *entrepreneur* into the fabric of popular mythology. They created a powerful new identity that broke with the old images of the robber baron and the organization man. They became celebrities in the truest sense of the term. They hobnob with movie stars, invite rock stars to play at their parties, and appear on late-night TV talk shows; Jobs's untimely death inspired some of the same frantic mourning as Elvis's, JKF Jr.'s, or Princess Di's.

Consider Paul Allen, one of the world's richest men. Setting aside his accomplishments at Microsoft, which he cofounded, his real estate interests, and the sports teams he owns, he has donated millions to the search for intelligent life in the universe and is the creator of Seattle's Experience Music Project, an interactive music museum designed by Frank Gehry, which was initially created as a tribute to Seattle native Jimi Hendrix but has now expanded to encompass genres from jazz and blues to hip-hop.[24] Consider the implications. Unlike powerful plutocrats of the past, Allen did not build an opera house or a library or a high-culture museum. He built a museum that celebrates the art of a man who taunted and disdained white-collar conservatives; who defied them to point "their plastic finger at me" and vowed to "wave my freak flag high."[25]

Other factors helped change the image of the engineer. A key early development was the massive infusion of technology into popular music—a blending of technological and artistic creativity. Les Paul, a tinkerer and inventor as well as a master musician, launched the process in the 1940s when he began producing unearthly sounds with his revolutionary solid-body electric guitar. He also pioneered studio techniques such as overdubbing and multitrack recording. Then came inventor-entrepreneurs like Robert Moog and Raymond Kurzweil with the synthesizer, and Amar Bose and Henry Kloss with their high-fidelity sound equipment. All became cult figures in the music world. So did the techno-wizards who put together the light shows for concerts in the 1960s and worked ever-greater magic with recorded tracks in the studios. Many of the most famous musicians of the 1960s, from the Beatles to Hendrix, experimented with new sounds and recording techniques in state-of-the-art studios built expressly for such experiments.

Another key development, of course, was the growth of computing. Here was a technology with double-feature appeal to the popular imagination. The big supercomputers had been perceived as remote and mysterious, even dangerous, like rockets or H-bombs, whereas personal computers were ubiquitous and charming, like TV. But unlike TV, these computers and their software kept changing and metamorphosing before our eyes, right there on our desks. And it was maverick engineers who were working the miracles, members of a new and awesome fellowship of the elect. They wrote code—a secret language!—and with it, they could do just about anything: start a company, make art, play games. Better still, you, too, could join them. Exactly as in rock music, you could hack away in your basement or garage with a couple of friends and dream of hitting it big.

So today we have the engineer as pop-culture hero. The very word *geek,* which *Webster's* dictionary defines as "a person often of an intellectual bent who is disliked," has lost its pejorative connotation, becoming a term of endearment and status. One of the hottest social events in Pittsburgh in the late 1990s was a bimonthly Geek Nite, packing upward of five hundred people into a local microbrewery. The event began drawing so many hangers-on and groupies, not to mention headhunters and service providers, that its organizers created a more exclusive event, Shadow Geek Nite, for the engineers, programmers, and other real geeks who wished to party in peace. As cyberpunk novels and films like *Neuromancer* and *The Matrix* glamorized cyberculture, computer nerds found their way into mainstream fiction as well. In Richard Powers's acclaimed 2000 novel *Plowing the Dark,* the heroes are Stevie, an ex-poet who finds the essence of poetry in computer code, and Adie, a disillusioned painter whose passion for art is rekindled when she discovers computer graphics. Artists become geeks and reconnect with their artistic creativity through technology: such a plot line would have been unthinkable just a few years before.[26] Jon Katz's 2000 bestseller *Geeks* celebrated the term in its very title.[27] More recently, Lisbeth Salander, the heroine of Stieg Larsson's best-selling *The Girl with the Dragon Tattoo,* is a hacker with a profoundly antisocial but highly charismatic and sexy personality.

Cultural icons in past eras tended to fall into two general types. The first was the romantic, rebellious outsider. Included here were the sailors and cowboys of the 1800s—lowly blue-collar types who eschewed the common workaday world to roam the wide sea or the Great Plains—as well as twentieth-century drifters like the characters played by Marlene Dietrich, Humphrey Bogart, and James

Dean. In real life, these icons were the bohemian artists and writers themselves, from Edgar Allan Poe and Vincent van Gogh to the punk rockers: rebels, with or without causes, but questing against the grain. The other type was the straight-arrow good guy, such as the young heroes of factory-produced Young Adult series, like the Hardy Boys and Nancy Drew; many of the movie characters played by Jimmy Stewart; the Cleaver family on TV's *Leave It to Beaver;* and real-life culture heroes such as Eisenhower. These heroes were builders and problem solvers: exemplars and upholders of the Protestant ethic, welcome in any living room or boardroom. And then, in a unique and unprecedented role, came the geek. Neither outsider nor insider, bohemian nor bourgeois, the geek is simply a technologically creative person.

The New Mainstream

Whether people define themselves as geeks or not, they are coming to see themselves as having deeply fused identities. This was brought home to me rather forcefully as I was working on this book, when I noticed that the Creative Class people I was interviewing, particularly the younger ones, did not like to be called Bobos—and that they bridled at the suggestion that they were in any way bohemian. Many of them hated the word: some urged me to find another one to use in the book.

At first I thought the problem was that bohemian sounded passé to them, conjuring up old images of beatniks with bongos or spaced-out hippies strumming acoustic guitars. Perhaps they wanted something more up-to-date, from an argot that belonged to their own generation. But that wasn't it. They disliked terms like alternative, too—and thus the real issue became clear. Bohemians are alienated people, living in the culture but not of it, and these people didn't see themselves that way at all—not even the immigrants who really *were* aliens. What they did like, however, was the notion that in whatever they did, they could be thought to be creative.

Are they cutting-edge? Definitely. On top of it, open to new ideas and to neglected old ones, too? Yes. Youthfully inventive and at times youthfully rebellious, walking into a situation and wondering why it has to be that way? Absolutely. At a fall 2001 meeting in Providence, Rhode Island, organized to help the city become more of a Creative Class center, one young man stood up in front of the city's leadership and said: "You say you want us here so long as we don't cause 'trouble.' It's our very nature to ask tough questions; so by our very nature, we're troublemakers."[28] The point is that these people want to contribute; they want to be heard. They are not drifters in our midst, nor by any means are they barbarians at the gates. They see no need to overthrow the established order when they will soon be joining their older counterparts at events like the Austin 360 Summit. They will be helping society run, and run on an even more powerful new work ethic—not on some nitro-burning strain of pure hedonism or narcissism.

The people we're seeing today are neither Baudelaire nor Babbitt. The synthesis that they are living is not just a matter of sticking a bohemian lifestyle onto an organization-man value set, like a bike rack on the back of a chrome-bumpered Country Squire station wagon. The melding has become so deep that the old components are no longer recognizable; the old categories no longer apply. The people of the Big Morph see themselves simply as creative people with creative values, working in increasingly creative workplaces, living essentially creative lifestyles. And, in this sense, they represent a new mainstream—and they are setting the norms and pace for much of society.

PART FOUR

COMMUNITY

CHAPTER 10

Place Matters

One fine spring day around the turn of the millennium, I was taking a stroll across the campus of Carnegie Mellon University when I came upon a table surrounded by young people, chatting and enjoying the spectacular weather. Several were wearing identical blue T-shirts with "Trilogy@CMU" printed across them, Trilogy being an Austin-based software company that often recruited our top students. I walked over to the table. "Are you guys here to recruit?" I asked. "No, absolutely not," they answered, seeming taken aback that I would even ask. "We're not recruiters. We're just hangin' out, playing a little Frisbee with our friends." How interesting, I thought. They've come all the way from Austin to Pittsburgh on a workday, just to hang out with some new friends.

I noticed one member of the group sitting slouched over on the grass, dressed in a tank top. This young man, an obvious slacker, had spiked multicolored hair, full-body tattoos, and multiple piercings in his ears. "So what's your story?" I asked. "Hey, man," he answered. "I just signed on with these guys." As I would later learn, he had inked the highest-paying deal of any graduating student in the history of his department, right at that table on the grass, with the recruiters who do not "recruit," because, of course, that would be pushy and not cool. What a change from my own college days, when students would put on their dressiest clothes and carefully hide any counterculture symptoms, in order to show recruiters that they could fit in. Here, the company was trying to fit in with the students. Trilogy had wined and dined this young man over margaritas in Pittsburgh and flown him to Austin for private parties at hip nightspots and aboard company boats. When I called the recruiters to ask why, they answered, "That's easy. We wanted him because he's a rock star." Moreover, "when big East Coast companies trek down here to see who is working on their project, we'll wheel him out"—blowing the customers' minds with his skill and coolness.

So it went in the heady days of the dot-com boom. But what struck me most forcibly at the time was the spectacle of yet another talented young person leaving Pittsburgh. That was exactly the problem that had started me on this line of research in the first place. Pittsburgh was filled with impressive assets, not least of them Carnegie Mellon where I taught for nearly two decades, one of the world's leading centers for information technology research. Close by is the University of Pittsburgh, with its world-class medical center. The city has three major sports franchises, renowned museums and cultural venues, a spectacular network of urban parks, remarkable industrial-age architecture, and truly great urban neighborhoods with an abundance of charming yet affordable housing. It is a friendly city, defined by strong communities and a strong sense of pride. But the best and brightest products of its universities were leaving as soon as they graduated.

With all of this whirring in the back of my brain, I asked the young man with the spiked hair why he was decamping to a smaller city in the middle of Texas, a place with no sports teams, museums, or high-art cultural amenities that were comparable to Pittsburgh's. The company is excellent, he told me. It has terrific people and the work is challenging. But this was the clincher: "It's in Austin!"

"Why is that good?" I asked. There are lots of young people, he explained, and a tremendous amount to do, a thriving music scene, ethnic and cultural diversity, fabulous outdoor recreation, and great nightlife. That's what mattered—not the symphony or the opera, which he enjoyed but would not feel comfortable attending. What's more, Austin was affordable, unlike Silicon Valley, another place that offered the kind of work he desired. (He was right: at the time, Austin ranked as the fourth-most-affordable place for information-technology workers like him. Its pay differential was more than $18,000 over the San Francisco Bay area when cost-of-living differences were taken into account.)[1]

"I can have a life in Austin," he concluded, not merely a job. When I asked him about Pittsburgh, where he had chosen to go to college, he replied that he had lived in the city for four years and knew it well. Although he had several good offers from Pittsburgh high-tech firms, the city lacked the lifestyle options, cultural diversity, and tolerant attitude that would make it attractive as a place to live. As he summed it up, "How would I fit in here?"

He has since gone on to quite a career, with stops at the Savannah College of Art & Design before heading back to Austin, where he works for Frog Designs, and founded the nonprofit Austin Center for Design.

His answer helped me frame the questions that formed the very heart of his book: How do we decide where to live and work? What really matters to us in making this kind of life decision? How has this changed—and why?

Most economists would say that we move in pursuit of jobs and financial rewards. But jobs are not the whole story. People balance a host of other considerations when deciding where to work and live. What we want today is different from what our parents wanted, and from what many of us once thought we wanted. And though the young man with the spiked hair and impressive tattoos is not representative of everyone in the Creative Class, my research shows that the kinds of things that he liked about Austin are what many of his fellow creatives are looking for when they are choosing a place to live.

Creative people do not move for traditional reasons. The physical attractions that most cities focus on building—sports stadiums, freeways, urban malls, and tourism-and-entertainment districts that resemble theme parks—are irrelevant, insufficient, or actually unattractive to them. What creatives look for are abundant high-quality amenities and experiences, an openness to diversity of all kinds, and above all else the opportunity to validate their identities as creative people. The communities that creatives are attracted to do not thrive for traditional economic reasons, such as access to natural resources or proximity to major transportation routes. Nor is their economic success tied to tax breaks and other incentives designed to lure businesses. A big part of their success stems from the fact that they are places where creative people want to live. This circumvents the age-old chicken-and-egg problem of what comes first, jobs or people. The answer is simple: it is not either-or, but both. Creative centers provide the integrated ecosystem or habitat where all forms of creativity—artistic and cultural, technological and economic—can take root and flourish.

This next section of the book will summarize my original research on the importance of place that informed the 2002 edition of this book, updating it with research that my team and I have conducted since. But before I get to the factors and motivations that shape the location decisions of the Creative Class, it's important to consider why, in spite of the many and varied predictions about how globalization and technology would make location irrelevant, place has not only endured but become more important.

Not that there is anything like a consensus on the issue—the debate over the role of place in our economy and society continues full force. Perhaps the greatest of all the New Economy myths is that "geography is dead." Thanks to advances in technology, the thinking goes, the global playing field has been leveled; all of us are potential players, no matter who we are or where we live. "When the world is flat," as Thomas Friedman famously put it, "you can innovate without having to emigrate."[2]

It's not a new idea. Since the advent of the telegraph and the telephone, the automobile and the airplane, commentators have remarked on the diminishing importance of place. In 1995, *The Economist* proclaimed The Death of Distance on its cover. "Thanks to technology and competition in telecoms," journalist Frances Cairncross prognosticated, "distance will soon be no object." Four years later, the same magazine and author announced the Conquest of Location: "The wireless revolution is ending the dictatorship of place," Cairncross declared.[3]

My own research has convinced me that this "end of place" view is unequivocally wrong. The most obvious challenge to the flat-world hypothesis is the explosive growth of cities and urban areas worldwide. The share of the world's population living in urban areas increased from just 3 percent in 1800 to 14 percent in 1900. By 1950, it had reached 30 percent. Today, this number stands at more than 50 percent, and in the advanced countries, cities and metros account for some three-fourths of the population. Cities are projected to grow at nearly double the rate of the rest of the world. More and more people are clustering in urban areas—and there's no evidence to suggest that this trend will slow down anytime soon. In "The World Is Spiky," an essay I published in *The Atlantic* in October 2005, and in my book *Who's Your City?* I presented detailed maps of light emissions, captured in satellite photographs, that clearly revealed the densely populated mega-regions that drive the world's economies, such as the Boston-Washington corridor (which produces more than $2 trillion in output), greater Tokyo ($2.5 trillion), and Europe's Amsterdam-Brussels-Antwerp ($1.5 trillion). The world is anything but flat and its spikes are getting higher and higher. At the same time, its valleys—the dark places on the maps that boast little, if any, economic activity—are mostly languishing.[4]

The reality is that globalization has two sides. The first and more obvious one is the geographic dispersion of routine economic functions such as straightforward manufacturing or service work (for example, making or answering telephone calls). The second, less obvious side to globalization is the tendency for higher-level economic activities such as innovation, design, finance, and media to cluster in a relatively small number of locations. Thinkers like Friedman focus on the ways that globalization spreads out economic activity (its centrifugal force, so to speak), missing the reality of this clustering (the centripedal force). Michael Porter, a Harvard Business School professor and expert on competitive strategy, dubs this the "location paradox." "Location still matters," he told *Business-Week* in August 2006. "The more things are mobile, the more decisive location becomes." "This point," he added, "has tripped up a lot of really smart people."[5] The mistake they make is to see globalization as an either-or proposition. It's not. The key to our new global reality lies in understanding that the world is both flat and spiky at the same time.

It all boils down to one simple fact: Place has replaced the industrial corporation as the key economic and social organizing unit of our time. Cities have always been important engines of economic growth, but they are assuming an even greater importance in today's knowledge-driven innovation economy, in which place-based ecosystems are critical to economic growth. Students of urban and regional growth have long pointed to the role of places as incubators of creativity, innovation, and new industries.[6] We've known for a while that the cities and metros that attract the most human capital prosper. But brainpower alone only tells part of the story. Even more key is the aptitude for marshaling and focusing all that raw intelligence that's on tap. Cities are not just containers for smart people; they are the enabling infrastructure where connections take place, networks are built, and innovative combinations are consummated.

Many local economies are characterized by clusters of like businesses. As the great nineteenth-century economist Alfred Marshall was the first to notice, companies benefit from the "agglomeration" economies that come from locating near each other—from being a part of a tight network of suppliers, users, and customers.[7] Such clusters can be found in the automotive industry in Detroit, the theater and garment districts in New York, and of course in Silicon Valley for high tech. Farther afield are the *maquiladora* electronics and auto-parts districts in Mexico, the clusters of disk-drive manufacturers in Singapore and of flat-panel displays in Japan. Porter has identified clusters of insurance companies in Hartford, casinos in Las Vegas, furniture manufacturing in High Point, North Carolina, and advanced imaging laboratories in Rochester, New York. As he told the Clinton Global Initiative in the summer of 2011: "There is no one US economy but a collection of local economies."

The question is no longer whether firms cluster, but why. Several answers have been proposed. Some believe that clustering captures the efficiencies generated from tight linkages between firms. Others say it has to do with the positive benefits of co-location, or what they call spillovers. Still others claim it is because certain kinds of economic activities require face-to-face contact.[8] All of these are true, but they provide only partial explanations. The real force behind this clustering is people.

The Jane Jacobs Economy

The study of economic growth is an arcane field, and until recently, it paid scant attention to the importance of location. Going back to 1776, Adam Smith's *The Wealth of Nations* argued that specialization, efficiency, and division of labor were the cornerstones of modern economic growth. Later, David Ricardo's theory of comparative advantage argued that not just firms but countries gain advantage by specializing in certain kinds of economic activity.[9] Economists and geographers have always acknowledged that economic growth is driven by and spreads from specific regions, cities, or even neighborhoods. The traditional view, however, is that places grow either because they are located on or near transportation routes or because they have endowments of natural resources that encourage firms to locate there. According to this conventional view, the economic importance of a place is tied to the efficiency with which companies can make things and do business there. Local governments employ this theory when they use tax breaks and highway construction to attract businesses. But these cost-related factors are no longer the key to success.

The great urban theorist Jane Jacobs[10] was not an academically trained economist, but her theory of growth made an indelible contribution to the field. In her eyes, it was new types of work and new ways of doing things that drove large-scale economic expansions. But while most economists located momentum in great companies, entrepreneurs, and nation-states, Jacobs identified great cities as the prime motor force behind innovation. Companies come under extraordinary pressure to specialize—to do things more cheaply, efficiently, and uniformly. But cities are host to a wide variety of talents and specialties, the broad diversity of which is a vital spur to creating things that are truly new. "The diversity, of whatever kind, that is generated by cities rests on the fact that in cities so many people are so close together, and among them contain so many different tastes, skills, needs, supplies, and bees in their bonnets," Jacobs argued. When asked in 2001 what she hoped to be remembered for, she responded:

If I were to be remembered as a really important thinker of the century, the most important thing I've contributed is, "What makes economic expansion happen?" This is something that has puzzled people always. I think I've figured out what it is, and expansion and development are two different things. Development is differentiation—new differentiation of what already existed. Practically every new thing that happens is a differentiation of a previous thing. Just about everything—from a new shoe sole to changes in legal codes—all of those things are differentiations. Expansion is an actual growth in size or volume of activity. That is a different thing.[11]

When the Nobel Prize–winning economist Robert Lucas went back to Jane Jacobs's early writings, he put cities and places front and center. "I will be following very closely the lead of Jane Jacobs, whose remarkable book, *The Economy of Cities*, seems to me mainly and convincingly concerned (although she does not use this terminology) with the external effects of human capital," he wrote. Building on Jacobs's fundamental contribution, Lucas identified the multiplier effects that stem from talent-clustering as the primary determinants of economic growth. Lucas contends that cities would be economically unfeasible if not for the productivity effects that are associated with endowments of human capital, what he called "Jane Jacobs externalities":

If we postulate only the usual list of economic forces, cities should fly apart. The theory of production contains nothing to hold a city together. A city is simply a collection of factors of production—capital, people and land— and land is always far cheaper outside cities than inside. . . . It seems to me that the "force" we need to postulate to account for the central role of cities in economic life is of exactly the same character as the "external human capital." . . . What can people be paying Manhattan or downtown Chicago rents for, if not for being near other people?[12]

Labor, capital, and technical knowledge are all well and good, he allowed, but none of those would amount to anything significant if people could not combine their talents, ideas, and energy in real places. The music industry provides a prime example. Musicians don't require a lot of equipment or capital; using the computer and the Internet, they can make and record music virtually anywhere they want. Every town and city needs at least some musicians—if not to make records, then to give piano lessons and provide entertainment in night spots and at weddings. The music business and musicians, to use Lucas's language, have every reason to fly apart. But they don't. In fact they have become more and more concentrated.

My colleagues and I have tracked the locations of musicians and musical groups in the United States, using data from a wide range of sources.[13] In 1970, despite its status as the capital of country and western, Nashville was not even among the top five regions for the music business. But by 2004, only New York and Los Angeles had more musicians and music businesses. In fact, Nashville—which had been busily expanding its reach to many other genres, particularly rock and pop—accounted for almost all of the industry's growth during those thirty-four years. Today, it is home to much of the world's best studio talent and has eclipsed even New York and LA as the go-to place for music writing, recording, and publishing.

Just as high-tech companies trek to Silicon Valley, a great deal of top musical talent eventually ends up in Nashville's orbit. In 2005, one of the most significant rock musicians of the past decade, Jack White, the founder of the White Stripes, relocated his newest band and recording project, The Raconteurs, from Detroit to Nashville. White had produced and performed on Loretta Lynn's highly regarded album *Van Lear Rose*, which was recorded in Nashville. Impressed by what he saw, he bought a house there. None of the other musicians in The Raconteurs are originally from Nashville, either. White and Brendan Benson are from Detroit; the drummer, Patrick Keeler, and bass player Jack Lawrence had been members of a Cincinnati band, The Greenhornes. When asked why he relocated, White said that Detroit's scene had become too negative and confining, that people who were once his friends and associates had become jealous of The White Stripes's success. Nashville was different, he said: it was more professional, less confrontational, less melodramatic. Like Silicon Valley, it was a place where the best and the brightest could collaborate with other top talent and make the most of its world-class infrastructure.

When talented and creative people come together, the multiplying effect is exponential; the end result is much more than the sum of the parts. Clustering makes each of us more productive—and our collective creativity and economic wealth grow accordingly.

Human Capital City

Human capital theory has been the dominant theory of regional growth over the past decade or so. The person most associated with it is Harvard professor Edward Glaeser, whose 2011 book *Triumph of the City* made an eloquent case for the proposition that what powers cities is not their great buildings, companies, or physical infrastructure but the concentrations of skilled and talented people they house.[14] Glaeser and other proponents of human capital theory argue that regional growth is best achieved by protecting and propagating local endowments of highly educated, productive people. There is more than anecdotal evidence to back this up. Cross-national studies of economic growth find a clear connection between the economic success of nations and their human capital, as measured by the level of education. And it is human capital clusters that lie behind the regional agglomerations of firms.[15] Firms concentrate to reap the advantages that stem from common labor pools—not merely to tap the advantages from linked networks of customers and suppliers, as is more typically argued. Research by one of Glaeser's former graduate students, Spencer Glendon, shows that a good deal of city growth over the twentieth century could be predicted by their levels of human capital at the beginning of the century.[16] Places with greater numbers of highly educated people grew faster and were better able to attract more talent.

My own theory shares much in common with human capital theory; I certainly agree that skilled and talented people are the keys to city and regional growth. As I mentioned back in Chapter 3, where human capital theory uses education as a proxy for skills, I look at the kinds of work that people actually do—a subject I'll return to in greater depth later.

Urban Metabolism

But what about the inevitable drawbacks and obstacles that arise from this clustering and concentration of talented people and other key assets? One problematic consequence is the accelerated sorting of people and cities into an economic hierarchy. Our society is not just becoming more unequal, its inequities are being etched into our economic geography.

Concentration and density contribute to all sorts of other problems, too, such as traffic congestion, rising crime rates, and unaffordable housing—all of them predictable by-products of big-city life. You would think such problems, or what economists sometimes refer to as urban diseconomies, would be enough to eventually kill a city; at the very least, they must pose significant barriers to its future development. Compelling research suggests otherwise. In my books *Who's Your City?* and *The Great Reset*, I wrote about the findings of a multidisciplinary team of researchers led by Geoffrey West of the Santa Fe Institute.

West and his team wondered whether cities and mega-regions, though not literally living things, might have a metabolism that increases as their populations do, allowing them not just to overcome the drawbacks associated with size but to continue to innovate and improve their productivity as they grow. To test this idea, they collected data from the United States, Europe, and China at a variety of different stages in their development and looked at a wide range of characteristics, such as crime rates, disease transmission, demographics, infrastructure, energy consumption, economic activity, and innovation. Sure enough, they found:

> Social organizations, like biological organisms, consume energy and resources, depend on networks for the flow of information and materials, and produce artifacts and waste. . . . Cities manifest power-law scaling similar to the economy-of-scale relationships observed in biology: a doubling of population requires less than a doubling of certain resources. The material infrastructure that is analogous to biological transport networks— gas stations, lengths of electrical cable, miles of road surface—consistently exhibits sublinear [less than one] scaling with population.[17]

This might have been expected. But what the researchers had not expected to see was that the correlation between population growth and characteristics that had fewer or no analogies in biology—such attributes as innovation, patent activity, the numbers of super-creatives, the levels of wages, and gross domestic product—was greater than one. In other words, a doubling of population resulted in more than twice the creative and economic output. They called this phenomenon "superlinear" scaling: the larger a city's population, they concluded, the greater the innovation and wealth per person.

The World According to Zipf

Urban metabolism is not the only paradox that helps explain the enigma of cities. One of the great remaining puzzles of urban economics and regional analysis revolves around Zipf's Law.[18] Named for its discoverer, George Zipf, it is also referred to as the rank-size rule. Zipf's Law says that the distribution of virtually all cities within a nation follows a simple power law: the second-largest city is roughly half the size of the largest; the third, roughly one-third the size of the largest; and so on. According to detailed empirical studies, Zipf's Law accurately describes the real size distribution of US cities over the past century, and of virtually every other advanced industrial nations' cities as well. Plotted on a log-arithmic graph, populations of cities form a nearly perfect line with a descending slope. There are some exceptions, of course—capitals or former capitals of empires, London, for example—tend to be disproportionately large; cities in highly planned economies, like China's, tend to fall off the scale as well. Also bear in mind that Zipf's Law applies to the relative sizes of cities, not metropolitan areas. The city of Los Angeles is about half the size of the city of New York; greater LA's population is much closer to New York's.

Try as they might, economists and social scientists have failed to develop plausible explanations for why Zipf's Law holds up as well as it does. In their book *The Spatial Economy*, the economists Masahisa Fujita, Paul Krugman, and Anthony Venables wrote: "Attempts to match economic theory with the data usually face the problem that the theory is excessively neat . . . whereas the real world throws up complicated and messy outcomes. When it comes to the size distribution of cities, however, the problem we face is that the data offer a stunningly neat picture, one that is hard to reproduce in any plausible (or even implausible) theoretical model." After devoting more than eight pages and scads of sophisticated mathematical formulas to this problem, they conclude: "At this point we have no resolution of the striking regularity in city size distributions. We must acknowledge that it poses a real intellectual challenge to our understanding of cities. . . . Nobody has come up with a plausible story about the process that generates the rank size rule."[19]

That is, until now. The remarkable computer models built by Robert Axtell shed new light on this enigma. Part computer scientist, part economist, and part physicist, Axtell, a former Carnegie Mellon student, is a professor at George Mason University, a frequent visitor to the Santa Fe Institute, and a leader in the field of agent-based modeling. Along with his Brookings Institution colleague Josh Epstein, he pioneered high-level computer programs to evaluate how people or organizations—which they refer to as agents—behave. Taking my creative capital theory as his point of departure, Axtell built a model of how cities form, based on the law of "preferential attachment," in which skilled and productive people attract other skilled and productive people. First, creative agents cluster around other creative agents, reinforcing each other's productivity. Then, these creative agents combine to form larger economic units or firms. These economic units or firms then locate in cities where they grow and develop. As they grow, they become the locations for still more creative agents and firms. As the computer runs thousands of iterations of this basic scenario, a discernible pattern for the size distribution of cities comes clearly into view— a hierarchical distribution that conforms almost perfectly to Zipf's Law and matches the real size distribution of US cities.[20] If its cause still remains mysterious, preferential attachment and creativity are clearly the mechanism by which Zipf's Law operates.

The Place of Creativity

The history of human creativity and of human progress is intimately intertwined with that of cities. *The Epic of Gilgamesh*—perhaps the oldest known work of literature—closes with an awed description of the walls of the city of Uruk. Plato's *Republic*—which envisioned an ideal city—was a product of the cultural and intellectual flowering of the earthly city of Athens, as well as a broadside against its politics. Dante, Petrarch, Boccaccio, Brunelleschi, da Vinci, and Michelangelo all were born in or near the city of Florence. Great thinkers, artists, and entrepreneurs rarely come out of nowhere. They cluster and thrive in places that attract other creative people and provide an environment that fosters and supports creative effort.

That environment is provided by cities. Cities have long functioned as critical containers and mobilizers of creativity, attracting creative people from the surrounding countryside while providing the structures, scenes, and ecosystems that undergird and support creative effort. As the great Swedish economic geographer Åke Andersson, a leading student of creativity and cities, puts it: "Creative people need creative cities."[21] He notes the flourishing of creativity in four different cities from four very different eras: Athens in 400 BC, Renaissance Florence, Enlightenment London, and fin de siècle Vienna. "The creative city as an informal and spontaneously evolving spatial organization has been the arena for all large-scale creative revolutions," he writes. "In the course of the past 2,500 years, a small number of relatively large cities have functioned as hotbeds of revolutionary creativity. These cities attracted a disproportionate share of migrants with creative inclinations, and they also facilitated the growth of creativity among those already present. Such cities were both used as arenas for presenting findings from elsewhere and as fertile locations for developing new ideas in collaboration with other creative people."

Even deeper in our past, the congregation of populations into progressively larger, denser, and less isolated groups may have been what enabled humanity's rise. Archaeologists and anthropologists have been aware of the incredible flowering of artistic and material creativity that occurred roughly 40,000 years ago in Europe, reflected in everything from cave paintings, figurines, and jewelry to the complex tools that allowed our ancestors to begin to transform nature. Some scientists have attributed this leap to evolutionary advances in cognition and memory alone. But more recent research puts communities—not genes—at the center of this evolutionary watershed.

Research by Stephen Shennan at University College London, Robert Boyd at UCLA, and others indicates that shifting demographics was an important cause of early leaps in human development. Shennan's research—which notes that artistic and technological leaps similar to the one in Europe had occurred in Africa and the Middle East and tens of thousands of years earlier—suggests that what all these leaps had in common was the growth of local population density beyond a certain threshold. Many of these cultural blooms withered, Shennan observes, when populations subsequently shrank. Boyd's research shows the close relationship between toolmaking advances and population size. As people gathered into larger groups and came into contact with one another more frequently, knowledge was shared, retained, and advanced more easily.[22]

Writing in the early decades of the twentieth century, Robert Park, the pioneering University of Chicago urban sociologist, noted the functional importance of loose ties and anonymous lifestyles in giving rise to what he called the "mobilization of the individual man."[23] "Great cities," wrote Park, "have always been melting pots of races and of cultures. Out of the vivid and subtle interactions of which they have been the centers, there have come the newer breeds and the newer social types. They have multiplied the opportunities for the individual man for contact and association with his fellows, but they have made these contacts and associations more transitory and less stable." He went on to point out the importance of these structures to the creative environment of the city:

This makes it possible for individuals to pass quickly and easily from one moral milieu to another, and encourages the fascinating but dangerous experiment of living at the same time in several different contiguous, but otherwise widely separated worlds.

All of this tends to give city life a dangerous and adventitious character; it tends to complicate social relations and to produce new and divergent individual types.

It introduces, at the same time, an element of chance and adventure which adds to the stimulus of city life and gives it, for young and fresh nerves, a peculiar attractiveness.

The lure of great cities is perhaps a consequence of stimulations which act directly upon the reflexes.

Park goes on to contrast the stasis of the small, tightly knit community with the dynamism of the city. "In a small community, it is the normal man, the man without eccentricity or genius, who seems most likely to succeed. The small community often tolerates eccentricity," he noted. "The city, on the contrary rewards it. Neither the criminal, the defective, nor the genius has the same opportunity to develop his innate disposition in a small town that he invariably finds in the big city."

In her fascinating and detailed study of Greenwich Village life in the 1920s, Carolyn Ware identified loose ties and quasi-anonymity as its fundamental feature: "Many who were drawn to the Village came to seek escape from their community, their families, or themselves," she wrote.[24] The Villagers were "intensely individualistic in both their social relations and their point of view," "independent of virtually all institutions." They scorned the "the joining habit" and took "full advantage of both the selectiveness and anonymity the city offered." They "avoided the usual casual contacts with family, friends, neighbors, or members of the same economic or social class and the relations growing out of institutional connections."

Rather than this more traditional life, "they maintained individual ties with friends scattered all over the city."

But cities do more than just attract creative people and provide a broad environment or ecosystem for creativity; they stimulate it as well. They do this in two key ways, according to Dean Keith Simonton.[25] First, they play a critical role in "creative development." Creators must be exposed to role models and mentors during adolescence and young adulthood. "To the extent that such mentors are more likely to be found in urban areas, this apprenticeship phase will necessarily occur in city environments," Simonton writes. "In fact," he adds, "research on talent development indicates how often exceptional gifts will have to move to metropolitan areas once they reach a certain stage in their intellectual or artistic growth."

Second, creativity requires cultural heterogeneity: it is enhanced by "early exposure to ideational diversity and conflict, enabling the individual to engage in cultural 'hybridization' or 'cross-fertilization' as an adult creator." Again, this is more likely to occur in urban settings, which have "educational or cultural institutions that help mix up the broth," not to mention an overflowing and ever-shifting spectacle of things to look at. When a solution to a problem is not forthcoming, a creative person will put it aside temporarily and resume the tasks of ordinary life. During this time, he or she is exposed to a host of stimuli that prime associations. Given sufficient time, Simonton writes, "one of these stimulated pathways may lead to a solution to the problem"—a eureka moment. "It goes without saying that an urban environment will afford a more diverse variety of potential priming stimuli than will a rural environment. The former, relative to the latter, is more likely to offer a world replete with different languages, cultures, religions and lifestyles."

The popular image of the solitary creator notwithstanding, much of the creativity in modern societies emerges in groups—in research laboratories, cinematic collaborations, and architectural teams, to name just a few examples. "Naturally, the members of these problem-solving or brainstorming groups are most often recruited from the immediate environment, whether suburb, town or city," Simonton observes. The more urban the setting, the more diverse and hence more creative such a group is likely to be.

CHAPTER 11

The Geography of Class

Many people like lists and maps, and I'm one of them. In this chapter, I investigate the geography of the Creative Class across America's cities and metro regions. This chapter and the next update all of the various measures for the Creative Class, the other classes, and the three T's of economic development: technology, talent, and tolerance.

Different kinds of people have always sorted themselves into different kinds of neighborhoods. There have always been ethnic enclaves, such as the Italian American community in Newark where I was born. There have long been artistic and cultural communities like New York's Greenwich Village, college towns like Madison and Boulder and manufacturing towns like Pittsburgh and Detroit. But when I was first researching this book over a decade ago, my data pointed me toward something new: a large-scale re-sorting of people geographically, based on class, that was becoming increasingly pronounced. This new geography of class, I noted, seemed to have a direct connection to a place's economic prospects. Regions with greater concentrations of the Creative Class were more likely to be economic winners. Those with larger Working Class concentrations were becoming economically stagnant; some were in the midst of grim downward spirals. Those with large Service Class concentrations, such as tourist destinations like Las Vegas, were attracting people and creating jobs at a rapid pace, but they were not really prospering. Many of the jobs they had were low skill and low pay: a job cleaning hotel rooms or even dealing cards, I wrote then, does not offer much of a ladder up into our economy's jet stream. I suspected that those Service Class centers were fated to become increasingly disconnected from the economic engine of our society. As this chapter and later ones will show, subsequent research, by me and by others, backs up those presentiments. The United States and the world have become more unequal, and that inequality is not only one of income, it reflects the increasingly uneven geography of class. Furthermore, we have learned that rapid population growth, such as occurred in many Sun Belt locations, does not necessarily lead to economic growth. Many Sun Belt metros added population like crazy but improved neither their productivity nor wages. Some built entire economies around the housing bubble and fell victim to the illusion of "growth without growth."

In the original edition, I found that the Creative Class made up more than 35 percent of the workforce in the leading metros as of 1999. By 2010, that figure had jumped to nearly 50 percent. Back then, the leading Creative Class metros (with populations over 1 million) were greater Washington, DC, Raleigh-Durham, Boston, Austin, San Francisco, Minneapolis, Hartford, Denver, Seattle, and Houston. I noted that large metros had not exclusively cornered the market for the Creative Class, despite their considerable advantages. In fact, a number of smaller regions ranked among the highest in Creative Class concentration, notably such college towns as Gainesville, East Lansing, and Madison. Other smaller-scale Creative Class centers were Bloomington, Illinois; Melbourne, Florida; Huntsville, Alabama; Santa Fe; and Boise. I also pointed out that the Creative Class was not limited only to well-known high-tech and artistic centers. Kansas City; Rochester, Minnesota; and Detroit, for example, numbered among the top twenty centers for the Cre-

Figure 11.1   Creative Class by Metro, 2010

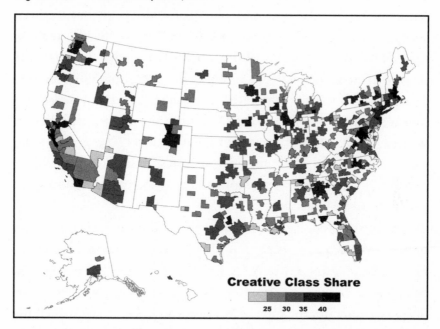

Source: US Department of Labor, Bureau of Labor Statistics, Occupational Employment
Statistics (OES) Survey, 2010. Available online at http://www.bls.gov/oes/. Analysis by
Kevin Stolarick. Map by Zara Matheson.

ative Class among large regions in 1999. Albany, Omaha, Little
Rock, Birmingham, and Baton Rouge ranked alongside Albu-
querque as leading Creative Class locations among medium-sized
metro regions (with populations between 500,000 and 1 million).

I now turn to the updated 2010 rankings for Creative Class metros
(see Figure 11.1). These new rankings were developed by Kevin
Stolarick, based on occupational data from the Bureau of Labor
Statistics. Two things are worth noting about them. First, instead
of separating larger and smaller metros, they are all ranked together.
And second, whereas our earlier rankings were based on broader
consolidated metropolitan areas (which combine certain metro
areas into bigger, more populous units), the new rankings cover

all of the individual metropolitan statistical divisions separately. (Appendix Table A.1 provides full data for all US metros.)

The Creative Class remains concentrated geographically, making up more than 40 percent of the workforce in eleven metros. It makes up more than 35–40 percent in another thirty-four metros. There are 105 metros where the Creative Class accounts for between 30 and 35 percent of the workforce and 162 where it makes up between 25 and 30 percent of the workforce. On the flip side, there is one metro where the Creative Class makes up less than 20 percent of the workforce and forty-eight where it accounts for between 20 and 25 percent.

The top-ranked region is Durham, where the Creative Class makes up 48.4 percent of the workforce (see Table 11.1, which provides a list of the top twenty Creative Class metros). It is followed by San Jose, greater Washington, DC; Ithaca, New York; and Boulder. Rounding out the top ten are Trenton, New Jersey (which includes Princeton); Huntsville, Alabama; Corvallis, Oregon; Boston, and Ann Arbor. Among the top twenty Creative Class metros are Tallahassee, Gainesville, Rochester, Minnesota; Charlottesville, Hartford, Bridgeport, San Francisco; Olympia, Washington; Madison, and Burlington, Vermont.

This list belies the fatalistic notion that geography is destiny. It includes many northern Frost Belt locations, among them Ann Arbor in the very shadow of Detroit. There are some noticeable absences among this top-tier group: greater New York ranks thirty-fourth, with 34.9 percent of its workforce in the Creative Class; Chicago is forty-fourth (35.1 percent); LA is sixtieth (34.1 percent); Greater Detroit, on the other hand, scores a surprisingly high rank of fifty-third—which bodes reasonably well for its future. Some of Detroit's suburbs have among the very highest concentrations of the Creative Class in the nation.

In the original edition of this book, I noted that among large metros, Las Vegas, Grand Rapids, and Memphis had the smallest con-

Table 11.1 Top Twenty Creative Class Metros, 2010

Metro	Creative Class Share
Durham, NC	48.4%
San Jose-Sunnyvale-Santa Clara, CA	46.9%
Washington-Arlington-Alexandria, DC-VA-MD-WV	46.8%
Ithaca, NY	44.6%
Boulder, CO	44.4%
Trenton-Ewing, NJ	42.9%
Huntsville, AL	42.7%
Corvallis, OR	41.7%
Boston-Cambridge-Quincy, MA-NH	41.6%
Ann Arbor, MI	41.3%
Tallahassee, FL	40.5%
Rochester, MN	40.0%
Charlottesville, VA	39.7%
Hartford-West Hartford-East Hartford, CT	39.7%
Bridgeport-Stamford-Norwalk, CT	39.5%
San Francisco-Oakland-Fremont, CA	39.4%
Gainesville, FL	39.3%
Olympia, WA	38.9%
Madison, WI	38.3%
Burlington-South Burlington, VT	37.9%

Source: US Department of Labor, Bureau of Labor Statistics, Occupational Employment Statistics (OES) Survey, 2010. Available online at http://www.bls.gov/oes/. Analysis by Kevin Stolarick.

centrations of the Creative Class as of 1999, and that the Creative Class had nearly abandoned a wide range of smaller regions in the outskirts of the South and Midwest. In 2010, Las Vegas had just 22.7 percent of its workforce in the Creative Class, placing it in the bottom ten of all US metros. Of large metros, Riverside, Memphis, Louisville, and Orlando had less than 30 percent of their workforce in the Creative Class. The places with the very lowest concentrations of the Creative Class remained small, mostly tourist destinations in the Sun Belt, such as Myrtle Beach, South Carolina; Dalton,

Georgia; Ocala and Naples, Florida; Houma, Louisiana; and Ocean City, New Jersey—and manufacturing towns in the old Rust Belt, like Elkhart, Indiana; Sandusky, Ohio; and Michigan City, Michigan.

There is considerable variation in Creative Class wages across metros, which is something that I did not track in the original edition. Figure 11.2 maps Creative Class wages for all metros across the United States, and Table 11.2 lists the top twenty. Not surprisingly, San Jose (Silicon Valley) tops the lists with Creative Class wages of more than $100,000. San Francisco is second, followed by Bridgeport-Stamford-Norwalk, Connecticut. The Washington metro area makes the list, as do college towns such as Boulder, Durham, and New Haven.

Figure 11.2   Creative Class Wages by Metro, 2010

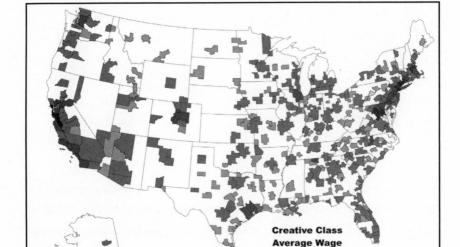

Source: US Department of Labor, Bureau of Labor Statistics, Occupational Employment Statistics (OES) Survey, 2010. Available online at http://www.bls.gov/oes/. Analysis by Kevin Stolarick. Map by Zara Matheson.

Table 11.2   Top Twenty Metros for Creative Class Wages, 2010

Rank	Metro	Average Annual Wages
1	San Jose-Sunnyvale-Santa Clara, CA	$101,827
2	San Francisco-Oakland-Fremont, CA	91,361
3	Bridgeport-Stamford-Norwalk, CT	90,713
4	Washington-Arlington-Alexandria, DC-VA-MD-WV	90,442
5	Napa, CA	87,765
6	New York-Northern New Jersey-Long Island, NY-NJ-PA	87,625
7	Boston-Cambridge-Quincy, MA-NH	84,403
8	Los Angeles-Long Beach-Santa Ana, CA	80,859
9	Trenton-Ewing, NJ	80,816
10	San Diego-Carlsbad-San Marcos, CA	80,036
11	Seattle-Tacoma-Bellevue, WA	79,455
12	Oxnard-Thousand Oaks-Ventura, CA	78,481
13	Boulder, CO	78,348
14	Santa Barbara-Santa Maria, CA	78,173
15	Hartford-West Hartford-East Hartford, CT	77,187
16	Durham, NC	77,132
17	Salinas, CA	77,086
18	New Haven, CT	76,826
19	Philadelphia-Camden-Wilmington, PA-NJ-DE-MD	76,694
20	Anchorage, AK	76,612

Source: US Department of Labor, Bureau of Labor Statistics, Occupational Employment Statistics (OES) Survey, 2010. Available online at http://www.bls.gov/oes/. Analysis by Charlotta Mellander.

The Creative Class share is also concentrated and uneven across the fifty states. (See Figure 11.3 and Table 11.3.) The District of Columbia tops the list, with 57.8 percent of its workforce in Creative Class occupations. This is not surprising because DC is a small geographic area with a high-skill workforce. Massachusetts is next, where the Creative Class makes up nearly four in ten workers (39 percent), followed by Maryland, Connecticut, and Virginia. Colorado, New Hampshire, New York, Washington, and Minnesota round out the top ten. Nevada is the state with the smallest percentage of the Creative Class (24.2 percent). Missouri, West Virginia, North and

Figure 11.3 Creative Class Share by State, 2010

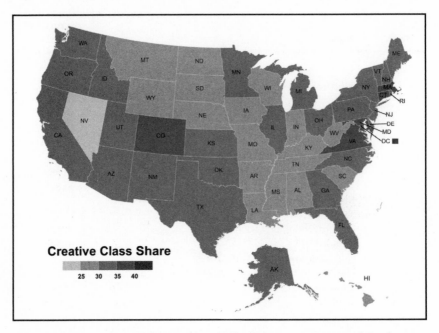

Source: US Department of Labor, Bureau of Labor Statistics, Occupational Employment Statistics (OES) Survey, 2010. Available online at http://www.bls.gov/oes/. Analysis by Kevin Stolarick. Map by Zara Matheson.

South Dakota, Wyoming, Mississippi, Arkansas, Louisiana, Indiana, and South Carolina number among the states with the lowest Creative Class concentrations.

The Creative Class is even more concentrated by county (see Figure 11.4). Counties are a smaller geographic unit than metros: there are more than three thousand counties in the United States, compared to several hundred metros. In 1999, I only had metro data to work with, but since then researchers such as David McGranahan and Tim Wojan and my own colleague Kevin Stolarick have been able to use data from the American Community Survey to chart the Creative Class by county.

Nationwide, the leading Creative Class county is Los Alamos, New Mexico, home to the famous laboratory that bears its name, with

Table 11.3   Leading and Lagging Creative Class States, 2010

Rank	State	Creative Class Share
Top Ten		
1	District of Columbia	57.8%
2	Massachusetts	39.0%
3	Maryland	38.0%
4	Connecticut	37.0%
5	Virginia	36.4%
6	Colorado	35.9%
7	New Hampshire	34.8%
8	New York	34.7%
9	Washington	34.7%
10	Minnesota	34.6%
Bottom Ten		
41	South Carolina	28.5%
42	Indiana	28.4%
43	Louisiana	28.2%
44	South Dakota	28.1%
45	Arkansas	28.1%
46	Mississippi	27.5%
47	Wyoming	27.4%
48	North Dakota	27.4%
49	West Virginia	27.3%
50	Missouri	27.1%
51	Nevada	24.2%

Source: US Department of Labor, Bureau of Labor Statistics, Occupational Employment Statistics (OES) Survey, 2010. Available online at http://www.bls.gov/oes/. Analysis by Kevin Stolarick.

nearly 70 percent of its workers employed in Creative Class occupations (see Table 11.4). Other counties with large concentrations (44 percent or more) of the Creative Class include DC and its suburbs of Arlington, Fairfax, and Loudon Counties in Virginia, and Howard and Montgomery Counties in Maryland; Kalawao, Hawaii;

Figure 11.4   Creative Class Share by County, 2010

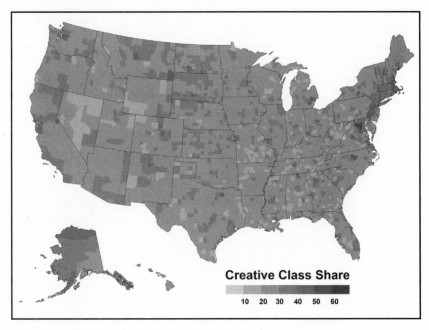

Source: US Department of Labor, Bureau of Labor Statistics, Occupational Employment Statistics (OES) Survey, 2010. Available online at http://www.bls.gov/oes/. Analysis by Kevin Stolarick. Map by Zara Matheson.

New York County, New York (which covers Manhattan); Carter County, Montana; San Francisco County and nearby Marin County in California; Douglas County, Colorado (outside Denver); Middlesex County, Massachusetts (which includes Cambridge and other Boston suburbs); and Orange County, North Carolina (which includes Chapel Hill and the University of North Carolina). On the flip side, the Creative Class accounts for less than 10 percent of the workforce in the lowest ranked county, and it composes less than one in five workers in more than 200 others.

The original edition of this book looked at the Creative Class as a whole and separated it into two main groups, the Super-Creative Core and Creative Professionals. Since that time, my colleagues and I have broken down the key types of Creative Class workers

Table 11.4 Top Twenty Creative Class Counties, 2010

County	Creative Class Share
Los Alamos County, NM	65.9%
Arlington County, VA	60.8%
Falls Church, VA	58.9%
District of Columbia	53.7%
Kalawao County, HI	52.5%
Alexandria, VA	53.4%
New York County, NY	51.9%
Fairfax County, VA	51.8%
Howard County, MD	51.6%
Loudoun County, VA	50.9%
Montgomery County, MD	51.0%
Fairfax County, VA	48.2%
Carter County, MT	47.0%
San Francisco County, CA	46.2%
Albemarle County, VA	45.3%
Douglas County, CO	44.4%
Middlesex County, MA	45.1%
York County, VA	44.9%
Marin County, CA	44.5%
Orange County, NC	44.1%

Note: Includes cities that are considered as "county equivalents" by the US Census.

Source: US Department of Labor, Bureau of Labor Statistics, Occupational Employment Statistics (OES) Survey, 2010, and US Census, American Community Survey, 2005–10. Available online at http://www.bls.gov/oes/. Analysis by Kevin Stolarick.

or occupational groups into smaller categories. My ever-pragmatic colleague Lou Musante came up with the acronym TAPE (technology, arts, professional, and eds and meds workers) to refer to them. Since writing the original edition of this book, we have been able to break out these key segments of the Creative Class and identify the leading regions for them (see Figure 11.5 and Table 11.5).

Technology: San Jose, Huntsville, and Boulder lead in science and technology; greater Washington, DC, Seattle, and Boston also boast large concentrations of technology workers.

Arts: LA, New York, San Francisco, Washington, DC, and Boston
   lead in arts, culture, media, and entertainment occupations.
Professionals: Washington, DC, San Francisco, Bridgeport, Hartford, and Trenton have the largest concentrations of business,
   management, financial, and legal professionals.
Eds and Meds: Not surprisingly, college towns dominate. The
   leaders are Ithaca, New York, home to Cornell University;

Figure 11.5   Major Creative Class Subgroups, 2010

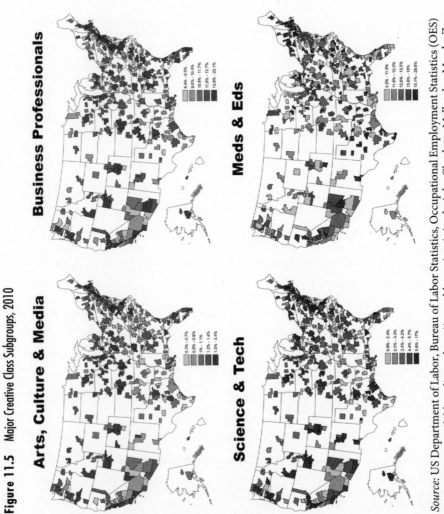

Source: US Department of Labor, Bureau of Labor Statistics, Occupational Employment Statistics (OES) Survey, 2010. Available online at http://www.bls.gov/oes/. Analysis by Charlotta Mellander. Map by Zara Matheson.

Gainesville (the University of Florida); Athens (University of Georgia); Rochester, Minnesota (the Mayo Clinic); and Ann Arbor (University of Michigan). Among large metros, the greatest concentrations of these occupations are in Rochester, Buffalo, Nassau-Suffolk, New York; Boston, and Providence.

Table 11.5   Leading Metros for Major Creative Class Subgroups, 2010

Creative Class Subgroup	Share of Total Employment
Technology and Science	
San Jose-Sunnyvale-Santa Clara, CA	17.0%
Huntsville, AL	16.5%
Boulder, CO	14.5%
Framingham, MA	13.4%
Lowell-Billerica-Chelmsford, MA-NH	13.0%
Arts, Culture, and Media	
Los Angeles-Long Beach-Glendale, CA	3.4%
New York-White Plains-Wayne, NY-NJ	2.8%
San Francisco-San Mateo-Redwood City, CA	2.7%
Washington-Arlington-Alexandria, DC-VA-MD-WV	2.4%
Boston-Cambridge-Quincy, MA	2.2%
Professionals	
Washington-Arlington-Alexandria, DC-VA-MD-WV	23.1%
San Francisco-San Mateo-Redwood City, CA	20.6%
Bridgeport-Stamford-Norwalk, CT	20.2%
Trenton-Ewing, NJ	18.8%
Tallahassee, FL	18.8%
Eds and Meds	
Ithaca, NY	29.6%
Gainesville, FL	22.1%
Athens-Clarke County, GA	21.1%
Rochester, MN	21.0%
Ann Arbor, MI	21.0%

Source: US Department of Labor, Bureau of Labor Statistics, Occupational Employment Statistics (OES) Survey, 2010. Available online at http://www.bls.gov/oes/. Analysis by Charlotta Mellander.

We've also been able to identify which of these key Creative Class groups add the most to regional development. Three of these groups—technology, business professionals, and arts and cultural workers—add considerably to regional economic output and wages.[1] The finding for artistic and cultural occupations is especially notable: these occupations are significantly associated with regional wages. Many simply presume that art follows wealth: richer cities and regions have more money to invest in the arts, hence they have more artists. That may have been true in the past, but today it works both ways. It is an empirical fact that arts, design, and entertainment occupations are among the most important contributors to regional income and wealth.

Many regions that lost manufacturing jobs have rebuilt their economies around meds and eds. In Rochester and Buffalo as well as Detroit, Cleveland, St. Louis, and Pittsburgh, the largest employers are colleges, universities, and hospitals. This would seem to bode well for these places—it offers a steady supply of good jobs for residents and a solid foundation for further growth. But according to our analysis, high concentrations of these meds and eds jobs add little to regional income. In fact, we found that regional earnings and incomes fall as a region's share of meds and eds jobs rises. The more Creative Class jobs in education and health care, the lower a region's wages tend to be. Why might this be? For one thing, eds and meds tend to monopolize a region's workforce—the demand for employees is so great that it leaves other sectors with smaller hiring pools. Like police and fire departments, eds and meds are basic necessities. Every place must devote some of its workforce to them. But out-of-state tuitions and government research grants notwithstanding, they bring in relatively little money from outside. Occupations like management science and engineering and even arts and culture tend to produce exportable products that can be sold far and wide.

Creative Class occupations are also highly clustered and concentrated, according to a 2011 study by economists Jaison Abel and Todd Gabe. This is especially true of the occupations that add the most to regional wages, those of artists, media workers, scientists, social scientists, information technology workers, environmental designers, and engineers.[2] The more clustered they are, the more wages they add.

My own research uncovered a related feature. When Charlotta Mellander and I examined the relationship between wages and metro size, we found that the wages for Working Class jobs tended to rise beyond the national average and then level off in communities where the labor market was about 120,000 people. The population threshold where wages passed the national average was much higher for the Creative Class—roughly 1 million for business professionals, scientists, and engineers, and more than 1.5 million for artistic, cultural, and entertainment occupations. The critical mass at which Creative Class wages rise, in other words, is as much as ten times higher than that for manufacturing. The Creative Economy thrives at a larger scale.

We have already seen that Creative Class workers earn a substantial premium even when their level of education is taken into account. And this, too, varies by region as well as industry. In a fascinating study, Gabe identified the key factors behind this Creative Class wage premium.[3] "Is it working around other creative workers in the same industry?" he asked. Or, "Is it interacting with other creative workers who reside in the same region?" The study found little evidence that the wage premium related to creativity was positively associated with industry effects—that is, the share of creative workers in the same industry or sector—and concluded that productivity gains from creativity are in fact diminished by working around other creative workers involved in producing the same good or delivering a similar type of service. But Gabe found evidence that

the creativity-based wage premium is driven up by the share of
Creative Class workers in the region. Even more importantly, the
study finds that Creative Class wages are higher in metros with a
diversity of Creative Class occupations; for example, where there
are more artists and cultural creatives as well as technological creatives and creatives in management and business. This makes intuitive sense as the interaction across varieties of Creative Class
work creates greater "knowledge spillovers" and higher rates of innovation, ultimately leading to higher wages.

Working Class Enclaves

The United States has witnessed a long decline in its share of Working Class jobs—high-paying, family-supporting jobs in production,
maintenance, and installation, as well construction, transportation,
and related fields. When I wrote the original edition of this book,
the Working Class still made up a substantial share of jobs—from
40 percent to more than 50 percent—in Elkhart, Indiana; Decatur,
Alabama; Fort Smith, Arkansas; Hickory, North Carolina; and
Houma, Louisiana. Working Class jobs accounted for roughly three
in ten workers, not just in older industrial metros like Milwaukee,
Buffalo, and Detroit, but in Nashville, Louisville, Charlotte, and
Salt Lake City.

Figure 11.6 maps the Working Class across US metros in 2010.
One thing is abundantly clear: the economic crisis has substantially
reduced the Working Class, even in its leading centers. The share
of the Working Class in Elkhart-Goshen fell from 55 percent in
1999 to 46 percent in 2010. It has shrunk even more in large metros. Its largest concentrations are found in Memphis (26.2 percent), Louisville (26.1 percent), and Houston (24.4 percent), where
the Working Class accounts for roughly one in four jobs. In the

Figure 11.6   The Working Class by Metro, 2010

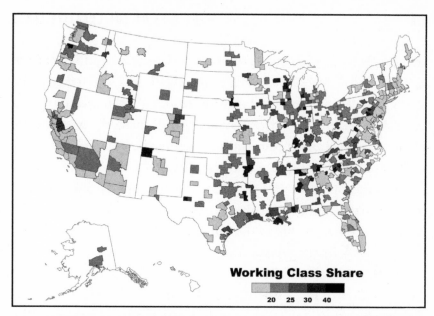

Source: US Department of Labor, Bureau of Labor Statistics, Occupational Employment Statistics (OES) Survey, 2010. Available online at http://www.bls.gov/oes/. Analysis by Kevin Stolarick. Map by Zara Matheson.

Table 11.6   Top Twenty Working Class Metros, 2010

Metro	Working Class Share
Elkhart-Goshen, IN	46.0%
Dalton, GA	45.6%
Pascagoula, MS	39.7%
Houma-Bayou Cane-Thibodaux, LA	39.0%
Morristown, TN	38.4%
Decatur, AL	37.1%
Fort Smith, AR-OK	36.1%
Hickory-Morganton-Lenoir, NC	35.3%
Odessa, TX	34.4%
Columbus, IN	34.3%
Holland-Grand Haven, MI	34.2%
Longview-Kelso, WA	33.3%
Gainesville, GA	33.3%
Decatur, IL	33.2%
Joplin, MO	32.9%
Farmington, NM	32.6%
Harrisonburg, VA	32.5%
Oshkosh-Neenah, WI	32.5%
Spartanburg, SC	32.4%
Sheboygan, WI	32.4%

Source: US Department of Labor, Bureau of Labor Statistics, Occupational Employment Statistics (OES) Survey, 2010. Available online at http://www.bls.gov/oes/. Analysis by Kevin Stolarick.

once-great industrial centers of Cleveland, Detroit, and Pittsburgh, just one in five workers belongs to the Working Class today.

The original edition of this book covered the Working Class overall. Although roughly one in five US workers (20.5 percent) are members of the Working Class, production workers compose a much smaller share—just slightly more than one in twenty (6.0 percent).

Not surprisingly, metros with high concentrations of production workers have a large Working Class in general. They tend to be smaller regions, mainly in the old South and the Midwest. There is one metro where production workers make up 30 percent of the workforce and another where they number more than 25 percent (see Figure 11.7 and Table 11.7). In no other metro do production workers make up more than one in five members of the entire workforce.

Figure 11.7   Production Workers by Metro, 2010

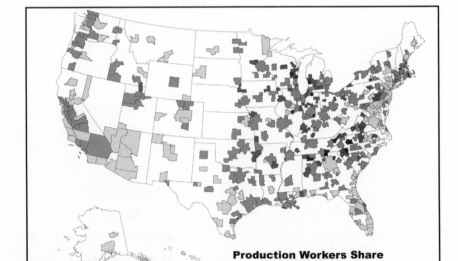

Source: US Department of Labor, Bureau of Labor Statistics, Occupational Employment Statistics (OES) Survey, 2010. Available online at http://www.bls.gov/oes/. Analysis by Charlotta Mellander. Map by Zara Matheson.

Table 11.7   Top Twenty Metros for Production Workers, 2010

Rank	Region	Production Occupation Share
1	Elkhart-Goshen, IN	30.3%
2	Dalton, GA	25.8%
3	Hickory-Lenoir-Morganton, NC	19.5%
4	Morristown, TN	18.3%
5	Columbus, IN	18.3%
6	Sheboygan, WI	17.6%
7	Holland-Grand Haven, MI	17.4%
8	Oshkosh-Neenah, WI	16.5%
9	Spartanburg, SC	16.3%
10	Decatur, AL	16.3%
11	Cleveland, TN	16.2%
12	Decatur, IL	15.9%
13	Gainesville, GA	15.1%
14	Racine, WI	15.0%
15	Fort Smith, AR-OK	14.8%
16	Anderson, SC	14.8%
17	Battle Creek, MI	14.8%
18	Logan, UT-ID	14.5%
19	Wausau, WI	14.3%
20	Florence-Muscle Shoals, AL	13.9%

Source: US Department of Labor, Bureau of Labor Statistics, Occupational Employment Statistics (OES) Survey, 2010. Available online at http://www.bls.gov/oes/. Analysis by Charlotta Mellander.

It is even more striking how far industrial work and production workers have fallen in the larger blue-collar metros that were once the bastions of America's manufacturing might. Production workers make up roughly 10 percent of the workforces in Milwaukee and Youngstown. They account for just 8 or 9 percent of the workforce in the industrial-era stalwarts of Toledo, Akron, and Cleveland, and Scranton, Pennsylvania. That's about the same level as in Napa, California—in fact, production workers make up a smaller share of Gary, Indiana's workforce than they do in that sunny center of wine and tourism. The share of production workers is lower still in Dayton, Detroit, Allentown, Syracuse, Rochester

and Buffalo—all of which have a smaller share of production workers than Augusta, Georgia, or Asheville, North Carolina. In my
former hometown of Pittsburgh, the heart and soul of America's
iron and steel industry, production workers make up just 5.7 percent of the workforce, about the same as in Eugene, Oregon;
Ann Arbor, and Charleston, South Carolina!

It's no wonder America's industrial workers feel like they've
been shunted aside—they have. A decade into the new millennium
and three years into the worst economic crisis since the Great Depression, both America's smokestack industries and the workers
who stoked them are increasingly on the margins.

Service Class Centers

In numbers, the Service Class is the largest class of all, employing
more than 45 percent of American workers. Back in 1999, when I
was first writing this book, Las Vegas was the country's preeminent
Service Class center, with nearly 60 percent of its workforce in Service Class occupations. The Service Class made up roughly one-
half or more of the workforce in some fifty metros, including West
Palm Beach, Orlando, Miami, Naples, Fort Myers, Daytona Beach,
Panama City, and Sarasota, Florida; Myrtle Beach, South Carolina;
and the towns on Cape Cod, Massachusetts. Few of them boasted
any significant concentrations of the Creative Class, save for visitors
on vacation. The Service Class also dominated employment in a
number of metros that were a far cry from tourist meccas, like
Shreveport, Louisiana; Rapid City and Sioux Falls, South Dakota;
Bismarck and Grand Forks, North Dakota; Pittsfield, Massachusetts;
Utica, New York; Chico, California; and Victoria, Laredo, Killeen,
and Lubbock, Texas. The economic and social future of these non-
tourist destinations, I wrote then, was troubling to contemplate.

Figure 11.8   The Service Class by Metro, 2010

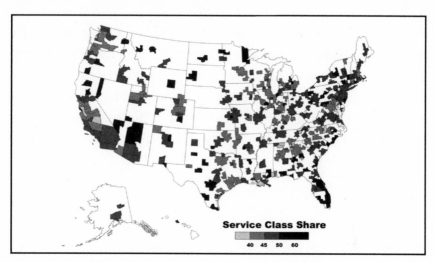

Source: US Department of Labor, Bureau of Labor Statistics, Occupational Employment Statistics (OES) Survey, 2010. Available online at http://www.bls.gov/oes/. Analysis by Kevin Stolarick. Map by Zara Matheson.

Table 11.8   Top Twenty Service Class Metros, 2010

Metro	Service Class Share
Myrtle Beach-Conway-North Myrtle Beach, SC	64.9%
Ocean City, NJ	62.7%
Atlantic City, NJ	62.0%
Punta Gorda, FL	60.9%
Naples-Marco Island, FL	59.3%
Las Vegas-Paradise, NV	59.1%
Laredo, TX	58.3%
Brownsville-Harlingen, TX	57.9%
Cape Coral-Fort Myers, FL	57.3%
Deltona-Daytona Beach-Ormond Beach, FL	57.2%
Ocala, FL	57.1%
Missoula, MT	56.3%
Barnstable Town, MA	56.1%
Dover, DE	55.9%
Panama City-Lynn Haven, FL	55.7%
Pittsfield, MA	55.7%
McAllen-Edinburg-Pharr, TX	55.6%
Sebastian-Vero Beach, FL	55.3%
Norwich-New London, CT	55.0%
Jacksonville, NC	54.8%

Source: US Department of Labor, Bureau of Labor Statistics, Occupational Employment Statistics (OES) Survey, 2010. Available online at http://www.bls.gov/oes/. Analysis by Kevin Stolarick.

Figure 11.8 charts the Service Class across US metros. Tourist destinations Myrtle Beach, Ocean City, Atlantic City, Punta Gorda and Naples, Florida, and Las Vegas, continue to top the list. But non-tourist destinations like Laredo, Brownsville, and McAllen, Texas, are present as well (see Table 11.6). These places continue to have among the least resilient and most vulnerable economies of anywhere.

The Role of Skills

One of the more interesting developments to occur since the original edition of this book appeared is our improved ability to zero in more precisely on the underlying skills that inform Creative Class and other types of work, allowing us to make finer distinctions and better understand the underlying nature of work. This was made possible by the incredible Occupational Information Network (or O*NET)[4] database developed by the Bureau of Labor Statistics, which provides richly detailed information on the mix and level of skills required for more than 800 occupations. My colleagues and I, as well as several other research groups, have used these data to identify the fundamental skills underlying Creative Class and other types of work, to chart the economic returns to these core skills, and ultimately to map their distribution across the US economic landscape.

There are three core types of skills. The first is one we are all familiar with—basic physical skill of the sort associated with traditional work. Its attributes include good hand-to-eye coordination, strength, and dexterity.

The other two types of skills are associated with Creative Class work. The second basic skill type—cognitive skill—is reasonably well understood. It involves the ability to acquire knowledge, process information, and solve problems. This basic intellectual and analytical horsepower has been identified as the core skill under-pinning the knowledge economy by writers from Peter Drucker and Daniel Bell to Robert Reich and Charles Murray.[5]

However, there is a third type of skill set that is less well under-stood, or even talked about, but even more critical. The O*NET system defines its core attributes as the "capacities used to work with people to achieve goals." My colleagues and I dubbed it social skill, or, to put it a bit more accurately, "social intelligence." Its salient characteristics are discernment, communications abilities, leadership, awareness, and the like. These are more than just people skills. Bartending, retail clerking, and waiting tables may require sociability and pleasantness, but not social intelligence. Highly de-veloped social skills include the capacity to bring the right people together on a project, persuasion, social perceptiveness, the ability to help develop other people, and a developed sense of empathy. These are the leadership skills that are needed to innovate, mobilize resources, build effective organizations, and launch new firms. So-cial skill and analytical skill are highly complementary—and indeed, the very highest paying jobs, and the most robust economies, usually require exceptional skills in both realms.

Even a cursory glance at the relationship between these skills and income confirms how far the US economy has evolved beyond the industrial age and toward the Creative Economy. Analytic and so-cial skills add greatly to wages and salaries, according to our analy-sis. Occupations that rank in the top quartile of analytic skill pay $25,600 more than those in the lowest quartile, on average; those that rank in the top quartile of social skill pay $34,600 more than those in the lowest 25 percent. Occupations in the top quartile of physical skill, on the other hand, pay $13,600 *less* than those that demand the least physical skill. That's not to say that an individual construction worker will make less as he or she becomes more skilled—the opposite is true. But by choosing an occupation in which physical skill is predominant, workers are, by and large, isolating themselves from the more dynamic and higher-paying parts of the economy. Higher levels of analytical and social skill are associated with higher wages, and not just for Creative Class work but for Working and Service Class jobs as well.

What's even more telling is the way that skills are distributed geographically. This has been probed in a series of fascinating studies by the University of Toronto economists William Strange, Marigee Bacolod, and Bernardo Blum; the economic geographer Allen Scott of UCLA; and my own team.[6] Jobs requiring physical skill cluster in smaller and medium-sized metro areas—industrial centers where land for factories is relatively inexpensive. Jobs featuring analytic skills are sparse in these places and heavily concentrated in the largest metro areas, indicating rising benefits from having larger numbers of well-educated, highly intelligent people working close together. And jobs requiring the highest level of social skill are the *most* concentrated in the very largest metro areas. In fact, these skills seem to grow ever-more essential as local economies grow larger and more complex. What this research has helped us understand is that it is not just the accumulation of knowledge or cognitive ability that drives the growth of cities, but the additional clustering of social-intelligence skill. This clustering of social-intelligence skill increases the quality of the combinations and recombinations that drive innovation and economic growth. In this sense, cities are like brains: their growth and development require the development of an increasingly dense web of synaptic connections.

We've known for a while that the cities and metros that attract the most highly educated populations prosper. But brainpower alone only tells part of the story. Even more key is being able to marshal and focus all that raw intelligence, the ability to inspire disparate groups of people to focus on a common goal, to persuade venture capitalists to underwrite a new idea or product and the public to buy shares in your company.

Think of it as the Steve Jobs side of cities. Jobs was certainly smart, though being a college dropout, he wouldn't have been captured by the standard economists' measure of human capital. But his analytical intelligence wasn't what made him who he was. Most of all, he was a connector and resource mobilizer, the quintessential attributes of an entrepreneur. When he toured Xerox's famous PARC laboratory, he saw all the various components of a personal computer waiting there to be put together. He enlisted Steve Wozniak and others to help him with the task and attracted venture capital to pay for it. What he possessed and what cities enable, in addition to cognitive skills, are the critical social or relational skills required for true innovation and creative destruction.

As many benefits as the Creative Class brings to cities, metros, and regions, they're not equally shared. The correlation between Creative Class and Working Class metros was negative and significant in 2002, and it has increased today, indicating that the different classes were and are continuing to sort themselves into distinct regional centers.[7] These patterns cut across the lines of race, nationality, and sexual orientation. Creative Class people of varied backgrounds are increasingly clustering in the same kinds of metros. More African American members of the Creative Class may head for Washington DC and Atlanta, and gay members may favor San Francisco, but all are attracted to regions with considerable concentrations of their own class.

The new geography of class might be giving rise to a new form of segregation—different from racial segregation or the old schism between central city and suburb, and perhaps even more threatening to national unity. Over the past decade and especially since the economic meltdown of 2008, this trend has only become more pronounced.

CHAPTER 12

The 3T's of Economic Development

The key to understanding the new economic geography of creativity and its positive effects on economic outcomes is what I call the 3T's of economic development: technology, talent, and tolerance. Each is a necessary but by itself insufficient condition for prosperity; for real innovation and sustained economic growth a place must offer all three. The 3T's explain why some cities fail to grow, despite their deep reservoirs of technology and world-class universities: they have not been sufficiently tolerant and open to attract and retain top creative talent. The interdependence of the 3T's also explains why others do not make the grade, even though they are lifestyle meccas: they lack the required technology base. The most successful places put all 3T's together. Together, these 3T's comprise my Creativity Index, an updated version of which I present at the end of this chapter. The appendix provides updated data for all 3T's and the Creativity Index for all US metros.

Technology

The first and also the least controversial of the T's is technology. Economists agree that technology is key to growth. First Karl Marx and then Joseph Schumpeter recognized that advances in technology are what enable capitalism to constantly revolutionize itself. "Capitalism not only never is but never can be stationary," Schumpeter wrote in 1942. MIT's Robert Solow won a Nobel Prize for his work that isolated technology as the driving force of growth. From new inventions like software, robotics, and biotechnology to improvements in manufacturing systems and processes, technology makes economies and societies more efficient and productive.[1]

Figure 12.1 shows how US metros stack up on the updated Technology Index. The index is a composite of the Milken Institute's Tech-Pole Index, a measure of high-tech industry, plus two measures of regional innovation, patents per capita and average annual patent growth.

Silicon Valley, home to leading-edge technology companies from Intel, Apple, and Cisco to Google and Facebook, and the world's largest center for venture capital, has been widely acknowledged as the nation's dominant center for high-tech innovation and entrepreneurship since the 1970s. But on the 2010 version of the Technology Index, its hegemony has been supplanted by greater Seattle—the home of Microsoft, Amazon, and many other high-tech powerhouses. San Jose takes second, followed by the greater San Francisco metro, which has gained ground as large numbers of key high-tech talent and firms have come to prefer more urban locations (a subject I will return to in greater detail in Chapter 15). Portland, Oregon, is fourth, and Austin, is fifth, followed by Raleigh, San Diego, and then Durham, at the other end of the Research Triangle from Raleigh. Boston and Boulder

Figure 12.1 The Technology Index by Metro, 2010

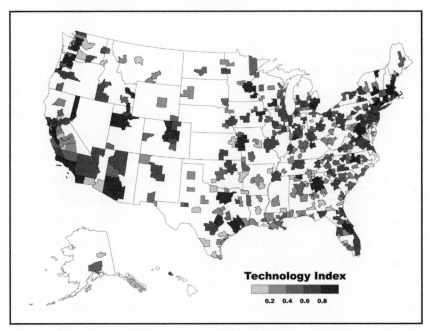

Source: Analysis by Kevin Stolarick. Map by Zara Matheson. See the appendix for full detail on sources.

round out the top ten. Completing out the top twenty are Burlington, Tucson, Provo, Corvallis, Huntsville, Poughkeepsie (home to IBM), Minneapolis–St. Paul, Madison, Oxnard–Thousand Oaks, and Manchester, New Hampshire (near Boston's Route 128).

In the original edition of this book, I noted the close correlations between the Creative Class and our technology indicators, and conversely the negative associations between high-tech and the Working Class. The same basic pattern continues a decade later, only it is even more accentuated. The Creative Class makes up more than 35 percent of the workforce in fourteen of the top twenty Technology Index metros, and exceeds 40 percent in six of them. The Creative Class remains positively correlated with all of the various measures of high-tech industry and innovation, whereas the correlations with Working Class share are negative across the board.[2]

The changing geography of US innovation can be seen in Figure 12.2, which is constructed from data charting trends in innovation (based on patents) for the top 10 US metros over roughly the past three decades, 1976 to 2009.[3] The level of innovation has fallen off considerably in older industrial regions like Pittsburgh and Detroit and in Sun Belt regions like Dallas and Houston. During the same period, innovation increased substantially in high-tech regions like Silicon Valley, San Francisco, and Seattle, and also in Los Angeles. Two other large regions—New York and Chicago—saw dramatic growth in the late 1990s, followed by precipitous drops in the 2000s that erased those gains. Overall, American innovation has become more geographically concentrated and spikier.

Talent

The second T is talent. Economists agree that skilled, ambitious, educated, and entrepreneurial people—whom they refer to as human capital—are a central force in economic progress. Whereas my original measure of talent combined the Creative Class and the conventional measure of human capital, essentially the number of college graduates, our updated index counts only the Creative Class. In the original edition of this book, I found a close association between Creative Class share, the Talent Index, and levels of high-tech companies and of innovations. The same is true today.

Tolerance

Tolerance is the third T. Economists have long recognized that diversity is important to economic performance, but they have usually

Table 12.1   Top Twenty Metros on the Technology Index, 2010

Metro		Technology Index Score
1	Seattle-Tacoma-Bellevue, WA	.996
2	San Jose-Sunnyvale-Santa Clara, CA	.983
3	San Francisco-Oakland-Fremont, CA	.976
4	Portland-Vancouver-Beaverton, OR	.956
5	Austin-Round Rock, TX	.955
6	Raleigh-Cary, NC	.952
7	San Diego-Carlsbad-San Marcos, CA	.945
8	Durham, NC	.940
9	Boston-Cambridge-Quincy, MA-NH	.933
10	Boulder, CO	.920
11	Burlington-South Burlington, VT	.918
12	Tucson, AZ	.912
13	Provo-Orem, UT	.909
14	Corvallis, OR	.898
15	Huntsville, AL	.894
16	Poughkeepsie-Newburgh-Middletown, NY	.893
17	Minneapolis-St. Paul-Bloomington, MN-WI	.891
18	Madison, WI	.891
19	Oxnard-Thousand Oaks-Ventura, CA	.886
20	Manchester-Nashua, NH	.885

Source: Analysis by Kevin Stolarick. See the appendix for full detail on sources.

meant the diversity of firms or industries. The economist John Quigley, for instance, argues that regional economies benefit from the location of a diverse set of firms and industries.[4] Jane Jacobs was among the first to highlight the role of diversity of both firms and people in powering innovation and city growth.[5] Tolerance and openness to diversity is part and parcel of the broad cultural shift toward post-materialist values identified by Ronald Inglehart.[6]

New ideas are generated most efficiently in places where different cognitive styles are tolerated—and different cognitive styles are linked to demographic diversity, as University of Michigan economist Scott Page has shown.[7] Tolerance—or, broadly speaking, openness to diversity—provides an additional source of economic

Figure 12.2 The Changing Geography of Innovation, 1976–2009

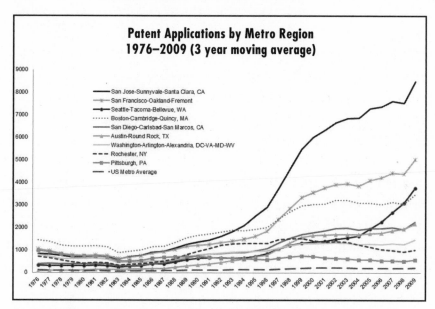

Source: US Patent and Trademark Office, various years. Data processed by Debbie Strumsky. Additional analysis and graph by Kevin Stolarick.

advantage that works alongside technology and talent. The places that are most open to new ideas and that attract talented and creative people from across the globe broaden both their technology and talent capabilities, gaining a substantial economic edge.

Most economists tend to see technology and talent as fixed stocks, like raw materials or natural resources, but the reality is that they are flows. Unlike seams of coal or natural harbors, talented people are not forever wedded to one place; they are mobile factors—they can and do move around. The fact that some places are better than others at generating, attracting, and holding onto talent has everything to do with how open, diverse, and tolerant they are. Our work finds a strong correlation between, on the one hand, places that are welcoming to immigrants, artists, gays, bohemians, and socioeconomic and racial integration, and, on the other, places that experience high-quality economic growth. Economists speak of the

importance of industries having low entry barriers, so that new
firms can easily enter and keep the industry vital. Similarly, I think
it's important for a place to have low entry barriers for people—
that is, to be a place where newcomers are accepted quickly into
all sorts of social and economic arrangements. Such places gain a
creativity advantage. All else being equal, they are likely to attract
and retain the sorts of people who power innovation and growth
(see Figure 12.3 and Table 12.2).

Openness to entrepreneurial individuals from around the globe
is a fabled hallmark of the United States. Immigrants have been
overrepresented among America's leading entrepreneurs since the
days of the steel magnate Andrew Carnegie. The Hungarian Jew
Andy Grove founded Intel in the 1960s; over the past two decades,
immigrants have been among the principals of more than half of

Figure 12.3   The Foreign-Born Index by Metro, 2010

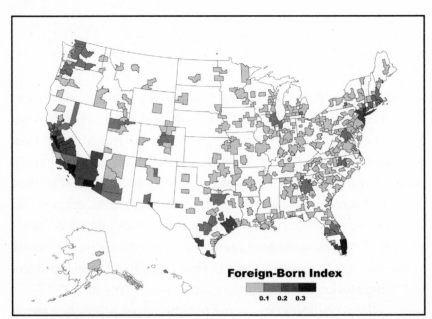

Source: US Census Bureau, American Community Survey, 2005–09. Analysis by Kevin
Stolarick. Map by Zara Matheson.

Table 12.2 Top Twenty Metros on the Foreign-Born Index, 2010

Rank	Metro	Foreign-Born Index Score
1	Miami-Fort Lauderdale-Miami Beach, FL	.365
2	San Jose-Sunnyvale-Santa Clara, CA	.356
3	Los Angeles-Long Beach-Santa Ana, CA	.342
4	El Centro, CA	.315
5	Salinas, CA	.296
6	San Francisco-Oakland-Fremont, CA	.291
7	McAllen-Edinburg-Pharr, TX	.286
8	Laredo, TX	.279
9	New York-Newark-Edison, NY-NJ-PA	.276
10	El Paso, TX	.266
11	Yuma, AZ	.250
12	Merced, CA	.247
13	Brownsville-Harlingen, TX	.244
14	Stockton, CA	.231
15	Naples-Marco Island, FL	.229
16	San Diego-Carlsbad-San Marcos, CA	.227
17	Visalia-Porterville, CA	.226
18	Santa Barbara-Santa Maria-Goleta, CA	.222
19	Oxnard-Thousand Oaks-Ventura, CA	.220
20	Napa, CA	.215

Source: US Census Bureau, American Community Survey, 2005–09. Analysis by Kevin Stolarick.

all Silicon Valley start-ups—like Google's Sergey Brin, who hails from Russia; Hotmail's Sabeer Bhatia, who grew up in Bangalore; Yahoo's Taiwan-born Jerry Yang; and eBay's Pierre Omidyar, who was born in Paris, France. Omidyar's highly talented parents, a surgeon and a linguistics professor, had immigrated to Paris from Iran; they moved on to the United States when Omidyar was six. Even though immigrants make up just 12 percent of the US population, they generate more than 25 percent of its global patents and account for nearly one-half (47 percent) of its science and engineering workers with PhDs.

With the economic crisis, some pundits and a growing share of Americans have come to believe that legal and illegal immigrants alike are taking jobs away from Americans and pushing down wages. In recent years, Arizona, Alabama, and several other states have instituted draconian measures to restrict immigration. But in fact there are more high-skill immigrants in the United States than low-skill ones, according to a June 2011 Brookings Institution report.[8] "In 1980, just 19 percent of immigrants aged 25 to 64 held a bachelor's degree, and nearly 40 percent had not completed high school," the report finds. "By 2010, 30 percent of working-age immigrants had at least a college degree and 28 percent lacked a high school diploma." Compared with their US-born counterparts, the report continues, "low-skilled immigrants have higher rates of employment and lower rates of household poverty." In more than four in ten of the nation's largest 100 metro areas, such as Washington, DC, and San Francisco, college educated immigrants outnumber those that did not complete high school by at least 25 percent.

Even more than its natural resources, native ingenuity, or other factors, what stood at the heart and soul of US prosperity historically is its openness to hardworking, ambitious, and talented immigrants of all stripes. And that includes low-skill immigrants. Careful studies by economist Giovanni Peri of the University of California at Davis have found that immigrants add rather than detract from American prosperity for the simple reason that "the skill composition of immigrants is complementary to that of natives." At the low-skill end of the spectrum, immigrants specialize in "manual intensive tasks such as cooking, driving, and building" that their American counterparts tend not to do, specializing instead in "in language-intensive tasks such as dispatching, supervising and coordinating." At the high-skill end of the spectrum, immigrants bring scientific, technical, and entrepreneurial skills that are in short supply and vital for America's innovative and entrepreneurial engine. A "more multicultural urban environment," Peri concludes, "makes U.S.-born citizens more productive."[9]

The Gay Index

When I first started looking at the patterns of economic development, I never imagined I would find connections between gay demography and high-tech industry. Then, as I recounted in the introduction to the first edition of this book, I met Gary Gates, who, along with economists Dan Black, Seth Sanders, and Lowell Taylor, had created a new measure that he called the Gay Index.[10] Gates has since become the world's leading authority on gay and lesbian demographic patterns; he is co-author of *The Gay and Lesbian Atlas* and a researcher at UCLA's Williams Institute.

Building upon a report Gates and I wrote for the Brookings Institution, the original edition of this book noted that the Gay Index[11] was closely associated with regional clusterings and concentrations of high-tech industry, as well as with its growth.[12] Four of the regions that ranked in the top ten for high-technology growth from 1990 to 1998 also ranked in the top ten on the Gay Index in both 1990 and 2000.[13] In addition, we found that the correlation between the Gay Index (measured in 1990) and the High-Tech Index (calculated for each year from 1990–2000) increased over time, suggesting that the benefits of openness to gays actually compounds.

Some of our critics argued that our results might be biased by the unique situation of San Francisco, which ranked highly (number 1, in fact) on both measures at the time. To check for this, we removed San Francisco from the analysis. The findings remained virtually the same. In fact, the correlation between the Gay Index and high-tech industry was strengthened. Overall, twelve of the top twenty Gay Index regions continued to rank among the top twenty high-tech regions, and ten of the top twenty Gay Index regions numbered among the top twenty centers for the Creative Class. The Gay Index was positively associated with the Creative Class in both periods; but it was negatively associated with the Working Class.[14] Figure 12.4 and Table 12.3 show the updated Gay-Lesbian Index for US metros.

It's amazing how consistently people have misconstrued what Gates and I have to say about the connection between gays and economic growth. Many seem to think we believe the connection is linear. But not once have either of us ever said that gays literally *cause* high-tech growth. Rather, we see a strong and vibrant gay community as a solid *leading indicator* of a place that is open to many different kinds of people. If gays feel comfortable in a place, then immigrants and ethnic minorities probably will, too, not to mention eggheads, eccentrics, and all the other non-white-bread types who are the sources of new ideas. As Bill Bishop put it, "Where gay households abound, geeks follow."[15]

Ronald Inglehart, who has studied the relationship between culture and economic growth for some four decades, has noted that

Figure 12.4   The Gay/Lesbian Index by Metro, 2009

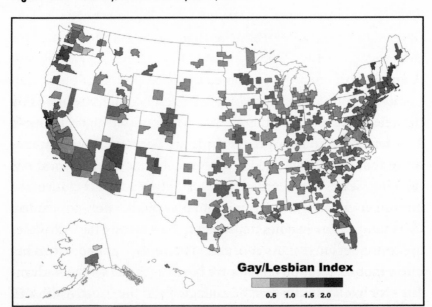

Source: US Census Bureau, American Community Survey, 2005–09. Analysis by Kevin Stolarick. Map by Zara Metheson.

the lack of societal acceptance of gays is the most significant remaining bastion of intolerance and discrimination around the world. Accordingly, places that accept gays are also likely to be accepting of all different types of people. Gates himself always said that gays can perhaps best be thought of as the veritable "canaries" of our high-tech, Creative Class centers.

My close friend Terry Nichols Clark, a sociologist at the University of Chicago, offered a more reasoned and nuanced critique of our findings on gays and high-tech location.[16] Using detailed information from thousands of US counties, Clark found that "gay relations with jobs appear strong in large metro areas, but fall in smaller metro areas." Gates and I have no quarrel with Clark's county-level results. It's in fact exactly why we designed our research the way we did. Metro areas are natural economic units, designated based on the journey to work. People can easily live in one county and commute to another. The metro, not the county, is the more appropiate unit from which to view the role of tolerance and diversity.

The Bohemian Factor

A number of studies have pointed to the role of amenities in economic growth. An early one by Paul Gottlieb found a relationship between the presence of amenities and high-tech companies in New Jersey.[17] Another by the economists Dora Costa and Matthew Kahn found that high-income power couples preferred locations with high levels of amenities.[18] In a detailed study of the rise of the consumer city, Edward Glaeser and his collaborators concluded: "The future of most cities depends on their being desirable places for consumers to live. As consumers become richer and firms become mobile, location choices are based as much on their advantages for workers as on their advantages for firms."[19] An April 2000

story in the *Economist,* "The Geography of Cool," pointed out that
cities that had long been centers of culture and fashion, from New
York to Berlin, had also emerged as leading destinations for talented
people and centers of certain new technology-intensive industries.[20]
All this was highly suggestive, but I wanted a more direct measure
for a place's artistic and creative climate.

One day Stolarick and I were sitting at my kitchen table in Pittsburgh, discussing our research on tolerance and economic growth,
when I blurted out a question: Could we actually chart the locations
where working artists, writers, designers, musicians, actors, and
the like cluster? The Bohemian Index that we created, as I noted
back in 2002, turned out to be quite strongly associated with both

Table 12.3 Top Twenty Metros on the Gay/Lesbian Index, 2009

Rank	Metro	Gay/Lesbian Index
1	San Francisco-Oakland-Fremont, CA	2.22
2	Burlington-South Burlington, VT	1.82
3	Barnstable Town, MA	1.80
4	Portland-South Portland, ME	1.78
5	Ithaca, NY	1.74
6	Santa Rosa-Petaluma, CA	1.68
7	Portland-Vancouver-Beaverton, OR-WA	1.63
8	Santa Fe, NM	1.63
9	Flagstaff, AZ	1.58
10	Santa Cruz-Watsonville, CA	1.55
11	Springfield, MA	1.50
12	Seattle-Tacoma-Bellevue, WA	1.50
13	Boston-Cambridge-Quincy, MA-NH	1.48
14	Billings, MT	1.47
15	Greeley, CO	1.47
16	Boulder, CO	1.46
17	Austin-Round Rock, TX	1.45
18	Asheville, NC	1.45
19	Napa, CA	1.45
20	San Diego-Carlsbad-San Marcos, CA	1.41

Source: US Census Bureau, American Community Survey, 2005–09. Analysis by Kevin
Stolarick.

high-technology and economic growth.[21] Five of the top ten and twelve of the top twenty Bohemian Index regions numbered among the nation's top twenty high-technology regions. Eleven of the top twenty Bohemian Index regions ranked among the top twenty most-innovative regions.[22] A region's 1990 Bohemian Index value predicted both its high-tech industry concentration and its employment and population growth between 1990 and 2000.

Figure 12.5 updates the Bohemian Index for 2009. Los Angeles takes the top spot, followed by New York, San Francisco, and Santa Fe. The list also includes Nashville, Seattle, and Portland, Oregon; Jersey City across the Hudson River from Manhattan; college towns like Boulder, Austin, Santa Cruz, and Iowa City; and somewhat less likely places like Stamford and Danbury, Connecticut; Pittsfield, Massachusetts; and Orange County, California (see Table 12.4).

My Colbert Controversy

A study I conducted with Charlotta Mellander in 2007, utilizing both the Gay Index and the Bohemian Index, earned me a berth on a top-rated Comedy Central show. I wrote about it in *Who's Your City?* "A disturbing new study has found a solution to the housing slump: Live next to gay people," Steven Colbert declared in his lead-in to our interview. "The study found that artistic, bohemian, and gay populations increase housing values in the neighborhoods and communities they inhabit," he continued. "I guess people these days want a house with a view of some goateed beatnik playing his bongos while he smokes a clove cigarette and chisels a sculpture of k.d. lang." It might have been good fodder for late-night TV, but the evidence didn't lie. The Gay Index and the Bohemian Index were amazing, indeed, shockingly powerful predictors of regional housing prices.[23]

There is no single national real estate market, and there are many reasons some places are more expensive than others. One key factor is income—where people have more money, they can buy more expensive housing. Housing prices tend to be higher in locations with higher levels of high-tech industry, as in Silicon Valley. Amenities and attractions—like scenic mountains or nearby beaches—also drive housing prices higher, a correlation pinpointed in 1982 by the economist Jennifer Roback, who found that amenities carried as much weight in determining housing prices as land costs and wages.[24] Whether it's a strip of beach or a chunk of Manhattan, prices will increase in accord with the basic law of supply and demand.

Edward Glaeser and his colleagues found that housing prices tend to rise faster than wages in cities. To explain this, they devised

Figure 12.5   The Bohemian Index by Metro, 2009

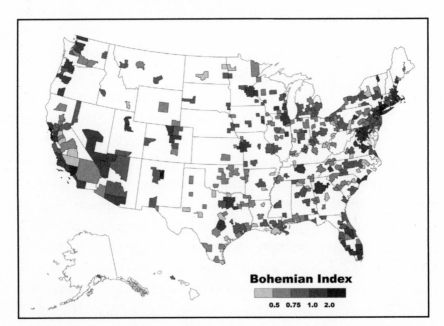

Source: US Census Bureau, American Community Survey, 2005–09. Analysis by Kevin Stolarick. Map by Zara Matheson.

a formula that assumes that urban housing demands a premium for both the improved productivity and the higher levels of amenities that are found in cities.[25] But my research was telling me that neither urban efficiencies nor location-specific amenities (beautiful beaches, shopping, bike trails) told the whole story.

"Want to know where a great place to invest in real estate will be five or ten years from now?" a 2007 *BusinessWeek* article asked. "Look at where artists are living now."[26] So we did. It really wasn't such a leap—urbanists have long recognized that gentrification (and the higher housing prices that follow) is set in motion by artists, creatives, and gays. Yet artistic and gay populations are relatively small, and evidence of their relation to housing prices is

Table 12.4   The Top Twenty Metros on the Bohemian Index, 2009

Rank	Metro	Bohemian Index
1	Los Angeles-Long Beach, CA	2.62
2	New York, NY	2.54
3	San Francisco, CA	2.46
4	Santa Fe, NM	2.45
5	Stamford-Norwalk, CT	2.11
6	Danbury, CT	1.78
7	Boulder-Longmont, CO	1.72
8	Jersey City, NJ	1.66
9	Santa Cruz-Watsonville, CA	1.57
10	Nashville, TN	1.51
11	Medford-Ashland, OR	1.47
12	Austin-San Marcos, TX	1.44
13	Seattle-Bellevue-Everett, WA	1.44
14	Iowa City, IA	1.41
15	Pittsfield, MA	1.37
16	Portland-Vancouver, OR, WA	1.36
17	Ventura, CA	1.36
18	Orange County, CA	1.35
19	Santa Barbara-Santa Maria-Lompoc, CA	1.35
20	Santa Rosa, CA	1.30

Source: US Census Bureau, American Community Survey, 2005–09. Analysis by Kevin Stolarick.

limited. As of 2000, there were approximately 1.3 million bohemians in the United States and 8.8 million self-identified gay and lesbian people, totaling roughly 4 percent of the country's adult population. Can groups this small really be so highly associated with housing prices?

Mellander and I looked closely at the associations between high-tech industry, human capital, high-paid workers and occupations, wages and incomes, and artist, bohemian, and gay populations across more than 300 US metropolitan regions. We used statistical techniques to isolate the correlations between each of these factors on housing values as well. The results were striking. We found that two factors combine to shape housing values. The first is pretty obvious: income—the wealthier the residents, the pricier the housing. But the correlation was to wealth, not salaries. Wages alone, in the absence of capital gains and other earnings, had little relation to housing values. For that matter, neither did levels of education, human capital, the presence of a Creative Class, or the mix of occupations.

The second and much larger factor is reflected by the combined Bohemian-Gay Index, which merges the concentration of artists, musicians, and designers with the concentration of gays and lesbians in a region. Regardless of which variables we applied, what version of the model we used, or which regions we looked at, the concentration of bohemians and gays consistently had a substantial correlation with housing values, even after controlling for income, human capital, jobs, and city size.[27]

Many people believe that bohemians and gays do not cause growth but are merely drawn to certain types of places. By using path models—advanced statistical tools that relate independent, intermediary, and dependent variables—we were able to isolate the relationships between the bohemian and gay populations and other factors on housing values, and on each other. Our initial findings were on target. The presence of bohemians and gays had a direct relation to housing values and also to income levels. In other words, the presence of these groups was not only related to higher housing values, but to greater regional wealth as well.

Why would this be? For two reasons, each of which sheds further light on the role of diversity, openness, and tolerance in regional growth and development. Artists and bohemians not only produce amenities but are attracted to places that have them. As selective buyers with eyes for amenities, authenticity, and aesthetics, they tend to concentrate in places where those things abound. The second reason is even more important: the openness that gay and bohemian populations not only reflect but signal. Places with large bohemian and gay populations possess low barriers to entry, allowing them to attract talent and human capital across racial, ethnic, and other lines. Artistic and gay populations also cluster in communities that value open-mindedness and self-expression. And, their status as historically marginalized groups means that artistic and gay populations tend to be highly self-reliant and receptive to newcomers. They've had to build networks from scratch, mobilize resources independently, and create their own organizations and firms.

For all of these reasons, regions in which artists and gays have migrated and settled are more likely than others to provide an environment that is more open to innovation, entrepreneurship, and new firm formation. It's not that gays and bohemians drive up housing simply by paying more (just as they do not directly stimulate the economy); their effect on housing prices, regional innovation, and prosperity is less direct. Bohemian and gay residents drive up housing values for the same reason they make areas more productive and innovative: they create a feedback loop. Their presence signals that a location has the very characteristics that drive innovation and growth, driving further innovation and growth.

The Tolerance Index

In the original edition of this book we used a combined measure of diversity and tolerance that we called the Composite Diversity Index (or CDI).[28] The CDI added together three diversity measures—the Gay Index, the Melting Pot Index (a measure of the concentration of immigrants), and the Bohemian Index. The CDI provided powerful support for the basic notion that diversity and creativity work together to power innovation and economic growth. Five of the top ten regions on the CDI were also top-ten high-tech regions: San Francisco, Boston, Seattle, Los Angeles, and Washington, DC. (see Table 12.5). The statistical correlation between the High-Tech Index and the CDI rankings was quite high,[29] and even when we factored in the percentage of college graduates in the region, population, and measures of culture, recreation, and climate, the CDI had a significant relationship to high-tech growth between 1990 and 1998.

For the updated paperback edition of this book in 2004, Stolarick and I revised the CDI, creating a new measure we called the Tolerance Index. In addition to the three key measures—the Gay Index, Bohemian Index, and Foreign-Born Index, we added a fourth new measure of the level of racial integration versus separation in a metro area, which we dubbed the Integration Index (the appendix provides a full description of its methodology). We did this because, as I've already had occasion to mention, unlike most other kinds of diversity, racial diversity is not associated with high-tech growth, innovation, and economic development. In fact my statistical research consistently found a negative correlation between concentrations of high-tech firms and the percentage of the nonwhite population, a particularly disturbing finding in light of the positive role that other dimensions of diversity play. The Creative Economy apparently does little to ameliorate the traditional divide between the white and nonwhite segments of the population. It might even make it worse.

Seattle topped the list on our new Tolerance Index in 2004, followed by Portland, Oregon; Boston, Minneapolis, and Providence. San Francisco, Austin, Denver, Orlando, and Los Angeles rounded out the top ten.

For this edition, we have revised the Tolerance Index slightly, removing the Bohemian Index from it. We did so because we believe that the Bohemian Index is already captured in our measure of the Creative Class, which includes the same arts and culture-related occupations that comprise the Bohemian Index. The 2010 Tolerance Index includes three key variables—the share of immigrants or foreign-born residents, the Gay Index, and the Integration Index (see Figure 12.6).

Figure 12.6   The Tolerance Index by Metro, 2010

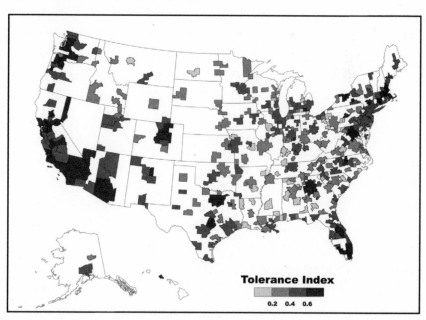

Source: Analysis by Kevin Stolarick. Map by Zara Matheson. See the appendix for full detail on sources.

San Diego is the top-ranked metro on the updated Tolerance Index, followed by Napa, Santa Rosa, Santa Cruz, and Santa Fe (see Table 12.5). Ithaca, Oxnard-Thousand Oaks, Cape Coral, Florida; Boulder, and Ann Arbor round out the top ten. Miami, Las Vegas, Portland, San Francisco, and Boston all rank in the top twenty. Seattle, Phoenix, Los Angeles, Orlando, and greater Washington, DC, all make the top thirty.

The relationship between tolerance and economic growth has been confirmed by several independent studies. Meric Gertler and Tara Vinodrai, working in collaboration with Gary Gates and me, found that the relationship between bohemians and high-tech growth not only held but was in fact markedly stronger among

Table 12.5   Top Twenty Metros on the Tolerance Index, 2010

Rank	Metro	Tolerance Index Score
1	San Diego-Carlsbad-San Marcos, CA	.751
2	Napa, CA	.747
3	Santa Rosa-Petaluma, CA	.739
4	Santa Cruz-Watsonville, CA	.738
5	Santa Fe, NM	.726
6	Ithaca, NY	.723
7	Oxnard-Thousand Oaks-Ventura, CA	.708
8	Cape Coral-Fort Myers, FL	.702
9	Boulder, CO	.701
10	Ann Arbor, MI	.693
11	Miami-Fort Lauderdale-Miami Beach, FL	.692
12	Greeley, CO	.691
13	Trenton-Ewing, NJ	.690
14	Fresno, CA	.687
15	Las Vegas-Paradise, NV	.686
16	Portland-Vancouver-Beaverton, OR-WA	.684
17	San Francisco-Oakland-Fremont, CA	.683
18	Worcester, MA	.680
19	Carson City, NV	.679
20	Boston-Cambridge-Quincy, MA-NH	.678

Source: Analysis by Kevin Stolarick. See the appendix for full detail on sources.

Canadian regions.[30] Independent research by the Australian think tank National Economics discovered the relationship among gays, bohemians, and tech growth to be quite substantial in their comparative analysis of Australian regions and urban centers. The Tolerance Index continues to be closely associated with many sorts of positive regional outcomes, from Creative Class share, innovation, and high-tech industry to higher regional incomes and wages, and even the level of happiness and well-being.[31]

Are You Open to Experience?

Psychologists have long noted the connection between self-expression and creativity. A large body of literature shows a strong correlation between the high levels of creativity that are found in artists, scientists, and entrepreneurs and a personality type that is curious and open to new experiences. "The Geography of Personality," a pathbreaking study by two psychologists, Jason Rentfrow of Cambridge University and Sam Gosling of the University of Texas, examined the geographic clustering of what psychologists dub the Big Five personality types: agreeableness, conscientiousness, extraversion, neuroticism, and openness to experience. Based on a large-scale survey of more than 600,000 people, they found that people with high levels of the open-to-experience characteristic were both more mobile and much more likely to cluster in specific geographic areas. Open-to-experience people were more likely to "attempt to escape the ennui experienced in small-town environments by relocating to metropolitan areas where their interests in cultures and needs for social contact and stimulation are more easily met." In other words, they move to and cluster in places that welcome them and offer them lots of exciting experiences and stimuli. They may not do this by design, but over time, certain areas develop large clusters of these kinds of people and more and more begin to reflect the characteristics that are associated with them.

A 2011 study by Rentfrow, "The Open City," explored the distribution of open-to-experience personality types by metro.[32] Table 12.6 shows the top ten and bottom ten metros on this score. San Francisco has the nation's largest concentration of open-to-experience people, followed by Los Angeles, Austin, New York, and San Diego. Each of these metros has a considerable concentration of the Creative Class. Of the top ten open-to-experience metros, only one, Las Vegas, has a low level of the Creative Class—it appears to be relatively unique in providing employment for open-to-experience people in the nightlife and gaming industries that lie outside the Creative Class occupations. At the opposite end of the spectrum, Detroit, Minneapolis, Cleveland and Columbus, and Pittsburgh have the nation's smallest concentrations of open-to-experience people. In research conducted jointly with Rentfrow, my team utilized even larger surveys to map the concentration and clustering of personality types within large cities and metropolitan areas like New York, Los Angeles, Toronto, and others. Confirming Rentfrow's and Gosling's original insight, we found extreme concentrations of open-to-experience people in downtown urban neighborhoods.

Seeing the strong clustering of personality types and learning more about the relationship between psychology and place caused a subtle shift in my own thinking. All my professional life, I'd looked at the ways that social and economic factors shape the world. I'd never thought that much about psychology—and certainly not about the ways that personal proclivities might affect innovation or economic development. But all of a sudden it was dawning on me that psychology plays a central role.

For years, I had sought to develop better and more refined measures of what economists refer to as human capital or skill. My measures of the Creative Class were my attempts to do just that. But psychology identifies another key factor over and above the level of

Table 12.6   Openness-to-Experience by Metro

Top 10	Creative Class Share
San Francisco	39.4%
Los Angeles	34.1%
Austin	34.4%
New York	35.8%
San Diego	35.6%
San Antonio	31.2%
Nashville	31.8%
Las Vegas	22.7%
Tampa	33.0%
Denver	37.6%

Bottom 10	Creative Class Share
Detroit	34.5%
Minneapolis	37.7%
Cleveland	32.2%
Columbus	34.0%
Pittsburgh	31.7%
Indianapolis	33.0%
Kansas City	34.8%
St. Louis	33.6%
Memphis	28.5%
Cincinnati	31.8%

Source: Jason Rentfrow, "The Open City," in Ake Andersson, David Andersson, and Charlotta Mellander (eds.), *Handbook of Cities and Creativity*, London: Elgar, 2011, pp. 117–127.

education or the kinds of work people do. Personality involves the capacity to acquire and perform certain tasks competently and effectively. The type of skills economists are interested in, Rentfrow notes, "implies something that can be acquired with proper training, talent, motivation, and resources." But, he adds, "it's more consistent with personality theory to argue that personality traits predispose people to acquire certain skills. For example, highly conscientious people have a disposition to be detail oriented, plan ahead, or stay organized. Openness influences people's ability to acquire new skills relatively quickly." Obviously, some people are more creative or more ambitious or more motivated than others. What separates a

Steve Jobs or a Bill Gates from most people is not their level of education or even the work they do; it is this "something else."

To get at the effects of personality on regional economic growth, my research team and I matched our metro-level data sets on innovation, human capital, and economic growth to Rentfrow's data on personality types. When Mellander and I ran correlations between openness-to-experience and these factors, we found that it was modestly associated with the Creative Class, college grads, and the Bohemian Index, and negatively associated with the Working Class. Openness was a bit more strongly related to high-tech industry and immigrants, and quite a bit more so for the Gay Index.[33] Rentfrow's study found similar associations and the correlations between openness-to-experience and three variables—the high-tech industry, percent foreign-born, and the Gay Index—held up even after controlling for the level of college graduates.[34]

Rentfrow's research suggests that there is a psychological dimension to creative cities that contributes to their ethos and character. It is not just that people sort themselves into places where they can find work, he notes; they seek out environments where they can pursue their personal as well as their professional interests. Clusters of open-to-experience personalities are associated with innovation, he suggests, because the "jobs at the center of innovation . . . such as design, engineering, science, painting, music, software development, writing and acting, appeal to individuals who are curious, creative, intellectual, imaginative, inventive and resourceful. These professions are primarily concerned with exploring, developing and communicating new ideas, methods and products." People who are high in openness are also adventurous, he adds: they are likely to generate new perspectives on old issues and are comfortable with and adaptable to change. It makes sense that places with high concentrations of highly open individuals would also be places with disproportionately large numbers of high-tech workers, artists, musicians, and designers, as well as foreign-born people and gays and lesbians, who also signal a high level of openness.

The more I thought about it, the more the connection between open places and open people became clear. At bottom, my measures of gay and bohemian concentrations not only signaled exciting amenity-rich places but places that had drawn broader clusters of open-to-experience people from all walks of life. Openness was literally imprinted on their psychological and cultural DNA.

The Creativity Index

The Creativity Index is my overall measure of regional economic potential. It combines the three major indexes discussed above: the Technology Index, the Talent Index, and the Tolerance Index. I use it as a baseline indicator of a region's economic development and longer-run economic potential (see Figure 12.7 and Table 12.7).

Boulder takes first place, followed by San Francisco and Boston. Believe it or not, there is a three-way tie for fourth place—Seattle, San Diego, and Ann Arbor. Rounding out the top ten are Corvallis, Durham, greater Washington, DC, and suburban Trenton. Ithaca is eleventh. And interestingly, Silicon Valley (San Jose) follows in twelfth place. Portland, Worcester, Burlington, Austin, Hartford, Minneapolis-St. Paul, Atlanta, and Tucson complete the top twenty. Madison, Los Angeles, Denver, and Raleigh make the top one-third, with New York City in thirty-first place.

Competing "Capitals"

In the original edition of this book, I cited the research of Robert Cushing, a former University of Texas sociologist and statistician

Table 12.7 Top Twenty Metros on the Creativity Index, 2010

Creativity Index Rank	Metro	Creativity Index Score	Technology Index Rank	Talent Index Rank	Tolerance Index Rank
1	Boulder, CO	.981	10	5	9
2	San Francisco-Oakland-Fremont, CA	.970	3	16	17
3	Boston-Cambridge-Quincy, MA-NH	.968	9	9	20
4	Seattle-Tacoma-Bellevue, WA	.961	1	22	22
4	San Diego-Carlsbad-San Marcos, CA	.961	7	37	1
4	Ann Arbor, MI	.961	25	10	10
7	Corvallis, OR	.959	14	8	25
8	Durham, NC	.953	8	1	45
9	Washington-Arlington-Alexandria, DC-VA-MD-WV	.947	27	3	30
10	Trenton-Ewing, NJ	.945	44	6	13
11	Ithaca, NY	.937	61	4	6
12	San Jose-Sunnyvale-Santa Clara, CA	.933	2	2	71
13	Portland-Vancouver-Beaverton, OR-WA	.930	4	59	16
14	Worcester, MA	.922	30	40	18
15	Burlington-South Burlington, VT	.918	11	20	61
16	Austin-Round Rock, TX	.916	5	54	34
16	Hartford-West Hartford-East Hartford, CT	.916	42	14	37
18	Minneapolis-St. Paul-Bloomington, MN-WI	.915	17	23	53
19	Atlanta-Sandy Springs-Marietta, GA	.912	23	33	42
20	Tucson, AZ	.909	12	64	26

Source: Analysis by Kevin Stolarick. See the appendix for full detail on sources.

Figure 12.7 The Creativity Index by Metro, 2010

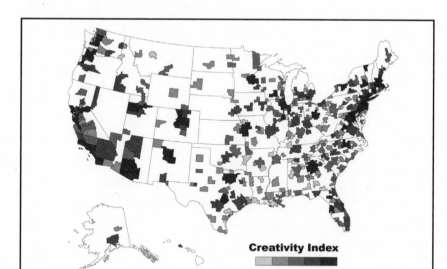

Source: Analysis by Kevin Stolarick. Map by Zara Matheson. See the appendix for full detail on sources.

who undertook a systematic comparison of the three main theories of regional growth—Glaeser's human capital theory, Putnam's social capital theory, and my own, which he referred to as creative capital theory. He built statistical models to determine the effects of human, social, and creative capital on regional growth between 1990 and 2000, including separate measures of education and human capital; occupation, wages, and hours worked; poverty and income inequality; innovation and high-tech industry; and creativity and diversity.

His results were striking. He found no evidence that social capital leads to regional economic growth; in fact, the effects were negative. In a related study, he found that leading high-tech regions had higher income and higher levels of growth but scored below average on almost every measure of social capital. They had less trust, less reliance on faith-based institutions, fewer clubs, less volunteering, less interest in traditional politics, and less civic leadership, but much higher levels of "protest politics" and "diversity of friendships." In his own words, "conventional political involvement and social capital seem to relate negatively to technological development and higher economic growth."

Both the human capital and creative capital models performed much better, according to his analysis. Turning first to the human capital approach, he found that though it did a good job of accounting for regional growth, "the interpretation is not as straightforward as the human capital approach might presume." Using creative occupations, bohemians, the Milken High-Tech Index, and innovations as indicators of creative capital, he found that the creative capital theory produced formidable results, with the predictive power of the Bohemian and Innovation Indexes particularly high. He concluded: "The creative capital model generates equally impressive results as the human capital model and perhaps better."[35] Many other studies have confirmed his results since.

Even so, several critics have questioned the connection between the Creative Class and regional growth. "Jobs data going back 20 years, to 1983," wrote one of them in 2004, "show that Florida's top ten cities as a group actually do worse, lagging behind the national economy by several percentage points, while his so-called least creative cities continue to look like economic powerhouses, expanding 60% faster than his most creative cities during that same period."[36]

First off, it bears repeating that there is wide consensus that skill—whether measured as human capital or the Creative Class—is the primary factor in economic growth and development. But more specifically, in my 2004 essay in *Next American City* titled "The Great Creative Class Debate" and in my follow-up book *The Flight of the Creative Class,* I reported the results of an analysis by Kevin Stolarick that blew those jobs numbers out of the water.[37] Stolarick examined the economic performance of two groups of regions. To keep things comparable, he confined his analysis only to the forty-nine regions that had more than 1 million people at the time. The first group was composed of the top eleven performers on the 2004 version of the Creativity Index; the second group included the eleven lowest-ranked regions. He used eleven instead of the more common top ten because two of the lowest-ranked regions were tied.

His findings speak for themselves. Between 1990 and 2000, the creativity leaders generated three times as many jobs as the lowest-ranked, 2.32 million versus 850,000 jobs. Even after controlling for the fact that those regions employed more people, they still generated jobs at more than twice the rate of the others, 22 percent versus 11 percent. Still, looking at job creation alone can be misleading. A place might create lots of jobs, but the quality of those jobs—the wealth they generate and the salaries they pay—also matters. Stolarick's analysis showed that the leading creative regions added more than $100 billion in total wages between 1999 and 2002, more than five times the $20 billion added by the lowest-ranked regions. Workers in the leading creative regions averaged over $5,000 more in wages and salaries than those in the lowest-ranked regions, $40,091 versus $34,383. Wages in the top-ranked creative regions grew at almost double the rate (5.1 percent) of the laggards (2.8 percent). This translates into a far better "raise" for workers in creative cities, who took home more than one-third (37 percent) more money than their counterparts in lower-scoring regions, $5,125 versus $3,129.

I asked at the time: Which city would you put your money on to be an economic powerhouse fifty years from now—Las Vegas, which had among the fastest population growth in modern memory, or a Creative Class center like San Francisco? It's true that between 1990 and 2000, Las Vegas ranked first in population growth and third in job growth. But look at it today. Aside from perhaps

Detroit, Las Vegas was the metro that was hardest hit by the economic crisis of 2008, experiencing one of the worst housing crises and staggeringly high unemployment. I would have made a heckuva lot of money had my critics been willing to take the bet.

For this latest edition of this book, Stolarick updated the numbers for the period 2005 through 2010, comparing the top ten and bottom ten metros on the Creativity Index. Needless to say, the economic crisis dramatically reshaped the jobs picture. The ten lowest-ranked regions lost 5 percent of their jobs and the leaders only showed slight gains. The picture for Creative Class jobs, however, was somewhat brighter. The leaders added 50,000 Creative Class jobs, as compared to just 9,000 for the lowest-ranked metros. Even controlling for population, the leaders added Creative Class jobs at more than double the rate of the laggards, 8.0 versus 3.6 percent. Average salaries were $12,631 higher in the top ten Creativity Index metros, $54,207 versus $41,576 for the bottom ten regions, growing by 27 percent in the former, compared to 20 percent in the latter. And the earnings gap was considerably higher in the most creative metros. Average salaries for Creative Class members were a full 25 percent higher ($16,435) in the leading Creativity Index regions, $82,242 versus $65,987.

Another set of critics questioned my theory on the grounds that it was not related to population growth. Creative Class cities and metros were not adding population as fast as many of their Sun Belt peers. How could my theory be right, they asked, if its top cities weren't expanding? When interviewed for a story in the *Boston Globe* in 2004, Edward Glaeser insisted that people prefer to live in sunny, dry climates and that they actually like car-centered cities. "In place of Florida's 'Technology, Talent, and Tolerance,'" the story noted, "Glaeser proposes a different recipe, 'Skills, Sun, and Sprawl.'" In 2009, Glaeser wrote, "There is no variable that predicts urban population growth in the 20th century better than January temperature."[38]

Having more people or adding them at a faster rate might make some city leaders and residents proud, but it is a terribly misleading measure of economic growth. A decade ago, the urban economist Paul Gottlieb coined a term for this disconnect between population and economic growth: "growth without growth."[39] When Gottlieb compared population growth to growth in real per-capita income in the one hundred largest US metropolitan areas, he found that they divided into four basic categories. Some—like Atlanta, Austin, and Dallas—were above the national average in both categories. Others, including many older Rust Belt metros, were below average in both. But it's the last two categories that were the deal breakers. Half of the one hundred largest metros divided into "population magnets" (places where populations grew but not income) and "wealth builders" (where incomes rose much faster than populations).

Real economic growth comes not from population growth, but from improvements in productivity. The gold standard for measuring productivity is economic output per capita. To get at this, Kevin Stolarick and I partnered with José Lobo, an urban economist at Arizona State University. When we compared the average annual growth in population against average annual growth in GDP per capita across America's 350-plus metros between 2001 and 2010, we found virtually no correlation between the two.[40] In fact, the disconnect Gottlieb discovered had become even more pronounced. Just one in three metro areas experienced gains in both productivity and population that exceeded the national average— and we found no statistical association at all between population growth and productivity growth, either for metros or states. This not only challenges the notion that population growth is a proxy for economic growth; it puts the lie to development strategies that encourage population growth as an end in itself. A rising population can create a false illusion of prosperity, as it did in so many Sun Belt metros, which built their house-of-cards economies around housing construction and real estate development, leaving ghost towns, mass unemployment, and empty public coffers in their wake when the bubble inevitably burst.

How has Creative Class theory fared since the crisis of 2008? To get at this, Charlotta Mellander and I examined the effect of the Creative Class and other factors on the growth in regional economic output between 2007 and 2010. We can start out with what's *not* associated with regional economic growth. The economic growth of metros between 2007 and 2010 had little or no relationship to population size, density, levels of innovation, wages, or places with warmer summers. It had only a weak relationship to high-tech industry and a weak negative association with housing prices. The most powerful factor in our analysis by far was Creative Class share. The correlation between it and regional economic growth was the strongest of any in our analysis.[41] Despite the strong showings posted by some traditional manufacturing metros like Elkhart, Indiana, economic growth was much less likely to occur in metros where the Working Class makes up a greater share of the workforce. In fact, regional economic growth was negatively associated with the share of Working Class jobs.

Despite hemming and hawing, mainly among non-academics, it is well established that skill, talent, and what economists refer to as human capital all drive economic development. My own work is squarely in line with that view. Still, a number of economists questioned my Creative Class measure. As we have seen, their concern was that it was a warmed-over version of the standard educational measure of human capital. But as Chapter 3 has shown, independent studies showed that although the two are indeed related, they measure different things; also, membership in the Creative Class adds to wages and salaries over and above the returns to education. To reiterate, the standard educational attainment measure does not account for individuals who are incredibly important to the economy but who for one reason or another did not go to or finish college, such as, for example, Bill Gates, Michael Dell, and Steve Jobs. Also, the conventional educational measure is too broad; it does not capture differences in types of skill. An occupation-based measure like mine has obvious empirical advantages, as we have seen, in that it identifies more precisely the kinds of skills or talent that add to regional productivity and wealth. My occupation-based measure has the added advantage of providing regions and their leadership with a practical tool that they can actually use to better identify, understand, and act on their unique advantages and disadvantages. Occupational cluster analysis is a tool that both complements industrial cluster analysis and goes beyond it in important ways.

Several careful empirical studies have compared my theory to human capital theory. Two economists affiliated with the US Department of Agriculture, David McGranahan and Timothy Wojan, used sophisticated statistical techniques to gauge the effects of the Creative Class versus human capital on regional growth. These techniques, they note, allowed them to undertake a "critical examination of the most cutting critique of Florida's analysis: that he is merely substituting employment in highly skilled occupations as a proxy for the endowment of human capital." To do so, they used systems of simultaneous equations rather than the conventional simple regression models to control for the endogeneity of population and employment growth as well as influences from a range of other local conditions and attributes. Their key findings overwhelmingly confirm the "strong independent influence on employment growth from both the initial share employed in the recast creative class occupations and its growth over the decade. By contrast, the statistical association with human capital variables is quite weak." And they add: "The econometric test of the creative class thesis provides strong support for the notion that creativity has an effect on growth independent of the endowment of human capital."[42]

Another detailed study, this one investigating regional development in the Netherlands, also found that the Creative Class considerably outperformed the standard human capital measure in accounting for employment growth. This led its authors to conclude that using Creative Class in analysis sets a "new standard" for measuring skill and talent, especially when considering regional labor productivity. "With our Dutch data set we do find evidence that Florida's creative class is a better predictor of city growth than traditional education standards," they wrote. "Therefore we conclude that Florida's major contribution is his successful attempt to create a population category that is a better indicator for levels of human capital than average education levels or amounts of highly educated people. The point is, as Florida stated, not which or how much education people can boast of, but what they really do in working life."[43]

Other critics have said that my approach falls victim to the proverbial chicken-and-egg problem. What typically come first, these critics argue, are the jobs. Once a region has those, the people—as well as the amenities, lifestyle, and tolerance—will follow. One conventional economic developer put it this way: "Create the jobs and diversity will follow." As I have said before, jobs-versus-people is a false dichotomy. The rationale behind my approach is worth reiterating: skills and skilled people are an incredibly mobile factor of production; they flow. The key question my theory poses is: what are the factors that shape that flow and determine the divergent levels of talent and skill across regions?

As far as I can determine, there are three basic answers. The first argues that amenities attract human capital. For example, a study by the economist Jesse Shapiro found that though "roughly 60 percent of the employment growth effect of college graduates is due to enhanced productivity growth," the "rest" is "caused by growth in quality of life," adding that: "this finding contrasts with the common argument that human capital generates employment growth in urban areas solely through changes in productivity." The second centers on the university's role in producing and concentrating human capital. But how is it that some regions have great universities and substantial amenities (symphony, ballet, opera, museums, professional sports, golf courses, and the like) but still experience a significant outflow of talented people?

This led me to a third answer, which I believe provides an even simpler and more basic explanation for the flow of talent and skill. I say that the key factor in the divergence or flow of human capital is the openness of a given place to human capital. If firms and markets benefit from low barriers to entry, why not people and labor markets? Thus, the more open a place is, the more likely it is to attract the kinds of people who power innovation and economic growth. There are two reasons this should be so. First, such places possess some underlying characteristics that allow individuals, including entrepreneurs, to readily mobilize resources. And second, they are oriented toward personal self-expression and openness to experience, which psychological studies show is a key characteristic of entrepreneurial behavior.

The most complete test of the Creative Class theory can be found in a detailed study I conducted with Charlotta Mellander and Kevin Stolarick entitled "Inside the Black Box of Regional Economic Development." We devised it to be the fullest and most accurate test of my theory versus human capital theory. We sought to show that it is not just the endowment of skill and talent that matters but its flow, and we wanted to test my notion that a low barrier to entry for human capital—reflected by openness to diversity—is a key factor for both talent and regional growth.

We used an advanced statistical technique called path analysis to examine the relative roles played by the Creative Class, the conventional measure of human capital, and tolerance on two key elements of regional growth—regional income and wages. These two measures can and do vary widely across metros. Wages refers to pay for work; income is a broad measure of wealth that includes capital gains, rents, interest, transfers, and the like, in addition to wages. Naples, Florida, for example, a tourist and second-home destination, has high income, of which only 32 percent comes from wages. Silicon Valley has one of the highest income levels in the nation, and more than 92 percent of it is made up of wages. In this sense, wages are a more direct measure of local productivity.

Our study was designed to identify the effects of three key classes of factors on regional incomes and wages. First, it tested for the differential effects of educational human capital and occupational class, enabling us to parse their relative effects vis-à-vis high-tech industry and technological innovation, which have also been shown to affect regional growth. Then, it tested for the effects of regional cultural and institutional factors—amenities, university, and openness—on talent, technology, and ultimately on regional incomes and wages.

Our models enabled us to not only identify the direct effects of these classes of factors but also to identify how they might relate to one another indirectly through other variables. A big limit of the standard regression techniques used in most studies is that they do not allow for these indirect effects. The nuanced effects of variables that work through other variables cannot be ascertained; key, if subtle, factors may register as insignificant. We did the analysis for all 300-plus US metro areas, running varied permutations of the model to examine the relative roles played by the Creative Class versus human capital, the role of high-tech industry, and the effects of tolerance. We defined openness as a combination of bohemian and gay concentrations. We added variables for technology of different kinds—taking both high-tech industry and patents per capita into account. We put all of that into our model and generated results that help us better understand the dynamics of the so-called black box of regional growth.

What did we find? First and foremost, we found that the Creative Class and human capital both play a role, but they seem to operate through different channels. Human capital relates more strongly to income, and the Creative Class relates more strongly to wages. This is a critical difference, as wages are a better gauge not just of wealth, which can be imported from elsewhere, but of the productivity of a region. Human capital may reflect richer places, but it seems that the Creative Class actually makes a place more productive.

In the next chapter, we will look at the Creative Class's growing global impact.

CHAPTER 13

Global Reach

In March 2003, I traveled to New Zealand to address a major forum on the future of the Creative Economy. I took advantage of the opportunity to meet with Peter Jackson, the Academy Award–winning director of the *Lord of the Rings* trilogy, at his studios in lush, green, otherworldly Wellington, a smallish but exciting cosmopolitan city of roughly 400,000, and one certainly not previously considered a global cultural capital. But Jackson's is one of the world's most sophisticated filmmaking complexes, and he built it in his hometown of Wellington for a reason. He realized, he told me, that the allure of the *Rings* movies could entice the best cinematographers, costume designers, sound technicians, computer graphic artists, model builders, editors, and animators from all over the world to relocate to New Zealand.

Jackson had figured out what many American cities discovered during the 1990s: that paradigm-busting creative industries could single-handedly change the way cities flourish while driving dynamic and widespread economic change. During my visit to Wellington, I saw dozens of Americans from places like Berkeley and MIT working alongside talented filmmakers from Europe and Asia. Many had begun the process of establishing residency in New Zealand, ready to relinquish their American citizenship for what they saw as greener creative pastures. One of them, a digital wunderkind from Silicon Valley, told me he was launching his new high-tech start-up in Wellington because of its technology infrastructure, which for his purposes had advantages that trumped even Silicon Valley. As we walked past a wall map with pins stuck in it showing the studio workers' native countries, the head of digital animation joked that the organization looked more like the United Nations than a film production studio.

My encounter with Jackson and his Wellington film complex had a big effect on me. A decade ago, when I was preparing the first edition of this book, I focused almost exclusively on the United States. I'm an American after all, and I knew my own country best. The United States has lots of cities—several hundred metros overall—so it provided a good test case on which to base my statistical research on the role and effects of the Creative Class and of the 3T's on economic development. When the original edition of this book came out, a number of commentators argued, and some still do, that its main findings and implications had scant relevance for other nations—especially ones that are smaller, have fewer large cities, and whose populations are less mobile. But within just a couple of years, international researchers began applying my framework to study the Creative Class in their own countries, confirming many of my insights. That was what had gotten me invited to New Zealand in the first place.

When I returned home, I immediately got to work with my colleagues and students to develop estimates of the Creative Class around the world. That work led directly to two things—"Europe in the Creative Age," a report I wrote with Irene Tinagli, the first serious census and analysis of the global Creative Class, and a new metric, the Global Creativity Index, which I unveiled in my 2004 book, *The Flight of the Creative Class*.[1] This chapter updates and revises them, this time covering eighty-two nations across the world.[2]

The Creative Class Around the World

Our statistics for the global Creative Class come from the International Labour Organization (ILO). The ILO collects the most detailed available data on occupations, breaking the workforce down into job categories like scientists and engineers, artists, musicians, architects, engineers, managers, professionals, and so forth. Although the ILO's occupational categories and definitions differ somewhat from the US-based statistics my team and I use in our domestic research, they are consistent across nations and therefore provide the best available measures of the extent and growth of creative occupations worldwide.

The Creative Class numbers 300 million workers in the eighty-two nations for which data are available. This is double the 150 million I estimated in *The Flight of the Creative Class* in 2005, mainly because our data now covers more countries. Still, this number should be interpreted carefully. It is a very rough estimate that in all likelihood still vastly underestimates the true number of Creative Class workers worldwide.

Although the United States leads in the total number of Creative Class workers, it ranks a dismal twenty-seventh in terms of its Creative Class share, with Creative Class workers making up roughly 35 percent of its workforce. (You will notice that this number differs somewhat from the figure used in most of this book. In order to make sure we are comparing apples to apples, this 35 percent Creative Class figure is based on the same ILO data we use for other nations.)

The highest-ranking countries have close to one-half of their workforce in the Creative Class. Singapore takes the top spot, with 47.3 percent of its workforce in the Creative Class, followed by the Netherlands with 46.2 percent and Switzerland with 44.8 percent. Australia is fourth, with 44.5 percent of its workforce in the Creative

Class. Scandinavian and Northern European countries take many of the top spots: Sweden (43.9 percent), Belgium (43.8 percent), Denmark (43.7 percent), Finland (43.4 percent), Norway (42.1 percent), and Germany (41.6 percent). Canada ranks twelfth, with 40.8 percent of its workforce in the Creative Class. Of the countries with newly advanced economic development—the BRICs (Brazil, Russia, India, China)—Russia ranks highest at twentieth (38.6 percent), Brazil is fifty-seventh (18.5 percent), and China is seventy-fifth (7.4 percent).

So much for countries: The real drivers of the Creative Economy are cities and metros. Unfortunately, we lack a single organized source of comparable data for cities worldwide—not just for the Creative Class, but for lots and lots of other factors we would like to measure. After *Rise* was published, researchers in a wide range of countries undertook projects to collect Creative Class data for their countries and regions.

A particularly notable effort to collect and organize data for Canada, Western Europe, and the Nordic countries was organized by Björn Asheim from Lund University in Sweden, with Ron Boschma of Utrecht University; Phillip Cooke of Cardiff University; Michael Fritsch of Friedrich-Schiller University, Jena; Meric Gertler from the University of Toronto; Arne Isaksen of Norway's University of Agder; Mark Lorenzen of the Copenhagen Business School; and Markku Sotarauta, University of Tampere, Finland. Using their data, we can compile an illustrative list of the Creative Class in cities and metro regions outside the United States. I need to emphasize that this list is illustrative only—there are many Creative Class regions, nations, and cities around the world where data are either unavailable, have not been organized or published, or of which I am not aware. Some of those cities may well have higher Creative Class shares than any of the ones here. Table 13.1, compiled by Mellander and me from the available data, shows twenty cities outside the United States for which Creative Class data are available.[3]

Table 13.1 The Creative Class in Global Cities

Region	Country	Creative Class Share
Amsterdam	Netherlands	46.0%
Stockholm	Sweden	46.0%
Helsinki	Finland	44.0%
Oxford	UK	42.8%
Munich	Germany	42.2%
London	UK	41.2%
Cambridge	UK	41.2%
Malmö-Lund	Sweden	41.0%
Berlin	Germany	39.3%
Hamburg	Germany	38.2%
Hannover	Germany	37.8%
Oslo	Norway	37.6%
Ottawa	Canada	37.6%
Bonn	Germany	37.3%
Toronto	Canada	37.1%
Copenhagen	Denmark	36.8%
Stuttgart	Germany	36.6%
Leicestershire	UK	36.2%
Leeds	UK	35.3%
Paris	France	35.1%

Sources: Analysis by Charlotta Mellander from various sources, but see in particular the European Science Foundation project, *Technology, Talent and Tolerance in European Cities: A Comparative Analysis.* The project was carried out over a three-year period, 2004–2006, and was coordinated by Björn T. Asheim, Lund University, Sweden, and supervised by Meric Gertler, University of Toronto (and also affiliated with the University of Oslo). The national project leaders were Ron Boschma, Utrecht University, the Netherlands; Phil Cooke, University of Cardiff, Wales; Michael Fritsch, Technical University Freiberg (now affiliated with Friedrich-Schiller University, Jena), Germany; Arne Isaksen, University of Agder, Norway; Mark Lorenzen, Copenhagen Business School, Denmark; and Markku Sotarauta, University of Tampere, Finland. Available online at http://www .esf.org/activities/eurocores/running-programmes/ecrp/ecrp-scheme-2001-2004.html. Also, see the special section in *Economic Geography,* Volume 85, Number 4, October 2009, pp. 355–442. Data for French metros provided by Sébastien Chantelot of ESC Bretagne Brest University.

Figure 13.1   The Global Creative Class Map

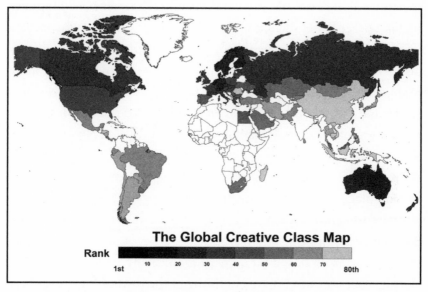

Source: Richard Florida, Charlotta Mellander, and Kevin Stolarick, *Creativity and Prosperity: The 2011 Global Creativity Index,* University of Toronto, Martin Prosperity Institute Report, October 2011. Available online at www.research.martinprosperity.org.

Amsterdam and Stockholm top the list, with 46 percent of their workforce in the Creative Class. The Creative Class makes·up more than four in ten workers in Helsinki, Oxford, Munich, Malmö, London, and Cambridge. This is roughly the same as the top ranked US metros at the time—Boulder and San Jose (Silicon Valley). The Creative Class made up between 35 and 40 percent of the workforce in Paris, Toronto, Hamburg, Berlin, Oslo, Copenhagen, and several other metros—more than Boston, greater Washington, DC, Austin, or San Francisco at the time.

Technology, of course, is the first of my three T's of economic development. From cutting-edge inventions in software, robotics, and biotechnology to improvements in manufacturing systems and processes, technology makes economies and societies more efficient and productive.

The Global Technology Index employs three key technology metrics—a Global R&D Investment Index (based on R&D spending as a percent of GDP), a Global Researchers Index (which measures professionals engaged in R&D, controlling for population), and a Global Innovation Index (patents per capita). The United States does much better here than it did on Creative Class share, ranking third overall. With its well-developed infrastructure for entrepreneurial venture-capital finance, the United States remains a technology leader.

Finland is first on the Global Technology Index and Japan takes second place. Israel ranks fourth. Its high ranking might come as a surprise to some, considering its small size, but as Dan Senor and Saul Singer's *Start-Up Nation* argues, Israel's economic development strategy has been based on launching innovative firms.[4] Israel has the highest concentration of engineers in the world—135 per 10,000 people, compared to 85 per 10,000 people in the United States. Sweden is fifth. Canada ranks eleventh.

Although much has been made of the ascendance of the BRIC countries—Brazil, Russia, and especially India and China—they do not rank highly on the Global Technology Index. Russia, in the twenty-eighth spot, ranks highest, and China is thirty-seventh, about the same as Latvia and Bulgaria. Brazil takes forth-eighth place and India, forty-ninth, just behind Serbia and Croatia.

Talent is the second T. In *The Flight of the Creative Class,* I predicted that the competition for global talent would soon supplant the competition for goods, investment, and resources as the key factor in global competition and found that the United States was already beginning to falter on this score. We measure talent with the Global Talent Index, a composite of the Creative Class and "tertiary education," which includes technical and vocational education as well as colleges and universities.

The United States ranks eighth on the Global Talent Index. The Scandinavian countries come out on the top, with Finland and Swe-

Figure 13.2 The Global Technology Index

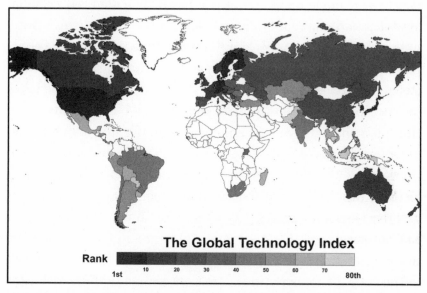

Source: Richard Florida, Charlotta Mellander, and Kevin Stolarick, *Creativity and Prosperity: The 2011 Global Creativity Index,* University of Toronto, Martin Prosperity Institute Report, October 2011. Available online at www.research.martinprosperity.org.

den taking first and second place. Singapore ranks third, Denmark fourth, New Zealand fifth, Norway sixth, and Australia seventh. Canada ranks seventeenth. Of the BRIC nations, Russia ranks highest at thirteenth, with Brazil in sixty-sixth, India in seventy-fifth, and China in seventy-sixth place.

Tolerance, the third T, is critical to a region's or nation's ability to attract and mobilize creative talent. Tolerance is more than a matter of political correctness—it's an economic growth imperative: places that welcome diversity foster creativity. We measure global tolerance as a combination of two variables, both taken from the Gallup World Poll. The first is the percentage of respondents who believe that the community where they live is a good place for ethnic and racial minorities to live. The second is the percentage that says that their community is a good place for gay and lesbian people to

live. A significant body of independent research confirms that openness to gays and lesbians is associated with higher levels of regional
as well as national economic performance.[5]

The United States ranks eighth on the Global Tolerance Index,
perhaps reflecting recent increases in anti-immigrant sentiment
and social conservatism toward gays and lesbians. Canada takes
the top spot, and Ireland ranks second. The Netherlands ranks
third: it is the only country among the top five that is more open
to gay and lesbian people (83 percent) than it is to racial and ethnic
minorities (73 percent). New Zealand ranks fourth, followed by
nearby Australia in fifth place. Both have open immigration systems
and have made it a priority to attract foreign talent. Spain, where
the Zapatero administration made tolerance and openness a priority, is in sixth place, followed by Sweden.

The Global Creativity Index, or GCI, brings all these measures
together, providing an integrated and comprehensive assessment
of a nation's standing on the 3T's of economic development (see
Figure 13.5). The United States takes second place, up from fourth
place in the original 2004 index. Sweden takes first, maintaining
the top position it held in 2004. Finland is third, followed by Denmark in fourth, and Australia in fifth place. New Zealand takes
sixth place; Canada ties with Norway for eighth; Singapore and the
Netherlands round out the top ten. Despite their rapid economic
rise, the BRIC nations still do not crack the upper tiers on the GCI:
Russia ranks thirtieth, Brazil forty-sixth, India fiftieth, and China
fifty-eighth.

Creativity and the Wealth and Happiness of Nations

Looking through the lens of the Global Creativity Index, two things
become clear. First, the more creative and innovative a country's
economy is, the more of an economic edge it enjoys. And second,

Figure 13.3 The Global Talent Index

Source: Richard Florida, Charlotta Mellander, and Kevin Stolarick, *Creativity and Prosperity: The 2011 Global Creativity Index*, University of Toronto, Martin Prosperity Institute Report, October 2011. Available online at www.research.martinprosperity.org.

the US model, which combines high levels of creativity and innovation with high levels of economic inequality, is not the norm: in fact, it is somewhat unique.

When we examined the relationship between overall creativity (measured on the GCI) and key gauges of economic output, innovation, and entrepreneurship we found that the GCI was closely related with the standard measure of economic output (gross domestic product per capita). The GCI was also closely associated with the Global Competitiveness Index (another GCI, confusingly) developed by Harvard professor Michael Porter for the World Economic Forum, which includes factors associated with economic output, innovation, efficiency, and business climate, among others.

Figure 13.4   The Global Tolerance Index

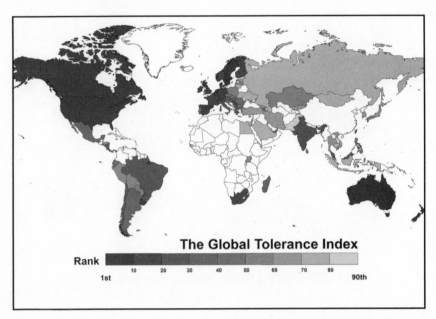

Source: Richard Florida, Charlotta Mellander, and Kevin Stolarick, *Creativity and Prosperity: The 2011 Global Creativity Index,* University of Toronto, Martin Prosperity Institute Report, October 2011. Available online at www.research.martinprosperity.org.

We then looked at the connection between creativity and entrepreneurship using the Global Entrepreneurship Index, which covers fifty-four nations, worldwide. The index shows the wide disparity in entrepreneurial activity across the nations of the world. Canada, Israel, and the United States have the highest levels of entrepreneurial activity, whereas Denmark, Finland, France, Germany, and Japan have the lowest. The correlation between the GCI and the Global Entrepreneurship Index was considerable.

Economic competitiveness is one thing, but what about broader concerns for happiness and well-being? To get at this, we examined the connection between the GCI and a comprehensive measure of happiness and life satisfaction collected by the Gallup Organization's World Poll. Once again, the correlation was very close.

Figure 13.5 The Global Creativity Index

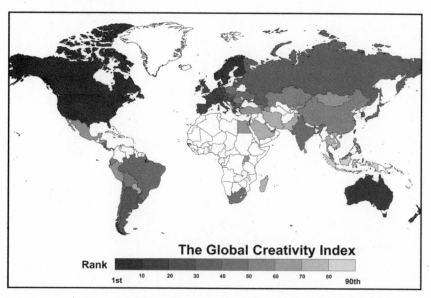

Source: Richard Florida, Charlotta Mellander, and Kevin Stolarick, *Creativity and Prosperity: The 2011 Global Creativity Index*, University of Toronto, Martin Prosperity Institute Report, October 2011. Available online at www.research.martinprosperity.org.

Many argue that the shift to a knowledge-intensive Creative Economy exacerbates levels of inequality as once high-paying, family-supporting manufacturing jobs inevitably decline and the labor market splits into higher-pay, higher-skill knowledge and professional jobs, on the one hand, and lower-pay, lower-skill service jobs, on the other. There is clear evidence that this is happening in the United States. But is this the case everywhere? Must more innovative and Creative Economies necessarily bring greater levels of economic inequality? To get at this, we examined the relationship between the GCI and a standard measure of income inequality, the Gini Index. Although it may come as a surprise to those familiar with the case of the United States, we found that the GCI is in fact systematically associated with *lower* levels of socioeconomic inequality—and hence

Figure 13.6 Creativity and Inequality Across Nations

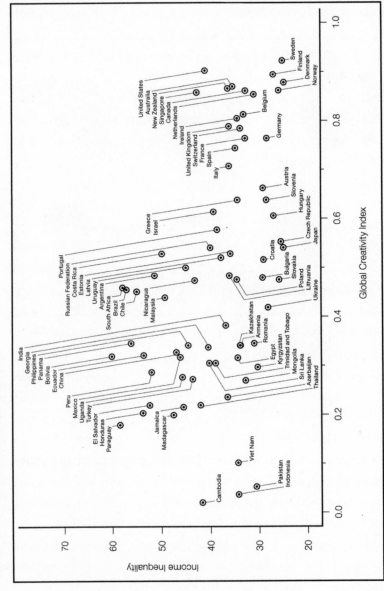

Source: Richard Florida, Charlotta Mellander, and Kevin Stolarick, *Creativity and Prosperity: The 2011 Global Creative Index,* University of Toronto, Martin Prosperity Institute Report, October 2011. Available online at www.research .martinprosperity.org.

greater equality—across the nations of the world. The correlation between inequality and the GCI is actually negative.[6]

Figure 13.6 plots the association between the Gini measure of income inequality and the GCI. On the one hand, there are countries like the United States, the United Kingdom, Singapore, and to a lesser extent, Australia and New Zealand, where high levels of creativity, productivity, and economic competitiveness go hand in hand with higher levels of inequality. But, on the other hand, there are also a large number of countries—mostly Scandinavian and Northern European nations, along with Japan—where high levels of creativity combine with much lower levels of inequality. In fact, this pattern appears to be the more general one, with the United States and Singapore appearing more as outliers. As Chapter 16 will show, US inequality appears to be at least in part driven not just by globalization, technology, and changes in the skills required of knowledge-based and creative jobs, but by concentrated poverty.

A high-road path to prosperity—an innovative and competitive economic system that causes far less severe socioeconomic divides than we are experiencing today in the United States—is not only possible, it is already in place in some of the world's most advanced and competitive nations.

In this respect, the United States has much to learn from other Creative Economies.

CHAPTER 14

Quality of Place

W hy do people—especially talented Creative Class people with lots of choices—opt to locate in certain places? What draws them to some places and not others? Economists and social scientists have paid a great deal of attention to the location decisions of companies, but they have virtually ignored how people, especially creative people, make the same choices. In search of answers, I began by simply asking people how they made their decisions about where to live and work. I started with my students and colleagues and then turned to friends and associates in other cities. Eventually, I began to ask virtually everyone I met. Ultimately, in the mid-2000s, I put the question at the heart of a major survey I conducted along with the Gallup Organization. The same answer came back, time and again.

Place itself, I began to realize, was the key factor. So much so, that I coined a term—*quality of place*—to sum it up. I use the term in contrast to the more traditional concept of quality of life. It refers to the unique set of characteristics that defines a place and makes it attractive. Over time, my colleagues and I have come to refer to it as the fourth T: "Territorial Assets." Generally, one can think of quality of place as cutting across three key dimensions:

What's there: the combination of the built environment and the natural environment; a proper setting for pursuit of creative lives.

Who's there: the diverse kinds of people, interacting and providing cues that anyone can make a life in that community.

What's going on: the vibrancy of street life, café culture, arts, music, and people engaging in outdoor activities—altogether a lot of active, exciting, creative endeavors.

Quality of place can be summed up as an interrelated set of experiences. Many of them, like the street-level scene, are dynamic and participatory. You can do more than be a passive spectator; you can be a part of the scene. The street buzz is right nearby if you want it, but you can also retreat to your home or some other quiet place, chill out in an urban park, or even set out for the country.

Many members of the Creative Class also want to have a hand in actively shaping their communities' quality of place. At that same meeting of the downtown revitalization group in Providence, Rhode Island, that I mentioned earlier, during which a member of the audience spoke about "troublemakers," another participant remarked: "My friends and I came to Providence because it already has the authenticity that we like—its established neighborhoods, historic architecture, and ethnic mix." He then implored the city leaders to make these qualities the basis of their revitalization efforts and to do so in ways that actively harness his and his peers' energy. Or as he aptly put it: "We want a place that's not *done*." Quality of place does not occur automatically; it is an ongoing dynamic process that engages a number of disparate aspects of a community. But like most good things, it is not all good—what looks like neighborhood revitalization from one perspective is gentrification from another; rising housing values often go hand in hand with the displacement of long-term residents, a serious problem that demands serious responses.

Some of my critics argue that my focus on quality of place is a distraction, pointing to tech enclaves like the suburbs of northern Virginia, Silicon Valley, or the outer rings of Seattle to make the point that the people who work in high-tech industries actually prefer traditional suburban lifestyles. My response is simple: all those places are located within major metropolitan areas that are among the most diverse in the country and that offer a wide array of lifestyle amenities. As colorless as those suburbs might appear to some, they are a product of the openness and diversity of their broader milieu. Silicon Valley can't be understood without reference to the counterculture of nearby San Francisco. Had it not been receptive to offbeat people like the young Steve Jobs years ago, it could not have become what it is today.

What people want is not an either-or proposition. Successful places do not provide just one thing; they provide a range of quality of place options for different kinds of people at different stages in their lives. Great cities are not monoliths; as Jane Jacobs said long ago, they are federations of neighborhoods. Think about New York City and its environs. When they first move to New York, young people live in relatively funky places like the East Village, South Slope, Williamsburg, or Hoboken, where there are lots of other young people, the rent is more affordable, and roommate situations can be found. When they earn a little more, they move to the Upper West Side or maybe Tribeca or SoHo; earn a little more and they can go to the West Village or the Upper East Side. Once marriage and children come along, some stay in the city while others relocate to bedroom communities in places like Westchester County, Connecticut, or the New Jersey suburbs. Later, when the kids are gone, some of these people buy a co-op overlooking the park or a duplex on the Upper East Side. Members of the Creative Class come in all shapes, sizes, colors, ages, and lifestyles. To be truly successful, cities and regions must offer something for all of them.

Social Capital and the City

I have mentioned Robert Putnam and his theory of social capital a number of times in the course of this book. Although I don't always agree with him, he is a distinguished scholar and a true public intellectual who has had a profound influence on my own thinking. I greatly admire his willingness to climb down from the ivory tower to address pressing social issues and stimulate informed public debate. The title of his widely read book *Bowling Alone* comes from his finding that from 1980 to 1993, league bowling declined by 40 percent, while the number of individual bowlers rose by 10 percent.[1] This, he argues, is just one indicator of a broader and more disturbing trend: a long-term decline in social capital. By this, he means that people have become increasingly disconnected from one another and from their communities. The decline is evident in everything from the loosening bonds between family, friends, and neighbors to declining participation in organizations of all sorts—churches, neighborhood associations, political parties, and recreational leagues. This social capital deficit is in turn rattling many aspects of our society, weakening our neighborhoods, affecting our health, making us less happy, damaging our educational system, threatening the well-being of our children, eroding our democracy, and threatening the very sources of our prosperity.

Putnam identified four key factors behind this civic malaise. First, longer working hours and increasing pressures of time and money mean we have less time to spend with one another. Second, rampant suburban sprawl keeps us farther away from family and friends and makes it harder for us to get to activities. Third, television and other electronic mass media take up more of our time, leaving less of it for more active pursuits and volunteer efforts. Fourth and most important, according to Putnam, is the "generational shift" from the "civic-minded generation of World War II" to "me-oriented" boomers and generation X-ers that followed.

Much of Putnam's account initially resonated with me. I grew up surrounded by relatives and friends in just the sort of community whose decline Putnam laments. My father belonged to the Italian-American Club; he was the manager of my Little League team, and my mother was a den mother for my Cub Scout troop. My brother and I played in our own rock band with some friends from Catholic school; we frequently entertained neighborhood kids in the basement of our family home. Pittsburgh, where I lived for nearly two decades, was filled with strong ethnic neighborhoods and bursting with community pride of the sort Putnam describes; it was thanks to its strong sense of community that it stayed as intact as it did in the wake of the near-total collapse of the region's steel and other heavy industries.

The Quasi-Anonymous Life

But as compelling as Putnam's story is, my own research led me to very different conclusions. The people in the focus groups and interviews I did when I was preparing the original edition of this book expressed little interest in living in tightly knit, social-capital kinds of communities; they did not want friends and neighbors peering over fences into their lives. Rather, they desired what I have come to call quasi-anonymity. Like the denizens of 1920s Greenwich Village whom Carolyn Ware described, they craved openness, diversity, and the ability to be themselves. Social structures that were the hallmark of community in the past were fading. Where strong ties among people were once important, weak ties are becoming the norm. Where old structures were once nurturing, they have become more and more restrictive and exclusionary. The life that Madison

Avenue and politicians encourage us to think of as distinctively American—close families and friends, tight neighborhoods, civic clubs, vibrant electoral politics, strong faith-based institutions, and a reliance on civic leadership—has been giving way to something new.

At the root of these changes is the distinction between two types of social bonds—strong versus weak ties. Strong ties are of long standing, marked by trust and reciprocity in multiple areas of life: the kinds of relationships we tend to have with family members, close friends, and longtime neighbors or coworkers. When you have strong ties with someone, you know each other's personal affairs and do things like trade visits, run errands, and do favors for one another. Practically all of us have at least a few such relationships; most people can manage between five and ten of them, according to sociologists who study such things. These are the friends you can confide in, the neighbor who watches your house while you're away, perhaps the uncle who gets you a job. The advantages of such relationships are obvious.

But weak ties are often more important. The modern theory of the "strength of weak ties" comes from the sociologist Mark Granovetter's classic research on how people find jobs.[2] When it comes to finding work, Granovetter discovered, weak ties matter more than strong ones. Other research on social networks has shown that weak ties are the key mechanism for mobilizing resources, ideas, and information, whether for finding a job, solving a problem, launching a new product, or establishing a new enterprise. The key reason that weak ties are so important is that we can manage so many more of them. Strong ties, by their nature, consume much more of our time and energy. Weak ties require less investment, and we can use them more opportunistically. Weak ties are critical to the creative environment of a city or region because they allow for rapid entry of new people and rapid absorption of new ideas.[3] The idea that proximity to total strangers is more important than connections to lifelong friends may seem strange until you think about it for a minute. Chances are, you and your close friends travel in mostly the same circles. You know the same people, frequent the same places, and hear about the same opportunities. Weak ties allow us to admit new people and new information into the equation, which exposes us to a larger set of novel and potentially unforeseen opportunities.

I am not advocating that we abandon our strong ties and opportunistically structure our lives around weak ones. That would be a lonely and shallow way of life, indeed, and it is the fate that Putnam fears we are facing. But most Creative Class people that I've met and studied do not aspire to such a life and don't seem to be falling into it. Most maintain a core of strong ties. They have significant others; they have close friends; they call Mom. But life in modern communities revolves around a larger set of looser ties, and interestingly enough, most people seem to prefer it that way.

The shift from small, homogeneous strong-tie communities to larger, more heterogeneous weak-tie communities is a basic fact of modern life, identified a century ago by the giants of modern social theory—Max Weber, George Simmel, and Emile Durkheim.[4] Writing in the 1930s, the influential German critical theorist Walter Benjamin quoted from a police report written in 1798 that lamented the fact that surveillance had become impossible because "each individual, unknown to all the others, hides in the crowd and blushes before the eyes of no one."[5] In his musings on nineteenth-century Parisian life, Baudelaire portrayed a city of passing encounters, fragmentary exchanges, strangers, and crowds where people could find relief from their "inner subjective demons." Although Baudelaire disliked many aspects of the city—the factories, the merchants, and the crowds—he "loved its freedom and its opportunities for anonymity and curious observation."[6] This aspect of city life was reflected in the *flaneur*—a citizen who is quasi-anonymous and free to enjoy the diversity of the city's experience.

The desire for such quasi-anonymous communities is not limited to urban enclaves. William Whyte identified it as a primary motivator behind the great migration of middle-class professionals from closely knit urban neighborhoods to the more transient suburbs in the 1950s. For Whyte, suburbia was a new kind of community—the preferred home of the new, upwardly mobile "transients" who could build the lives they desired, unencumbered by close family and ethnic-group ties.[7]

What People Really Want

So if creative people no longer want to live in a culture that revolves around a big corporation during the working day, and the church league and the Oddfellows and the Garden Club the rest of the time, what *do* they want? What draws them to some places rather than others?

Thick Labor Markets

Yes, jobs still matter. But it is not just a question of a single job. As we have seen, the old employment contract has broken down; people recognize that the idea of a job for life is a thing of the past. When I asked about the role that jobs and employment opportunities play in location decisions in interviews and focus groups, I kept hearing the same things. My subjects told me they could not settle for a location that provided just one good job; they needed to go to a place that offered many and varied employment opportunities. The reason, they told me, was simple. They did not expect to stay with the same company for very long. Companies are disloyal, and careers are increasingly horizontal. To be attractive, a place needed to offer a job market that is conducive to a horizontal career path.

In this way, place solves a basic puzzle of our economic order: It facilitates the matching of creative people to economic opportunities, providing a labor pool for companies that need people and a thick labor market for people who need jobs. Place has become the central organizing unit of our economy and society, taking on a role that used to be played by the large corporation. The gathering of people, companies, and resources into particular places with particular specialties and capabilities generates both the efficiencies and the innovations that power economic growth.

Lifestyle

The people in my focus groups told me they consider lifestyle alongside employment when choosing where to live. Many said that they had turned down jobs or decided not to look for them in places that did not afford the variety of scenes they desired—music, art, technology, outdoor sports, and so on. Some recounted how they or their friends had taken jobs for economic reasons, only to quit and move elsewhere for lifestyle reasons. In the course of my research, I have come across many people who moved somewhere for the lifestyle and only *then* set out to look for employment. This has been independently confirmed in systematic empirical research conducted since the original edition of this book. The most comprehensive study of the subject, "The Young and the Restless" by Joe Cortright and Carol Coletta found that though jobs and economic growth are important, highly educated young singles place a "higher priority on quality of life factors." Furthermore, their findings show that almost 60 percent of the time, well-educated young people are "more likely to move to a place with slower job growth than the place they left."[8]

People expect more from the places where they live than they used to. In the past, many were content to work in one place and vacation somewhere else, getting away for weekends to ski, enjoy a day in the country, or sample nightlife and culture in another city. Remember Clement Hayes, commuting between his job in Pittsburgh and his life in New York City, hundreds of miles away. The idea seemed to be that some places are for making money and others are for fun. This is no longer sufficient. The sociologists Richard Lloyd and Terry Nichols Clark of the University of Chicago note that "workers in the elite sectors of the postindustrial city make 'quality of life' demands, and increasingly act like tourists in their own city."[9] One reason is the nature of modern creative work. Of course, people still go away at times, but given their flexible and unpredictable work schedules, they want ready access to recreation on a just-in-time basis. They may need an extended break in the middle of a long, grueling workday to recharge their batteries and go for a bike ride or a run. For this, a beach house or country getaway spot doesn't do them much good. They require trails or parks close at hand.

Nightlife is another important part of the mix. A survey conducted by one of my former students found that for one-third of the respondents, nightlife is indeed an important component of a city's lifestyle and amenity mix. Defining nightlife as "all entertainment activities that happen after dark," the survey examined what younger Creative Class people (respondents ranged in age from early twenties into their thirties) desire in urban nightlife. The highest-rated nightlife options were cultural attractions from the symphony and theater to music venues and late-night dining, followed by small jazz and music clubs and coffee shops. Bars, large dance clubs, and after-hours clubs ranked much farther down the list. Most of the respondents desired a gestalt of entertainment options and safe and reliable "after-hours transportation."[10]

Time and again, the people I speak with, informally and in interviews and focus groups, say that the availability of a wide mix of cultural attractions is the signal that a place "gets it"—that it embraces the culture of the Creative Age; that it is a place where they can fit in. Interestingly, some of the biggest complaints I heard in my focus groups were about cities where the nightlife closes down too early. Not that most of those people were all-night partyers, but with long work hours and late nights, they wanted to have options around the clock.

Social Interaction

Not surprisingly, the ability to meet people and make friends is one of the most important factors that determines our happiness with our lives and communities. Human beings crave interaction, but as Putnam reminds us, modern society isolates us; satisfying interactions and social support are harder to find than they once were. As I mentioned in my book *Who's Your City?* a 2006 study by sociologists from the University of Arizona and Duke University found that the share of Americans who feel socially isolated in their communities (defined by having no one to talk to about personal matters) increased from 10 percent in 1985 to more than 25 percent in 2004.[11] Highly educated middle-class families felt this lack the most, possibly as a consequence of their longer commutes and working hours. The authors note that people are spending more time "interacting with multiple computers in the home, instead of with each other." But the biggest change since 1985, the study reports, has been the momentous decline in ties between neighbors. An increasing number of people live alone, and many of them lack friends or family nearby. A 2012 book by the sociologist Eric Klineberg, *Going Solo: The Extraordinary Rise and Surprising Appeal of Living Alone*, documents the substantial increase in the number of people living alone in America over the past several decades—from four million in 1950, slightly less than 10 percent of US households, to 32.7 million today, or 28 percent of US households.

One reason our cities and communities are changing is to help to fill that void. Ethan Watters has suggested that what he calls "urban tribes"[12]—close-knit groups of friends—are assuming the roles that families once did. "If our tribes were maximizing our weak ties within a city," Watters writes, "might we be creating the social science equivalent of dark matter—a force that was invisible but was nonetheless critical to holding everything together?" Furthermore, Watters argues, the urban tribe meets members' needs for self-expression and self-actualization in ways that actual parents and siblings sometimes suppress. As a young woman I interviewed in Chicago put it: "You don't get to pick your family. But you do get to pick your new family—your friends."

There are not just people we can turn to but places where we can go to allay our sense of isolation. The sociologist Ray Oldenburg identified the role played by "third places." Neither home nor work (the "first two" places), venues like coffee shops, bookstores, and cafés make up "the heart of a community's social vitality," places where people "hang out simply for the pleasures of good company and lively conversation." Barbershops, beauty parlors, and nail salons fill this role in many urban neighborhoods.[13]

Creative Class people in my focus groups and interviews report that such third places play critical roles in making a community attractive. Home life is less stable than it once was—many couples both have demanding jobs; many more people are single. And work life is changing as well. Even if we are lucky enough to have a secure job, more and more of us do not work on fixed schedules and many of us work in relative isolation—for instance, in front of a keyboard at home, as I often do. Human contact is harder to come by, and e-mail or phone interruptions only go so far. When I feel myself going stir crazy, I take a break and head to the coffee shop down the street, where I'm likely to run into someone I know. Many people I interviewed described doing pretty much the same thing.

Writing in the *Daily Beast* in July 2010, I noted the rise of the *fourth place*—a venue that integrates work and community. I defined it as a place where creative workers can go not just to "escape from work but to do some: to check our e-mail, post a tweet, to grab an impromptu meeting . . . it's ironic but true: it's hard to get any real work done in an office."[14] Real estate developers are beginning to respond to freelancers' and travelers' needs for temporary offices and meeting facilities, making cubicles, offices, and conference rooms available for rent on an as-needed basis.

The Mating Market

Another factor that's so basic that it's hard to imagine why it's so often overlooked is the need to be in a place where you might find people to date or, if you desire, a life partner. For young people, or older people who are looking for a second chance, the thickness of the mating market is as important as the thickness of the job market. Our odds of meeting a compatible partner are better in some locations than others. Not only are we more likely to make connections with people that we have something in common with—race, national origin, religion, job, education, lifestyle—but some places simply have more single people than others, as well as more amenities and activities that bring singles together.

In 2006, *National Geographic* published its wildly popular "Singles Map," which plotted the metros where single men outnumber single women, and vice versa. The metropolitan region with the best ratio for heterosexual men was New York's, which includes New York City and its suburbs in Long Island, Westchester, New Jersey, and Connecticut. Together, those areas housed 165,000 more single women than men. Other places where single women outnumbered single men were Boston, Washington, DC, Philadelphia, Baltimore, Miami, Chicago, Detroit, St. Louis, and San Francisco. On the other hand, the best ratio for heterosexual women was in greater Los Angeles, where single men outnumbered single women by 40,000. Other places favorable to single women included San Diego, Portland, Seattle, Dallas, Houston, and Austin.[15]

Diversity

If commonalities are important for mating, my focus group and interview participants consistently listed diversity as among the most important factors in their choice of locations. People were drawn to places that were known for diversity of thought and open-mindedness, and they looked for signs of it when evaluating communities—among them, a mix of ages, people of different ethnic groups and races, people with different sexual orientations and alternative appearances, such as significant body piercings or tattoos. Small wonder that when I polled a group of my Carnegie Mellon students about where they wanted to live after graduation, highly diverse Washington, DC, was the clear favorite. A Korean student liked it "because there's a big Korean community," meaning Korean religious institutions, Korean grocery stores, and Korean children for his children to play with. An Indian student favored it for its large Indian population, an African American for its large black professional class, and a gay student for the community around DuPont Circle. But there's more at work here than expatriates and minorities who want to be around people like themselves. The differences are important, too. A young female pre-med student of Persian descent summarized the many criteria for diversity:

> I was driving across the country with my sister and some friends. We were commenting on what makes a place the kind of place we want to go, or the kind of place we would live. We said: It has to be open. It has to be diverse. It has to have a visible gay community; it has to have lots of different races and ethnic groups. It has to have people of all ages and be open to young people. It has to have people who *look* different.[16]

Like the diverse workplace, a diverse community is a sign of a place that is open to outsiders. Just as domestic partner benefits convey that a potential employer is open and tolerant, a visible gay presence conveys that a community is broad-minded. Younger women in particular said they liked to live in gay neighborhoods because they feel safe. As with employers, visible diversity sends a signal that a community embraces the open meritocratic values of the Creative Age.

Diversity also means excitement and energy. Creative-minded people enjoy a mix of influences. They want to hear different kinds of music and try different kinds of food. They want to meet and socialize with people unlike themselves, to trade views and spar over issues. A person's circle of closest friends may not resemble the Rainbow Coalition—in fact, it usually doesn't—but creatives want the rainbow to be available.

An attractive place doesn't have to be a big city, but it does have to be cosmopolitan—a place where anyone can find a peer group to be comfortable with and other groups to be stimulated by, seething with the interplay of cultures and ideas, where outsiders can quickly become insiders. In her book *Cosmopolitan Culture*, Bonnie Menes Kahn says a great city has two hallmarks: tolerance for strangers and intolerance for mediocrity.[17] These are precisely the qualities that appeal to members of the Creative Class—and they also happen to be qualities conducive to innovation, risk taking, and the formation of new businesses.

Authenticity

Places are also valued for their authenticity and uniqueness. Authenticity comes from several aspects of a community—historic buildings, established neighborhoods, a distinctive music scene, or specific cultural attributes. It especially comes from the mix—urban grit alongside freshly renovated buildings, the commingling of young and old, longtime neighborhood characters and yuppies, fashion models and street people.

People in my interviews and focus groups often define authenticity as the opposite of generic. They equate authentic with being real, as in a place that has real buildings, real people, real history. A place that's full of chain stores, chain restaurants, and chain nightclubs is seen as inauthentic: Not only do these venues look pretty much the same everywhere, they offer the same experiences you could have anywhere. One of my Creative Class interview subjects, emphasizing the way people are attracted to the authenticity and uniqueness of a city, put the two terms together and used them as a portmanteau word:

> I'm thinking in particular of the Detroit Electronic Music Festival. Here was a free concert that drew a million people the first year . . . and featured a stellar lineup of Detroit and some national performers and DJs, a great boon to the city and its image. This year, they . . . start to drop Detroit artists in favor of more well-known national acts. So more people come, but the event is losing much of the uniqueness/authenticity that makes people want to come to this event from around the world.[18]

Music is a key part of what makes a place authentic. The phrase "audio identity"[19] refers to the identifiable musical genre or sound associated with local bands, clubs, and so on that give a city a unique sound track: electric blues in Chicago, Motown in Detroit, grunge in Seattle, Philadelphia soul, Austin's Sixth Street, second-line brass bands and R&B in New Orleans, bluegrass in greater DC. This is the first thing many people associate with these cities; it is also one of the principal ways that they promote themselves.

Music, in fact, plays a central role in the creation of identity and the formation of real communities. Musical memories are some of the strongest and most easily evoked. You can often remember events in your life by what songs were playing at the time. Simon Frith writes that music "provides us with an intensely subjective sense of being sociable. It both articulates and offers the immediate experience of collective identity. Music regularly sound tracks our search for ourselves and for spaces in which we can feel at home."[20]

It is hard to think of a major high-tech region that doesn't have a distinct audio identity. Consider the San Francisco Bay area, home to perhaps the most creative music scene of the 1960s, with the Grateful Dead, Jefferson Airplane, Big Brother and the Holding Company and Janis Joplin, Santana, The Mamas and the Papas, and the seminal Monterey Pop Festival. Chapel Hill, at the heart of the Research Triangle, was recently recognized for having one of the best local music scenes in the country. Technology and music scenes go together because they reflect a place that is open to new ideas, new people, and creativity. It is for this reason that I like to tell city leaders that finding ways to help support a local music scene can be just as important as investing in high-tech business and far more effective than building a downtown mall.

Scenes

Other kinds of sound tracks are important besides music. A big, exciting city can and does throw up countless scenes, which shift over time and space. Scenes enable talented people to collaborate and compete with one another—to seek inspiration, to look over and learn from each other's work. Authentic, locally grounded scenes help to establish a creative environment and the buzz of a place.

The dynamics of scenes are similar in some respects to the clusters and agglomerations of firms, people, and businesses. As the Harvard economist Richard Caves explains in his book *Creative Industries*, art, music, theater, design, and the like are characterized by high levels of uncertainty: it is nearly impossible to predict what will be a hit in advance. That makes it very difficult to organize these businesses and industries in a vertically integrated style like, say, automotive or steel production. Instead, they tend to take shape around clusters, agglomerations, and local scenes. As my former student Elizabeth Currid-Halkett points out in her insightful book, *The Warhol Economy*, these scenes are not just about going out and having fun but equally about work—building connections, learning from one another, networking, and building a career. Instead of doing this in companies and offices or at breakfast and lunch meetings at expense-account restaurants, this kind of social networking takes place in a local environment of clubs and performance venues.[21]

But scenes have social and psychological, and creative, dimensions, not just economic ones. Scenes are places where experiences are made and enjoyed—"modes of organizing cultural production and consumption," according to Daniel Silver, Terry Clark, and Lawrence Rothfield, who have written widely on them.[22] "Cafés, theatres, parks, music venues, restaurants, markets, shops, and other amenities," they write, "define a range of possible experiential qualities that give meaning and value to a given place." The value of scenes, in their view, comes from the way they make places more than just spaces for living and working. Scenes become "affective arenas for sharing, affirming or rejecting feelings, sensibilities and values" and provide "a range of symbolic meanings." They distinguish between different types of scenes—from highly authentic local scenes to self-expressive and highly glamorous and charismatic scenes. "Film festivals, high fashion, and movie stars may, for example, indicate the presence of a glamorous scene," whereas "tattoo parlours, punk music venues, body art studios and piercing salons" are associated with self-expressive scenes. "Local crafts stores, farmers markets, community centres and arts festivals" signal a crunchier, more environmentally aware, authentic scene.

A related study documents the ways that scenes directly and indirectly contribute to local economies. Bohemian neighborhoods, for example, are not just centers of arts and artiness, but provide key economic functions. Such neighborhoods—"filled with used clothing boutiques, late night bars, tattoo parlours, smoke shops, galleries, ethnic restaurants and marginal individuals" function as veritable "laboratories for generating new consumption styles," affording insight into what is cutting edge, youth-oriented, edgy, and retro. They provide companies access to edgy designers but also clued-in marketers who "can go to the bars and find out what is (about to be) hip" and who can "consume on the edge of accepted conventions, without themselves having to be artists or revolutionaries." Their research finds an especially close connection between "self-expressive scenes" and economic growth. In their analysis of the effects of more than twenty separate variables on the economic performance of thousands of neighborhoods (measured at the zip code level) across the United States, they found that self-expressive scenes had the biggest impact of all—more than "such urban development staples as growth and level of human capital, arts jobs, technology jobs, population density, and commute times." And they found that the economic effects of such scenes went beyond their role in attracting talented and creative people. No other "single variable" they concluded, "showed as consistently strong and broad a set of economic impacts" as the presence of self-expressive scenes.[23]

Identity

As the sociologist Manuel Castells noted in his seminal *The Power of Identity*, an elusive, varied sense of self has become a defining feature of our insecure, constantly changing, postmodern world, where so many traditional institutions no longer provide meaning, stability, and support.[24] In the old economy, many people took their cues from the corporation and found their identity there. Others lived in the towns where they grew up and could draw on the strong ties of family and long-term friends.

Today, where we choose to live as opposed to what we do has become our main element of identity. I travel by plane a lot and have noticed that the standard conversation-starter has changed. Twenty years ago, people were likely to ask, "Where do you work?" Today it's "Where do you live?"

With the demise of the company-dominated life, a new kind of pecking order has developed around places. Place, of course, has always been a source of status; the right neighborhoods in cities like Paris, London, and New York City have always been highly desirable. But if most people were content to substitute the status that came from having a good job with a prestigious company for the status of place, this is no longer the case. Most of the people in my focus groups and interviews told me they hope to trade up to a higher-status location.

As noted, many Creative Class people also express a desire to be involved in their communities. This is not so much the result of a do-gooder mentality as a reflection of their desire to establish their own identities in places, and to build places that reflect and validate those identities. In Pittsburgh, for instance, a group of young people in creative fields, ranging from architecture and urban design to graphics and high-tech, formed a loose association they dubbed Ground Zero. The group emerged on its own out of a series of brainstorming sessions that I organized in early 2000 to gain insight into the lifestyle and other concerns of young Creative Class people. The group's initial impetus was to combat a redevelopment plan that would have replaced an authentic downtown shopping district with a generic urban mall, but then it shifted its focus to reshaping the creative climate and identity of the whole city. From organizing edgy community arts events to working to organize a shuttle system to establish connectivity between the various neighborhoods that make up Pittsburgh's street-level mix—they called it the Ultra-Violet Loop—they sought to implant their creative identity into the urban fabric of the city.

The role of place in our identity is also evident in the growing struggles over who controls places. I got a firsthand taste of the passions that so-called gentrification inspires one warm night in Seattle's up-and-coming Belltown neighborhood in May 2000. Walking down newly fashionable First Avenue, with its mix of high-tech companies, high-end residences, and nice restaurants, our group came upon a ragtag band banging on drums and bellowing: "Say no to the construction noise." Jolted by the commotion, well-dressed yuppies emerged onto the street to see what it was about. A boisterous debate broke out between them and the protesters over who were the neighborhood's "true" residents.

Soul of the Community

Back when this book was first published, my views on quality of place stoked quite a backlash. Conservative social critics and even a number of self-proclaimed urbanists complained that I was urging cities to squander money on frivolities that only the urban gentry, bohemian gays, and feckless, spoiled young people really cared about. Most Americans, they said, continued to opt for good schools, safe streets, and a family-friendly environment. Although it has been debated endlessly, this is a question that can in fact be settled empirically. As I mentioned earlier, in the mid-2000s, I undertook a large-scale study with the Gallup Organization.

The survey led us to several important insights. One is that place itself is an important contributor to our happiness and subjective well-being. Subjective well-being is a clunky-sounding locution, but it is how psychologists describe an individual's self-reported level of happiness. In his book *Stumbling on Happiness*, Harvard psychologist Daniel Gilbert lists the three most important decisions that most of us will make in our lives: "where to live, what to do, and with whom to do it."[25] Place, in his telling, is the first leg in the triangle of a happy and fulfilled life—something that my research objectively confirms.

Our second insight revolves around the attributes or characteristics of places that contribute to our happiness and satisfaction. We looked at a wide array of factors that fell into five major categories: physical and economic security, that is, the presence of a thriving job market, low crime rate, and so forth; basic services, like schools, trash removal, and road repair; leadership, or the forward-looking qualities of community stakeholders and politicians; openness to immigrants, minorities, gay people, and the like; and quality of place, meaning natural scenery, parks, architecture, and so on.

What we found might shock those who still subscribe to the view that the basics trump everything else. The most highly valued attributes of cities weren't basic services or economic opportunities, but a place's social and cultural amenities, its friendliness, and its natural and physical beauty. This isn't just me talking. With financial support from the Knight Foundation, Gallup has expanded and updated the survey that we originally undertook together. It is now called the Soul of the Community Study.[26] "After interviewing close to 43,000 people in twenty-six communities over three years, Gallup concluded in 2011, "the study has found that three main qualities attach people to place: social offerings, such as entertainment venues and places to meet, openness (how welcoming a place is) and the area's aesthetics (its physical beauty and green spaces)."[27]

Gallup's and Knight's findings actually make a great deal of intuitive sense. Most people expect their communities to provide basic services, and most communities do. Because we expect basic services to be provided, we end up valuing aesthetics a little higher. Economists call this a beauty premium.[28] As for openness, the survey probed it in detail by asking respondents how they would rate their city or area as a place to live for families with children, racial and ethnic minorities, gays and lesbians, immigrants, the poor, young singles, recent college grads, and so on. As the level of tolerance toward each group rose, the overall happiness of the community increased. One finding did surprise us. The group that communities were least open to was recent college graduates looking for work. Although cities and towns around the country have upped their efforts to battle brain drain, the reality is that most are less than welcoming to the young talented people who do choose to live in them. I'll have more to say about this in the next chapter.

The key conclusions of the Soul of the Community Survey are so interesting and powerful that they are worth quoting at length.

> After three years of research, the results have been very consistent, and possibly surprising. First, what attaches residents to their communities doesn't change much from place to place. While we might expect that the drivers of attachment would be different in Miami, Fla., from those in Macon, Ga., in fact, the main drivers of attachment show little difference across communities. In addition, the same drivers have risen to the top in every year of the study.
>
> Second, these main drivers may be surprising. While the economy is obviously the subject of much attention, the study has found that perceptions of the local economy do not have a very strong relationship to resident attachment. Instead, attachment is most closely related to how accepting a community is of diversity, its wealth of social offerings, and its aesthetics. This is not to say that jobs and housing aren't important. Residents must be able to meet their basic needs in a community in order to stay. However, when it comes to forming an emotional connection with the community, there are other community factors which often are not considered when thinking about economic development. These community factors seem to matter more when it comes to attaching residents to their community.
>
> And finally, while we do see differences in attachment among different demographic groups, demographics generally are not the strongest drivers

of attachment. In almost every community, we found that a resident's perceptions of the community are more strongly linked to their level of community attachment than to that person's age, ethnicity, work status, etc.

Quality of life features define the very soul of a successful community. And though they are factors that the Creative Class in particular desires, they are things that everyone wants in their communities, regardless of their demographic or economic status. This is not to say that great schools, good jobs, and safe streets do not also matter. Quite the contrary. But those who continue to frame the issue as an either-or between quality and basic services offer a false choice. In *Who's Your City?* I likened what we want in our communities to psychologist Abraham Maslow's hierarchy of needs. Just as we want more from our lives than the mere basics of bodily subsistence, we also desire more from our communities. Quality of place, it turns out, is less a frivolity and more a necessity.

CHAPTER 15

Building the Creative Community

O ne of the questions I get asked most frequently is: how do you actually do it, how do you build a truly creative community—one with real quality of place—that can survive and prosper in this still-emerging new economic order? There is no easy, silver-bullet answer, but one thing is for certain: the old approaches simply will not work. It's not enough to just provide good schools or a family-friendly environment, just as it is not enough merely to have an environment that's teeming with restaurants and bars. Neither gargantuan downtown stadiums and convention centers nor gleaming arts centers, leafy suburbs ringed with high-tech industrial parks, and upscale shopping malls are sufficient unto themselves. It makes no sense to use precious public funds to lure companies from state to state or even across national borders: research shows those efforts typically cost more than they are worth. Trying to be the next Silicon Somewhere seldom pays off, either, as countless communities have learned.

The rise of the Creative Economy has altered the rules of the economic development game. Cities used to measure their status by the number of corporate headquarters they were home to. Although companies remain important, they no longer call all the shots. As I've said repeatedly, it's people who are increasingly key. In the original edition of this book, I quoted Robert Nunn, then the CEO of a major semiconductor company, who told the *Wall Street Journal* that the "key element of building a technology business is attracting the right people to the company. It's a combination of experience, skill set, raw intelligence, and energy. The most important thing is to be somewhere where you have a pool of people to draw that."[1]

The bottom line is that cities need a *people climate* as much as, and perhaps even more than, they need a business climate. By a people climate I mean a general strategy aimed at attracting and retaining people, especially, but not limited to, creative people. The benefits of this kind of strategy are obvious. Openness costs nothing. Whereas companies that get financial incentives—and sports teams, for that matter—can pull up and leave at virtually a moment's notice when an even more attractive inducement materializes somewhere else, investments in broad amenities like urban parks last for generations while benefiting a broad swath of the population.

There is no one-size-fits-all model for a successful people climate. As we have seen, the Creative Class is diverse across the dimensions of age, ethnicity and race, marital status, and sexual orientation. An effective people climate cannot be restrictive or monolithic. Truly creative communities appeal to many different groups. Building a creative community is something of an organic process, one that cannot be dictated in any top-down fashion. It's a matter of providing the right conditions, planting the right seeds, and then letting things take their course. A decade ago, I pointed out that I had yet to find a community whose leaders and citizens have sat down and written out an explicit strategy for building a people climate. Most communities, however, do have a de facto one. If you ask most community leaders what kinds of people they'd most want to attract, they'd likely say successful married couples in their thirties and forties—people with good middle- to upper-income jobs and stable family lives. And this in fact is what many communities (particularly suburban ones) actually do, by emphasizing services like good school systems, parks with plenty of amenities for children, and strict (read: exclusionary) zoning for single-family housing. I certainly think it is important for cities and communities to be good for children and families, and I am fully supportive of better schools and parks. But as we have seen, less than one quarter of all American households consist of traditional nuclear families. Communities that want to be economically competitive need to cast their nets wider, to appeal to all the diverse groups of people that make up both the Creative Class and American society at large.

And as mentioned in the previous chapter, one group that has been sorely neglected by most communities, at least until recently, is young single people. Young workers have typically been thought of as transients who contribute little to a city's bottom line. But in the Creative Age, they matter for several reasons. Young people are workhorses: they are able to work longer and harder and are more prone to take risks, precisely because they are young and childless. In rapidly changing industries, it's often the recent graduates who have the most up-to-date skills. This is why so many leading companies aggressively target them in their recruiting strategies. In Washington, DC, it's often quipped that twenty-three-year-olds run the country.

Single people make up a large and growing segment of our demography. In the early 1960s, approximately 80 percent of Americans lived in households headed by married couples. As of 2010, that number had fallen to just a bit less than one-half—48.4 percent—or 56.6 million out of 116.7 million total households. As noted previously, people are marrying later and staying single longer.

Younger people are the most mobile group in society. The likelihood that someone will move peaks at around age twenty-five, declines steeply for the next two decades, and then continues to trail off into retirement and old age. A twenty-five-year-old is three times more likely to move than a forty-five- or fifty-year-old, according to a 2005 study.[2] Highly educated young people are the most mobile of all.

The mathematics of this do not bode well for cities and regions that are content to watch their young people move away in search of fun and adventure, complacently believing that they will be able to lure them back once they hit their thirties and are ready to settle down and start families. The likelihood that they will move back diminishes with each year they spend away. The winning places are the ones that establish an edge early on, by attracting and retaining residents in their mid-twenties.

But in the end, age is less relevant than most people think. What does matter is that cities and regions have a people climate that values every type of person and every type of family. Creative Class people don't give up their lifestyle preferences as they age. They don't stop bicycling or running, for instance, just because they have children. When they put their children in child seats or jogging strollers, amenities like traffic-free bike paths become more important than ever. They don't stop valuing diversity and tolerance, either. The middle-aged and older people I speak with may no longer hang out in nightspots until 4:00 AM, but they enjoy stimulating, dynamic places with high levels of cultural interplay. And if they have children, that's the kind of environment they want them to grow up in. Some things that benefit young people are even supported by those old enough to be their grandparents. When a colleague of mine spoke to a group of senior citizens in Pittsburgh about the importance of lifestyle amenities like bike paths, he got a fascinating response. The seniors were enthusiastic about the idea, because the bike lanes would keep the cyclists off the sidewalks, where the seniors were frightened by them and sometimes even knocked down.

A woman from Minneapolis whom I interviewed put the age issue into perspective. She originally came to Minneapolis as a young single because of the lifestyle it offered. She liked being able to engage in active outdoor recreation in the city's fabulous park system and being able to walk from her house to bars and clubs. She never thought she would want to raise a family there. But when she got married and had children, she was more than pleasantly surprised to discover that some of the same lifestyle amenities she had enjoyed when she was single—the parks and walkable neighborhoods—were even more attractive to her as a new parent.

Lots and lots of families prefer to stay in urban settings. In my book *Who's Your City?* I quoted a 2007 *New York Times* report that found that the number of children under age five living in Manhattan had increased by nearly one-third since 2000. The borough that was the "glamorous and largely childless locale for *Sex and the City*" was starting to more closely resemble "a decidedly upscale and even more vanilla version of 1960s suburbia in *The Wonder Years*," it added.[3] A 2006 Yankelovich survey found that young married couples with children were as open to moving to urban neighborhoods close to downtown as to small towns and suburbs— as anyone who has ever tried to negotiate the stroller-clogged sidewalks of Park Slope, Brooklyn, well knows.[4]

True, many of those families tend to leave the city when their kids reach school age. The demography of urban America resembles a barbell, with singles and empty-nesters bulging at both ends of the age spectrum. But what's important to remember is that families themselves are increasingly diverse; cities that attract diverse people necessarily attract families. While some maintain that my findings regarding gays and regional growth put me at odds with family values, they miss the fact that many gay and lesbian households are families with children. Roughly half of lesbians and gay men in the United States, between 4 and 5 million people, were members of same-sex couples in 2011, including an estimated 160,000 who are married, according to Gary Gates's detailed studies. And nearly one in five of those same-sex couple households were

Table 15.1 Leading Metros for Same-Sex Households with Children, 2010

Rank	Metro	Same-Sex Couples with Children	Creative Class Share
1	San Antonio-New Braunfels, TX	33.9%	31.2%
2	Jacksonville, FL	32.4%	30.4%
3	Raleigh-Cary, NC	29.5%	37.6%
4	Las Vegas-Paradise, NV	28.4%	22.7%
5	Providence-New Bedford-Fall River, RI-MA	28.1%	31.3%
6	Rochester, NY	28.1%	35.1%
7	Houston-Sugar Land-Baytown, TX	27.2%	33.0%
8	Hartford-West Hartford-East Hartford, CT	26.7%	39.7%
9	Riverside-San Bernardino-Ontario, CA	25.7%	27.4%
10	Oklahoma City, OK	25.4%	33.0%
11	Buffalo-Niagara Falls, NY	24.9%	31.3%
12	Dallas-Fort Worth-Arlington, TX	24.9%	34.3%
13	Baltimore-Towson, MD	24.8%	37.7%
14	Detroit-Warren-Livonia, MI	24.5%	34.5%
14	Kansas City, MO-KS	24.2%	34.8%

Source: Gary Gates, "How Many People Are Lesbian, Gay, Bisexual and Transgender?" UCLA Williams Institute, April 2011.

raising children.[5] Table 15.1, provided by Gates, shows the fifteen metros that have the largest percentage of same-sex couples with children under eighteen years old. The densest concentrations of such families are not necessarily in the places where you'd expect to find them. Especially surprising are the metros that don't make the cut—for instance, San Francisco and New York.

The University as Creative Hub

The potential of the university as an engine for regional economic development has captured the fancy of business leaders, policy makers, and academics—and it has led them astray. A theory of sorts has been handed down that assumes a linear pathway from university research to commercial innovation to an ever-expanding network of newly formed companies. This is a naive and mechanistic view of the university's contribution to economic development.

The university is indeed a key institution of the Creative Economy, but what's not so widely understood is the multifaceted role that it plays. It doesn't simply crank out research projects that can be spun off into companies. To be an effective contributor to regional growth, the university must play three interrelated roles that reflect the 3T's of creative communities.[6]

Technology: Universities are centers for cutting-edge research in fields from software to biotechnology and important sources of new technologies and spin-off companies.

Talent: Universities are amazingly effective talent magnets. By attracting eminent researchers and scientists, universities in turn attract graduate students, generate spin-off companies, and encourage other companies to locate nearby in a cycle of self-reinforcing growth.

Tolerance: Universities foster a progressive, open, and tolerant people climate that helps attract and retain members of the Creative Class. College towns from Austin to Iowa City have always been places where gays and other outsiders in those parts of the country could find a home.

In doing these things, universities help to establish the broader quality of place of the communities in which they are located.

In my view, major research universities are key—if not *the* key—hubs of the Creative Economy. The Boston high-tech miracle would not have happened without MIT. Silicon Valley would be unthinkable without Stanford University, its longtime creative nucleus. Many of the places that score high on my Creativity Index are home to major research universities. This includes large metros like San Francisco, greater Washington, DC, Seattle, Boston, and classic college towns like Madison, Burlington, Boulder, and Ann Arbor.

In late 2011, New York City hosted a competition to lure a major engineering and technology campus to Roosevelt Island, which drew proposals from Stanford University and Carnegie Mellon among others, before a consortium of Cornell University and Technion Israel Institute of Technology was selected. "This is Mayor Michael Bloomberg's attempt to create a locus of entrepreneurial education that would mate with venture capital to spawn new enterprises and enrich the city's economy," is the way the *New York Times*'s Bill Keller put it. The mayor himself noted: "New York City's goal of becoming the global leader in technological innovation is now within sight. By adding a new state-of-the-art institution to our landscape, we will educate tomorrow's entrepreneurs and create the jobs of the future. This partnership has so much promise because we share the same goal: to make New York City home to the world's most talented workforce."

But a university cannot do it alone—it is a necessary but insufficient condition for generating high-tech firms and growth. Although many places generate new knowledge, relatively few of them can absorb and apply it. The surrounding community must also have the capacity to exploit the innovation and technologies that the university generates, and the will to put in place the broader lifestyle amenities and qualities of place the Creative Class seeks. The economist Michael Fogarty has found that patented intellectual property consistently migrates from universities in older industrial regions such as Detroit and Cleveland to high-technology regions such as the greater Boston area, the San Francisco Bay region, and the New York metropolitan area. To turn intellectual property into economic wealth, the creative communities surrounding the universities must be able to utilize it within a social structure of creativity.

The university is only one part of this social structure. It is up to communities to put the other pieces into place: both the economic infrastructure and the quality of place to retain the talent the university attracts. Stanford did not transform the Silicon Valley area into a high-tech powerhouse on its own, nor did MIT make Cambridge what it is. The once run-down Kendall Square area around MIT had to be refurbished and renovated, its abandoned factories and warehouses turned into homes for start-up companies and venture-capital funds, not to mention restaurants, microbreweries, cafés, and hotels. Regional leaders in Austin undertook aggressive measures to create not only incubator facilities and venture capital but outdoor amenities and the quality of place that creative people demand. A pioneering initiative in Philadelphia, Campus Philly, has worked to make the city and region more attractive to college students and to retain as well as attract recent college grads. And the city's major universities, especially the University of Pennsylvania, have devised new and more cooperative approaches for revitalizing their surrounding neighborhoods by investing in local schools, supporting home and storefront improvements, and opening their health centers and other facilities to residents as well as students and faculty. University and regional leaders in cities like Providence, Pittsburgh, and Baltimore have worked hard to develop quality of place in and around their universities.

Revenge of the Squelchers

So why are so many communities unable to leverage the considerable creative assets they have? It's not that these places don't want to grow. In most cases, their leaders are doing everything they think they can to spur innovation and high-tech growth. But most of the time, they either can't or won't do the things required to create an environment or habitat that is attractive to the Creative Class. They pay lip service to the need to attract talent but dedicate their resources to underwriting big-box retailers, subsidizing downtown malls and convention centers, and recruiting corporations to relocate their call centers to their corporate parks. Or they try to reinvent themselves as facsimiles of quirkiness and charm, erasing their old, authentic neighborhoods and retail districts and replacing them with the generic and new—and in so doing driving the resident Creative Class away.

At a time when genuine political will seems difficult to muster for virtually anything, city after city across the country can generate the political capital to underwrite hundreds of millions of dollars of investment in professional sports stadiums. The ostensible economic goal of these facilities is one to which they are sublimely irrelevant. Recent studies show that, far from producing wealth, stadiums actually reduce local incomes.[7] Ponder, just for a moment, the opportunity costs of these facilities. Imagine what could be accomplished if those hundreds of millions of dollars had been spent on something genuinely productive, like university research, or on more finely grained neighborhood improvements and lifestyle amenities that can actually attract and retain talented people. Not once during any of my focus groups and interviews did a member of the Creative Class mention professional sports teams as playing even a marginal role in their choice of where to live and work. Why are most civic leaders unable to muster the will to pursue the things that really matter to their communities and their economic futures— or even to imagine that such things exist?

The answer is simple. These cities are trapped by their pasts. The economist Mancur Olson long ago noted that the decline of nations and regions is a product of an organizational and cultural hardening of the arteries that he called "institutional sclerosis."[8] Places that grow and prosper in one era, he argued, find it difficult, oftentimes impossible, to adopt new organizational and cultural patterns, regardless of how beneficial they might be. Consequently, innovation and growth shift to new places, which can adapt to and harness these shifts for their benefit. This is why the United States surpassed England as the world's great economic power, he contends. Olson's prophetic diagnosis explains the decline of cities like Detroit, Cleveland, and Pittsburgh, the great stars of the Organizational Age, and the rise of creative centers like Silicon Valley and Austin, and the adaptability of great cities like New York and Los Angeles, which have eclipsed and supplanted them. The cultural and attitudinal norms that drove their success became so engrained that they prevented the new norms and attitudes of the Creative Age from becoming generally accepted. Instead of nurturing their cities' creativity, their leaders stamped it out, causing talented people to seek out more congenial and challenging places. Their departure, in turn, removed much of the impetus for change.

When traveling to cities for speaking engagements, I have come up with a handy metric to distinguish the cities that are a part of the Creative Age from those that are not. If city leaders tell me to wear whatever I want, take me to a casually contemporary café or restaurant for dinner, and, most important, encourage me to talk openly about the role of diversity and gays, I am confident their city will be able to attract the Creative Class and prosper in this emerging era. If, on the other hand, they ask me to "please wear a business suit and a tie," escort me to a private club for dinner, and ask me to "play down the stuff about bohemians and gays," I can be reasonably certain that they will have a hard time making it.

Not long after the first edition of this book was published, I was invited to Toronto to participate in a public conversation with Jane Jacobs, humorously billed as "Lunch with Dick and Jane." Before we went on I asked her, why do some places make it and others get trapped? She told me that all communities are filled with deep reservoirs of creative energy. But what holds so many back, she added, are "Squelchers"—overly controlling types who believe that they and they alone know what's best for their city or region. They use the word *no* a lot and respond to new initiatives or ideas with comments like, "That's not how we do things here"; "That will never fly"; or "Why don't you just move someplace else?"

Writing in the preface to the Australian edition of this book, the Australian entrepreneur Terry Cutler described some of these Squelchers at work in his account of a presentation he made before a gathering of distinguished intellectuals and civic leaders. "Summoning my courage," he writes, "I described Florida's findings about the correlation between bohemianism and diversity in the location of high-tech firms. The palpable recoil around the room at such a radical and distasteful recipe for success left me in no doubt that these civic leaders would clearly prefer to drift into a genteel poverty."[9]

The venture capitalist Paul Graham, the founder of Y Combinator, Silicon Valley's premier start-up funding firm, has thought long and hard about what makes for a successful start-up hub. Most places that aspire to be the next Silicon Valley, he writes, have amounted to little more than "roach motels" for start-ups: "Smart ambitious people went in, but no start-ups came out."[10] It is as if, Graham wrote, those places were sprayed with "start-upicide." What makes Silicon Valley and a very few other places different, he noted, is that they embrace an ethos that encourages rather than crushes start-ups and the broader mentality from which they grow. "The problem is not that most towns kill start-ups. It's that death is the default for start-ups and most towns don't save them," he explains. "Instead of thinking of most places as being sprayed with start-upicide, it's more accurate to think of start-ups as all being poisoned, and a few places being sprayed with the antidote."

The Great Creative Class Debate

I would have never imagined that my theory relating openness and tolerance to economic growth would become so controversial when I was first writing this book. And yet I opened a floodgate. One critic quipped that it was ridiculous to put street buskers with T-shirts and jeans at the center of regional growth. Another claimed that I am wrongly focused on "singles, young people, homosexuals, sophistos, and trendoids." In the decade since the original edition of this book was published, I have been accused of attacking traditional family values, of promoting a gay agenda, and of undermining the foundations of Judeo-Christian civilization.

I have taken flack from the right as a pseudo-leftist:

> To a new generation of liberal urban policymakers and politicians who favor big government, Florida's ideas offer a way to talk economic-development talk while walking the familiar big-spending walk. . . . Now comes Florida with the equivalent of an eat-all-you-want-and-still-lose-weight diet. Yes, you can create needed revenue-generating jobs without having to take the unpalatable measures—shrinking government and cutting taxes—that appeal to old-economy businessmen, the kind with starched shirts and lodge pins in their lapels. You can bypass all that and go straight to the new economy, where the future is happening now. You can draw in Florida's creative-class capitalists—ponytails, jeans, rock music, and all—by liberal, big-government means: diversity celebrations, "progressive" social legislation, and government spending on cultural amenities.[11]

And from the left as a proverbial sellout:

> Florida's proposals ultimately amount to a plea for grassroots agency with a communitarian conscience amongst a privileged class of creatives, lubricated

by modest public-sector support for culturally appropriate forms of gentrification and consumption. There is no challenge to the extant "order" of
market-oriented flexibility. . . . Florida is not asking for a blank check for
new government programs, for major concessions to be made to the non-
creative underclasses, nor even for regulatory transformation. His calls for
creative empowerment can be met in relatively painless ways—by manip-
ulating street-level façades, while gently lubricating the gentrification processes. This, critics justly complain, is cappuccino urban politics, with plenty
of froth.[12]

An attack piece in the *American Prospect* accused me of essentially
fleecing the rubes, giving speeches, consulting with economic development groups in hard-hit Rust Belt towns, and then pronounc-
ing them dead in the water.[13] The alleged smoking gun was a single
sentence in my 2009 cover story in *The Atlantic,* "How the Crash
Will Reshape America": "We need to be clear that we can't stop
the decline of some places, and that we would be foolish to try."[14]
The gist of my remarks was aimed at the federal government's
bailout of the big automakers who had managed themselves into
financial ruin. My larger point was that the crisis had blighted
the prospects of some places—not just older industrial cities but
the Sun Belt's cities of sand as well—whereas others would rebound
more quickly.

I have spent my entire life living, working, and studying in industrial cities. I adore the realness and authenticity of these great
cities. I have always believed and still believe that they can return
to prosperity, if not to their former grandeur. As we have seen,
some already have. But today's key drivers and revivers of economic
growth are not massive government programs aimed at reviving
old industries, but rather community-based efforts to cultivate diversity and harness human creativity from all possible quarters. As
Ryan Avent of the *Economist* responded to the piece at the time:

The man went from city to city encouraging leaders to be gay-friendly, to support artists, to encourage creativity, and to build amenities like bike lanes. Perhaps he was wrong to suggest that these measures would deliver an economic turnaround. I'd say he was less wrong about the secret to urban success than those urging cities to throw tax incentives at potential employers, or those suggesting that we ought to adopt an industrial policy aimed at returning Midwestern cities to manufacturing glory.[15]

To which the urbanist Aaron Renn added:

I might even suggest that if there is any scamming going on, the arrow is pointing the other direction. Cities go hire a big name like Florida to give a speech or two and do a few flash in the pan arts projects, all for a very small sum of cash. They trumpet that as showing Something Is Being Done and that change will happen Real Soon Now. Then they go back to doing what it is they really want to do—namely spending money on all those other things.[16]

The *American Prospect* essay didn't just criticize me, but also the allegedly circular nature of my theory, writing: "A tautology lies at the heart of Florida's theory that has limited its instructive value all along: Creative people seek out places that draw a lot of creative people. Florida has now taken this closed-loop argument to another level by declaring that henceforth, the winners' club is closed to new entrants."[17] But in fact this tautology is the very mechanism by which cities, urbanization, and economic development works. Renn describes it as a positive feedback system. "Mathematical truths like '2 + 2 = 4' are tautologies," he writes. "A positive feedback system is one where an effect tends to produce more of itself." Avent adds:

That tautology doesn't just lie at the heart of Florida's theory; it describes the actual functioning of urban economies. The value in economically dynamic cities is the people that populate them. Where once, firms would pay high land prices to be near coal deposits or harbors, based on the economic advantages those amenities conferred, they now pay high land prices to be near talent. This yen to concentrate in particular areas has a number of dynamics. Firms want to be near customers and clients. Workers want to be near firms. Firms want to be near workers. Where there are lots of firms and workers, there will also be businesses serving those workers—in business and in the provision of consumption opportunities—and those services attract additional firms and workers. Everyone wants to be where everyone is, and it's tough for anyone to go somewhere else because somewhere else is where people aren't. The result is an urban geography that's very lumpy. People clump together, because there are gains to doing so.[18]

I'm an open book. I harbor no hidden agendas. Over the course of a more than three decades long academic career, my work has been concerned with one thing: identifying the key factors that drive economic growth. When I find myself in front of audiences primarily interested in arts, culture, or diversity issues, I always begin with an apology: I am not a student of those subjects, I say, I have only a cursory understanding of them. The reason I came to arts, culture, and diversity issues (rather late in my career) is because I found them to be fundamental to the process of economic growth.

In the interest of full disclosure, I should say that I'm politically independent, fiscally conservative, socially liberal, and a believer in vigorous international competition and free trade. As I write, I'm middle-aged, white, Italian-American, married, and straight. I have voted for and served under Democrats, Republicans, and independents, and I work closely with mayors, governors, and business, political, and civic leaders from both sides of the aisle on economic development issues. The members of my core team of colleagues and collaborators include Canadian, Swedish, and other international researchers, as well as Americans, registered

Democrats and Republicans, far left socialists, staunch conservatives, liberals and libertarians, married and single people who are both straight and gay, recent college graduates and the middle-aged. What binds us together is not a political agenda but our common determination to identify the factors that drive economic development and rising standards of living.

Let me be clear on where I stand. I believe in markets but recognize government has an important role to play. That said, I don't advocate giving government a blank check. I have unequivocally maintained that large, top-down development projects are a major part of the problem. I roundly criticize public boondoggles like stadium-building efforts, giant convention centers, and urban casinos; in fact, I've called for a moratorium on all such government mega-projects. Real economic development is people oriented, organic, and community-based. Nor do I believe in favoring the Creative Class over any other group. My theory says that we need to harness the creativity of each and every person. I have pointed to the rising inequality of wages, the unaffordability of housing, and the increasing spikiness of our world as perhaps the key issue of our time, one that new institutions and a new social compact are required to solve. I urge communities everywhere to spend their money wisely, to do the small things that matter, and to focus on being open to everyone.

Back to the City

In the original edition of this book, I identified the beginning of a back-to-the-city movement fueled by the rise of the Creative Class and the Creative Economy. I pointed to data from the 2000 US Census that documented the trend in cities as diverse as New York and Oakland, California. I cited the 2000 *State of the Cities* Report by the Department of Housing and Urban Development, which found that high-tech jobs made up almost 10 percent of all jobs in central cities, roughly the same as in the suburbs, and that high-tech job growth in cities had increased at three times the national average in the 1990s.[19] I used Seattle to illustrate the trend. Nearly one-half of all high-tech jobs in Seattle were located in the city (most of them in the central business district, Pioneer Square, and Belltown), versus 35 percent in the suburbs, according to a 2000 study by Paul Sommers and Daniel Carlson of the University of Washington.[20] The study found that many high-tech companies prefer the urban environment for its "vertical character, specialty shops, street life, entertainment and proximity to a great mixture of businesses and cultural activities." Because so many employees preferred to live downtown, Microsoft had initiated a bus service to take employees to its suburban Redmond headquarters. I quoted the city's former mayor, Paul Schell, who noted that the key to success lay in "creating a place where the creative experience can flourish."[21]

Cities were leveraging their diversity. Significant numbers of people were moving back downtown in some twenty-one large American cities, according to a 2001 study.[22] When Gary Gates and I compared HUD's State of the Cities Report's findings to our own measures of innovation and diversity, we found a clear set of correlations. Metros with thriving downtowns were positively correlated with our own measures of high-tech industry; metros with high levels of downtown living also scored high on our Gay Index and the Bohemian Index, as well as on our Composite Diversity Index.[23]

The back-to-the-city movement has only accelerated since. Many large US cities saw their fastest growth in the wake of the economic crisis of 2008. A 2010 Brookings Institution study found that nearly two-thirds of the cities with more than 1 million people, "including New York, Los Angeles, and Chicago—grew faster in 2008–2009 than the year before, and 23 grew faster than at mid-decade when many migrants were following the boom to suburbs, exurbs, and smaller places. Chicago, Dallas, Denver, Seattle, and Washington, DC, each exhibited their fastest growth of the decade in the past year." As a consequence, the study added, "the growth rate differential between suburbs and cities narrowed considerably over the latter half of the decade (1.1 percent versus 1.0 percent in 2008–2009, compared with 1.3 percent versus 0.6 percent in 2004–2005)."[24]

Urban Tech

When I wrote the original edition of this book, the suburban nerdistan remained the predominant high-tech industrial model. Since that time there has been a substantial shift to what I have come to call *urban tech*. In Seattle, where the shift to more central locations was already afoot in the early 2000s, it became more pronounced. The city's South Lake Union District development, pioneered by Paul Allen, has become a major center for technology, with Amazon's new headquarters at its hub. San Francisco began to vie with Silicon Valley as a location for both tech talent and new start-ups, such as Twitter, which is located in the city. Twitter co-founder Jack Dorsey highlighted the shift when he tweeted in February 2012: "I love the idea of an urban corporate campus with all the energy and variety that provides."

And the shift to urban tech was not confined to the United States. London's Silicon Roundabout became one of Europe's leading high-tech districts, and the older, once bohemian districts of Berlin did so as well.

Leading high-tech companies also sought out more urban locations. Google, for example, expanded beyond its Silicon Valley Googleplex, adding successful centers in New York, London, Toronto, and other major urban centers. Google's New York location was so successful that in 2010 it purchased the entire building where it was renting office space for $1.8 billion, adding 2,390,000 square feet to the 550,000 it was already occupying (the building, at 111 Eighth Avenue in Chelsea, has more floor space than the Empire State Building). A 2010 article in the *Harvard Business Review,* headlined "Back to the City," noted that for a growing number of companies "the suburbs have lost their sheen." The article cautioned that "businesses that don't understand and plan for it may suffer in the long run."[25]

Some commentators have even gone so far as to suggest that the shift to urban tech has advantaged New York over Silicon Valley. Rather than suggesting that New York would supplant Silicon Valley as the nation's and the world's preeminent tech center, these commentators were simply pointing out that more urban settings such as New York's have their own considerable virtues.

Writing in his *Washington Post* blog on September 21, 2011, Dominic Basulto noted that "some of the most exciting new start-ups over the past two years have been companies like Foursquare, Etsy, Tumblr, Gilt Groupe, Boxee and Kickstarter—all of which got their start in New York. At a time when the cost of launching a start-up has dropped to nearly nothing, New York's young Creative Class has been starting new companies at an astonishing pace. And, in the process, they are transforming entire industries from media to food to fashion to the arts." Whether Silicon Valley's hegemony is in jeopardy or not, there can be little doubt that high-tech has taken on much more of an urban cast in the first decade of the twenty-first century.

In a 2006 speech, Silicon Valley icon Paul Graham noted that for all its advantages and power, Silicon Valley has a great weakness. The "paradise Shockley found in 1956 is now one giant parking lot," he noted. "San Francisco and Berkeley are great, but they're forty miles away. Silicon Valley proper is soul-crushing suburban sprawl. It has fabulous weather, which makes it significantly better than the soul-crushing sprawl of most other American cities. But a competitor that managed to avoid sprawl would have real leverage."[26] He could not be more right. "The entire world is now a rival to Silicon Valley," the venture capitalist Fred Wilson declared in the *New York Times* in summer 2011. "No country, state, region, nor city has a lock on innovation in technology anymore." Or as Basulto spells it out:

> Silicon Valley is unquestionably still the role model around the world. It is the place where foreign dignitaries visit when they want to export "innovation" back to their homeland. Yet, the New York model might be more flexible for European cities trying to become innovative hubs—especially if those cities already have the type of urban density that makes something as simple as a "check-in" worthwhile. One thinks immediately of densely populated cities like Mumbai and Shanghai—where a Silicon Alley model may make more sense than a Silicon Valley model.[27]

The data bear this out, at least to some extent. On July 20, 2011, *Crain's New York Business* reported that New York City had surpassed Boston as the nation's second-largest technology hub. "A cool $642.2 million in venture capital funding flooded the New York metro area during the second quarter, with more than $416 million going to 48 Internet-based companies, according to a report released by PricewaterhouseCoopers and the National Venture Capital Association. A total of 98 companies in the area received venture capital funding. This is compared to the New England area, where 22 Internet-based companies received $290 million."[28] It was not a one-time occurrence: It was the third consecutive quarter that the New York metropolitan area, mainly Manhattan, had attracted more than $500 million in venture capital. And it continued a trend. New York actually edged past Boston in venture capital in 2010, taking in $896 million, compared with $866 million for Boston. Then, in the first nine months of 2011, New York venture capital surged to $2.2 billion, more than double the figure for the entire previous year, according to a follow-up report in *Crain's*. Despite the rapid growth in venture funding to New York start-ups, this amount was but one-fourth of the more than $8 billion in venture funding raked in by Silicon Valley firms over the same period.[29]

In the Boston area as well, venture capital has shifted from the outlying suburbs around Route 128 to the urban core. In 2011, start-up companies in the city limits raised almost $600 million in venture capital, roughly the same amount as firms located in the Route 128 suburbs.[30]

Driving this trend is the fact that a growing number of cities and urban centers have become ever-more powerful talent magnets, the locations of choice for talented young people. Since 2000, the number of college-educated young people between the ages of 25 and 34 years old increased twice as fast in the urban centers (defined as the three miles surrounding the urban core) as in other parts of America's 51 largest metros, according to a 2011 study by CEOs for Cities.[31] The number of young adults with a four-year degree living in those close-in urban neighborhoods increased by 26 percent from 2000 to 2009, compared to 13 percent in outlying neighborhoods. In five metros—New York, Washington, Boston, Chicago, and San Francisco—more than two-thirds of the residents of the urban core had college degrees.

What a remarkable change from the past. During the 1970s and 1980s, when I was in college and graduate school, many of my professors maintained that structural changes in society and industry had dealt most American cities a death blow. Multistory factories of the sort found in neighborhoods like New York's SoHo or Cleveland's Flats had been rendered redundant by the shift to large-scale horizontal factories in Greenfield locations, the Sun Belt, or abroad that offered the advantages of mass production and economies of scale. Government policies encouraging home ownership and extensive freeway subsidies had helped to fuel a shift to the suburbs that was accelerated by white flight in the 1960s.

City leaders tried to stanch the trend by buttressing the one economic activity left in cities: building taller and denser central business
districts that were increasingly filled with government or nonprofit
activities. As failing mixed-use neighborhoods were bulldozed in the
name of urban renewal, cities were transformed into skyscraper ghost
towns—filed with workers by day but empty and dangerous after
5:00 PM, when middle-class workers climbed into their cars and drove
back to their lives in the suburbs, leaving the city to the underclass.

I saw those changes play out in my own life. I was born in 1957,
in Newark, New Jersey, the city that became the nation's poster
child for urban decay. The Newark of my youth—the place that
Philip Roth has written about so eloquently—was a wonderland
for a little boy, a mix of industries, thriving multiethnic neighborhoods, and a prosperous downtown. On weekends, our extended
family would gather at my grandmother's home in the predominantly Italian American neighborhood of North Newark. On warm
nights, we'd take in the professional bicycle races in Branch Brook
Park; during holiday season, we shopped in the retail district at department stores like Bamberger's. Among the times I recall most
fondly were Saturdays with my father, especially when he took me
to Newark Public Library, and turned me loose in the stacks, where
I would eventually devour volume upon volume on urban America.

Then, almost all at once, everything changed. I can vividly recall
driving through downtown Newark with my father during the summer of 1967, when I was ten. The once-bustling streets were barri-
caded, many buildings were in flames. Everywhere, I could see
police, National Guardsmen, and armored vehicles brought in to
quell the riots. The *Newark Star Ledger* office building where my
mother worked—a place I had often visited—had been transformed
into a barbed-wire fortress.

In subsequent years, I witnessed the fall of Victory Optical, the
once-grand factory where my father worked, which had provided

solid livelihoods for ethnic families in Newark and surrounding communities for years. For many people who grew up as I did, the decline of manufacturing and of America's great urban centers signaled the end of this country's golden age.

But the past decade has seen a dramatic turnaround in the fortunes of urban America. In defiance of expert pessimism, cities are back. Many have become preferred destinations for creative people and creative companies. Not all cities and not all creative people, for sure—there are still many who prefer suburbs and rural areas—but for quite a considerable number. Several forces have combined to bring people and economic activity back to urban areas. For one thing, crime is down to its lowest level in forty years. Part of the reason for this lies in better policing, but much of it can be attributed to the growing diversity and improved conditions of the cities themselves.[32] Couples now push baby carriages down city blocks where not so long ago even the hardiest urban dwellers feared to tread.

Cities are cleaner than they were—there are no more coal-fired furnaces and incinerators and fewer smokestack industries; they are also greener and more environmentally efficient, as David Owen and others have shown.[33] Multifamily dwellings that share walls are easier to heat than detached single-family houses; density discourages car use and promotes mass transit and walking. People picnic in urban parks, Rollerbladers and cyclists whiz along trails where trains used to roll, and water-skiers jet down once-toxic rivers.

Beyond the Size Fetish

There is no denying the advantage of size. Bigger cities have bigger markets. They have more people and more resources to throw at problems. They generate higher densities, which put people in closer physical contact and which also increase their energy and resource efficiency. Bigger cities also have higher levels of well-educated individuals. But it is possible to make too much of this: many economists, urbanists, and city leaders suffer from a size fetish. Edward Glaeser argues that cities need to grow bigger and higher still, because "tall buildings enable the human interactions that are at the heart of economic innovation, and of progress itself." Land-use restrictions should be eased, he wrote in *The Atlantic* in March 2011, because they tie "cities to their past and limit the possibilities for their future. If cities can't build up, then they will build out. If building in a city is frozen, then growth will happen somewhere else."[34]

It's an understandable mistake, seeing the raw compacting of people into space as the key to urban economic advantage, because marginal returns to scale do seem to be ever-increasing. But density does in fact have its limits. Giant buildings and massive skyscrapers can, and often do, function as vertical suburbs where it's much easier to conduct your business and life inside, muting the spontaneous, freewheeling encounters that give cities so much of their energy. Asia's great cities are the biggest and densest in the world, but their innovative and creative impetus pales in comparison to places like New York and London in finance, to Paris in fashion, Milan in design, or Silicon Valley in technology. The advantage for cities lies in their pedestrian-friendly scale, which features mixed use and mid-rise structures, abundant bars, cafés, and other third places, and an active street life that facilitates human interaction.

"Does Density Matter?"—that's the critical question that Peter Gordon and Sanford Ikeda ask in a detailed empirical study of the subject. They contrast two types of density. The first is "crude density" of the sort associated with taller and taller buildings. Density in and of itself, they note, will not generate innovation, new firm formation, and economic development. "If it could," they write, "county prisons or the streets around Yankee Stadium as fans crowd into and out of games would be economically diverse and dynamic places—they are not. The former are not dynamic for obvious reasons while the latter lacks dynamism because it fails to provide the foundation for dynamic long-term growth, although it may sustain businesses such as baseball cap and hot dog sales." Too much density can stifle the exchange and flow of information and ideas, just as too little does. It is only when density goes hand in hand with walkability, pedestrian scale, and the like that it can yield real cultural and economic benefits.

The second type of density they refer to simply as "Jane Jacobs density." I call it "street-level serendipity." This kind of density, in their words, maximizes the "potential informal contacts of the average person in a given public space at any given time."[35] Density of this sort not only provides the all-important "eyes on the street" and facilitates networking and informal exchanges of knowledge and information, it actively creates demand for local products. In this way, it leads to diversity, and not just of populations and ethnic groups, but of tastes, preferences, and demand. "Jacobs density" cannot be achieved in the absence of diverse land uses and economic functions that are authentic and "unique enough to attract people from outside the locality."

As Jacobs herself put it: "Densities can get too high if they reach a point at which, for any reason, they begin to repress diversity instead of to stimulate it. Precisely this can happen, and it is the main point in considering how high is too high." And she added: "In the absence of a pedestrian scale, density can be big trouble."[36]

Creative Suburbs and Rural Areas

The idea that clustering only happens in Manhattan-style urban centers is shortsighted and parochial, however. None of America's three largest metros—New York, Los Angeles, or Chicago—crack the top thirty on my Creativity Index. And though all innovative activity requires interaction, not every kind of interaction has to occur at the pedestrian scale. Silicon Valley—the most innovative place on earth—is chronically car dependent. Music industry types who have relocated to Nashville cite the ease of getting around by car—zipping off to meet for lunch, to get to the studio, or to go over to a venue to see a new act—as a big part of its draw. Car-based suburban models necessarily become less effective at larger scales, but that doesn't mean that they cannot work.

Many suburbs have extraordinary endowments of the Creative Class and human capital. The level of college graduates approaches 50 percent of all adults in just a handful of metros—Boulder and San Jose, Danbury and Stamford. But more than eight in ten adults in the suburb of Bethesda are college grads, as are roughly three-fourths of the adults in Princeton, New Jersey; Highland Park, Texas; Park Forest, Illinois; and Palo Alto, California. Roughly two-thirds of adults hold college degrees in the Detroit suburb of Birmingham; and in Reston, Virginia; Coral Gables, Florida; Evanston, Illinois; and Santa Monica, California.

Some of these suburbs are actively fostering their creative economies. Ferndale, Michigan, just outside of Detroit, has focused on promoting its arts scene and has been building affordable housing and marketing itself as gay friendly. Arlington, Virginia, has added density by building mixed-use high-rise complexes at its eleven Metrorail stations, while encouraging the development of independent businesses in its older neighborhoods. It is a place of exhilarating contrasts, with funky coffee shops, vintage clothing stores, and places to hear Indie bands, close upon gleaming office towers and chain restaurants. Bellevue, Washington, just across from Seattle, which has been retrofitting and adding density and mixed land use to its downtown for some time, recently launched a major core-building initiative, the "Bel-Red Area Transformation," a nine-hundred-acre urban infill project that will bring mixed-use development, light rail, new streets, parks, and open spaces to a disused stretch of highway.

But as car dependent as suburbs are, the ones that are doing the best are the most walkable. A 2008 Brookings study by Christopher B. Leinberger identified more than 150 walkable suburbs in America's thirty largest metros.[37] More than one-third of Americans say that they would prefer to live in walkable communities, according to research by Jonathan Levine of the University of Michigan and his collaborators. Houses in walkable neighborhoods command higher prices than houses in more distant, less dense locations. A 2009 study by urbanist Joe Cortright for CEOs for Cities analyzed the sales of 90,000 homes in fifteen major metros. In twelve out of fifteen of them, walkability commanded premiums—of as much as hundreds of thousands of dollars in some DC suburbs.[38] Charlotta Mellander and I found that metros with walkable suburbs had greater economic output, higher incomes, and higher housing prices; higher levels of human capital, higher membership in the Creative Class; higher levels of patented innovations and of high-tech industries and employees; not to mention higher levels of happiness.[39]

Walkable suburbs offer many of the features of great urban neighborhoods but with much less of the hassle. Many move to them from the city when they have families, hoping to gain safety and access to good schools without giving up the amenities they left behind. Whether they move to these suburbs specifically *because* of their walkability, their urban virtues of mixed use and generally medium-scale density ensure that the innovation and productivity-enhancing effects of clustering continue to be available to them. The most successful suburbs share attributes of the kinds of street-level serendipity that are found in the best urban neighborhoods. Just as they do in the city, people bump into each other in coffee shops and other such third places; they discuss projects and make deals.

In fact, the best urban and suburban neighborhoods look strikingly more similar than different.

More than half of Americans would prefer to walk more and drive less, a 2003 national survey reported.[40] Still, most suburbanites don't want to move to the city. They'd like the best aspects of city life—its liveliness, its amenities, its walkability—to come to them.

Walkability's appeal is also being driven by the downsizing brought on by the housing crisis. Much has been made of the shift to a so-called new normal, where consumers scale back on debt, purchase fewer material things, spend more time with family and friends, and seek greater meaning in their lives. It may sound like the wishful thinking of ivory-tower pundits—but it really is happening. According to an eye-opening 2009 survey commissioned by *Builder* magazine, home buyers are no longer willing to drive to the farthest edges of development to buy the biggest house they can afford. In fact, those are precisely the kinds of homes that are *not* selling. Today's buyers—surprising numbers of them single women—are looking for smaller houses that are closer in, with access to parks and cultural amenities. There is a rapidly growing market for super-energy-efficient homes under 1,300 square feet— quite a departure from the 5,000–6,000 square foot McMansions of just a few years past. "We are entering a new era of home building, where buyers look for spiritual satisfaction rather than material gain," the *Builder* study concludes—not the kind of language we're used to hearing from the construction industry.

But not all suburbs are prospering, far from it. Many, if not most, do not have the option of developing compact cores along old streetcar lines or near commuter-train stations; not all are filled with wonderful old housing stock that is ripe for gentrification. Many are sprawling, relatively characterless places, with spread-out populations living in cookie-cutter houses on large lots, who commute long distances to work. With millions of homes underwater or in foreclosure, suburbs and exurbs have taken some of the most visible hits from the great recession. Even as many inner city areas are being gentrified, blight and intransigent poverty are moving out to the suburbs, where one-third of the nation's poor now reside— 1.5 million more than in cities. Suburban poverty populations are growing at five times the rate of those in cities, according to a recent Brookings study.[41] But even if some of our most stressed suburbs might have passed the tipping point—like those brand-new unsalable houses on the far-out fringes of Los Angeles that were bulldozed to the ground not too long ago, double-paned windows, granite countertops, whirlpool baths, and all—most of them aren't about to fade away.[42] For better or worse, our suburbs are here to stay.

A question I am frequently asked is: how do rural areas factor into your theory, and are they being left behind by the Creative Age? The short answer is that their fortunes are divided: some are prospering; others are falling further behind. A large-scale study by David McGranahan and Timothy Wojan of the US Department of Agriculture compared the rural and metropolitan Creative Class across 3,000-plus US counties. They found that the Creative Class accounted for 20 percent of rural or "nonmetropolitan" employment, less than the 31 percent in metropolitan areas.[43] But composed as it is mainly of "managers, high-end sales positions, scientists, engineers, college professors, artists and designers," this "rural Creative Class" was "similar in occupational structure to the urban Creative Class." The main difference is that the rural Creative Class had lower levels of college graduates and was older than its more urban counterpart. Their research also found that rural counties with large concentrations of the Creative Class tended to have leading universities and colleges (they mention Cornell in Ithaca, New York) and rich endowments of outdoor amenities, such as mountains, lakes, and other attractive landscape.

Remaking the 'Burbs

Remaking our fading suburbs and rural areas might well turn out to be the biggest urban revitalization challenge of modern times— far larger in scale, scope, and cost than the revitalization of our inner cities. In their book *Retrofitting Suburbia,* Ellen Dunham-Jones of Georgia Tech and June Williamson of City College of New York highlighted some of the most promising approaches.[44] In Phoenix, Arizona, for example, three abandoned strip malls, clustered at the corner of Fortieth and Campbell Streets, were converted into a restaurant, an upscale grocery, a chic bakery, and a cocktail bar. The development is called Le Grande Orange, and it has become a huge attraction for diners, shoppers, and local home buyers who want to live within walking distance of it. National Harbor, a mix of hotels, residential units, marinas, parks, stores, and indoor and outdoor entertainment venues, is being built on the footings of two previous failed projects in Prince George's County, Maryland. When completed, it will extend along 1.25 miles of the Potomac River.

A PricewaterhouseCoopers study found that one in five malls was dead or dying—a situation that has only worsened since the economic crash.[45] But some of them have become the sites of a wave of renewal. Outside of St. Paul, the parking lot that surrounded a dead shopping center built on landfill was turned back into wetlands—which in turn attracted a new "lakefront" townhome development. In Lakewood, a suburb of Denver, Colorado, a dead mall on a single 103-acre superblock is being transformed into Belmar—twenty-two urban blocks with parks, bus lines, restaurants, stores, and 1,300 new households—the downtown that Lakewood never had. Eight of the thirteen regional malls in the Denver area are now planning or have completed makeovers.

Perhaps the biggest retrofit of all is happening in Tysons Corner, Virginia, the virtual archetype of an auto-dependent, sprawling edge city. Located near the junctions of three major highways, it boasts 25 million square feet of office space and 4 million square feet of retail space, including one of the largest malls on the East Coast. Although only 18,500 people live there, the town's population swells to 120,000 on weekdays. Decades ago, developers hailed Tysons Corner as the wave of the future—one of hundreds of new stretched out, auto-dependent satellite centers that would render our old downtown commercial centers obsolete. But for all the jobs it supports, stores it houses, and tax revenue it generates, Tysons Corner has been losing out of late. Its perpetual traffic gridlock and its lack of human energy have caused home buyers to choose other places; some of the companies that were headquartered there have even moved back into the District of Columbia.

When the DC Metro announced plans to build an extension to Dulles Airport that would pass through Tysons Corner, the biggest debate was not about whether or not it was needed, but whether to bury it underground—an expensive proposition, but one that would free up land for densification. On June 22, 2010, the Fairfax County Board of Supervisors adopted a comprehensive plan that will transform the town from "a sprawling suburban office park" to a "24 hour urban center where people live, work and play." Its retrofit is being led by its major developers and landowners who are seeking to make it more walkable, denser with a more integrated mix of uses, and more connected to the city via transit. There is a certain irony in this. America's archetypal Edge City is seeking to reinvent itself as a place whose hallmarks will be walkability, green construction, access to public transportation, and abundant public amenities, like parks and bicycle trails—something that sounds very much like a real city.

There are countless other opportunities for reclamation all across America. Disused golf courses can be transformed into parks and nature sanctuaries; abandoned car dealerships can be landscaped and developed as new, mixed-use neighborhoods. Whole commercial corridors, as Dunham-Jones and Williamson put it, "are being retrofitted in ways that integrate rather than isolate uses and regenerate underperforming asphalt into urban neighborhoods." Developers are decking over the parking lots at commuter rail stations and building high- and mid-rise office/commercial/residential complexes atop them; they are cutting streets through formerly walled-off corporate campuses and adding restaurants, stores, and public spaces. Although the recession has slowed down many of the most ambitious suburban renewal projects, it's provided further impetus for community service and greening efforts. Abandoned big-box stores are being made over into senior centers and schools and libraries—amenities that are just as essential for neighborhoods as eateries and boutiques. This type of strip commercial redevelopment will be the major development feature of the next generation. Most of these retrofits, of course, are a far cry from the organic authenticity of real cities, Dunham-Jones and Williamson note, but they build community and lay the groundwork for still further redevelopment. Writ large and multiplied across hundreds of other metros, they are remaking the way Americans live and laying the groundwork for future economic prosperity.

Talent in Cities and Suburbs

Although we have long known that human capital is central to economic growth, most studies have measured it across either nations or metropolitan regions. But how is human capital distributed *within* metros? And how might that affect regional development?

Metros vary widely in terms of their shape as well as their size. Some have concentrated central cities or cores—for example, within the greater New York metropolitan area, Manhattan has heavy concentrations of business and also significant concentrations of higher-income, higher-skill, higher-human-capital individuals. Others, like Los Angeles and Atlanta, are more sprawling, with higher-income, higher-skill, higher-human-capital individuals residing mainly in the suburbs.

In a 2011 study, Charlotta Mellander, Kevin Stolarick, and I used statistical models to examine the effects on regional incomes and housing values of the distribution of human capital in the suburbs and cities of metro areas. We found that both suburbs and cities play different but important roles in regional development. Suburban human capital is the key factor in smaller and medium-sized metros, those with fewer than one million people. This makes sense, actually. It is easier to get around in smaller metros; there is less congestion and less pressure for central locations. Skilled people can live further out and easily get to the center when needed.

But once metro populations surpass one million people, human capital in the center city begins to play a bigger role. In these larger metros, center city human capital was more strongly related to regional incomes and housing values. And the effect grew stronger as metros got bigger. Metros with more than three million people had nearly twice the density of human capital as those between one and three million. This, too, makes intuitive sense. Commutes are longer and congestion worse in larger metros, causing higher skilled, higher human-capital people to begin to seek out more central locations.

Overall, we found that the distribution of human capital between suburbs and cities had a greater effect than we expected on a metro's overall economic performance. In virtually every permutation of our analysis, the results were stronger when we separated center-city and suburban shares than when we looked at a metro's overall level of human capital.

Metro Nation

Take it from me, a card-carrying, dyed-in-the-wool urbanist who has lived in inner cities for most of my adult life: my urbanist fellow travelers are making a big mistake when they impugn the suburbs wholesale. Just over one-half of Americans live in the suburbs, and the great majority of them are content to stay there. More than two-thirds (68 percent) of suburbanites are "satisfied" or "very satisfied" with where they live; 57 percent rated their communities as the "best" or "near-best," according to a survey I conducted with the Gallup Organization and report in my book *Who's Your City?*. A separate Pew survey identified the group of Americans that is most satisfied with their living choices as college-educated suburbanites—62 percent of whom said there was no better place for them to live.[46]

As Bruce Katz of the Brookings Institution says, "the real America isn't found in cities or suburbs or small towns, but in the metropolitan areas or 'metros' that bring all these places into economic and social union. We are not a nation of cities vs. suburbs but a metro nation."[47] I heartily concur. A metro, or a metropolitan area, encompasses not just a center city but its suburban rings. Suburbs don't grow at the expense of cities; suburbanization and urbanization alike are parts of the same larger process. Suburbs no longer draw most of their populations from inner cities, according to the research findings of the Brookings Institution's Audrey Singer, but grow by attracting people from small towns and rural areas further out, as well as immigrants from foreign countries, more than 50 percent of whom bypass cities and settle directly in the suburbs of larger metro areas.[48]

Great metropolitan areas are like economic suns; their gravitational appeal is irresistible. Suburbs and cities are mutually dependent. We need to stop debating which is better and start building the stronger, more tightly connected metropolitan areas that are the key to our future competitiveness. This task becomes even more important as our metropolitan areas morph into ever larger mega-regions, like the gargantuan Bos-Wash corridor that is home to 50-plus million people and generates more than $2 trillion in economic output.[49]

Building the Creative Community

So after all that, how *do* you build a creative community? Certainly not all at once and from the top down—most of what defines and shapes creative communities emerges gradually over time. But that does not mean that strategy and public policy do not matter. Quite the contrary. Smart strategies that recognize and enhance bottom-up, community-based efforts that are already working can help accelerate the development of creative communities, as we can see in the following cases.

Austin City Limits

A good case in point is Austin, Texas. Although much of what occurred there happened organically, over time the city developed an integrated strategy for harnessing the 3T's and leveraging quality of place. It started with the first T, technology. During the 1980s and 1990s, Austin went to great lengths to bolster its technology base. It began, as many places do, by recruiting branches of firms from other places—IBM, Intel, and Motorola to name a few.[50] The city's leadership made benchmarking visits to leading high-tech regions, both to learn from their best practices and to pay visits to companies they wanted to attract. Austin was selected as the home of two major research consortia, MCC (the Microelectronics and Computer Technology Corporation) and SEMATECH (Semiconductor Manufacturing Technology), both of them supported by the federal government and leading firms in those fields. But the effort did not stop there. Under the leadership of fabled entrepreneur George Kozmetsky and others, the region built a thriving entrepreneurial climate. It also invested heavily in the second T, talent, by building up the University of Texas and attracting hundreds of millions of dollars in federal and state research dollars.

The Austin story would not be complete without the third T, tolerance. Ask the average person the following question: what is the first thing that comes to your mind when you hear about Austin? Most people don't answer Dell, Trilogy, or any other high-tech company. Many of them mention *Austin City Limits,* the live music broadcast on public TV, or perhaps the South-by-Southwest Festival. Alongside efforts to develop technology and tolerance, the region has made considerable investments in its lifestyle and music scene—right down to the clubs and bars of Sixth Street. The city's downtown running trail features a bronze sculpture of a famous regional figure, the late guitarist Stevie Ray Vaughn. When one high-tech company, Vignette, expanded into a new facility in downtown Austin, it agreed to establish a $1-million fund to support the local music scene.[51]

After I delivered a speech in Austin in spring 2000, a group of business and political leaders invited me to join them for "Hippie Hour" at a local club. Delighted, I replied that I was certainly ready for "Happy Hour." "It's not Happy Hour," they pointedly corrected me, "we said Hippie Hour." We ended up at the Continental Club, a ramshackle old place on South Congress Street, hanging out with a crowd of musicians, Latinos, politicians, high-tech business types, and even a few hippies—a veritable cauldron of creativity where everyone could let their hair down and be themselves.

More than ten years later, Austin continues to attend to its unique cultural qualities as well as its economic growth. "Ronnie Johnson, my bass player, used to say, 'Austin is a good place to leave your stuff,'" the alt country performer James McMurtry wrote on his blog in 2011.

> I can't imagine a better place for a musician to grow up than Austin. There are so many live music venues. A kid with ample talent and drive can find a gig here. . . . After my Tuesday night show, I usually hang around to hear the Ephraim Owens Trio, three incredible jazz players. I don't know what they're doing, but I like it. Through the plate glass window, I can see our rapidly changing skyline, new glass high-rises climbing skyward. The remains of Liberty Lunch and countless other clubs are buried somewhere under that glass, metal, and stone. Ronnie Johnson leaves his stuff in Marfa now, Austin having grown expensive for a side man. It's not the same town, but the music carries on. I'll stay a while yet.[52]

U2 and High-Tech

Dublin, Ireland, provides another interesting case of a city that consciously cultivated its creative development.[53] In the 1970s, Ireland suffered from double-digit unemployment, stagnant incomes, and a brain drain of its best and brightest. Then it began recruiting global high-tech companies through a policy of "industrialization by invitation." Financial and tax-related incentives helped attract high-tech giants, including IBM, Lotus, Intel, Microsoft, Dell, Gateway, and Oracle, which were also lured by the thick talent pool emerging from the country's world-class universities. The Irish government formed a body called Enterprise Ireland to support entrepreneurship and venture capital and foster an indigenous high-tech industry. By 2000, the Irish software industry included some 900 firms, employing over 30,000 people.

But these traditional economic development efforts would not have worked if Ireland had not buttressed them with a major lifestyle effort. First, the basic idea of recruiting technology companies and entrepreneurs was extended to the artistic and cultural scene of actors, writers, and musicians. By offering tax breaks to culturally creative people and a high-quality place to live and work, the country has not only retained its growing legion of native celebrities, such as U2, Van Morrison, and Liam Neeson, but also plays host—and home—to many international stars. The second step revolved around building true quality of place, grounded in history and authenticity. Dublin began by restoring its Temple Bar district, utilizing $25 million in European Union tourism funds to revitalize the pubs where James Joyce, Bram Stoker, and Samuel Beckett might once have enjoyed a pint. As the *New York Times* reported in October 2000, "Planners were determined not to turn the neighborhood into a Euro-Disney of faux-Georgian architecture, but to encourage innovative design."[54] Today, the district is hipper and more energetic than ever.

The Irish economy took a body blow during the financial crisis, and the country has seen its real estate values tumble and much of its wealth disappear. But there is widespread agreement that its Creative Economy provides the only way forward.

Back in 2000, when I was first writing this section, I could never have imagined that in fall 2011, at the Global Irish Economic Forum, Bono, on a panel with Bill Clinton, would cite *The Rise of the Creative Class* by name, as he made the case that the Irish people were "very, very well suited for the 21st century." "Hierarchical societies don't translate well into the 21st century," he continued. "The industrial revolution may sit well with some of our neighbours, but the Irish have never been good at fitting into it. We're not good at taking orders, perhaps. But we are great anarchic thinkers. . . . We have an environment that creative people want to be around—like Richard Florida talks about in *The Creative Class*. There is an environment that people want to be around and music and culture are part of that."[55]

Zappos and Las Vegas

Far from the glitz and bling of the Strip, an intriguing transformation has been under way in Las Vegas's struggling downtown core.

Las Vegas, as Chapter 11 showed, has the lowest Creative Class concentration of any large metro in the United States—but perhaps not for long. Zappos is moving its headquarters from an outlying suburb to the old City Hall building and CEO Tony Hsieh's goal is to create a vibrant, urban district in the surrounding area.

As I wrote in my 2010 book, *The Great Reset*, Zappos has been a leader in upgrading low-pay, low-skill service jobs. Most of Zappos' employees work in fulfillment and customer service—taking customer orders and packing and shipping shoes. Zappos's base pay for unskilled work is $11.00 an hour, well above the average. The company works hard to recruit the right people and has adopted a radical policy to screen them even further—a week after a new person starts, he or she is offered a $1,000 bonus to quit. Employees who take the company up on "The Offer" prove that they don't have the commitment that Zappos demands. Zappos offers extensive in-house training and development programs so employees can gain higher wages and advance their careers through promotion from within; at the same time, team members are encouraged to be themselves by embracing their differences.

Hsieh and his partners plan to invest as much as $350 million in redeveloping downtown Las Vegas, according to several accounts published in early 2012. In addition to $60 million in renovations to the City Hall Building, where some 1200 Zappos workers will be employed, another $100 million will be dedicated to residential development, $50 million for high tech startups, and $50 million for other small businesses like cafes, bars, book stores, restaurants, and other third places to help flesh out the character and texture of the neighborhood. Another $50 million has been set aside for education and upgrading local schools. *Fortune* called Hsieh a "combination of Steve Wynn meets Walt Disney meets Jane Jacobs." Hsieh responded, "This isn't so different than what we built at Zappos. We're just scaling it."[56]

Hsieh wants as many Zappos employees to move downtown as possible, so one of the first uses he put all that money to was to take over the leases for 50 apartments in The Ogden, one of the neighborhood's most desirable high-rise buildings. Apartments are offered to Zappos employees at subsidized rents. Hsieh and his Downtown Project team have already moved into the top floor.

Zappos' urban-renewal project is two-pronged. On the one hand, the company is building a facility and importing Creative and Service Class jobs. On the other, it is working to turn Las Vegas itself into an idea center. Hsieh has entered into a partnership with a company that leases small jets to start a new airline that will shuttle techies and entrepreneurs between the Bay Area and Las Vegas. Zappos has invested in a monthly downtown arts festival and has spurred a local start-up incubator program. Its employees have partnered with local tech groups on regular exchanges and seminars.

Hsieh believes that serendipitous interactions—what he calls "collisions" between people—facilitate relationships and spark ideas. "When you're in a city, the bar or the restaurant becomes an extended conference room," he says. Since downtown Las Vegas didn't have that, he explained, "The idea went from 'let's build a campus' to 'let's build a city.'"

An article in *Forbes* magazine dubbed these efforts a new form of "corporate neo-urbanism"—a way of "reviving, in an interesting new form, a kind of intimate relationship between corporations and cities." The article contrasts this with two previous paradigms of company community interaction. At the beginning of the Industrial Revolution, rising manufacturers literally built company towns from the bottom up for their workers. During the Organizational Age, the suburbs became virtual dormitories for their managers. "In the third era, corporations need creative talent, and here they run into an immediate problem. Unlike the blue-collar worker of the first generation company towns, or the docile Organization Man types of second-generation suburban towns, the Creative Class workforce needs a far more stimulating environment to function," it notes.[57] Hsieh's and Zappos' solution, the article concludes, is to adapt and absorb a small, relatively manageable and inexpensive city, Las Vegas, to this new model. All in all, it is an interesting and important experiment that may point the way to the revitalization of many other struggling downtown urban centers.[58]

Pittsburgh—Still the Base Case

In the original edition of this book, I used my then hometown of Pittsburgh as my base case about the transition from an old industrial age economy and society to a creative community. If a city with all of Pittsburgh's assets—great universities, industrial age architecture, splendid natural amenities, and emerging human creativity—can't make it in the Creative Age, I wrote, then the future does not bode well for other older industrial cities. Back then, it looked like Pittsburgh might be on the wrong track. Too much of its precious creative capital (graduates of the University of Pittsburgh and Carnegie Mellon) were leaving, along with the start-up companies they'd founded. Although the city had made some important strides in self-reinvention, and indeed ranked near the top of some magazines' lists of the "Best Places to Live," it had been hurt by its long legacy of top-town redevelopment, such as the transformation of the Homestead Steel Works into a giant waterfront mall featuring islands of big-box retail stores amid yawning acres of parking lots.

I noted the conflict between the Squelchers who ran the town— the old capitalists who frequented the Duquesne Club—and the emerging energy of the region's Creative Class. In the 1990s, when I lived there, the Squelchers were promoting a revitalization plan that turned on spending $1 billion for two new sports stadiums and a convention center, even after their initial proposals had been soundly rejected by a popular vote. The National Center for Historic Preservation singled out their "Fifth and Forbes" downtown plan— which sought to raze several blocks in the center of downtown and replace them with an urban mega-mall, complete with a Nordstrom's, multiplex cinema, and chain nightspots like a Hard Rock Café and a Planet Hollywood—as perhaps the worst example of urban renewal of the past forty years.

But there were good things, too. I was involved with some of them while I was living there, and many of them have since borne fruit. As my friend and colleague Don Carter, the architect, professor, and director of Carnegie Mellon's Remaking Cities Institute, recounts:

> Something else was happening—an unprecedented bubbling up of quality of life initiatives from individuals, volunteer groups, and non-governmental organizations, many of which were in turn funded by the corporations and foundations. There was receptivity to new things and willingness to take risks. This bottom-up energy was especially exhibited by young adults in their twenties and thirties who began populating older neighborhoods, renovating houses, creating art, and starting new businesses. Two important civic groups, PUMP (Pittsburgh Urban Magnet Program) and GroundZero Action Network, were created by and for young adults. Word of mouth fed

a trickle and then a steady flow of young expatriate Pittsburghers back home ("boomerangs") and young newcomers eager to take advantage of the low cost of living, available jobs, and a vibrant cultural scene.

Pittsburgh has made signal progress on the arts, culture, and community development front. The Andy Warhol Museum and the Mattress Factory, a museum-work space devoted to large-scale installation art, have both achieved worldwide recognition. Pittsburgh Filmmakers and the Manchester Craftsmen's Guild, which started as grassroots efforts more than thirty years ago, have become nationally known. Smaller visual-arts collectives like the Brew House (which originated as a squatter-artist project) have thrived, as have a multitude of small theater companies.

Street-level culture has gained a growing foothold in Pittsburgh, too, as main street corridors in several older Working Class districts have been transformed. Along Carson Street on the South Side, a former steel-mill neighborhood once best known for having a polka named after it, galleries, theaters, and cafés have sprung up amid the older stores and bars; as one local wit has observed, this is now a place where "blue-hairs of both types converge." Similar street-level scenes have cropped up elsewhere, notably along Penn Avenue in Garfield, long one of the city's poorest neighborhoods, and predominately black.

Carter points to Lawrenceville as another particularly promising neighborhood. "It is attracting hipsters, blue-collar families, professional families, artists, cool restaurants, architects, students, faculty, renovators and landlords, bicyclists, and most importantly, private and public investment," he notes. "Lawrenceville has many neighborhood celebrations: Art All Night; 16 to 62 Design Zone; Disposable Film Festival; Doo Dah Festival (honoring Stephen Foster, who grew up in Lawrenceville); Joy of Cookies Tour; Annual House Tour; Annual Artist Tour, etc." As a result, Pittsburgh has moved from a laggard to a leader in locally oriented creativity and quality of place. Its architecture and urban design community has become much more vocal about the need to preserve historic buildings, invest in neighborhoods, and institute tough design standards. And it has developed exemplary initiatives for green building and the conversion of old rail lines to bike trails.

On the economic development front, Pittsburgh has shifted its attention from downtown to the universities and has embraced start-ups, innovation, and creativity. It worked hard to attract and retain the Creative Class. It has generated high-tech companies and has navigated the current economic crisis very well. Pittsburgh ranked as one of the top twenty strongest-performing metro regions in spring 2009, at the peak of the economic crisis, according to the Brookings Institution's Metro Monitor. A 2010 study by the University of Pittsburgh's University Center for Social and Urban Research, comparing the educational attainment of workers age twenty-four to thirty-four in the country's top forty metropolitan areas, found that nearly one-half (48.1 percent) of Pittsburgh residents in that cohort had obtained at least a bachelor's degree.[59] This puts Pittsburgh in fifth place, after Boston, San Francisco, Washington, DC, and Austin.

Many pundits have begun to single out Pittsburgh as an example of successful transformation from an older industrial to a more knowledge-based economy. *Newsweek*'s Howard Fineman, a Pittsburgh native, has taken to invoking Pittsburgh as a model for revitalizing older industrial cities and even for urban policy in the age of Obama. "Before jetting off to the Middle East and Europe," Fineman wrote in spring 2009, "President Obama took care of another piece of international diplomatic business: He announced the city in which the United States will host the next G20 summit in September. His choice drew laughter and puzzlement from reporters and diplomats alike. Pittsburgh? Are you serious? As a proud native," Fineman continued, "I understand and agree with the president's decision. Pittsburgh's story is inspiring and impressive. It was a rusting steel-making behemoth that, through struggle, pain and creativity, retooled itself as a surprisingly vibrant, 21st-century leader in education, computer science, medical research, sports entertainment and boutique manufacturing. By most measures—unemployment and foreclosure rates, to name two—Pittsburgh is an island of calm in the raging recession."[60]

But Pittsburgh's transformation, though successful, is not yet complete. As of 2010, Pittsburgh's population was just 305,704, less than one-half its 1950 level of 676,806 people. And the region remained one of the least diverse in the country, with a population that is 87 percent white, the third-whitest of America's 100 largest metro areas, according to a Brookings Institution study.[61]

Regional economic transformation takes a long time. Greater Boston's revitalization, which began in the 1940s and 1950s, didn't turn the corner until the 1980s or 1990s, and it is still ongoing. Viewed in this light, Pittsburgh's transition is midstream. As John Craig, the former editor of the *Pittsburgh Post-Gazette* wrote in the *Washington Post,* "When I think about the lessons that the Steel City's 30-year economic transformation may hold for Detroit, another town built on an industry beaten by competition and confronting bankruptcy, I have to say that the first and hardest lesson for the Motor City is this: Fundamental change will be much longer in coming than you can imagine."

A headline in the *Pittsburgh Post Gazette* on January 15, 2012, proclaimed how far the city had come. "Watch Out Portland—Pittsburgh's Lookin' Hip." Its subtitle added the necessary coda: "Is It Really Possible We are Actually, Authentically Cool?"[62] The jury is still not in, but things in Pittsburgh are going in a much better direction than they were a decade ago.

PART FIVE

CONTRADICTIONS

CHAPTER 16

The Geography of Inequality

One evening in 2002, I found myself in a Zen-style garden in one of Northern California's most upscale neighborhoods. Enclosed by high walls, with flowering plants and small sculptures artfully placed amid beds of raked sand, the garden adjoined the home of a Palo Alto venture capitalist. The audience facing me could have served as a group portrait for the Creative Class. There were engineers and entrepreneurs, artists and musicians, businesspeople and venture capitalists. Many were tastefully clad in black or neo-hippie garb. Everyone looked permanently young in that ineffably California way. They asked challenging and provocative questions, most of them having little to do with their own status in life. Mostly, they wanted to know what the Creative Age had in store for people like the ones who tended the garden we were sitting in and who had prepared the finger foods we were enjoying—and who were being left further and further behind by the onslaught of technology-based growth and rising housing prices.

I'd had a firsthand look at those left behind myself, just a few hours before, when my cab driver had taken a wrong turn and we found ourselves in East Palo Alto. The streets were lined with shabby storefronts with signs for check-cashing services and *cerveza fria*, and instead of people who looked forever young, I saw teenagers who looked too old too soon. East Palo Alto was a poster child for rising inequality. Granted, it's hardly the poorest place on earth. Most of its adult residents have jobs—indeed, some have more than one. Many are immigrants, and they come from places where living conditions and life prospects are much worse. But their poverty is deepening and their numbers are vast—in East Palo Alto, in neighborhoods up and down the Silicon Valley, and all over the country and the world.

I had intended to include a chapter on inequality in the original edition of this book, but my editor at the time informed me that the book had already run to a quite substantial length. The original edition did touch on some aspects of it. I cited a February 2000 story in the *New York Times,* reporting the housing affordability crisis faced by Working and Service Class people in Silicon Valley.[1] I cited another report that found that roughly one-third of the estimated 20,000 homeless people in Santa Clara County (the heart of Silicon Valley) had full-time jobs. And I noted that at the very height of the technology boom in the late 1990s, the Valley's No. 22 bus had become known as "the rolling hotel" because a growing number of workers had nowhere else to sleep.[2] I cited Rebecca Solnit and Susan Schwartzenberg's 2001 book, *The Hollow City,* which argued that rising rents were undermining San Francisco's unique advantage as a creative center by driving out artists, musicians, small shopkeepers, and people with children. "When the new economy arrived in San Francisco," they wrote, "it began to lay waste to the city's existing culture."[3]

I did take up the issue of inequality in my 2004 follow-up, *The Flight of the Creative Class.* There, I cited a Brookings Institution study that traced inequality in US cities (as opposed to metros) between 1979 and 1999.[4] Only thirteen cities had a balanced class structure, it found. Eight cities, including San Jose and Raleigh, had class structures strongly tilted to the high-end groups, and seven additional cities, including Washington, DC, and San Francisco, had divided class structures, characterized by an extreme U-shaped distribution of wealth between the rich and poor. Forty-three cities had become repositories for predominantly low-income households.

That book also introduced a new metric of wage inequality across metros developed by my colleague Kevin Stolarick, which compared the wages of Creative Class members to those in the other classes. What he found was disconcerting. Metros that ranked highest on the Creativity Index also tended to have the highest levels of inequality. San Jose was the most unequal metro in the nation, New York was second, and greater Washington, DC, Raleigh-Durham, Austin, and San Francisco all ranked among the most unequal metros in the country.

In a 2006 essay in *The Atlantic,* I showed that America's economic and social fabric was being reshaped by a realignment that is as significant as the historical migrations of pioneers westward, of African Americans from the rural South to the urban North, and of postwar families from cities to suburbs to exurbs. I called it the "means migration"—the mass relocation of highly skilled, highly educated, and highly paid Americans to a relatively small number of metropolitan regions and a corresponding exodus of the traditional lower and middle classes from these same places.[5]

I noted that the geographic sorting of people by their economic potential on this large a scale is simply unprecedented. I quoted Wharton School economist Joseph Gyourko, who told me that this "spatial sorting will affect the nature of America as much as the rural-urban migration of the late nineteenth century did." I cited a 2005 study that documented the growing divergence in human capital among US metros over the past four decades.[6] In 1970, most metros had similar levels of college graduates. Eleven percent of

American adults had a college degree at the time, and the figure was between 9 and 13 percent in fully half of metros. By 2000, there were metros with more than 40 percent college graduates and others with less than 10 percent. By 2010, three metros had more than 50 percent college grads, and nineteen had more than 40 percent. In *Flight of the Creative Class*, I cited the research of Robert Cushing, who used tax-return data from the IRS to chart the means migration. He found that households moving from Austin to Kansas City in the 1990s earned an average of $25,912 a year, for example. Those going in the other direction, from Kansas City to Austin, earned over $65,000. The same basic pattern was occurring in other creative centers, from San Francisco and Los Angeles to Boston and Seattle.

Inequality moved from the margins to the very front and center of American life in 2011. The rise of the Occupy Movement shone a powerful light on the humongous gap between the top 1 percent and remaining 99 percent. "The upper 1 percent of Americans are now taking in nearly a quarter of the nation's income every year," is how the Nobel Prize–winning economist Joseph Stiglitz summed up the situation. "In terms of wealth rather than income, the top 1 percent control 40 percent," he said, adding that "twenty-five years ago, the corresponding figures were 12 percent and 33 percent." And then he cautioned: "One response might be to celebrate the ingenuity and drive that brought good fortune to these people, and to contend that a rising tide lifts all boats. That response would be misguided. While the top 1 percent have seen their incomes rise 18 percent over the past decade, those in the middle have actually seen their incomes fall. For men with only high-school degrees, the decline has been precipitous—12 percent in the last quarter-century alone. All the growth in recent decades—and more—has gone to those at the top."[7]

In his speech on the economy in Osawatomie, Kansas, on December 6, 2011—where Theodore Roosevelt delivered his New Nationalism speech in 1910—Barack Obama framed the issue in moral and pragmatic terms: "In the last few decades, the average income of the top one percent has gone up by more than 250 percent, to $1.2 million per year," he said. "For the top one-hundredth of one percent, the average income is now $27 million per year." Then he added: "And yet, over the last decade, the incomes of most Americans have actually fallen by about 6 percent. This kind of inequality—a level we haven't seen since the Great Depression—hurts us all."[8]

Although much popular attention and conversation has focused on the avarice and privileges of the top 1 percent, most economists argue that rising inequality has been driven by broader structural

Figure 16.1   The Metro Wage Inequality Map, 2010

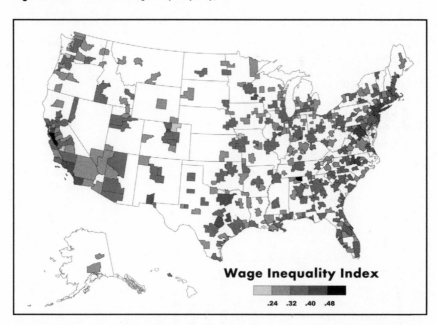

Source: US Department of Labor, Bureau of Labor Statistics, Occupational Employment Statistics (OES) Survey, 2010. Available online at http://www.bls.gov/oes/. Analysis by Kevin Stolarick. Map by Zara Matheson.

changes in the economy. The combination of globalization and the shift of manufacturing to lower-wage counties like China, dubbed the world's factory, new technologies of robotics and automation, and increases in productivity and efficiency have eliminated millions of formerly low-skill but high-paying jobs. As the middle has disappeared, the job market has literally been split in two. On one side are higher-paying, professional, knowledge and creative jobs that require considerable education and skill. On the other are an even larger and faster-growing number of more routine jobs in fields like personal care, retail sales, and food service that pay much lower

Table 16.1   Most Unequal Metros by Wage Inequality, 2010

Rank	Metro	Wage Inequality Index
1	Hunstville, AL	.500
2	San Jose-Sunnyvale-Santa Clara, CA	.481
3	College Station-Bryan, TX	.473
4	Boulder, CO	.446
5	Durham, NC	.446
6	Bridgeport-Stamford-Norwalk, CT	.432
7	Las Cruces, NM	.428
8	Decatur, IL	.426
9	Austin-Round Rock, TX	.418
10	Oxnard-Thousand Oaks-Ventura, CA	.417
11	New York-Northern New Jersey-Long Island, NY-NJ-PA	.413
12	San Diego-Carlsbad-San Marcos, CA	.409
13	Los Angeles-Long Beach-Santa Ana, CA	.409
14	Raleigh-Cary, NC	.408
15	Washington-Arlington-Alexandria, DC-VA-MD-WV	.407
16	Columbus, IN	.406
17	Dallas-Fort Worth-Arlington, TX	.406
18	Rochester, MN	.404
19	San Francisco-Oakland-Fremont, CA	.401
20	Fort Collins-Loveland, CO	.399

Source: US Department of Labor, Bureau of Labor Statistics, Occupational Employment Statistics (OES) Survey, 2010. Available online at http://www.bls.gov/oes/. Compiled by Kevin Stolarick.

Figure 16.2   The Metro Income Inequality Map, 2010

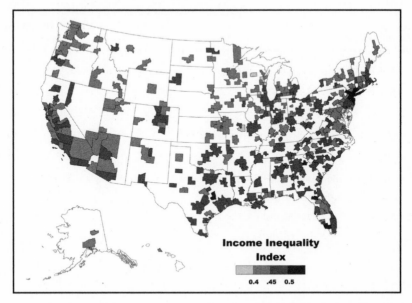

Source: US Census Bureau, American Community Survey, 2008–2010. Analysis by
Charlotta Mellander. Map by Zara Matheson.

wages. This process, one of "skill-biased technical change," according
to MIT economist David Autor, has shaped the huge rise in wage
inequality, which in turn underpins a broader set of social, cultural,
geographic, income, and other inequalities.

Whereas most studies of inequality have focused exclusively on
its manifestations on a national or international scale, much can be
learned by examining its appearance across US metros. Figure 16.1
updates the Metro Wage Inequality Index for 2010, and Table 16.1
lists the top twenty most unequal metros on this metric.[9] The pattern remains basically the same as it was in 2004. The list of unequal
metros reads like a who's who of Creative Class centers. Silicon
Valley is now second, and Huntsville is on top. Boulder is fourth,
Durham fifth, Austin ninth, New York eleventh, and Los Angeles
is tied with San Diego for twelfth. Raleigh is fourteenth, greater
Washington DC is fifteenth, and San Francisco is nineteenth.

Table 16.2   Most Unequal Metros by Income Inequality, 2010

Rank	Metro	Income Inequality Index
1	Bridgeport-Stamford-Norwalk, CT	.539
2	Naples-Marco Island, FL	.522
3	College Station-Bryan, TX	.515
4	Athens-Clarke County, GA	.514
5	Gainesville, FL	.508
6	New York-Northern New Jersey-Long Island, NY-NJ-PA	.503
7	Miami-Fort Lauderdale-Pompano Beach, FL	.498
8	McAllen-Edinburg-Mission, TX	.497
9	Brownsville-Harlingen, TX	.496
9	Sebastian-Vero Beach, FL	.496
11	Morgantown, WV	.494
12	Monroe, LA	.489
13	Corvallis, OR	.487
14	Tallahassee, FL	.486
15	Auburn-Opelika, AL	.485
15	Los Angeles-Long Beach-Santa Ana, CA	.485
15	Midland, TX	.485
18	Bloomington, IN	.484
18	Santa Fe, NM	.484
18	Shreveport-Bossier City, LA	.484

Source: US Census Bureau, American Community Survey, 2008–2010. Analysis by Charlotta Mellander.

Even though the wage gap is greater in more highly skilled, knowledge-based metros, those at the bottom of the wage scale also do better. A metro's average wage overall is higher in more highly skilled Creative Class metros—the correlation between the two is off the chart. Housing prices tend to be higher in Creative Class metros, however, which migrates this effect for service and working class workers to some degree. Still, there is no getting around the fact that wages across the board are higher in Creative Class locations.[10]

Figure 16.3 Comparing Metros on Wage and Income Inequality

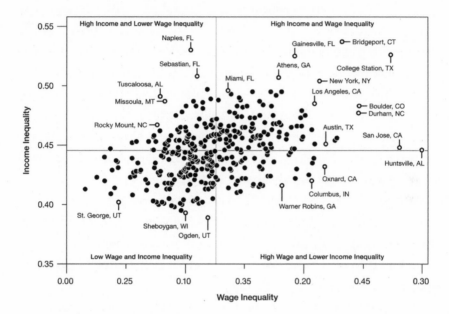

Source: US Census Bureau, American Community Survey, 2010, and US Department of Labor, Bureau of Labor Statistics, Occupational Employment Statistics (OES) Survey, 2010. Analysis by Charlotta Mellander. Design by Michelle Hopgood.

But when we turn to a second measure of inequality, the picture changes substantially. Whereas wage inequality considers the differences between salaries only, income inequality as measured by the Gini coefficient takes rents, royalties, as well as dividends into account. Figure 16.2 maps the Income Inequality Index across American metro areas, and Table 16.2 lists the twenty most unequal metros based on income inequality across the country.

It is striking how different the two maps are. Bridgeport-Stamford, Connecticut, has the highest level of overall income inequality in the nation—no surprise to anyone who has made the short drive from leafy Westport to gritty, downtown Bridgeport. Greater New

York is sixth, and Miami, seventh. But those three are the only metros with more than 1 million people to make the list. The majority of metros on this list are much smaller, for example, second, fifth, and ninth place Naples, Gainesville, and Vero Beach, Florida, and third place College Station, Texas. College Station and Gainesville are far from the only college towns represented—Athens, Georgia; Morgantown, West Virginia; Corvallis, Oregon; Auburn, Alabama; and Monroe, Louisiana, score relatively high, along with some industrial metros like Brownsville, Texas. High-tech, knowledge-based metros are conspicuously absent from this list.

The differences between the two inequality measures, two maps, and two lists could not be more striking. Figure 16.3 shows this, comparing the way metros fall out on these two inequality metrics. It arrays into four basic quadrants. Metros in the upper right-hand corner—College Station, Bridgeport, New York City, Gainesville, and Boulder—face the double whammy of high income and high wage inequality. Metros in the lower right—Oxnard, California, and Columbus, Indiana, for example—have relatively high levels of wage inequality alongside relatively lower levels of income inequality. Metros in the upper left—for example, Tuscaloosa, Alabama, and Naples, Florida—have high income inequality alongside relatively lower levels of wage inequality. Lastly, metros in the lower left—for example, Sheboygan, Wisconsin, and Ogden and St. George, Utah—have relatively low levels of both.

Our statistical analysis uncovers only a modest association between these two measures of inequality. When Mellander ran a simple regression analysis she found that wage inequality accounts for 15 percent of the variation in income equality across regions. What accounts for the other 85 percent?

A number of studies have looked beyond the increasingly divergent returns to high- and low-skill jobs brought on by technology and globalization. A couple of decades ago, Bennett Harrison and

Barry Bluestone pointed to the declining rate of unionization. Unionization was a key factor in the postwar social compact that elevated the wages of manufacturing workers and others. In their book *The Great U-Turn*, they argued that attacks on unions by corporations and the right had led to a weakening of this core institutional support for wages, driving them downward.[11]

It might not be so much the growing divide between high- and low-skill jobs that drives inequality, but the endemic poverty of the people that William Julius Wilson identifies in *The Truly Disadvantaged*, who don't have jobs at all or who scrape by in the underground economy.[12]

Geography also seems to be at play. As we have seen, Christopher Berry and Edward Glaeser noted the divergence of human capital levels across cities in 2005, and I wrote about the "means migration" in *The Atlantic*. In his book *The Big Sort*, Bill Bishop showed how America is becoming increasingly sorted and divided by skill, economic position, and political differences.[13]

The size and density of cities has also been shown to be a factor in inequality. Large cities and metros have distinct advantages when it comes to attracting high-skill people, high-tech jobs, and other economic assets in more global knowledge-based economies. An important study by Nathaniel Baum-Snow of Brown University and the National Bureau of Economic Research and Ronni Pavan of the University of Rochester finds a close connection between city size and inequality.[14] City size alone accounted for roughly 25 to 35 percent of the total increase in economic inequality over the past three decades, after taking into account the role of skills, human capital, industry composition, and other factors.

With help from Charlotta Mellander, I looked at the associations between wage inequality and income inequality, as well as the factors that bear on each of them from skills and human capital to unionization, poverty, and race as well as metro size and density. Our findings are striking along a number of fronts. Wage and income inequality, we found, are completely different beasts.[15]

Wage inequality is closely associated with the shift to more high-tech, human capital, knowledge-based economies—as one would expect it to be. It is closely associated with the percent of adults who are college grads and even more so with the Creative Class. Wage inequality is also closely associated with both of the key skill sets associated with Creative Class work—analytical skill and social skill. It is even more closely associated with the concentration of high-tech industry.[16] Wage inequality, not surprisingly, also follows the affluence of metros, being closely associated with region incomes, wages, and output per person. Wage inequality is significantly associated with the density and even more so with the size of metros. Although many believe large disparities in housing costs across cities and metros are part of the problem, wage inequality is only modestly related to housing costs as a share of income.[17]

But when we turn to income inequality, the story is different. Surprisingly income inequality bears little if any relation to the wealth of regions. There is no correlation whatsoever between income inequality and average incomes and wages, and only a weak relationship to economic output per capita. In striking contrast to wage inequality, income inequality is not driven so much by rising average levels of wealth and affluence.

The broader shift to an innovative, skill-driven, human-capital-powered economy plays a much smaller role than expected in income inequality as well. The correlation between human capital and income inequality is less than half of that between human capital and wage inequality. There is even less of a correlation to the Creative Class. Income inequality is only modestly related to social skill and not at all to analytical skill, the two skill types that are associated with Creative Class work and that are most advantaged by the process of skill-biased technical change.[18]

The size and density of cities and metros also has little if any relation to income inequality. Income inequality is only modestly related to the size of a metro and has no correlation whatsoever to density. And income inequality has no relation at all to the share of income devoted to housing costs.

So which among the factors we analyzed appear to play the biggest role in income inequality? Unions, race, and poverty. Let's take them one at a time. Unions mitigate income inequality, according to our analysis. Overall income inequality is lower where unions are stronger.[19]

Tellingly—and ominously, for its implications about the state of the nation—income inequality is linked considerably to both poverty and race. Income inequality is significantly associated with the share of the population that is black,[20] and poverty plays an even larger role.[21] When Mellander ran a regression for income inequality, poverty and race remained significant factors alongside wage inequality.

What it boils down to is this: although the broad structural transformation of our economy splits the labor market and increases the wage gap between the major classes, it has only a modest effect on income inequality broadly. In fact, the least-skilled and lowest-paid workers—the members of the Working and Service Classes—are actually economically better off in more affluent and knowledge-based regions with higher concentrations of the Creative Class, even if the wage gap is wider. To really understand the problem of income inequality, it is necessary to look at the bottom of the socioeconomic order rather than just the top, where we are confronted with the tragedy of endemic poverty.

CHAPTER 17

The Inclining
Significance of Class

T he late *New York Times* architecture critic Herbert Muschamp
once wrote that "just by daring to use the word class," I had
"changed the framework for discussing social and economic
inequality."[1] In the cold war environment of the 1950s and 1960s,
class had become something of a dirty word in America. In 1959,
the sociologist Robert Nisbet declared that "the term social class
. . . is nearly valueless for the clarification of data on wealth, power
and status."[2] Daniel Bell proclaimed not just the end of class but
of ideology.[3] A 2001 book was titled simply *The Classless Society.*[4]
Sociologists supplanted the older construct of class with a new, empirically grounded construct of "socioeconomic status," based on
education, income, and other factors, and referred to by the short-
hand SES. A wide range of categories—"lower," "middle," and
"upper," and many combinations thereof—was formulated to capture and parse people's position in the social order. Class came to
be viewed less in terms of the kind of work we do and more in terms
of what we buy or how we identify ourselves.

But whether we sweep it under the rug or not, class remains a
major force in our economy and society. As this book has shown,

the members of the three major classes today, the Creative Class, the Working Class, and the Service Class, each have very different connections to the economy. They live different kinds of lives, and they pursue them in very different kinds of places. The more I look at the reality of today's society, the more I'm reminded of the Italian Marxist thinker Antonio Gramsci's famous aperçu, "Hegemony here is born in the factory."[5] Gramsci, like Marx before him, reminds us of an essential point: the reality of everyday life is structured to a large degree by the very mode of how we work. And as this chapter will show, class structures everything, from where we live and how much we pay for housing to our very health and happiness.

One clear line of class demarcation is politics. Political commentators have long pointed to the underlying social and economic sorting that underpins America's growing Red-Blue divide. In his influential book *Red State, Blue State, Rich State, Poor State,* Andrew Gelman of Columbia University helps unpack this phenomenon: whereas rich *voters* trend Republican, rich *states* trend Democratic.[6]

Based on large-scale surveys, the Gallup Organization tracks the numbers of Americans who identify themselves as "conservatives," "moderates," and "liberals" across the fifty states.[7] Conservatism is clearly growing across America. In February 2011, Mississippi became the first state in which more than half of all residents identified as conservative, with Idaho, Alabama, Wyoming, and Utah approaching that level. In Arkansas, South Carolina, North Dakota, Louisiana, and South Dakota (the rest of Gallup's top-ten conservative states), conservative identification was 45 percent or higher. The Gallup data found conservatives outnumbering liberals in even the most liberal-leaning states (excluding the District of Columbia): Vermont (30.7 percent conservative to 30.5 percent liberal), Rhode Island (29.9 conservative to 29.3 percent liberal), and Massachusetts (29.9 to 28.0 percent).

When Charlotta Mellander and I used the Gallup data to examine the factors that shape these state-by-state patterns, we found class to be a key driver of the rising conservatism. Conservative political affiliation was strongly and positively correlated with the Working Class and religion (measured as the share of state population for which religion is an important part of daily life) and negatively associated with Creative Class and college grads. Conservative states were also far less tolerant and diverse. Conservative political affiliation was highly negatively correlated with the percent of the population composed of immigrants or gays and lesbians. Conservatism was most pronounced in America's least well-off, least educated, most blue-collar, most economically hard-hit states. More and more, it had become the default ideology of the economically left behind.

Class also registers itself powerfully in the politics of our cities. In the original edition of this book, I noted that as our cities were becoming increasingly sorted and divided, place itself was coming to supplant the factory and workplace as the fundamental site of class conflict. This process has only accelerated over the past decade. Serious political tensions were already erupting over gentrification in the late 1990s and early 2000s, and I cited some of them.[8] In summer 2000, for example, a powerful anti-high-tech development coalition emerged in San Francisco's SoMa and Mission Districts and quickly spread. A coalition of artists, club owners, and neighborhood residents held more than three dozen rallies and protests—including one outside City Hall, in which a group of demonstrators smashed a computer with a baseball bat. In a protracted battle that ultimately came to be known as the SoMa Wars, the coalition collected more than 30,000 signatures across the city to place Proposition L on the ballot—a measure to ban high-tech development and other forms of gentrification from SoMa, the Mission, and other largely residential neighborhoods. The measure was defeated by less than 1 percent of the vote.[9] Back in 2002, I noted the prospect of a new set of "place wars" that were likely to emerge in other creative centers.

But I could not anticipate the riots that broke out in London during the summer of 2011. Commentators on the right mostly put the blame on hooliganism, whereas those on the left cited frustrations with the United Kingdom's faltering economy and newly imposed fiscal austerities. But it seemed to me that more than youth, ethnicity, or even race, the riots were about class and the growing divide among classes.

Globalization has made the world smaller and brought its economies and peoples closer together. But instead of reducing and flattening economic and class distinctions, it has made them sharper, bringing them into ever-clearer relief. We make a big mistake when we look out across the peaks of privilege from our aeries in London or New York or Los Angeles to Tokyo, Shanghai, Singapore, and Mumbai and tell ourselves that the playing field is level. The defining feature of our world is that it is spiky—and it is getting spikier and more divided all the time. Those worsening class divisions are ferociously at work in microcosm within our cities.

What happened in London is a tale of two immigrations, which themselves cut across class lines. On the one hand, the great global metropolises are magnets for the international super-rich on the lookout for tax shelters and shopping opportunities. On the other hand, they attract less-skilled immigrants, hungry for better lives. In between are the local populations, left behind by fast-moving economic change. London certainly has its rich and poor districts. But in contrast to the physical divides and segregation that you see in most American cities, London's rich and poor often live right on top of each other in rapidly gentrifying enclaves. Rising housing costs, the concentration of wealth, and divergent life prospects are there for all to see. As the multinational global super-rich skate by, virtually unscathed by the economic crisis, the young and the less-skilled immigrants are out of work for longer and longer periods, their life prospects fading as the economy worsens and budget cuts take hold. London's riots were a global conflict, played out on a local scale.

The riots were also a reaction to the unvarnished corporate re-making of London. Like so many other global cities, the vast majority of London's political energy seems to be directed toward the needs and interests of an elite sliver of its population. The transformation of London into an "Olympic City" involves not just the redevelopment of stadium and venue sites but the physical relocation of groups and populations. With the social compact eroding and a lack of viable mass political institutions to channel the mounting resentment, what comes out is not a coherent voice or movement, but inchoate rage.

And then there's this: our greatest cities are not bland monocultures; some of the very features that make them so dynamic also contribute to their instability. Eric Hobsbawm long ago noted that density and the closeness of the poor to centers of political influence and power made old cities centers of insurrection. Scattered incidents of flash-mob violence in Philadelphia, Baltimore, and other US cities are almost certainly harbingers of worse things to come; the London riots should serve as a wake-up call to our great global cities and the people who run them. Our urban centers have become increasingly divided and unstable. Left to its own devices, the unbridled operation of the free market will only make those divides worse. Simply upping the police presence is a recipe for even greater disaster.

What's needed is the recognition that along with the great economic rewards of globalization comes substantial responsibilities. The long-term prosperity of London and other great global cities requires more than new condominiums, sports complexes, and cultural districts. Real opportunities must be provided for all residents, so that the rewards and promises of the creative city can be shared more equally.

In 2010, Toronto elected a new mayor, not just a conservative or a Tea Partier, but perhaps the most anti-urban mayor ever elected in a major North American city. Rob Ford rode to office with the support of lower-middle-class, working-class, and new-immigrant voters who resented the urban rich, downtown yuppies and hipsters, and unionized public-sector workers. Styling himself as a man of the people, Ford vowed to cut spending and go after the government-sponsored "gravy train." Upon assuming office, he declined to attend the city's famed gay pride festival. Adding injury to insult, his brother Doug, his close adviser, slighted Toronto's leading literary light Margaret Atwood, who gave them the handle "twinfordmayor(s)." Their plan to turn Toronto's waterfront into a mega-mall complete with a monorail, Ferris wheel, and boat-in hotel sparked a public fury (of which I was a part) and was quickly shelved.

All of this shocked and challenged me because I had long seen Toronto as a bastion of progressive urbanism, notable for its commitment to justice and fairness for all of its residents. But when my Martin Prosperity Institute research team prepared a map that overlaid Toronto voting patterns with the locations of its Creative Class, Working Class, and Service Class jobs, it all became clear. I could see that Toronto is completely divided. The Creative Class is densely concentrated in a T-shaped pattern in and around the downtown core and closely clustered along its east-west and north-south subway routes. This is where Ford's liberal and left-leaning challengers are located. The Service and Working Classes are pushed off to the periphery in more outlying areas. Only a handful of districts where Working Class jobs predominate are left in the city, and one of them is the mayor's. In the United States, the political divide is also a jurisdictional divide, pitting city against suburb. But in Toronto, it was all happening within the city itself.

If the world is taking on a Hobbesian cast, it's because globalization, poverty, and affluence have given rise to a new sorting process that geographically separates economic and social classes, both domestically and globally. Social cohesion is eroding within cities and countries as well as across them. It's little wonder we find ourselves living in an increasingly fractured society, in which growing numbers are ready to vote—or tear—down what they perceive to be the economic elite of our cities and the world.

Class, Health, and Happiness

The original edition of this book focused on conventional gauges of economic development like innovation, income, and employment. Over the past decade, a growing number of scholars have suggested that we need broader, less materialistic measures of social and economic well-being. There is growing interest in the field of happiness. Early studies found that happiness was not simply a function of rising incomes at the national level. The famous Easterlin Paradox[10] described the fact that while rich people are much happier than poor people, rich societies are only a little happier than poor societies, and countries as a whole don't get happier when they get richer. Other studies, notably research by economists Justin Wolfers and Betsy Stevenson, find a continuing connection between income and happiness.

A great deal of my recent research has focused on the connection between class and happiness. It finds that class plays a fundamental role in happiness—over and above that of income. Income matters, of course, but only up to a point. Once a basic threshold of income is met, then class kicks in. Nations with higher levels of the Creative Class post higher levels of happiness and subjective well-being. Where the Working Class is larger, happiness levels are lower.

But what about cities and metro areas? In a 2011 study, "The Happiness of Cities," Charlotta Mellander, Jason Rentfrow, and I probed the factors that shape metro happiness with statistical models that controlled for the effects of income, home ownership, commuting times, age, unemployment, human capital, and other factors. According to our analysis of data from the Gallup's City Well-Being tracking poll,[11] we found that human capital played by far the most significant role in the happiness of metros, outperforming income and every other variable.[12] Happiness was strongly positively associated with the Creative Class share as well as with income. Boulder, Colorado, for instance, ranked first on happiness as well as the Creative Class. Happiness was also negatively associated with the Working Class. Interestingly enough, it was also negatively associated with warmer temperatures, belying the notion that people are happier in places with warmer, sunnier climes.[13]

From the TV series *The Biggest Loser* to Oprah's documented struggles with her weight, fitness is a signal obsession of American popular culture. We suffer from no dearth of health, fitness, and nutritional experts; celebrities, politicians, and even first ladies exhort us to eat better and exercise more. But we need to face up to the fact that healthy or unhealthy lifestyles are not simply the result of good or bad individual decisions. They are inextricably tied up with the nature and structure of our society. America's increasingly uneven geography of fitness is yet another symptom of its fundamental economic and class divide.

Smoking and obesity are two of the most significant—if not the most significant—health problems we confront. Although smoking has been trending downward, more than 46 million Americans, about one in five adults, still smoke. Obesity has reached epidemic proportions: 17 percent of American children (12.5 million) and 33.3 percent of American adults (72 million) now meet the Centers for Disease Control's criteria for obesity—percentages that have doubled since 1980. Both smoking and obesity are associated with cancer, heart disease, and diabetes. Smoking takes an average of ten years off Americans' average life spans, and obesity reduces life spans by between five and twenty years, depending on age and race. Each year, about 443,000 Americans die from smoking-related diseases; some 300,000 premature deaths are attributed to obesity. The Centers for Disease Control estimates that smoking and obesity combined generate annual health costs of more than $300 billion.

We used data from the Centers for Disease Control to build a Metro Health Index based on smoking and obesity rates across US metros.[14] We measured smoking as the percentage of people who smoke every day, and obesity as the percent of the population with a Body Mass Index of thirty or more (see Table 17.1). San Jose and Santa Cruz are the most healthy metros, and Boulder comes in third. The least healthy metros are St. Joseph, Missouri, and Decatur and Gadsen, Alabama. Not surprisingly, smoking and obesity themselves are closely correlated with one another.[15] In a more detailed statistical study I conducted with Mellander, we found that smoking is lower in metros with a higher share of the Creative Class and higher levels of human capital, and obesity levels are higher in metros with higher Working Class concentrations.[16]

Using data from a comprehensive measure of metro fitness—the American Fitness Index—Mellander and I tracked the relations between class and other factors on fitness.[17] Metro fitness was strongly positively associated with the Creative Class and negatively associated with the Working Class. This is a little counterintuitive, perhaps, because Working Class people put more physical effort into their jobs, but as discussed in these pages, sedentary professionals are much more likely to pursue vigorous exercise in their leisure time. Fitter metros had higher levels of college graduates, more high-tech industry, and higher levels of innovation—all characteristics of Creative Class locations. They were also more affluent. Although many people presume fitness goes along with warmer locations, we found just the opposite. Each of the top five fitness metros is pretty chilly, and the top-ranked Twin Cities are among the coldest locations in the United States—certainly compared to warm and sunny LA, which languishes in forty-first place. Fitness was strongly related to happiness as well.[18]

Table 17.1   America's Healthiest and Unhealthiest Metros, 2010

Ten Healthiest Metros	Healthy Metros Index	Creative Class Share
San Jose-Sunnyvale-Santa Clara, CA	.982	46.9%
Santa Cruz-Watsonville, CA	.982	32.1%
Boulder, CO	.980	44.4%
Napa, CA	.968	27.4%
Bend, OR	.966	28.6%
San Francisco-Oakland-Fremont, CA	.965	39.4%
Bridgeport-Stamford-Norwalk, CT	.948	39.5%
San Luis Obispo-Paso Robles, CA	.946	30.1%
Corvallis, OR	.943	41.7%
Los Angeles-Long Beach-Santa Ana, CA	.943	34.1%

Ten Unhealthiest Metros	Healthy Metros Index	Creative Class Share
Gadsden, AL	.040	25.1%
Decatur, AL	.046	23.3%
St. Joseph, MO-KS	.052	25.1%
Gulfport-Biloxi, MS	.052	27.8%
Huntington-Ashland, WV-KY-OH	.054	28.5%
Pascagoula, MS	.054	23.4%
Muskegon-Norton Shores, MI	.054	26.6%
Anniston-Oxford, AL	.058	23.3%
Flint, MI	.073	29.9%
Goldsboro, NC	.073	30.1%

Source: Smoking data are from the Centers for Disease Control, Behavioral Risk Factor Surveillance System (BRFSS), 2002–2008. Obesity data are based on a Body Mass Index (BMI) greater than 30 and are from the National Center for Chronic Disease Prevention and Health Promotion, 2006–2008. Compiled by Charlotta Mellander.

When rates of smoking and obesity are used as a proxy for health and wellness, they reflect more than a medical problem—they are a socioeconomic problem as well. The geography of health in America varies considerably and consistently with income, education, class, and race. Tragically, the very Americans who are paying the greatest cost for these afflictions—in health-care expenses, lost wages, and general suffering—are the ones who can afford it the least. We can tell people to smoke less, eat better, and exercise more, but the United States will not solve its health problems—or reduce its skyrocketing health-care costs—until it comes to grips with class. As America's class divide worsens, so, too, does its health outcomes.

Commuting and Class

Class is also evident in the way we get to work. Across the board, nearly nine in ten (86 percent) Americans commute to work by car and more than three-fourths (76.1 percent) drive to work by themselves. Just 5 percent use public transit, fewer than 3 percent walk, and fewer than 1 percent ride their bikes to work. But these patterns vary widely across metros. It's no surprise that eight in ten Manhattan workers get to their places of employment via public transit, bicycle, or on foot. But more than four in ten (43 percent) of all commuters in the greater New York metro don't use cars, either. Neither do 25 to 30 percent of workers in San Francisco, Boston, and greater Washington, DC. Fewer than 3 percent (2.9) of Americans walk to work, but more than 5 percent of New Yorkers do. And in the college town of Ithaca, New York, 14 percent do. Only a little more than one-half of one percent (0.6) of Americans ride their bikes to work. But more than 5 percent do in Eugene, Oregon, and Fort Collins, Colorado. In the Portland, Oregon, metro, more than 2 percent of commuters cycle to work, and in San Francisco and San Jose, roughly 1.5 percent do. Walking and biking to work are especially prevalent in compact college towns with high percentages of the Creative Class, including Boulder, Ann Arbor, Madison, Iowa City, Corvallis, Gainesville, Burlington, State College, Pennsylvania, and Lafayette, Indiana.

I never expected the way we commute to be shaped by class, but it is. Economist Todd Gabe ran a series of statistical analyses to gauge the effects of class as well as weather conditions, density, and other factors that one might think to be associated with how we get to work. You'd think that density would matter—transit is more available and it's easier for commuters to walk or bike to work in cities and metros that have less sprawl. Weather and climate should also play a role. Who wants to cycle or walk to work in wet, cold, and snowy places? It's much easier and more pleasurable to use your feet to get to work when the weather is nice. But "what you'd think" isn't always what is. Gabe found that class plays a much bigger role than either density or weather and climate—in fact, class plays the biggest role of all. The correlation between the Creative Class and biking to work is the highest of any in his analysis. Population density increases public transportation usage but has no effect on walking and biking. Weather and climate play a role, but not necessarily in the way that one might think. People are more likely to drive to work in places where the weather is warm or wet. Public transit use as well as walking and biking are more common in drier climates but also in places with colder January temperatures. The longer the commute, the more likely people are to use public transit, but—not surprisingly—the less likely they are to bike or walk. Rapidly growing cities of sprawl (those which built the most houses during the height of the bubble) are much more car dependent than other places. We can see this when we look at another set of correlations, between the share of housing units built between 2000 and 2006 and the percentage of people who bike, walk, or take public transit to work, which is negative.[19]

America is becoming more and more divided and unequal—by income, by the kind of work we do, by our levels of education, by our politics and culture, and perhaps most dangerously, by our very health and happiness.

The Geography of Guns

Every once in a while a terrible shooting—like that of Congress-woman Gabrielle Giffords and eighteen bystanders, six of them fatally, in January 2011—focuses national attention on the horrible costs of gun violence. But gun violence is something that happens every day. In 2007, 10.2 out of every 100,000 people were killed by firearms across the United States. When Charlotta Mellander and I charted the statistical correlations between firearm deaths and a variety of psychological, economic, social, and political characteristics of states, one in particular stood out: firearm deaths were far less likely to occur in states with higher levels of the Creative Class and more college grads and far more likely to occur in Working Class states and those with higher levels of poverty.

Images of drug-crazed gunmen are commonplace in the media. Guns, mental illness, and drug abuse are presumed to go together. But that's not borne out in our analysis. We found no statistical association between gun deaths and mental illness or stress levels, and none between gun violence and the proportion of neurotic personalities. We found no association between illegal drug use and death from gun violence at the state level. And for all the terrifying talk about violence-prone immigrants, states with more immigrants have *lower* levels of gun-related deaths. Some might think gun violence would be higher in states with higher levels of unemployment and higher levels of inequality. But, again, we found no evidence of any such association with either of these variables.[20]

Overlaying gun deaths with voting patterns from the 2008 presidential election, we found a striking pattern: Firearms-related deaths were positively associated with states that voted for John McCain and negatively associated with states that voted for Barack

Obama. This might infuriate some, but the statistics are plain to see. Partisan affiliation alone cannot explain the phenomenon; most likely it stems from two broader, underlying factors—the economic and employment makeup of the states and their policies toward guns and gun ownership.

The Great Dental Divide

There's seemingly no end to the dimensions of America's class divide—religious versus secular, Starbucks versus Dunkin' Donuts, NPR versus the NRA, NASCAR versus World Cup Soccer. But one is particularly striking. Data released by the Gallup Organization[21] in September 2011, based on some 177,000 interviews, portrayed an additional axis of class cleavage, between those who regularly go to the dentist and those who do not.

When Mellander and I looked at the data, we found a strikingly familiar pattern. You would expect income to play a role in oral health, and it does. We found a close correlation between state income levels and how often their residents go to the dentist. But income is not the only factor. Frequency of dental office visits tracked closely with class, being much higher in Creative Class states and those with more college grads and much lower in Working Class states, and even more so where inequality is highest. Oral health also reflects America's political divide. Visits to the dentist were positively associated with states that voted for Obama in 2008 and negatively associated with McCain states.

Poor oral health is a big problem—one that is linked to heart disease, stroke, atherosclerosis, rheumatoid arthritis, and diabetes. Our analysis found close associations between oral health and two key health factors, smoking and obesity. Visits to the dentist were negatively associated with both smoking and obesity. And not surprisingly, more frequent dental visits are associated with higher levels of overall happiness and subjective well-being.[22]

Access to dental care stands as a remarkably stark divide in American life, but it shouldn't come as a surprise. More than four in ten Americans pay their dental bills themselves, and the past decade or so has seen a vicious "oral cost spiral," as *Slate*'s June Thomas puts it,[23] with the costs of dental care far outpacing both the rate of inflation and overall medical cost increases. With incomes falling, unemployment rising, and poverty increasing, dental care has become a luxury that fewer and fewer Americans can afford—and this despite the high premium that we put on appearance. "We rarely think about our teeth, but without them many of us would be up a creek socially and economically," writes Ylajali Hansen at Generation Bubble blog. "For many Americans, a tooth can make the difference between security and destitution. That's right: lose a tooth in the United States and you lose your chance to live the dream."[24]

Class remains a key feature of American life, shaping everything from our politics to our health and happiness. Overcoming these divides requires nothing less than a new set of institutions and a wholly new social compact that can leverage the full potential the new Creative Economy holds out, while mitigating the substantial divides and costs it imposes.

CONCLUSION

CHAPTER 18

Every Single
Human Being Is Creative

Ten years ago, I concluded this book with a challenge. It's past time, I said, that we members of the Creative Class recognize that our economic function makes us the natural—indeed, the only possible—leaders of twenty-first century society. But being newly emergent, we don't yet have the awareness of ourselves as a class that we need. We're even a little squeamish about identifying ourselves as such, as though to do so were to undercut our egalitarian values.

Then I threw down the gauntlet: it's time for the Creative Class to grow up, I declared. We must evolve from an amorphous group of self-directed, albeit high-achieving individuals into a more cohesive, more responsible collective. We must recognize that despite our differences, we share vital interests and concerns.

I imagined at the time that the dot-com crash and the events of 9/11 might turn out to be our generation's defining experience— what World War II was to the Greatest Generation, or Vietnam and the Civil Rights Movement was for many boomers. Little did I know about the even bigger temblor that was yet to come—the deep crisis that emanated from the bursting of the real estate and credit bubbles in 2008, events that we now recognize as the terminal spasms of a whole economic order.

But if I could not predict the violence of the crisis, I wasn't taken by surprise. The tectonic shift we are witnessing is the result not just of financial shenanigans but of a deeper and more fundamental shift—the passing of the old industrial order as it gives way to the emerging Creative Economy. If we wish to build a new prosperity, we cannot rely on market forces and the Invisible Hand to guide us. Left alone, as it has been, the new economic and social order—like the rise of other new social and economic systems before it—has generated and will continue to generate greater and greater inequalities; the social and economic divides within, across, and between cities and nations will only grow worse. The grand challenge of our time is to build new institutional structures that can guide its emergence and channel its energies in ways that benefit society and its people broadly.

Inequality has reached levels not seen in the United States since the Gilded Age. While much attention has been paid to the abuses taking place at the very top, its persistence today is as much a factor of stagnation at the bottom of the economic ladder—of endemic and persistent poverty. Although all developed nations face some level of inequality, the United States is a statistical outlier when it comes to its depth and severity. Creativity and inequality, innovation and immiseration don't have to go together.

New institutions are needed to harness such powerful economic forces, to address worsening class divides, and to make society and the economy work for all of us.

The Creative Compact

The key to all of this is a new social compact—a new set of institutions that can provide a Creative Economy analog to the great social compact of the 1930s, 1940s, and 1950s, which expanded and accelerated the growth of the industrial economy and led to the last great golden age of prosperity. This Creative Compact would be dedicated to the *creatification* of everyone. It would expand participation in the Creative Economy to industrial and service workers, leverage new private and public investment in human infrastructure, innovation, education, and our cities, while reaffirming and maintaining America's long-held commitment to diversity. It would restructure education, moving away from rote learning and overly bureaucratic schools and creativity-squelching standards. It would set in place a new social safety net that invests in people and provides mobile benefits that follow workers from job to job. It would recast urban policy as a cornerstone of economic policy and ensure that America remains a beacon for the best, brightest, most energetic and ambitious people in the world.

The Creative Compact would help unleash the innovative and productive potential of people—our most precious economic resource—while addressing the many and worsening inequities that have been caused by our failure to adapt to new structures and realities.

Despite the incredible outpouring of innovation, productivity, and wealth the Creative Economy has produced to date, most of its benefits have been enjoyed by a privileged economic and geographic cohort. It doesn't have to be this way. The challenges we face today may be different in their specifics, but they are by no means new. We have been through this before. The Industrial Revolution generated new technologies, new industries, and new productive potential alongside gross economic inequalities—which Marx wrongly believed would ultimately prove to be capitalism's undoing. Before the nascent industrial age could reach its full potential, the development of a much more broadly based urban-industrial society, in which great masses of people could participate, was required.

This industrial society did not emerge on its own but was gradually spurred into existence, over the emphatic and sometimes violent

objections of entrenched groups, by a broad social compact—the
creation of new institutions and policies that coped with and mit-
igated its most onerous and divisive aspects, extending the benefits
of its productivity to blue-collar workers, turning once terrible low-
paying manufacturing jobs into good family-supporting ones, allowing workers to organize and collectively bargain for their rights,
and ultimately linking wage increases to productivity gains. It also
established Social Security for older people, provided benefits for
the disabled and basic social welfare for the truly needy, while protecting health and safety in the workplace. It spurred human capital
accumulation by massively expanding the system of higher education, while providing federal investments for scientific research and
development, a cornerstone of the innovation economy.

This new social compact squared the circle, turning the once-
divided industrial economy into a middle-class society by allowing
the broad base of the population to participate in it, while enabling
its tremendous expansion. Far from undermining business and
subverting capitalism, by making home mortgages more available
and investing in the development of the interstate highway system,
this social compact encouraged the expansion of key mass production industries, from cars to appliances.

It's worth recalling that this new social compact did not stoke but
actually banked the fires of class warfare. It emerged at a time when
capitalism was not only in crisis but when fascism and communism
were fighting to supplant it. Although some still cherish nostalgia
for the fiery idealism of the revolutionary movements of the early
twentieth century, the long sweep of history suggests that what appeared as a meeker, more tepid reformist impulse was not only more
pragmatic but better, comparatively speaking. Efforts to overthrow
capitalism—either from the right or the left—devolved into chaos
and unprecedented disasters. Efforts to temper capitalism—to harness its innovative Schumpeterian engines while spreading its benefits more widely—certainly didn't solve all of its problems or

inequities, but they led to unprecedented prosperity and freedom. If Fordism was ultimately unsustainable, the foundational principle of this social compact—that workers must receive a level of compensation that allows them to participate in the economy—underpinned what we still look back on as the golden age of economic prosperity.

The challenges facing us today require something even bigger and bolder. A new Creative Compact for our time must be built across six key principles. I offer them as a series of overarching precepts, not as a full-blown plan. The most effective strategies will emerge from the nitty-gritty, trial-and-error efforts that happen in the real world.

Invest in Developing the Full Human Potential and Creative Capabilities of Every Single Human Being

First and foremost, before the United States or any other advanced nation can recover, prosper, and thrive, it must strive to tap the full creative capabilities of every one of its people. We can't simply write off the tens of millions of workers who toil in low-wage service jobs. The United States and other nations will have to find ways to bring the service and manufacturing sectors more fully into the Creative Age. The more creative they become, the more productive they will be. This means enabling and tapping the intellectual and social skills of each and every worker.

The manufacturing jobs that pay best today look a lot more like knowledge work than traditional factory work. In fact high paid manufacturing work—guiding and maintaining advanced machinery, engaging in problem solving and continuous improvement with other workers and engineers—increasingly is knowledge work. "If you look at what people are doing in manufacturing today, they are running robots, designing tools, programming computers," Judith Crocker, director of education at the Manufacturing Advocacy & Growth Network, or MAGNET, a manufacturing promoter in

Cleveland, told a reporter from *The Cleveland Plain Dealer.*[1] This is true for every kind of job, including service work. As we saw in Chapter 11, adding analytical and social skills to just about any job raises both its productivity and its wages.

Every job can and must be *creatified*; every worker must be able to harness his or her own inner entrepreneur. We did it before in manufacturing. We turned low-wage, low-skill work in horrific, exploitative factories into the good family-supporting jobs workers pine for today. We need to do the same for services—for the more than 60 million Americans and countless others around the globe, who toil for low wages in everything from food preparation and home health care to retail sales. Some will counter that this will only make services more expensive. My response is simple: we can't afford not to do it. Decades ago, we collectively conceded that we would have to pay more for manufactured goods so that workers could have better wages and a broad middle class could be born. The demand and productivity it spurred moved the whole economy forward. The same can be done today for low-skill service jobs. Tapping into the innovative and creative capabilities of service workers and engaging them more fully will ultimately make them more productive. If we paid more for cars and consumer goods, why can't we pay a little bit more collectively to the people who prepare our food, look after our homes, and take care of our children and aging parents? Doing so will build a stronger middle class, enhance social cohesion, and create the demand that can help drive the economy forward. The service sector is the last frontier of innovation in our economy; it needs to be brought up to date, and upskilling its workers and upgrading their jobs is key to that. Creativity is our most precious resource; we can't afford to waste it in any sector of the economy.

Paul Romer and other leading students of innovation have shown that investments in innovations and ideas have extraordinary rates of return and pay incredible dividends, precisely because they are public goods; the benefits they confer are broad and reverberate throughout the entire economy. We need to get beyond the notion that innovation is something that only occurs among scientists working in a lab. Innovation happens anywhere and everywhere, and more often than not it comes from small things. We need to see all members of society as potential innovators, stoke their innovative potential, and extend the definition of innovation beyond technology and R&D to include investment in the arts, in culture, and in every other form of creativity.

We similarly need to put entrepreneurialism front and center on the economic agenda. Although many debate the relative merits of large versus small companies, it is clear that it is dynamic new firms that drive innovation, create new industries, and generate a huge share of all jobs. When policy makers think of entrepreneurship, they think in terms of high-tech start-ups of the Silicon Valley variety. Those are important. But we must support every kind of entrepreneurship.

Fewer and fewer of us have the economic security once provided by large corporations to fall back on. If industrial age schools readied our children for the workforce, Creative Age schools must prepare them to manage their careers and build businesses of their own. The goal can no longer just be to get a job but rather to create a job—and to create more jobs for others. A huge percentage of new businesses fail, but we can help increase the odds of their success. We provide all sorts of assistance to technology-based entrepreneurs, so why not extend this to all new businesses? Instead of just building incubators for high-tech companies, why not for neighborhood restaurants, mom-and-pop shops, and hair and nail salons? Why not extend support to personal trainers, dieticians, therapists, musicians, artists, and lawn service providers? The list goes on and on. What kills new business is poor management, inattention to cost control, lack of marketing and sales skills. We need to offer all Americans, young and old, rich and poor, the tools they need to survive and thrive as creative entrepreneurs.

Make Openness and Diversity and Inclusion a
Central Part of the Economic Agenda

A growing body of economic research shows that diversity and openness power economic growth.[2] Immigrants from foreign countries spearhead innovations and enterprise in everything from steel making to semiconductors and all forms of high tech. As we have seen, literally half of all Silicon Valley start-ups involve immigrants. Our policy makers need to do what the venture capitalist John Doerr said they should: staple a green card to the diploma of every immigrant who graduates from one of our engineering schools.[3] More than that, we need to make this country welcoming to *all* enterprising, energetic, and ambitious people. This is the biggest no-brainer of them all.

Build an Education System That Spurs, Not Squelches, Creativity

The most important investments we make are not in bridges, highways, and other physical assets but in our human assets. Everyone agrees that education is important, but our definition of education must be broadened. Just as the United States once sank vast amounts of public and private funds into canals, railroads, highways, and other physical infrastructure to power industrial growth, the country today needs to massively increase its investments in its human creative capital. The scale of the effort required is enormous—it will need to dwarf the public education system, land grant colleges, and GI bills of previous generations.

Our current system of elementary and high-school education, as many have observed, is badly broken. It is not hard to see why: it is a complete and total relic of the industrial age, developed to stamp out workers for the Fordist industrial machine as if they were so many widgets on a, well, assembly line. As Sir Ken Robinson argues in his book *The Element*,[4] our current approaches to education are "stifling some of the most important capacities that young people now need to make their way in the increasingly demanding world of the 21st century—the powers of creative thinking."

"All children start their school careers with sparkling imaginations, fertile minds, and a willingness to take risks with what they think," he told the *Guardian*. "Most students never get to explore the full range of their abilities and interests. . . . Education is the system that's supposed to develop our natural abilities and enable us to make our way in the world. Instead, it is stifling the individual talents and abilities of too many students and killing their motivation to learn."[5]

We need to rebuild our education system from the ground up—and on the principles of creativity and the Creative Economy. That means an educational system that is less focused on test scores and standards and more around active learning. We need to pay much more attention than we have to early childhood learning and development; these are the most critical years, when creative abilities are shaped. We horde our kids into schools, as a form of institutionalized day care, so their parents can work. But too small a part of the school day is devoted to actual creative development. As Robinson says, a Creative Age educational system needs to connect with kids' real interests and passions. Kids need to become emotionally attached to learning.

And we need to stop blaming teachers for problems created by an outmoded system. A large-scale economic study that tracked more than 2.5 million students over two decades found that good teachers—those who are fully engaged in their work and rewarded by their schools—generate not only better-performing students but effect a wide range of social outcomes. The study developed new, comprehensive measures for tracking "teacher value-added," separating out excellent, average, and poor teachers. After controlling for a wide range of factors, including students' family backgrounds, which play an important role in academic achievement and success, it found that students with top teachers were not only more likely to go to college and earn more income over the course of their careers, they were less likely to become pregnant as teenagers.[6]

Build a Social Safety Net for the Creative Economy

The Creative Age is not an Ayn Rand fantasy of rugged individualists making their own way; no viable system or society can ever be. A decade ago, Creative Class freelancers were hailed as the vanguard of an army of liberating entrepreneurs who were finding fun, freedom, and fulfillment on their own. The truth, as it always is, is much more complicated.

A new social safety net is needed, one that does for the new reality of creative work what the New Deal safety net did for blue-collar workers eighty years ago. Not only must today's creatives and freelancers provide their own health care, disability insurance, and pensions, or do without, as Sara Horowitz of the Freelancers Union notes. There is "no unemployment during lean times; no protections from age, race, and gender discrimination; no enforcement from the Department of Labor when employers don't pay; and the list goes on."[7] This must change.

It no longer makes sense to tie benefits to a single employer. The reality of employment today is mobility. A new social compact must start from the flexible, hyper-individualized, and contingent nature of work. That means health benefits that move with workers, and retirement accounts that do the same. This is good for workers, good for companies, and good for society as a whole. Canada, for example, has a higher rate of self-employment than the United States; this is one of the key things that has helped bolster its economy over the course of the economic crisis. One thing that helped make this possible is that every Canadian has health care; workers do not need to depend on employers to provide it.

This new safety net must ensure that the truly disadvantaged are provided with adequate living standards, and even more so, with real opportunities. Such a system cannot confine itself to material needs alone. Income from Social Security for the elderly and income support for the truly disadvantaged are certainly important. But what we need to do goes much further. And here I am not only talking about the United States but also societies that many admire for their more extended social safety nets, such as those in Scandinavia, Northern Europe, and Canada. A Creative Compact must provide more than minimal security for those who fall through the cracks; it must invest in everyone and provide them with opportunities to develop and fully utilize their human talents and potential.

Some will counter that such a system will promote slacking, as it has in some societies. But here is the bargain I envision: society will invest all that is needed to enable you to develop your talents and passions. But you as an individual must keep your part of the bargain. You must use those talents and that social investment to contribute productively to society. The Creative Compact recognizes that all people have the capacity to develop and utilize their talents; it should recognize self-expression as a fundamental human right and provide education and training to foster it.

Strengthen Cities; Promote Density, Clustering, and Concentration

Channelling Jane Jacobs, Felix Salmon said it best. "Jobs require cities." We can no longer count on companies to create the millions of new jobs that are needed; job generation increasingly comes from cities. Cities are the key economic and social organizing units of the Creative Age. They give rise to the clustering, density, and interaction that generate economic growth. They speed the metabolism of daily life, and they accelerate the combinations and recombinations that spur innovation, business formation, job creation, and economic growth.

But so much of public policy either promotes sprawl and decentralization or sees cities as urban basket cases filled with social pathologies. Cities must be a centerpiece of economic policy, not an afterthought.

We need to stop taxing the productive potential of our cities and metro areas to subsidize dumb sprawling growth. At the same time, we must be careful not to go too far, building massive skyscraper complexes that isolate people in vertical suburbs. At the local level, cities and communities need to stop subsidizing stadiums, convention centers, and other mega-projects that add little to their economies and stop encouraging bland, generic development. They need to invest in people climates as well as business climates; cultivate all 3T's; promote density, transit-oriented development, and walkability; create green spaces and other public spaces; encourage diversity; and build real quality of place.

Our cities are not just economic engines; they are key to our health and well-being. We need to invest in more green space, greater livability, energy efficiency, and sustainability. We need to expand transit, reducing the need to drive, and promote walking and biking, activities that not only save energy but also improve our health. We need to better connect our cities and suburbs with transit, and connect our metro areas, especially those that are part of larger megaregions, to each other with high-speed rail. Our older industrial-age cities are potentially cauldrons of creativity—filled with just the sorts of warehouses, factories, and other buildings that can become the figurative garages where start-ups are incubated. We can only succeed if we look at them as opportunities and not blights. Such investments are win-win-win propositions: they reinvigorate our older centers, take the pressure off the new ones, and result in a stronger system of cities overall.

This is not just an agenda for big cities and downtown areas. Quality of place, density, walkability, and open-mindedness and diversity are things large numbers of people not only desire but are willing to pay more for. This is an agenda that all kinds of communities—suburbs as well as cities, Sun Belt as well as Rust Belt places—can embrace and prosper from.

Our cities are also fulcrums for social and political innovation. Everyone recognizes that America's national government is dysfunctional. But cities and community governments actually work. When I meet local officials in my travels through America and around the world, I often can't tell who is a Democrat or a Republican, a liberal or a conservative. The most important policy innovations no longer come from national legislatures or federal bureaucracies, but from cities and mayors crafting pragmatic, nonideological solutions to pressing social and economic problems. Benjamin Barber put it best: "If mayors ruled the world, we'd have a better chance of solving the world's problems."

Since its inception, America's decentralized federalist system has encouraged experimentation and learning across states and cities. We may have more problems than we know what to do with, but we also have plenty of latitude to figure out how to deal with them. Countries with more centralized planning have never brought the kind of social and political creativity to the table that the United States has been able to muster. Our cities, competitive laboratories of democracy as they are, will continue to be the source of truly innovative solutions to our problems—from education and crime and safety to innovation and economic development.

The Brookings Institution's Alice Rivlin long ago said that we'd be much better off with a more decentralized approach to economic innovation and productivity policy.[8] Mayors, council people, economic developers, business leaders, union officials, and laypeople are the ones who know the most about their economies. Just as the best companies decentralize decision making to work groups on the factory floor, we must give cities and neighborhoods the tools and resources they need to build their economies and in doing so help rebuild the broader economy from the bottom up.

From Dumb Growth to True Prosperity

We need to get beyond the idea, handed down from the Industrial Revolution, that growth is good in and of itself. We have had our share of dumb growth. We have polluted our environment, degraded our human as well as our natural assets, overbuilt housing, and watched our economy crater and collapse. For too long, pundits pointed to Sunbelt cities of sand and sprawl whose economies were fueled solely by home building as beacons of growth—until the bubble burst and they turned into virtual ghost towns. As the Nobel Prize–winning economist Edmund Phelps put it, "It used to be the business of America was business. Now the business of America is home ownership." "To recover and grow again," he added, "America needs to get over its house passion."[9]

But it goes even deeper than that. Our obsession with housing and the whole housing-automobile-energy complex of Fordism is but a symptom of a deeper problem: how we think of, measure, and account for economic growth. Back in the industrial age, pounding out more steel, more cars, and more consumer durables seemed good proxies for growth. Wasted energy and pollution were accepted as unfortunate but unavoidable by-products.

That no longer holds today in an era where knowledge, innovation, creativity, and human potential drive the economy. We need to value and measure what really matters. The idea of getting beyond our current crude conception of Industrial Age growth is not a fringe idea. More and more economists—smart, leading Nobel

Prize–winning economists—and other social scientists and thinkers are coming around to the idea that prosperity turns on more than gross domestic product. New and better metrics of creativity, human potential, and well-being are badly needed. Just as we came up with new metrics for productivity, innovation, and growth during the Industrial Age, we need metrics that can capture the essence of prosperity in the Creative Age.

Nicolas Sarkozy's Commission on the Measurement of Economic Performance and Social Progress was recently tasked "to identify the limits of GDP as an indicator of economic performance and social progress, including the problems with its measurement; to consider what additional information might be required for the production of more relevant indicators of social progress; to assess the feasibility of alternative measurement tools, and to discuss how to present the statistical information in an appropriate way."

The Commission's chairman, Nobel laureate Joseph Stiglitz, noted:

> What we measure affects what we do; and if our measurements are flawed, decisions may be distorted. Choices between promoting GDP and protecting the environment may be false choices, once environmental degradation is appropriately included in our measurement of economic performance. So too, we often draw inferences about what are good policies by looking at what policies have promoted economic growth; but if our metrics of performance are flawed, so too may be the inferences that we draw.[10]

My own measures, from the 3T's to the Creativity Index, are aimed at just this. We need better measures of true prosperity, not just of raw output, but of happiness and well-being, measurements that help us maximize human potential and capture the real costs of growth.

"There might be a problem even deeper than statistical narrowness," Harvard's Kenneth Rogoff wrote of our obsession with growth. That is "the failure of modern growth theory to emphasize adequately that people are fundamentally social creatures. They evaluate their welfare based on what they see around them, not just on some absolute standard."[11] The University of Chicago economist Raghu Rajan sums it up nicely: "The advanced countries have a choice. They can act as if all is well, except that their consumers are in a funk, and that 'animal spirits' must be revived through stimulus. Or they can treat the crisis as a wake-up call to fix all that has been papered over in the last few decades. For better or worse, the narrative that persuades these countries' governments and publics will determine their future—and that of the global economy."[12]

This is not an either-or. It is making growth work for us, broadening it, making it smarter. We cannot stop the clock of history from ticking; we cannot impede the logic of capitalism, but we can and must move from dumb (Industrial Age) growth to smarter (Creative Age) growth—growth that fully utilizes human capabilities, that makes us happier, that provides more and better experiences, and brings greater purpose and meaning into our lives, not just more stuff.

That's what a new Creative Compact would do. It would build new institutions that would fix all that has been papered over. But it cannot spring into life on its own. Building the necessary new institutions requires, as it always has, political action and human agency, both of which have been in short supply.

The Creative Class Comes of Age

There are signs that the Creative Class may at last be coming of age. The year 2011 was the turning point. The first half of the year saw the uprisings of the Arab Spring, which toppled some regimes and profoundly shook others. Then, in the fall, the Occupy Wall Street movement began in Manhattan's Zucotti Park and by October 15 had spread to 951 cities in eighty-two countries. The vanguards of both movements were middle-class students and young professionals—highly educated, digitally savvy members of the Creative Class, though there were certain numbers of anarchists, dropouts, and frustrated Working Class people involved as well. Their outcry was for more democracy and greater opportunity; their outrage was directed against old-line dictatorships in the Arab world and the obscene perquisites of the 1 percent. "It reminds me of 1848—another self-propelled revolution which started in one country, then spread all over the continent in a short time," the historian Eric Hobsbawm remarked of the Arab Spring. "Two years after 1848, it looked as if it had all failed," he added. "In the long run, it hadn't failed. A good deal of liberal advances had been made. So it was an immediate failure but a longer term partial success—though no longer in the form of a revolution."[13]

If the impetus for these uprisings came from the Creative Class, the movement also had a decidedly urban cast. Although social media—Facebook and Twitter—may have provided the fuel, these movements were conceived and brought to life in specific places. And not just any places—they took root in some of the very largest and densest cities on the planet, New York, London, and Cairo.

This is not unprecedented. Social and political movements have long arisen in cities—consider the Boston Massacre of 1770, the Paris Commune of 1871, the October Revolution of 1917 in St. Petersburg, the Chicago Convention in 1968, the Tiananmen Square uprising of 1989. At a time when technology was supposed to have erased place, it is staggering to see how rapidly these place-based movements came to the fore, how quickly they spread to other cities, and how the Occupy Movement in particular literally branded itself by city and place. Such activism is a product of cities, of their density and ability to push people together in public spaces.

All of this seems to signal that the Creative Class may at long last be developing what Marx would have called class consciousness; that the dynamic issue of becoming a class *for* itself may be overtaking the more academic questions of class *of* itself.

We are living, as they say, in interesting times, at the dawn of a broad and fundamental transformation not just of our lifestyles but of the ways that production and consumption have underpinned them. It is a time of tremendous potential, but also of terrible risks. Many a revolution has begun in hope and devolved into chaos. If the Creative Age is a revolutionary epoch, there can be no question that its beginnings have been less than auspicious. The old regime has left us with a degraded environment, a broken financial system, and a sclerotic political culture in thrall to special interests and its own prejudices. Two decades and counting after the fall of communism and the so-called end of history, the West is as culturally, economically, and politically riven as it's ever been—but its potential is literally without limits.

Today, for perhaps the first time in human history, we have the opportunity to align economic and human development. This is embedded in and driven by the very underlying logic of the Creative Economy—its further development turns on its ability to utilize ever more talent and more creative capacity. In the meantime, living as we are amid the ruins of the old order, we feel stuck and frustrated.

But the clock of history never stops ticking. Sooner or later, some city or nation is going to figure out what it takes to fully engage the full creative potential of its people. If we want to gain the advantages of precedence, we need to accelerate that process. Our future prosperity depends upon it. Our time, as they say, is now.

APPENDIX
Defining and Measuring the Creative Class

All figures for the Creative Class and the Creativity Index are updated using the latest available data. These data were compiled and analyzed by Kevin Stolarick.

The classes are defined according to the same categories used in the original edition, using the occupational categories of the Bureau of Labor Statistics (BLS) Occupational Employment Survey (OES).

Creative Class:

SUPER-CREATIVE CORE

Computer and mathematical occupations
Architecture and engineering occupations
Life, physical, and social science occupations
Education, training, and library occupations
Arts, design, entertainment, sports, and media occupations

CREATIVE PROFESSIONALS

Management occupations
Business and financial operations occupations
Legal occupations
Health-care practitioners and technical occupations
High-end sales and sales management

Working Class:

Construction and extraction occupations
Installation, maintenance, and repair occupations
Production occupations
Transportation and material moving occupations

Service Class:

  Health-care support occupations
  Food preparation and food-service-related occupations
  Building and grounds cleaning and maintenance occupations
  Personal care and service occupations
  Low-end sales and related occupations
  Office and administrative support occupations
  Community and social services occupations
  Protective service occupations

Agriculture:

  Farming, fishing, and forestry occupations

  The metro data for the classes are based on data from the 2010 BLS OES data available online at www.bls.gov/oes/.

Historical Time Series:

  The historical time series data for the classes has been updated and expanded to cover the period 1800–2010 and are drawn from sources that are fully listed in the endnotes.[1]

The Creativity Index

This edition of the book updates the Creativity Index and the measures for the 3T's—technology, talent, and tolerance.

  Technology is measured with three variables: the Tech-Pole Index, a measure of high-tech industry concentration originally developed by the Milken Institute[2] based on data from 2009 County Business Patterns, and two measures of regional innovation—patents per capita and average annual patent growth based on data from the US Patent and Trademark Office for the years 2005–2009. The overall Technology Index combines these three measures.

  Talent is measured as the Creative Class (defined above).

  Tolerance is measured with three key variables—the share of immigrants or foreign-born residents, the Gay and Lesbian Index, and the Integration Index. The Gay and Lesbian Index is based on the Gay Index, originally developed by Gary Gates and others.[3] The Integration Index, developed by Stolarick, measures level of integration versus segregation of a metro area. It compares diversity of race/ethnicities within the census tracts of a metropolitan region to the distribution of those same groups across the entire region. The index measures the distribution of racial and ethnic groups within a single metro; it does not consider the overall diversity of that metro relative to the rest of the country. In other words, it only measures the level to which a metro's given racial and ethnic groups are mixed together, and does not take into account the region's overall level of diversity—this is what the other two tolerance measures do. An Integration Index value of 0 identifies a high degree of segregation, whereas an index value of 1 reflects a high level of integration. The Integration Index is calculated using detailed census tract data for every metropolitan area. All three measures are from the American Community Survey, 2005–2009.

The Creativity Index is a composite measure based on these variables.

Table A.1 The Class Structure for All Metros

Rank	Metro	Creative Class Share	Employment	Working Class Share	Employment	Service Class Share	Employment	Total Employment
1	Durham, NC	48.4%	128,900	12.6%	33,630	38.9%	103,500	266,200
2	San Jose-Sunnyvale-Santa Clara, CA	46.9%	396,820	16.3%	137,640	36.6%	309,880	845,540
3	Washington-Arlington-Alexandria, DC-VA-MD-WV	46.8%	1,328,240	12.8%	362,950	40.3%	1,144,430	2,836,790
4	Ithaca, NY	44.6%	21,840	12.1%	5,900	42.9%	20,990	48,920
5	Boulder, CO	44.4%	67,000	13.7%	20,740	41.7%	62,860	150,870
6	Trenton-Ewing, NJ	42.9%	91,830	12.1%	25,810	45.0%	96,190	213,960
7	Huntsville, AL	42.7%	85,280	19.5%	38,930	37.9%	75,730	199,940
8	Corvallis, OR	41.7%	12,730	11.6%	3,560	45.9%	14,040	30,560
9	Boston-Cambridge-Quincy, MA-NH	41.6%	1,002,440	14.9%	360,440	43.4%	1,047,280	2,411,070
10	Ann Arbor, MI	41.3%	74,140	14.7%	26,340	44.1%	79,220	179,700
11	Tallahassee, FL	40.5%	63,880	11.6%	18,360	47.6%	75,110	157,680
12	Rochester, MN	39.9%	39,500	16.0%	15,820	44.0%	43,470	98,880
13	Charlottesville, VA	39.7%	34,980	14.8%	13,050	45.2%	39,780	88,070
14	Hartford-West Hartford-East Hartford, CT	39.7%	216,870	16.9%	92,090	43.4%	237,230	546,360
15	Bridgeport-Stamford-Norwalk, CT	39.5%	159,480	15.2%	61,290	45.4%	183,440	404,210
16	San Francisco-Oakland-Fremont, CA	39.4%	747,790	16.5%	312,380	44.1%	836,680	1,898,410
17	Gainesville, FL	39.3%	46,360	13.3%	15,670	47.4%	55,870	117,970
18	Olympia, WA	38.9%	36,250	13.9%	12,950	46.8%	43,600	93,120

Table A.1 The Class Structure for All Metros (continued)

Rank	Metro	Creative Class		Working Class		Service Class		Total
		Share	Employment	Share	Employment	Share	Employment	Employment
19	Madison, WI	38.3%	123,730	17.5%	56,590	44.0%	141,920	322,680
20	Burlington-South Burlington, VT	37.9%	40,970	18.9%	20,420	43.0%	46,510	108,140
21	Baltimore-Towson, MD	37.7%	465,460	17.6%	217,260	44.7%	551,750	1,235,390
22	Seattle-Tacoma-Bellevue, WA	37.7%	602,700	19.8%	317,360	42.3%	677,410	1,599,720
23	Minneapolis-St. Paul-Bloomington, MN-WI	37.7%	630,960	18.3%	306,350	44.1%	738,420	1,675,730
24	Raleigh-Cary, NC	37.6%	183,320	17.4%	84,900	44.9%	219,350	488,130
25	Denver-Aurora, CO	37.6%	443,720	17.9%	212,100	44.5%	525,810	1,181,630
26	College Station-Bryan, TX	37.4%	34,480	18.5%	17,080	43.8%	40,380	92,180
27	Colorado Springs, CO	37.0%	88,540	16.0%	38,410	46.9%	112,480	239,610
28	Springfield, IL	36.8%	38,580	15.2%	15,930	47.9%	50,230	104,870
29	Athens-Clarke County, GA	36.7%	27,770	18.1%	13,720	45.0%	34,030	75,680
30	Sacramento-Arden-Arcade-Roseville, CA	36.6%	299,700	15.4%	125,950	47.6%	390,170	819,940
31	Albany-Schenectady-Troy, NY	36.5%	154,920	16.4%	69,380	47.0%	199,420	423,950
32	Fort Collins-Loveland, CO	36.5%	45,290	17.8%	22,130	45.5%	56,450	124,040
33	Atlanta-Sandy Springs-Marietta, GA	36.3%	798,550	19.8%	434,970	43.8%	964,350	2,199,250
34	New York-Newark-Edison, NY-NJ-PA	35.8%	2,903,800	16.0%	1,295,520	48.1%	3,899,040	8,100,530
35	New Haven-Milford, CT	35.8%	94,510	18.8%	49,630	45.3%	119,560	263,830
36	Warner Robins, GA	35.8%	20,260	26.1%	14,790	38.1%	21,560	56,660
37	San Diego-Carlsbad-San Marcos, CA	35.6%	440,190	17.0%	210,570	47.2%	584,850	1,238,060

Table A.1 The Class Structure for All Metros (continued)

Rank	Metro	Creative Class Share	Creative Class Employment	Working Class Share	Working Class Employment	Service Class Share	Service Class Employment	Total Employment
38	Kennewick-Richland-Pasco, WA	35.5%	33,450	23.1%	21,800	41.3%	38,950	94,200
39	Ames, IA	35.5%	13,220	20.6%	7,670	43.4%	16,180	37,250
40	Worcester, MA	35.5%	83,610	18.8%	44,310	45.7%	107,730	235,740
41	Manchester-Nashua, NH	35.5%	34,490	18.1%	17,600	46.4%	45,140	97,260
42	Palm Bay-Melbourne-Titusville, FL	35.4%	67,140	17.0%	32,250	47.5%	90,020	189,410
43	Des Moines, IA	35.2%	111,310	18.8%	59,590	45.9%	145,110	316,460
44	Rochester, NY	35.1%	168,680	19.1%	91,640	45.6%	218,950	479,950
45	Chicago-Naperville-Joliet, IL-IN-WI	35.1%	1,460,040	21.4%	891,010	43.4%	1,803,920	4,156,840
46	Boise City-Nampa, ID	35.0%	89,180	19.3%	49,290	45.0%	114,790	254,880
47	Richmond, VA	34.9%	203,010	19.5%	113,160	45.5%	264,300	581,250
48	Kansas City, MO-KS	34.8%	330,590	19.9%	189,240	45.3%	430,610	951,030
49	Columbia, MO	34.7%	26,950	17.8%	13,830	47.3%	36,740	77,680
50	Lansing-East Lansing, MI	34.6%	67,570	19.6%	38,170	45.6%	89,070	195,140
51	Philadelphia-Camden-Wilmington, PA-NJ-DE-MD	34.6%	904,360	17.8%	467,020	47.5%	1,243,120	2,616,760
52	Kokomo, IN	34.5%	12,880	23.7%	8,870	41.8%	15,600	37,350
53	Detroit-Warren-Livonia, MI	34.5%	580,180	20.7%	347,960	44.8%	754,640	1,683,390
54	Austin-Round Rock, TX	34.4%	246,120	16.5%	118,350	49.0%	350,490	715,400
55	Champaign-Urbana, IL	34.4%	33,640	20.3%	19,850	45.0%	43,990	97,810
56	Dallas-Fort Worth-Arlington, TX	34.3%	969,680	21.5%	608,080	44.2%	1,248,770	2,826,530
57	Santa Fe, NM	34.3%	20,700	12.0%	7,230	53.7%	32,410	60,340
58	Dayton, OH	34.2%	122,680	20.5%	73,370	45.2%	162,250	358,590

Table A.1 The Class Structure for All Metros (continued)

Rank	Metro	Creative Class Share	Employment	Working Class Share	Employment	Service Class Share	Employment	Total Employment
59	Portland-Vancouver-Beaverton, OR-WA	34.2%	328,520	21.7%	209,150	43.8%	421,710	961,860
60	Los Angeles-Long Beach-Santa Ana, CA	34.1%	1,765,410	19.5%	1,007,910	46.3%	2,394,530	5,172,400
61	Columbus, OH	34.0%	301,170	19.3%	170,980	46.5%	411,730	884,780
62	Jefferson City, MO	34.0%	24,200	21.1%	15,000	44.9%	31,960	71,250
63	Portland-South Portland, ME	34.0%	64,980	18.5%	35,380	47.4%	90,740	191,360
64	Tucson, AZ	33.9%	116,930	16.5%	57,050	49.5%	170,830	345,040
65	Iowa City, IA	33.8%	27,550	19.5%	15,870	46.5%	37,860	81,400
66	Anchorage, AK	33.8%	55,570	20.4%	33,450	45.8%	75,280	164,300
67	Las Cruces, NM	33.8%	21,880	15.1%	9,770	49.4%	32,000	64,740
68	Salt Lake City, UT	33.7%	199,120	21.5%	127,190	44.8%	264,650	591,220
69	St. Louis, MO-IL	33.6%	421,810	20.1%	252,890	46.2%	580,640	1,256,020
70	Charlotte-Gastonia-Concord, NC-SC	33.6%	271,490	21.8%	175,970	44.6%	360,960	808,950
71	Topeka, KS	33.5%	35,270	20.0%	21,010	46.2%	48,540	105,140
72	Provo-Orem, UT	33.2%	55,500	19.9%	33,290	46.8%	78,150	167,080
73	Fort Walton Beach-Crestview-Destin, FL	33.2%	24,580	15.5%	11,490	51.2%	37,940	74,070
74	Columbia, SC	33.2%	109,610	19.9%	65,710	46.7%	154,300	330,330
75	Birmingham-Hoover, AL	33.1%	152,870	22.5%	104,050	44.2%	203,920	461,550
76	Cedar Rapids, IA	33.1%	44,810	23.9%	32,380	42.9%	58,070	135,420
77	Houston-Baytown-Sugar Land, TX	33.0%	825,000	24.4%	610,250	42.5%	1,061,070	2,497,100

Table A.1 The Class Structure for All Metros (continued)

Rank	Metro	Creative Class Share	Creative Class Employment	Working Class Share	Working Class Employment	Service Class Share	Service Class Employment	Total Employment
78	Indianapolis, IN	33.0%	281,210	23.3%	198,720	43.6%	370,820	851,240
79	Jackson, MS	33.0%	78,640	20.4%	48,650	46.4%	110,440	238,080
80	Oklahoma City, OK	33.0%	181,930	21.6%	118,850	45.3%	249,570	551,010
81	Winston-Salem, NC	33.0%	65,460	22.5%	44,650	44.5%	88,220	198,330
82	Tampa-St. Petersburg-Clearwater, FL	33.0%	359,710	17.0%	185,500	49.8%	542,420	1,089,900
83	Milwaukee-Waukesha-West Allis, WI	33.0%	258,660	23.0%	180,690	44.0%	344,660	784,010
84	Santa Rosa-Petaluma, CA	32.9%	56,160	19.7%	33,600	45.9%	78,340	170,490
85	Albuquerque, NM	32.9%	121,750	18.1%	66,840	48.9%	180,880	369,860
86	Syracuse, NY	32.9%	97,950	21.1%	62,840	45.9%	136,680	297,670
87	Phoenix-Mesa-Scottsdale, AZ	32.7%	549,790	19.1%	321,430	48.0%	807,000	1,681,990
88	Oxnard-Thousand Oaks-Ventura, CA	32.6%	92,180	19.0%	53,840	45.9%	129,900	282,880
89	Honolulu, HI	32.4%	135,780	16.9%	70,960	50.6%	211,660	418,710
90	Lexington-Fayette, KY	32.4%	77,090	22.9%	54,420	43.8%	104,200	237,950
91	Harrisburg-Carlisle, PA	32.4%	98,490	20.7%	63,030	46.8%	142,320	304,280
92	Binghamton, NY	32.3%	34,250	20.2%	21,430	47.4%	50,160	105,890
93	Greenville, NC	32.3%	22,650	17.4%	12,190	50.2%	35,220	70,180
94	Cleveland-Elyria-Mentor, OH	32.2%	311,700	21.2%	205,080	46.5%	450,410	967,590
95	Little Rock-North Little Rock, AR	32.2%	105,310	20.5%	67,180	47.2%	154,350	327,160
96	Cheyenne, WY	32.2%	13,080	23.6%	9,590	44.3%	18,000	40,670
97	Omaha-Council Bluffs, NE-IA	32.1%	142,290	22.0%	97,610	45.8%	203,130	443,550
98	Morgantown, WV	32.1%	18,110	20.5%	11,570	47.3%	26,730	56,470
99	Santa Cruz-Watsonville, CA	32.1%	26,350	15.7%	12,880	51.5%	42,370	82,200

Table A.1 The Class Structure for All Metros (continued)

Rank	Metro	Creative Class Share	Creative Class Employment	Working Class Share	Working Class Employment	Service Class Share	Service Class Employment	Total Employment
100	Virginia Beach-Norfolk-Newport News, VA-NC	31.9%	227,930	21.0%	150,120	46.9%	334,940	713,630
101	Blacksburg-Christiansburg-Radford, VA	31.8%	19,250	23.8%	14,370	44.2%	26,730	60,460
102	Lafayette, IN	31.8%	25,120	24.9%	19,640	43.2%	34,100	78,970
103	Nashville-Davidson-Murfreesboro, TN	31.8%	223,240	22.1%	155,220	46.0%	322,950	701,810
104	Cincinnati-Middletown, OH-KY-IN	31.8%	305,070	21.8%	209,140	46.4%	445,250	959,460
105	State College, PA	31.8%	21,090	17.1%	11,380	50.9%	33,770	66,400
106	La Crosse, WI-MN	31.7%	21,890	20.8%	14,380	47.5%	32,750	69,020
107	Pittsburgh, PA	31.7%	345,720	20.2%	220,170	48.1%	524,760	1,091,460
108	Springfield, MA	31.6%	88,870	20.9%	58,790	47.5%	133,500	281,160
109	Poughkeepsie-Newburgh-Middletown, NY	31.6%	76,190	18.7%	45,090	49.6%	119,590	241,270
110	Bremerton-Silverdale, WA	31.6%	24,810	22.4%	17,570	46.0%	36,130	78,600
111	Santa Barbara-Santa Maria-Goleta, CA	31.6%	51,830	16.6%	27,300	47.9%	78,600	164,260
112	Carson City, NV	31.5%	8,110	17.2%	4,420	51.3%	13,190	25,720
113	Flagstaff, AZ	31.5%	17,100	16.3%	8,870	52.2%	28,350	54,320
114	Muncie, IN	31.5%	13,620	18.8%	8,140	49.7%	21,510	43,270
115	Lincoln, NE	31.4%	49,680	21.9%	34,600	46.7%	73,860	158,300
116	Augusta-Richmond County, GA-SC	31.3%	63,110	22.3%	44,850	46.2%	93,090	201,370

Table A.1 The Class Structure for All Metros (continued)

Rank	Metro	Creative Class		Working Class		Service Class		Total
		Share	Employment	Share	Employment	Share	Employment	Employment
117	Providence-New Bedford-Fall River, RI-MA	31.3%	166,140	19.1%	101,540	49.6%	263,360	531,220
118	Fayetteville-Springdale-Rogers, AR-MO	31.3%	59,670	26.5%	50,570	41.8%	79,720	190,830
119	Peoria, IL	31.3%	51,840	25.2%	41,830	43.5%	72,070	165,810
120	Buffalo-Cheektowaga-Tonawanda, NY	31.3%	164,390	19.5%	102,520	49.2%	258,840	525,910
121	Salem, OR	31.2%	44,440	19.1%	27,230	47.8%	67,930	142,230
122	Bismarck, ND	31.2%	19,220	17.8%	10,950	50.8%	31,340	61,640
123	San Antonio, TX	31.2%	258,480	18.6%	154,090	50.1%	415,670	829,120
124	Bangor, ME	31.2%	18,940	19.1%	11,630	49.2%	29,920	60,780
125	Eugene-Springfield, OR	31.1%	42,060	19.4%	26,150	49.0%	66,140	135,100
126	Knoxville, TN	31.1%	99,150	22.7%	72,460	46.2%	147,360	319,200
127	Akron, OH	31.1%	95,220	21.7%	66,620	47.2%	144,690	306,640
128	Rome, GA	31.0%	10,920	24.6%	8,650	44.2%	15,540	35,180
129	Killeen-Temple-Fort Hood, TX	30.9%	37,350	19.2%	23,180	49.9%	60,400	120,980
130	New Orleans-Metairie-Kenner, LA	30.9%	155,310	22.9%	115,460	46.1%	232,170	503,430
131	Bloomington, IN	30.8%	21,640	21.3%	14,980	47.9%	33,690	70,310
132	Hinesville-Fort Stewart, GA	30.8%	5,100	21.7%	3,590	47.6%	7,890	16,580
133	South Bend-Mishawaka, IN-MI	30.8%	38,140	23.4%	29,040	45.8%	56,840	124,020
134	Tulsa, OK	30.7%	124,880	24.8%	100,550	44.5%	180,730	406,160
135	Idaho Falls, ID	30.6%	14,210	21.5%	9,980	46.8%	21,700	46,370

Table A.1 The Class Structure for All Metros (continued)

| Rank | Metro | Creative Class | | Working Class | | Service Class | | Total |
		Share	Employment	Share	Employment	Share	Employment	Employment
136	Macon, GA	30.6%	27,560	18.7%	16,840	50.4%	45,320	89,950
137	Charleston-North Charleston, SC	30.4%	83,630	20.8%	57,210	48.7%	133,640	274,660
138	Miami-Fort Lauderdale-Miami Beach, FL	30.4%	651,990	16.2%	347,900	53.0%	1,136,120	2,142,570
139	Jacksonville, FL	30.4%	172,820	19.7%	112,010	49.8%	283,320	568,570
140	Wichita, KS	30.4%	84,240	24.6%	68,250	45.0%	124,780	277,420
141	Kalamazoo-Portage, MI	30.4%	39,160	22.5%	29,080	47.0%	60,620	129,000
142	Ogden-Clearfield, UT	30.3%	57,480	25.2%	47,870	44.4%	84,360	189,890
143	Johnson City, TN	30.3%	22,260	19.8%	14,530	50.0%	36,750	73,540
144	Kankakee-Bradley, IL	30.2%	12,360	21.0%	8,570	48.8%	19,970	40,900
145	Tyler, TX	30.2%	27,140	21.3%	19,210	48.3%	43,460	89,990
146	Pensacola-Ferry Pass-Brent, FL	30.2%	44,730	17.5%	25,970	52.2%	77,490	148,350
147	Elizabethtown, KY	30.1%	12,920	22.6%	9,680	47.3%	20,260	42,860
148	San Luis Obispo-Paso Robles, CA	30.1%	26,910	18.2%	16,220	49.6%	44,280	89,300
149	Goldsboro, NC	30.1%	12,810	23.3%	9,940	46.2%	19,670	42,570
150	Spokane, WA	30.1%	58,860	19.7%	38,510	50.2%	98,320	195,690
151	Lawrence, KS	30.0%	13,360	17.2%	7,660	52.8%	23,520	44,540
152	Grand Rapids-Wyoming, MI	29.9%	106,970	27.5%	98,090	42.5%	151,850	357,170
153	Davenport-Moline-Rock Island, IA-IL	29.9%	52,830	27.3%	48,260	42.7%	75,340	176,630
154	Flint, MI	29.9%	37,710	18.9%	23,820	51.3%	64,730	126,260
155	Fayetteville, NC	29.9%	37,010	22.6%	27,960	47.6%	58,950	123,950
156	Salisbury, MD	29.8%	15,420	21.0%	10,880	48.8%	25,230	51,700
157	Jackson, MI	29.8%	14,720	22.9%	11,300	47.3%	23,350	49,370

Table A.1 The Class Structure for All Metros (continued)

Rank	Metro	Creative Class Share	Creative Class Employment	Working Class Share	Working Class Employment	Service Class Share	Service Class Employment	Total Employment
158	Allentown-Bethlehem-Easton, PA-NJ	29.8%	97,400	22.4%	73,270	47.7%	155,900	326,810
159	Fort Wayne, IN	29.8%	57,850	27.4%	53,300	42.7%	82,980	194,240
160	Baton Rouge, LA	29.8%	105,450	25.6%	90,850	44.5%	157,790	354,420
161	Springfield, MO	29.7%	53,910	21.8%	39,620	48.4%	87,780	181,440
162	Lubbock, TX	29.7%	36,110	17.0%	20,740	52.8%	64,290	121,760
163	Orlando, FL	29.6%	284,250	17.0%	163,010	53.2%	510,530	959,410
164	Niles-Benton Harbor, MI	29.6%	16,610	23.8%	13,360	46.6%	26,110	56,080
165	Florence, SC	29.6%	22,600	23.7%	18,080	46.3%	35,420	76,420
166	Redding, CA	29.5%	17,580	17.6%	10,500	51.9%	30,930	59,560
167	Louisville, KY-IN	29.5%	171,450	26.1%	151,760	44.3%	257,420	581,210
168	Montgomery, AL	29.5%	46,400	23.3%	36,630	47.0%	74,010	157,440
169	Greeley, CO	29.4%	21,830	29.9%	22,210	40.3%	29,940	74,240
170	Hattiesburg, MS	29.4%	16,040	19.0%	10,390	51.5%	28,110	54,610
171	Sioux Falls, SD	29.4%	38,450	22.4%	29,270	48.1%	63,040	130,950
172	Lawton, OK	29.3%	12,130	20.4%	8,430	50.3%	20,820	41,380
173	Columbus, GA-AL	29.3%	31,960	20.6%	22,460	50.0%	54,560	109,110
174	Wilmington, NC	29.3%	39,180	20.4%	27,250	50.3%	67,390	133,890
175	Duluth, MN-WI	29.2%	35,370	18.6%	22,570	52.0%	62,980	121,090
176	Chattanooga, TN-GA	29.2%	63,970	25.8%	56,530	45.0%	98,580	219,160
177	Dover, DE	29.2%	14,660	14.6%	7,340	55.9%	28,090	50,240
178	Waco, TX	29.2%	28,620	25.1%	24,640	45.6%	44,730	98,120
179	Billings, MT	29.2%	23,050	21.6%	17,110	49.1%	38,850	79,070
180	Logan, UT-ID	29.1%	13,690	28.1%	13,210	42.6%	20,030	47,000

Table A.1 The Class Structure for All Metros (continued)

Rank	Metro	Creative Class Share	Creative Class Employment	Working Class Share	Working Class Employment	Service Class Share	Service Class Employment	Total Employment
181	Sherman-Denison, TX	29.1%	11,690	21.7%	8,700	49.2%	19,760	40,150
182	Waterloo-Cedar Falls, IA	29.1%	24,540	28.2%	23,800	42.5%	35,870	84,310
183	Chico, CA	29.1%	19,620	15.3%	10,340	54.0%	36,420	67,420
184	Auburn-Opelika, AL	29.1%	13,230	23.3%	10,610	47.3%	21,540	45,530
185	Abilene, TX	29.0%	17,840	18.9%	11,630	51.8%	31,790	61,420
186	Greenville, SC	29.0%	82,940	27.2%	77,810	43.6%	124,550	285,890
187	Utica-Rome, NY	29.0%	35,970	19.8%	24,620	51.1%	63,390	124,090
188	Toledo, OH	28.9%	81,080	23.7%	66,520	47.3%	132,810	280,730
189	Prescott, AZ	28.8%	15,400	20.0%	10,690	51.0%	27,240	53,380
190	Eau Claire, WI	28.8%	21,260	23.6%	17,380	47.5%	35,000	73,740
191	Yuba City-Marysville, CA	28.8%	10,660	19.0%	7,050	49.4%	18,280	37,040
192	Fargo, ND-MN	28.7%	33,550	21.9%	25,600	49.0%	57,230	116,870
193	Burlington, NC	28.7%	15,450	27.0%	14,510	44.4%	23,880	53,840
194	Pocatello, ID	28.7%	9,460	23.7%	7,820	47.6%	15,690	32,970
195	Green Bay, WI	28.6%	46,300	27.1%	43,740	44.1%	71,300	161,630
196	El Paso, TX	28.6%	76,530	20.7%	55,210	50.6%	135,370	267,340
197	Bend, OR	28.6%	16,720	18.5%	10,830	52.4%	30,620	58,450
198	Winchester, VA-WV	28.6%	14,350	25.1%	12,600	46.3%	23,280	50,230
199	Bowling Green, KY	28.6%	15,700	25.7%	14,120	45.7%	25,110	54,980
200	Memphis, TN-MS-AR	28.5%	167,210	26.2%	153,520	45.1%	264,320	585,690
201	Norwich-New London, CT	28.5%	35,510	16.4%	20,460	55.0%	68,470	124,440
202	Huntington-Ashland, WV-KY-OH	28.5%	30,440	22.6%	24,070	48.9%	52,180	106,690
203	Savannah, GA	28.5%	41,220	23.1%	33,390	48.3%	69,900	144,580

Table A.1 The Class Structure for All Metros (continued)

Rank	Metro	Creative Class Share	Creative Class Employment	Working Class Share	Working Class Employment	Service Class Share	Service Class Employment	Total Employment
204	Charleston, WV	28.5%	40,100	25.7%	36,230	45.7%	64,400	140,800
205	Alexandria, LA	28.5%	17,310	21.6%	13,150	49.4%	30,040	60,780
206	Roanoke, VA	28.5%	41,580	24.4%	35,670	47.0%	68,690	146,070
207	Gainesville, GA	28.5%	19,070	33.3%	22,300	38.3%	25,640	67,010
208	Bloomington-Normal, IL	28.4%	20,150	17.2%	12,190	54.2%	38,470	70,970
209	Battle Creek, MI	28.3%	14,650	27.7%	14,320	43.9%	22,710	51,680
210	Reno-Sparks, NV	28.3%	53,530	20.8%	39,310	50.7%	95,810	188,860
211	Kingston, NY	28.3%	16,560	18.1%	10,580	53.3%	31,150	58,430
212	Bakersfield, CA	28.3%	70,610	22.0%	54,970	40.7%	101,520	249,580
213	Rockford, IL	28.3%	38,550	30.9%	42,080	40.9%	55,720	136,390
214	Fresno, CA	28.3%	87,980	19.6%	61,030	43.7%	136,100	311,380
215	Amarillo, TX	28.2%	30,260	23.3%	24,990	48.2%	51,700	107,200
216	Greensboro-High Point, NC	28.2%	94,500	27.4%	91,940	44.3%	148,310	334,950
217	Johnstown, PA	28.2%	15,330	21.1%	11,480	50.7%	27,580	54,440
218	Asheville, NC	28.1%	46,560	22.5%	37,180	49.3%	81,570	165,450
219	Barnstable Town, MA	28.1%	26,100	15.8%	14,640	56.1%	52,090	92,920
220	Jackson, TN	28.1%	15,240	28.0%	15,210	43.7%	23,760	54,310
221	Erie, PA	28.0%	34,670	22.7%	28,120	49.2%	60,830	123,660
222	Hot Springs, AR	28.0%	9,960	18.1%	6,440	53.9%	19,160	35,560
223	Mobile, AL	28.0%	46,660	27.3%	45,530	44.6%	74,320	166,690
224	Decatur, IL	28.0%	13,800	33.2%	16,370	38.9%	19,170	49,340
225	Medford, OR	28.0%	20,380	21.4%	15,630	50.0%	36,460	72,870
226	Jonesboro, AR	27.9%	12,690	24.0%	10,900	47.6%	21,620	45,410

Table A.1 The Class Structure for All Metros (continued)

| Rank | Metro | Creative Class | | Working Class | | Service Class | | Total |
		Share	Employment	Share	Employment	Share	Employment	Employment
227	Pine Bluff, AR	27.9%	9,440	28.2%	9,560	42.9%	14,530	33,850
228	Grand Forks, ND-MN	27.8%	12,890	21.2%	9,830	50.6%	23,430	46,290
229	Lima, OH	27.8%	13,670	27.0%	13,260	45.2%	22,180	49,110
230	Gulfport-Biloxi, MS	27.8%	28,010	20.6%	20,700	51.5%	51,900	100,700
231	Lynchburg, VA	27.8%	27,050	26.2%	25,470	45.8%	44,630	97,340
232	Saginaw-Saginaw Township North, MI	27.8%	22,210	22.3%	17,810	49.9%	39,860	79,930
233	Midland, TX	27.7%	17,720	28.2%	18,010	44.0%	28,100	63,870
234	Kingsport-Bristol, TN-VA	27.7%	31,130	27.0%	30,290	45.2%	50,720	112,320
235	San Angelo, TX	27.7%	11,410	21.6%	8,880	50.6%	20,840	41,180
236	St. Cloud, MN	27.7%	24,700	27.2%	24,290	44.9%	40,060	89,200
237	Vallejo-Fairfield, CA	27.7%	32,460	22.2%	25,980	49.8%	58,440	117,250
238	Wichita Falls, TX	27.7%	15,380	22.6%	12,580	49.7%	27,630	55,590
239	Lewiston, ID-WA	27.6%	6,180	26.5%	5,930	44.6%	9,980	22,370
240	McAllen-Edinburg-Pharr, TX	27.6%	60,400	15.9%	34,800	55.6%	121,590	218,830
241	Dubuque, IA	27.6%	14,170	26.8%	13,740	45.4%	23,330	51,360
242	Pueblo, CO	27.6%	15,110	19.2%	10,510	53.2%	29,150	54,770
243	Modesto, CA	27.5%	40,260	25.5%	37,280	43.0%	62,830	146,140
244	Sarasota-Bradenton-Venice, FL	27.5%	64,650	17.8%	41,840	54.4%	127,770	234,900
245	Reading, PA	27.5%	43,730	27.8%	44,160	44.6%	70,930	159,040
246	Shreveport-Bossier City, LA	27.5%	46,690	22.7%	38,590	49.7%	84,420	169,860
247	Lewiston-Auburn, ME	27.5%	12,800	22.8%	10,630	49.6%	23,140	46,620
248	Riverside-San Bernardino-Ontario, CA	27.4%	312,510	23.6%	268,470	48.5%	552,930	1,139,750

Table A.1 The Class Structure for All Metros (continued)

Rank	Metro	Creative Class Share	Creative Class Employment	Working Class Share	Working Class Employment	Service Class Share	Service Class Employment	Total Employment
249	Monroe, LA	27.4%	20,000	21.0%	15,360	51.2%	37,340	72,990
250	Madera, CA	27.4%	9,910	16.3%	5,910	41.6%	15,040	36,170
251	Napa, CA	27.4%	16,570	20.9%	12,650	47.2%	28,560	60,500
252	Danville, IL	27.4%	7,360	29.5%	7,920	43.0%	11,550	26,880
253	Cumberland, MD-WV	27.4%	10,020	20.2%	7,410	52.4%	19,170	36,600
254	Wausau, WI	27.3%	17,430	31.4%	20,020	41.0%	26,130	63,750
255	Glens Falls, NY	27.3%	13,900	22.9%	11,660	49.6%	25,230	50,870
256	Fairbanks, AK	27.3%	8,710	23.6%	7,520	49.2%	15,700	31,930
257	Oshkosh-Neenah, WI	27.3%	23,180	32.5%	27,600	40.2%	34,160	85,030
258	Lakeland-Winter Haven, FL	27.2%	51,290	23.3%	43,950	47.7%	89,890	188,570
259	Elmira, NY	27.2%	9,920	23.5%	8,590	49.3%	17,970	36,480
260	Dothan, AL	27.2%	14,990	26.5%	14,620	45.9%	25,310	55,160
261	Clarksville, TN-KY	27.1%	20,840	25.8%	19,810	46.9%	36,020	76,770
262	Jacksonville, NC	27.1%	11,800	17.9%	7,800	54.8%	23,840	43,500
263	Albany, GA	27.1%	15,940	25.2%	14,830	47.7%	28,040	58,810
264	Missoula, MT	27.0%	13,500	16.7%	8,320	56.3%	28,100	49,920
265	Rapid City, SD	27.0%	15,690	20.6%	11,940	52.1%	30,240	58,020
266	Monroe, MI	26.9%	9,260	24.2%	8,330	48.9%	16,860	34,450
267	Mount Vernon-Anacortes, WA	26.8%	11,200	23.7%	9,870	48.8%	20,340	41,720
268	Victoria, TX	26.8%	12,410	29.0%	13,440	44.2%	20,460	46,310
269	Parkersburg-Marietta, WV-OH	26.8%	17,440	27.0%	17,590	46.2%	30,120	65,150
270	Wenatchee, WA	26.8%	9,840	23.8%	8,750	49.4%	18,180	36,770
271	Canton-Massillon, OH	26.8%	41,990	24.7%	38,750	48.5%	76,070	156,970

Table A.1 The Class Structure for All Metros (continued)

Rank	Metro	Creative Class Share	Creative Class Employment	Working Class Share	Working Class Employment	Service Class Share	Service Class Employment	Total Employment
272	Grand Junction, CO	26.7%	15,160	23.8%	13,510	49.3%	27,960	56,680
273	Hagerstown-Martinsburg, MD-WV	26.7%	24,710	21.0%	19,400	52.2%	48,250	92,430
274	Holland-Grand Haven, MI	26.7%	25,790	34.2%	33,060	38.4%	37,040	96,570
275	Great Falls, MT	26.6%	9,290	19.8%	6,890	53.3%	18,590	34,860
276	Lafayette, LA	26.6%	37,580	28.2%	39,910	45.1%	63,740	141,310
277	Bellingham, WA	26.6%	19,400	23.2%	16,930	49.8%	36,380	73,000
278	Muskegon-Norton Shores, MI	26.6%	14,620	24.2%	13,290	49.3%	27,110	55,020
279	Corpus Christi, TX	26.5%	45,820	25.2%	43,500	48.1%	83,130	172,720
280	Spartanburg, SC	26.5%	29,500	32.4%	36,110	41.0%	45,700	111,390
281	Brownsville-Harlingen, TX	26.5%	32,570	15.4%	18,980	57.9%	71,250	123,110
282	Janesville, WI	26.4%	15,690	28.5%	16,930	45.0%	26,750	59,430
283	Terre Haute, IN	26.4%	17,390	25.0%	16,470	48.5%	31,980	65,930
284	Brunswick, GA	26.3%	9,990	19.6%	7,440	53.9%	20,510	38,030
285	Columbus, IN	26.2%	9,730	34.2%	12,710	39.5%	14,670	37,110
286	Port St. Lucie-Fort Pierce, FL	26.2%	30,460	18.7%	21,760	53.3%	61,960	116,250
287	Coeur d'Alene, ID	26.1%	13,270	22.1%	11,210	51.5%	26,170	50,780
288	Texarkana, TX-Texarkana, AR	26.1%	13,630	28.0%	14,630	45.7%	23,830	52,180
289	Deltona-Daytona Beach-Ormond Beach, FL	26.1%	38,960	16.6%	24,870	57.1%	85,370	149,380
290	Casper, WY	26.0%	8,100	22.8%	7,090	51.2%	15,920	31,110
291	Fond du Lac, WI	26.0%	10,570	28.2%	11,470	45.6%	18,570	40,720
292	Scranton-Wilkes-Barre, PA	25.9%	64,150	25.4%	62,850	48.6%	120,090	247,300
293	Beaumont-Port Arthur, TX	25.9%	40,100	29.6%	45,800	44.4%	68,690	154,670
294	Owensboro, KY	25.9%	11,910	28.9%	13,300	45.0%	20,680	45,970

Table A.1 The Class Structure for All Metros (continued)

Rank	Metro	Creative Class Share	Creative Class Employment	Working Class Share	Working Class Employment	Service Class Share	Service Class Employment	Total Employment
295	Evansville, IN-KY	25.9%	42,920	32.1%	53,370	41.9%	69,620	166,030
296	Yakima, WA	25.8%	20,320	25.4%	20,020	44.4%	34,960	78,680
297	Sebastian-Vero Beach, FL	25.8%	11,380	16.5%	7,260	55.3%	24,380	44,100
298	Salinas, CA	25.8%	39,310	15.0%	22,870	41.6%	63,470	152,470
299	Longview, TX	25.7%	23,560	31.2%	28,550	43.1%	39,450	91,610
300	Stockton, CA	25.6%	50,670	26.7%	52,770	44.3%	87,690	197,750
301	Appleton, WI	25.4%	28,070	30.3%	33,480	44.1%	48,670	110,370
302	Mansfield, OH	25.4%	12,500	26.8%	13,180	47.8%	23,480	49,160
303	York-Hanover, PA	25.3%	42,520	31.5%	52,870	43.1%	72,270	167,840
304	Tuscaloosa, AL	25.3%	22,460	31.1%	27,590	43.3%	38,440	88,700
305	Anderson, SC	25.3%	13,980	31.1%	17,160	43.6%	24,100	55,240
306	Rocky Mount, NC	25.3%	13,940	28.1%	15,470	46.2%	25,450	55,120
307	Hanford-Corcoran, CA	25.2%	9,510	19.1%	7,200	47.8%	18,020	37,700
308	Harrisonburg, VA	25.2%	14,280	32.5%	18,420	41.6%	23,610	56,700
309	St. Joseph, MO-KS	25.1%	12,910	28.1%	14,420	46.5%	23,910	51,380
310	Wheeling, WV-OH	25.1%	15,560	21.5%	13,330	53.4%	33,060	61,950
311	Gadsden, AL	25.1%	8,410	29.3%	9,810	45.4%	15,220	33,500
312	Bay City, MI	25.0%	8,270	21.0%	6,950	54.0%	17,850	33,070
313	Punta Gorda, FL	25.0%	9,590	14.1%	5,420	60.9%	23,360	38,370
314	Vineland-Millville-Bridgeton, NJ	25.0%	14,560	27.1%	15,780	47.9%	27,940	58,280
315	Lebanon, PA	24.9%	11,350	31.3%	14,230	43.5%	19,790	45,530
316	St. George, UT	24.9%	11,050	21.9%	9,690	53.1%	23,540	44,330
317	Youngstown-Warren-Boardman, OH-PA	24.9%	53,240	24.3%	51,990	50.7%	108,270	213,590

Table A.1 The Class Structure for All Metros (continued)

Rank	Metro	Creative Class Share	Creative Class Employment	Working Class Share	Working Class Employment	Service Class Share	Service Class Employment	Total Employment
318	Pittsfield, MA	24.8%	7,630	19.5%	6,000	55.7%	17,130	30,760
319	Sumter, SC	24.8%	8,200	29.2%	9,660	46.0%	15,230	33,090
320	Racine, WI	24.8%	17,330	30.1%	21,050	45.2%	31,610	69,990
321	Joplin, MO	24.8%	18,290	32.9%	24,330	42.3%	31,230	73,890
322	Lake Charles, LA	24.7%	21,470	27.9%	24,250	47.4%	41,200	86,950
323	El Centro, CA	24.7%	11,870	17.8%	8,550	45.2%	21,750	48,140
324	Valdosta, GA	24.7%	12,010	23.4%	11,400	51.1%	24,910	48,720
325	Altoona, PA	24.6%	13,900	25.0%	14,130	50.4%	28,470	56,500
326	Springfield, OH	24.6%	11,470	26.4%	12,310	49.0%	22,870	46,650
327	Visalia-Porterville, CA	24.6%	31,930	19.4%	25,190	38.7%	50,290	129,960
328	Danville, VA	24.5%	8,970	29.1%	10,640	46.2%	16,870	36,540
329	Cleveland, TN	24.5%	8,560	31.5%	11,000	44.0%	15,340	34,900
330	Lancaster, PA	24.4%	53,920	29.8%	65,770	45.4%	100,340	220,800
331	Atlantic City, NJ	24.4%	32,920	13.5%	18,250	61.9%	83,570	134,910
332	Sheboygan, WI	24.4%	13,390	32.4%	17,780	43.1%	23,660	54,880
333	Florence-Muscle Shoals, AL	24.3%	12,350	30.0%	15,230	45.3%	23,000	50,720
334	Laredo, TX	24.3%	20,270	17.4%	14,510	58.3%	48,580	83,360
335	Merced, CA	24.2%	13,650	26.5%	14,970	43.7%	24,690	56,510
336	Yuma, AZ	24.1%	13,150	17.9%	9,740	44.5%	24,290	54,560
337	Weirton-Steubenville, WV-OH	24.1%	9,420	27.6%	10,810	48.3%	18,910	39,140
338	Panama City-Lynn Haven, FL	24.0%	15,260	20.3%	12,930	55.7%	35,470	63,660
339	Williamsport, PA	23.9%	11,780	29.1%	14,350	46.9%	23,180	49,380

Table A.1 The Class Structure for All Metros (continued)

Rank	Metro	Creative Class Share	Creative Class Employment	Working Class Share	Working Class Employment	Service Class Share	Service Class Employment	Total Employment
340	Odessa, TX	23.8%	13,480	34.4%	19,460	41.8%	23,680	56,620
341	Anderson, IN	23.6%	8,800	23.3%	8,670	53.1%	19,740	37,210
342	Sioux City, IA–NE–SD	23.5%	16,470	30.8%	21,550	45.2%	31,660	70,070
343	Pascagoula, MS	23.4%	12,300	39.7%	20,880	36.9%	19,370	52,550
344	Fort Smith, AR–OK	23.3%	26,760	36.1%	41,360	40.3%	46,220	114,670
345	Anniston-Oxford, AL	23.3%	10,450	32.1%	14,400	44.6%	19,990	44,840
346	Decatur, AL	23.3%	11,980	37.1%	19,090	39.5%	20,290	51,430
347	Morristown, TN	23.2%	9,890	38.4%	16,380	38.3%	16,330	42,640
348	Hickory-Morganton-Lenoir, NC	22.9%	31,460	35.3%	48,450	41.6%	57,060	137,220
349	Cape Coral-Fort Myers, FL	22.8%	41,710	19.4%	35,520	57.3%	104,700	182,690
350	Farmington, NM	22.8%	10,820	32.6%	15,510	44.3%	21,090	47,560
351	Longview-Kelso, WA	22.7%	7,600	33.3%	11,150	42.2%	14,140	33,500
352	Las Vegas-Paradise, NV	22.7%	183,050	18.2%	147,030	59.1%	476,720	806,910
353	Michigan City-La Porte, IN	22.7%	9,290	26.6%	10,910	50.5%	20,670	40,960
354	Sandusky, OH	22.6%	7,280	23.9%	7,700	53.3%	17,180	32,240
355	Naples-Marco Island, FL	22.1%	22,700	18.6%	19,020	59.3%	60,810	102,530
356	Houma-Bayou Cane-Thibodaux, LA	22.1%	19,890	39.0%	35,150	38.8%	34,970	90,110
357	Elkhart-Goshen, IN	21.8%	21,580	46.0%	45,600	32.2%	31,880	99,120
358	Ocean City, NJ	21.8%	8,130	15.5%	5,800	62.7%	23,430	37,360
359	Ocala, FL	21.2%	17,620	21.2%	17,650	57.1%	47,530	83,300
360	Dalton, GA	21.1%	13,270	45.6%	28,750	33.3%	20,970	62,990
361	Myrtle Beach-Conway-North Myrtle Beach, SC	17.1%	17,410	18.0%	18,290	64.9%	66,020	101,720

Source: See pages 401–403 for full detail on sources. Data analysis by Kevin Stolarick.

Table A.2 The Creativity Index for All Metros, 2010

Rank	Metro	Creativity Index	Technology Index Rank	Talent Index Rank	Tolerance Index Rank
1	Boulder, CO	.981	10	5	9
2	San Francisco-Oakland-Fremont, CA	.970	3	16	17
3	Boston-Cambridge-Quincy, MA-NH	.968	9	9	20
4	Ann Arbor, MI	.961	25	10	10
5	Seattle-Tacoma-Bellevue, WA	.961	1	22	22
6	San Diego-Carlsbad-San Marcos, CA	.961	7	37	1
7	Corvallis, OR	.959	14	8	25
8	Durham, NC	.953	8	1	45
9	Washington-Arlington-Alexandria, DC-VA-MD-WV	.947	27	3	30
10	Trenton-Ewing, NJ	.945	44	6	13
11	Ithaca, NY	.937	61	4	6
12	San Jose-Sunnyvale-Santa Clara, CA	.933	2	2	71
13	Portland-Vancouver-Beaverton, OR-WA	.930	4	59	16
14	Worcester, MA	.922	30	40	18
15	Burlington-South Burlington, VT	.918	11	20	61
16	Hartford-West Hartford-East Hartford, CT	.916	42	14	37
17	Austin-Round Rock, TX	.916	5	54	34
18	Minneapolis-St. Paul-Bloomington, MN-WI	.915	17	23	53
19	Atlanta-Sandy Springs-Marietta, GA	.912	23	33	42
20	Tucson, AZ	.909	12	64	26

Table A.2 The Creativity Index for All Metros, 2010 (continued)

Rank	Metro	Creativity Index	Technology Index Rank	Talent Index Rank	Tolerance Index Rank
21	Madison, WI	.907	17	19	67
22	Los Angeles-Long Beach-Santa Ana, CA	.901	26	60	24
23	Oxnard-Thousand Oaks-Ventura, CA	.898	19	88	7
24	Denver-Aurora, CO	.896	42	25	48
25	Sacramento-Arden-Arcade-Roseville, CA	.894	49	30	38
26	Manchester-Nashua, NH	.889	20	41	62
27	Raleigh-Cary, NC	.887	6	24	95
28	Bridgeport-Stamford-Norwalk, CT	.886	39	15	71
29	Santa Rosa-Petaluma, CA	.878	48	84	3
30	Fort Collins-Loveland, CO	.872	34	32	74
31	New York-Newark-Edison, NY-NJ-PA	.871	52	34	57
32	Phoenix-Mesa-Scottsdale, AZ	.869	34	87	23
33	Dallas-Fort Worth-Arlington, TX	.865	46	56	47
34	Olympia, WA	.861	94	18	41
35	Santa Cruz-Watsonville, CA	.858	54	99	4
36	Albany-Schenectady-Troy, NY	.857	28	31	99
37	Santa Barbara-Santa Maria-Goleta, CA	.850	21	111	33
38	Rochester, NY	.849	72	44	50
39	Santa Fe, NM	.849	104	57	5
40	Baltimore-Towson, MD	.837	55	21	103
41	Kansas City, MO-KS	.837	24	48	106
42	Champaign-Urbana, IL	.834	49	55	78
43	Gainesville, FL	.830	80	17	88

Table A.2 The Creativity Index for All Metros, 2010 (continued)

Rank	Metro	Creativity Index	Technology Index Rank	Talent Index Rank	Tolerance Index Rank
44	Palm Bay-Melbourne-Titusville, FL	.829	32	42	112
45	Chicago-Naperville-Joliet, IL-IN-WI	.829	62	45	79
46	Charlottesville, VA	.826	58	13	119
47	Salt Lake City, UT	.823	41	68	86
48	Albuquerque, NM	.820	56	85	56
49	Columbus, OH	.819	64	61	73
50	Philadelphia-Camden-Wilmington, PA-NJ-DE-MD	.806	64	51	97
51	Tampa-St. Petersburg-Clearwater, FL	.805	77	82	55
52	Houston-Baytown-Sugar Land, TX	.794	33	77	116
53	Detroit-Warren-Livonia, MI	.787	36	53	145
54	Poughkeepsie-Newburgh-Middletown, NY	.787	16	109	109
55	Lexington-Fayette, KY	.785	45	90	100
56	Des Moines, IA	.784	66	43	127
57	Orlando, FL	.784	47	163	27
58	Iowa City, IA	.782	97	65	76
59	New Haven-Milford, CT	.778	68	35	139
60	Rochester, MN	.777	22	12	211
61	Honolulu, HI	.776	128	89	29
62	Greeley, CO	.774	66	169	12
63	Miami-Fort Lauderdale-Miami Beach, FL	.772	101	138	11
64	Provo-Orem, UT	.769	13	72	168
65	State College, PA	.768	100	105	49

Table A.2 The Creativity Index for All Metros, 2010 (continued)

Rank	Metro	Creativity Index	Technology Index Rank	Talent Index Rank	Tolerance Index Rank
66	Tallahassee, FL	.766	83	11	162
67	Colorado Springs, CO	.765	103	27	128
68	Milwaukee-Waukesha-West Allis, WI	.763	62	83	112
69	Lafayette, IN	.762	78	102	81
70	Reno-Sparks, NV	.761	31	210	21
71	Portland-South Portland, ME	.757	53	63	150
72	Cedar Rapids, IA	.757	29	76	161
73	Bremerton-Silverdale, WA	.756	73	110	84
74	Huntsville, AL	.748	15	7	254
75	Syracuse, NY	.745	85	86	108
76	Indianapolis, IN	.744	80	78	120
77	Charlotte-Gastonia-Concord, NC-SC	.736	88	70	130
78	Providence-New Bedford-Fall River, RI-MA	.733	90	117	85
79	Flagstaff, AZ	.732	121	113	58
80	Las Cruces, NM	.727	177	67	53
81	San Luis Obispo-Paso Robles, CA	.727	105	148	46
82	Carson City, NV	.720	175	112	19
83	Eugene-Springfield, OR	.716	120	125	66
84	Lansing-East Lansing, MI	.714	127	50	136
85	Springfield, MA	.703	148	108	68
86	Springfield, IL	.695	138	28	166
87	Binghamton, NY	.693	118	92	125
88	Richmond, VA	.692	99	47	191

Table A.2 The Creativity Index for All Metros, 2010 (continued)

Rank	Metro	Creativity Index	Technology Index Rank	Talent Index Rank	Tolerance Index Rank
89	Blacksburg-Christiansburg-Radford, VA	.689	51	101	187
90	Boise City-Nampa, ID	.685	106	46	192
91	Harrisburg-Carlisle, PA	.683	70	91	185
92	Athens-Clarke County, GA	.680	227	29	94
93	Spokane, WA	.680	94	150	105
94	Anchorage, AK	.679	220	66	64
95	Cleveland-Elyria-Mentor, OH	.676	87	94	173
96	Kennewick-Richland-Pasco, WA	.672	74	38	246
97	Bend, OR	.672	56	197	104
98	Kingston, NY	.667	125	211	28
99	Napa, CA	.665	112	251	2
100	San Antonio, TX	.663	123	123	121
101	Greenville, SC	.659	60	186	126
102	Nashville-Davidson-Murfreesboro, TN	.658	117	103	152
103	Columbia, MO	.657	235	49	89
104	Ames, IA	.656	110	39	225
105	Lawrence, KS	.655	161	151	64
106	Oklahoma City, OK	.645	185	80	122
107	Winston-Salem, NC	.645	123	81	182
108	Omaha-Council Bluffs, NE-IA	.645	71	97	218
109	Jacksonville, FL	.645	134	139	115
110	Vallejo-Fairfield, CA	.644	115	237	36
111	Riverside-San Bernardino-Ontario, CA	.642	110	248	32

Table A.2 The Creativity Index for All Metros, 2010 (continued)

Rank	Metro	Creativity Index	Technology Index Rank	Talent Index Rank	Tolerance Index Rank
112	Grand Rapids-Wyoming, MI	.641	129	152	111
113	Chico, CA	.634	181	183	34
114	Cincinnati-Middletown, OH-KY-IN	.633	79	104	216
115	College Station-Bryan, TX	.633	180	26	195
116	St. Louis, MO-IL	.632	84	69	249
117	Allentown-Bethlehem-Easton, PA-NJ	.627	75	158	174
118	Salem, OR	.626	218	121	69
119	Bloomington, IN	.625	39	131	238
120	Sarasota-Bradenton-Venice, FL	.616	131	244	43
121	Tyler, TX	.602	119	145	170
122	Midland, TX	.601	131	233	70
123	Fort Wayne, IN	.596	126	159	156
124	Cheyenne, WY	.591	191	96	158
125	Idaho Falls, ID	.587	37	135	277
126	Wichita, KS	.587	86	140	224
127	Virginia Beach-Norfolk-Newport News, VA-NC	.586	107	100	244
128	Knoxville, TN	.584	108	126	220
129	Fayetteville-Springdale-Rogers, AR-MO	.582	206	118	132
130	Ogden-Clearfield, UT	.582	109	142	204
131	Las Vegas-Paradise, NV	.580	91	352	15
132	Prescott, AZ	.577	197	189	74
133	Bangor, ME	.575	184	124	155

Table A.2 The Creativity Index for All Metros, 2010 (continued)

Rank	Metro	Creativity Index	Technology Index Rank	Talent Index Rank	Tolerance Index Rank
134	Port St. Lucie-Fort Pierce, FL	.572	93	286	87
135	Bakersfield, CA	.569	144	212	112
136	Kalamazoo-Portage, MI	.566	150	141	181
137	Bellingham, WA	.566	112	277	83
138	Fresno, CA	.565	246	214	14
139	Columbia, SC	.564	198	74	203
140	Barnstable Town, MA	.564	162	219	93
141	Logan, UT-ID	.560	37	180	262
142	Akron, OH	.558	58	127	296
143	Pittsburgh, PA	.557	76	107	300
144	Lincoln, NE	.557	152	115	215
145	New Orleans-Metairie-Kenner, LA	.555	202	130	152
146	Sebastian-Vero Beach, FL	.555	137	297	51
147	Kankakee-Bradley, IL	.554	187	144	154
148	Columbus, IN	.554	157	285	44
149	Asheville, NC	.553	179	218	90
150	Kokomo, IN	.548	133	52	307
151	Medford, OR	.547	192	225	77
152	Flint, MI	.545	130	154	212
153	Dayton, OH	.544	152	58	286
154	Tulsa, OK	.543	136	134	228
155	Louisville, KY-IN	.536	168	167	171
156	Morgantown, WV	.534	92	98	318

Table A.2 The Creativity Index for All Metros, 2010 (continued)

Rank	Metro	Creativity Index	Technology Index Rank	Talent Index Rank	Tolerance Index Rank
157	Charleston-North Charleston, SC	.533	194	137	178
158	Salisbury, MD	.529	265	156	92
159	Niles-Benton Harbor, MI	.529	80	164	266
160	South Bend-Mishawaka, IN-MI	.528	102	133	279
161	Bloomington-Normal, IL	.527	173	208	133
162	Davenport-Moline-Rock Island, IA-IL	.526	140	153	223
163	Memphis, TN-MS-AR	.523	69	200	251
164	Pensacola-Ferry Pass-Brent, FL	.521	228	146	146
165	Birmingham-Hoover, AL	.517	141	75	310
166	Augusta-Richmond County, GA-SC	.517	135	116	275
167	Gainesville, GA	.517	221	207	96
168	Warner Robins, GA	.514	316	36	176
169	Norwich-New London, CT	.512	170	201	160
170	Wilmington, NC	.510	172	174	187
171	Buffalo-Cheektowaga-Tonawanda, NY	.502	154	120	266
172	Fort Walton Beach-Crestview-Destin, FL	.500	257	73	214
173	Salinas, CA	.498	142	298	106
174	Elmira, NY	.491	146	259	148
175	Greensboro-High Point, NC	.490	158	216	179
176	Roanoke, VA	.489	158	206	190
177	Savannah, GA	.487	199	203	157
178	Naples-Marco Island, FL	.484	167	355	40
179	El Paso, TX	.482	245	196	123

Table A.2 The Creativity Index for All Metros, 2010 (continued)

Rank	Metro	Creativity Index	Technology Index Rank	Talent Index Rank	Tolerance Index Rank
180	Lubbock, TX	.477	262	162	143
181	Eau Claire, WI	.476	162	190	216
182	Peoria, IL	.474	122	119	332
183	Myrtle Beach-Conway-North Myrtle Beach, SC	.470	164	361	52
184	Toledo, OH	.469	183	188	207
185	Stockton, CA	.469	247	300	31
186	Deltona-Daytona Beach-Ormond Beach, FL	.466	173	289	118
187	Redding, CA	.461	297	166	124
188	Cape Coral-Fort Myers, FL	.461	230	349	8
189	Rockford, IL	.460	156	213	218
190	Killeen-Temple-Fort Hood, TX	.459	291	129	169
191	Fargo, ND-MN	.458	89	192	309
192	Reading, PA	.457	211	245	135
193	Billings, MT	.452	231	179	184
194	Greenville, NC	.450	189	93	316
195	La Crosse, WI-MN	.450	258	106	233
196	Little Rock-North Little Rock, AR	.444	238	95	272
197	Pocatello, ID	.440	216	194	197
198	Utica-Rome, NY	.440	228	187	194
199	Johnson City, TN	.439	208	143	260
200	Elizabethtown, KY	.438	293	147	172
201	Hinesville-Fort Stewart, GA	.432	248	132	237

Table A.2 The Creativity Index for All Metros, 2010 (continued)

Rank	Metro	Creativity Index	Technology Index Rank	Talent Index Rank	Tolerance Index Rank
202	Madera, CA	.431	310	250	58
203	Decatur, IL	.427	170	224	229
204	Auburn-Opelika, AL	.426	187	184	253
205	Rome, GA	.424	305	128	193
206	Burlington, NC	.422	307	193	129
207	Chattanooga, TN-GA	.421	254	176	200
208	Mount Vernon-Anacortes, WA	.419	234	267	130
209	York-Hanover, PA	.418	97	303	232
210	Pueblo, CO	.417	189	242	201
211	Waterloo-Cedar Falls, IA	.416	158	182	293
212	Green Bay, WI	.415	215	195	227
213	Modesto, CA	.415	296	243	98
214	Holland-Grand Haven, MI	.415	115	274	247
215	Gulfport-Biloxi, MS	.413	203	230	206
216	Fayetteville, NC	.412	250	155	233
217	Lancaster, PA	.410	147	330	164
218	Duluth, MN-WI	.406	214	175	257
219	St. George, UT	.402	193	316	142
220	Springfield, MO	.398	212	161	280
221	Macon, GA	.397	288	136	231
222	Bismarck, ND	.396	205	122	330
223	Muncie, IN	.395	345	114	197
224	Waco, TX	.391	282	178	201

Table A.2 The Creativity Index for All Metros, 2010 (continued)

Rank	Metro	Creativity Index	Technology Index Rank	Talent Index Rank	Tolerance Index Rank
225	Sioux Falls, SD	.389	200	171	293
226	St. Cloud, MN	.389	262	236	164
227	Oshkosh-Neenah, WI	.389	139	257	268
228	Lawton, OK	.388	350	172	144
229	Dover, DE	.386	314	177	176
230	Visalia-Porterville, CA	.386	280	327	60
231	Columbus, GA-AL	.384	287	173	210
232	Lakeland-Winter Haven, FL	.382	304	258	110
233	Ocala, FL	.377	217	359	102
234	Lewiston-Auburn, ME	.376	331	247	100
235	Yakima, WA	.374	346	296	39
236	Appleton, WI	.374	145	301	235
237	Winchester, VA-WV	.369	231	198	255
238	Canton-Massillon, OH	.367	96	271	320
239	Yuba City-Marysville, CA	.362	317	191	186
240	Baton Rouge, LA	.360	244	160	292
241	Erie, PA	.360	204	221	271
242	McAllen-Edinburg-Pharr, TX	.360	318	240	137
243	Goldsboro, NC	.357	361	149	189
244	Spartanburg, SC	.356	207	280	213
245	Missoula, MT	.355	242	264	196
246	Odessa, TX	.351	225	340	139
247	Amarillo, TX	.347	285	215	209

Table A.2 The Creativity Index for All Metros, 2010 (continued)

Rank	Metro	Creativity Index	Technology Index Rank	Talent Index Rank	Tolerance Index Rank
248	Saginaw-Saginaw Township North, MI	.344	143	232	337
249	Topeka, KS	.343	338	71	306
250	Sherman-Denison, TX	.342	290	181	245
251	Jackson, MS	.341	277	79	360
252	Bowling Green, KY	.339	255	199	265
253	Grand Junction, CO	.338	209	272	239
254	Hot Springs, AR	.333	298	222	204
255	Mobile, AL	.331	273	223	230
256	Hagerstown-Martinsburg, MD-WV	.331	279	273	175
257	Lafayette, LA	.329	166	276	288
258	Pittsfield, MA	.329	186	318	225
259	Evansville, IN-KY	.327	114	295	323
260	Vineland-Millville-Bridgeton, NJ	.327	327	314	91
261	Jefferson City, MO	.323	333	62	341
262	Dubuque, IA	.323	150	241	344
263	Abilene, TX	.321	295	185	258
264	Panama City-Lynn Haven, FL	.321	250	338	148
265	Janesville, WI	.319	260	282	197
266	Elkhart-Goshen, IN	.319	243	357	141
267	Hanford-Corcoran, CA	.318	353	307	82
268	Rocky Mount, NC	.315	165	306	274
269	Farmington, NM	.314	231	350	163
270	Kingsport-Bristol, TN-VA	.312	213	234	301

Table A.2 The Creativity Index for All Metros, 2010 (continued)

Rank	Metro	Creativity Index	Technology Index Rank	Talent Index Rank	Tolerance Index Rank
271	Atlantic City, NJ	.311	182	331	236
272	Brownsville-Harlingen, TX	.309	311	281	158
273	Corpus Christi, TX	.307	294	279	180
274	Harrisonburg, VA	.307	308	308	138
275	Laredo, TX	.306	341	334	79
276	Wenatchee, WA	.305	318	270	166
277	Montgomery, AL	.303	256	168	334
278	Dalton, GA	.303	335	360	63
279	Scranton-Wilkes-Barre, PA	.298	169	292	302
280	Jackson, MI	.295	277	157	331
281	Longview-Kelso, WA	.291	177	351	242
282	Glens Falls, NY	.284	241	255	280
283	Monroe, MI	.284	154	266	357
284	Coeur d'Alene, ID	.283	210	287	280
285	Battle Creek, MI	.283	302	209	268
286	Shreveport-Bossier City, LA	.283	201	246	333
287	Wausau, WI	.278	261	254	270
288	Texarkana, TX-Texarkana, AR	.272	352	288	151
289	Huntington-Ashland, WV-KY-OH	.271	300	202	291
290	Sheboygan, WI	.271	176	332	285
291	El Centro, CA	.270	337	323	134
292	Florence, SC	.269	273	165	356
293	Charleston, WV	.269	282	204	308

Table A.2 The Creativity Index for All Metros, 2010 (continued)

Rank	Metro	Creativity Index	Technology Index Rank	Talent Index Rank	Tolerance Index Rank
294	Hickory-Morganton-Lenoir, NC	.268	196	348	252
295	Racine, WI	.266	148	320	329
296	Lynchburg, VA	.262	221	231	348
297	San Angelo, TX	.259	321	235	250
298	Grand Forks, ND-MN	.256	268	228	311
299	Yuma, AZ	.255	357	336	117
300	Williamsport, PA	.255	221	339	248
301	Punta Gorda, FL	.254	315	313	183
302	Sioux City, IA-NE-SD	.249	252	342	222
303	Rapid City, SD	.246	240	265	314
304	Alexandria, LA	.242	332	205	287
305	Merced, CA	.241	343	335	146
306	Jackson, TN	.239	253	220	354
307	Johnstown, PA	.237	267	217	345
308	Hattiesburg, MS	.235	324	170	335
309	Fond du Lac, WI	.235	219	291	322
310	Longview, TX	.235	292	299	241
311	Lebanon, PA	.233	224	315	295
312	Parkersburg-Marietta, WV-OH	.231	268	269	297
313	Brunswick, GA	.231	344	284	208
314	Casper, WY	.229	288	290	259
315	Anderson, IN	.229	276	341	221
316	Joplin, MO	.227	235	321	283

Table A.2 The Creativity Index for All Metros, 2010 (continued)

Rank	Metro	Creativity Index	Technology Index Rank	Talent Index Rank	Tolerance Index Rank
317	Mansfield, OH	.226	299	302	240
318	Wichita Falls, TX	.225	328	238	276
319	Beaumont-Port Arthur, TX	.224	266	293	284
320	Jacksonville, NC	.217	237	262	351
321	Youngstown-Warren-Boardman, OH-PA	.216	195	317	340
322	Terre Haute, IN	.213	309	283	263
323	Fairbanks, AK	.212	336	256	264
324	.St. Joseph, MO-KS	.197	225	309	337
325	Houma-Bayou Cane-Thibodaux, LA	.194	258	356	261
326	Tuscaloosa, AL	.191	239	304	336
327	Danville, IL	.189	324	252	303
328	Monroe, LA	.183	285	249	353
329	Sumter, SC	.183	271	319	298
330	Lima, OH	.179	359	229	304
331	Morristown, TN	.176	248	347	299
332	Jonesboro, AR	.172	322	226	351
333	Anderson, SC	.167	280	305	319
334	Springfield, OH	.167	262	326	314
335	Clarksville, TN-KY	.166	303	261	342
336	Cleveland, TN	.166	334	329	243
337	Victoria, TX	.164	351	268	289
338	Lewiston, ID-WA	.163	358	239	312
339	Bay City, MI	.160	275	312	326

Table A.2 The Creativity Index for All Metros, 2010 (continued)

Rank	Metro	Creativity Index	Technology Index Rank	Talent Index Rank	Tolerance Index Rank
340	Cumberland, MD-WV	.158	323	253	339
341	Muskegon-Norton Shores, MI	.156	324	278	313
342	Owensboro, KY	.150	305	294	324
343	Pine Bluff, AR	.137	356	227	355
344	Wheeling, WV-OH	.135	284	310	346
345	Albany, GA	.132	330	263	349
346	Fort Smith, AR-OK	.129	329	344	273
347	Valdosta, GA	.125	349	324	278
348	Anniston-Oxford, AL	.125	301	345	305
349	Great Falls, MT	.119	354	275	328
350	Decatur, AL	.117	268	346	343
351	Ocean City, NJ	.114	347	358	256
352	Sandusky, OH	.104	272	354	347
353	Dothan, AL	.103	355	260	359
354	Gadsden, AL	.103	342	311	320
355	Danville, VA	.100	360	328	290
356	Pascagoula, MS	.096	312	343	327
357	Lake Charles, LA	.086	313	322	358
358	Altoona, PA	.084	320	325	349
359	Michigan City-La Porte, IN	.071	339	353	317
360	Weirton-Steubenville, WV-OH	.070	347	337	325
361	Florence-Muscle Shoals, AL	.048	340	333	361

Source: See pages 401–403 for full detail on sources. Data analysis by Kevin Stolarick.

NOTES

Notes to Preface to The Rise of the Creative Class, Revisited

1. See http://blog.linkedin.com/2011/12/13/buzzwords-redux/.

2. Erick Schonfeld, "The Rise of the 'Creative' Class," *TechCrunch,* December 14, 2011, available online at http://techcrunch.com/2011/12/14/creative-class/.

3. Joseph Stiglitz, "The Book of Jobs," *Vanity Fair,* January 2012.

4. See Kenneth Rogoff and Carmen Reinhart, *This Time Is Different: Eight Centuries of Financial Folly* (Princeton: Princeton University Press, 2009); and my own *The Great Reset: How New Ways of Living and Working Drive Post-Crash Prosperity* (New York: Harper, 2010).

5. See, for example, Ronald Inglehart, "Post-Materialism in an Environment of Insecurity," *American Political Science Review* 75 (4) (December 1981): 880–900.

6. Andrew Whitehead, "Eric Hobsbawm on 2011," BBC World Service News, December 22, 2011, available online at www.bbc.co.uk/news/magazine-16217726.

Notes to Chapter One

1. For a careful empirical comparison of technological change at the turn of the twentieth century versus modern times, see Robert Gordon, "Does the New Economy Measure Up to the Great Inventions of the Past?" Working Paper No. 7833, National Bureau of Economic Research, Cambridge, MA, August 2000. His answer is a resounding no. The great majority of the technological inventions in the National Academy of Engineering's "Greatest Engineering Accomplishments of the 20th Century" occurred prior to 1950. Only two of the top ten occurred after World War II (semiconductor electronics, number five; and computers, number eight), whereas the Internet ranked number thirteen in 2000.

2. Among the most popular works in this vein are: Sinclair Lewis, *Main Street* (New York: Harcourt, Brace, 1920); and *Babbitt* (New York: Harcourt, Brace and World, 1922); William H. Whyte Jr., *The Organization Man* (New York: Simon and Schuster, 1956); David Riesman, *The Lonely Crowd: A Study of the Changing American Character* (New Haven: Yale University Press, 1950); C. Wright Mills, *White Collar: The American Middle Classes* (New York: Oxford University Press, 1951); John Kenneth Galbraith, *The New Industrial State* (New York: Houghton-Mifflin, 1967). Also see Anthony Sampson, *Company Man: The Rise and Fall of Corporate Life* (New York: Times Books, 1995).

3. Dean Keith Simonton, "Creativity: Cognitive, Developmental, Personal, and Social Aspects," *American Psychologist* 55 (2000): 151–158; and his "Big-C Creativity in the Big City," in David Emanuel Andersson, Åke Emanuel Andersson, and Charlotta Mellander, eds. *Handbook of Creative Cities* (Cheltenham, UK: Edward Elgar, 2011), pp. 72–84.

4. There are many statements of the free agent view, but the most notable is Daniel Pink, *Free Agent Nation: How America's New Independent Workers Are Transforming the Way We Live* (New York: Warner Books, 2001).

5. Again there are many statements of this view, but for a contemporary one see Kevin Kelly, *New Rules for the New Economy: Ten Radical Strategies for a Connected World* (New York: Viking, 1998).

6. Fiorina preceded me in speaking to the Annual Meeting of the National Governors Association in Washington, DC, in winter 2000, where she made these remarks.

7. The classic statement here is that of Karl Marx in both *Capital* and *The Communist Manifesto,* among his many other works.

8. Daniel Bell, *The Coming of Post-Industrial Society* (New York: Basic Books, 1973).

Notes to Chapter Two

1. See Paul Romer, "Economic Growth," in *The Fortune Encyclopedia of Economics,* David R. Henderson, ed. (New York: Time Warner Books, 1993), p. 9; "Ideas and Things," *Economist,* September 11, 1993, p. 33; "Beyond the Knowledge Worker," *Worldlink* (January-February 1995), also available at his website. The classic statement is Romer, "Endogenous Technical Change," *Journal of Political Economy* 98 (5) (1990): 71–102.

2. Joseph Schumpeter, *Capitalism, Socialism and Democracy* (New York: Harper and Row, first edition 1942, second [revised] edition 1947, third and final author's revision 1950); quotes are from Harper Torchbooks edition of the latter, 1975, pp. 132–134.

3. Personal interview, summer 2000.

4. See, for example, Arthur Koestler, *The Act of Creation* (London: Hutchinson, 1964); Margaret Boden, *The Creative Mind: Myths and Mechanisms* (New York: Basic Books, 1990); Robert J. Sternberg, ed., *Handbook of Creativity* (New York: Cambridge University Press, 1999); Dean Keith Simonton, *Origins of Genius: Darwinian Perspectives on Creativity* (New York: Oxford University Press, 1999); Carl R. Rogers, "Toward a Theory of Creativity," chap. 19 in his *On Becoming a Person: A Therapist's View of Psychotherapy* (Boston: Houghton Mifflin, 1961); Douglas Hofstader, *Godel, Escher, Bach: An Eternal Golden Braid* (New York: Basic Books, 1979); Silvano Arieti, *Creativity: The Magic Synthesis* (New York: Basic Books, 1976).

5. See Antonio Preti and Paolo Miotto, "The Contribution of Psychiatry to the Study of Creativity: Implications for AI Research," at http://cogprints.org/2026/, p. 2. Also see F. Barron and D. M. Harrington, "Creativity, Intelligence and Personality," *Annual Review of Psychology* 32 (1981): 439–476; D. W. McKinnon, "The Nature and Nurture of Creative Talent," *American Psychologist* 17 (1962): 484–494; M. Dellas and E. L. Gaier, "Identification of Creativity in Individuals," *Psychological Bulletin* 73 (1970): 55–73.

6. See Boden, *The Creative Mind*; Arieti, *Creativity: The Magic Synthesis*; and S. A. Mednick, "The Associative Basis of the Creative Process," *Psychological Review* 69 (1968): 220–232.

7. Boden, *The Creative Mind,* p. 255. Also see Thomas Kuhn, *The Structure of Scientific Revolutions* (Chicago: University of Chicago Press, 1962).

8. Joel Mokyr, *The Lever of Riches: Technological Creativity and Economic Progress* (New York: Oxford University Press, 1990). Schumpeter initially advanced this distinction in his article "The Creative Response in Economic History," *Journal of Economic History* 7 (1947): 149–159.

9. Boden, *The Creative Mind,* p. 245.

10. Ibid., pp. 255–256.

11. Simonton, *Origins of Genius*.

12. As quoted in Boden, *The Creative Mind*, p. 254.

13. Boden, *The Creative Mind*, pp. 254–255.

14. Wesley Cohen and Daniel Levinthal, "Fortune Favors the Prepared Firm," *Management Science* (February 1994): 227–251.

15. Anthony Storr, *Churchill's Black Dog, Kafka's Mice: And Other Phenomena of the Human Mind* (New York: Grove Press, 1988), p. 103.

16. Teresa M. Amabile, *Creativity in Context* (Boulder: Westview Press, 1996), p. 15. Originally published as *The Social Psychology of Creativity*, 1983.

17. Cited in Thomas P. Hughes, *American Genesis: A Century of Invention and Technological Enthusiasm* (New York: Viking, 1989), p. 29.

18. Simonton, *Origins of Genius*, pp. 206–212.

19. Mokyr, *The Lever of Riches*, p. 16; this warning is reprised in Epilogue, p. 301.

20. Paul Romer, "Ideas and Things," *Economist*, September 11, 1993, online version, p. 2.

21. A comprehensive review of the new growth theory is presented in Joseph Cortwright, "New Growth Theory, Technology and Learning: A Practitioner's Guide to Theories for the Knowledge Based Economy," report prepared for the US Economic Development Administration, Washington, DC, 2000.

22. Lawrence Lessig, *The Future of Ideas* (New York: Random House, 2001).

23. Adam Smith, *The Wealth of Nations*, 1776, entire text online at The Adam Smith Institute, www.adamsmith.org.uk. Quote is from book 5, chap. 1, part 3, article II.

24. John Seely Brown and Paul Duguid, *The Social Life of Information* (Boston: Harvard Business School Press, 2000).

25. William H. Whyte Jr., *The Organization Man* (New York: Simon and Schuster, 1956).

26. Jane Jacobs, *The Death and Life of Great American Cities* (New York: Random House, 1961).

27. Interview by James Kunstler, September 6, 2000, Toronto, Canada, for *Metropolis Magazine*, March 2001. Available online at www.kunstler.com/mags_jacobs1.htm.

28. Peter Drucker, *Post-Capitalist Society* (New York: Harper Business, 1993), quote from p. 8; also "Beyond the Information Revolution," *Atlantic Monthly* 284 (4) (October 1999): 47–57; "The Next Society," *Economist*, November 1, 2001 (*Economist Survey*), pp. 1–20. Fritz Machlup is often credited with the term from his 1962 book, *The Production and Distribution of Knowledge in the United States* (Princeton: Princeton University Press, 1962). There are many others who have written on the knowledge economy: see, for example: Ikujiro Nonaka and Hiroetaka Takeuchi, *The Knowledge Creating Company: How Japanese Companies Create the Dynamics of Innovation* (New York: Oxford University Press, 1995); Alan Burton Jones, *Knowledge Capitalism: Business, Work and Learning in the New Economy* (Oxford: Oxford University Press, 1999). Steven Brint provides a comprehensive review of this entire field in his article "Professionals and the Knowledge Economy: Rethinking the Theory of the Postindustrial Society," *Current Sociology* 49 (1) (July 2001): 101–132.

29. "The Creative Economy," *Business Week*, special double issue: *The 21st Century Corporation*, *Business Week Online*, August 28, 2000, pp. 1–5.

30. John Howkins, *The Creative Economy* (New York: Allen Lane, Penguin Press, 2001). There is also an interesting report, "The Creative Economy Initiative," by the New

England Council, June 2000, that uses the term "Creative Economy." But the New England Council report limits its definition of the Creative Economy to artistic and cultural fields.

31. Others had written on the intellectual capital economy; see, for example, Thomas A. Stewart, *Intellectual Capital: The New Wealth of Organizations* (New York: Doubleday/Currency, 1997); and Leif Edvinsson and Michael S. Malone, *Intellectual Capital: Realizing Your Company's True Value by Knowing Its Hidden Brainpower* (New York: Harper-Collins, 1997).

32. There are many studies of the new role of knowledge and intelligence in the factory. See, for example, Shoshana Zuboff, *In the Age of the Smart Machine: The Future of Work and Power* (New York: Perseus Books, 1989); Dorothy Leonard-Barton, *Wellsprings of Knowledge: Building and Sustaining the Sources of Innovation* (Boston: Harvard Business School Press, 1995); James Womack, Daniel Jones, and Daniel Roos, *The Machine That Changed the World* (New York: Rawson/Macmillan, 1990); Michael Dertouzos, Richard Lester, and Robert Solow, *Made in America: Regaining the Productive Edge* (Cambridge: MIT Press, 1989); Richard Lester, *The Productive Edge: How U.S. Industries Are Pointing the Way to a New Era of Economic Growth* (New York: W.W. Norton, 1998).

33. On Japanese transplant factories, see Martin Kenney and Richard Florida, *Beyond Mass Production: The Japanese System and Its Transfer to the United States* (New York: Oxford University Press, 1993). On environmental innovation, see Richard Florida and Derek Davison, "Gaining from Green: Environmental Management Systems Inside and Outside the Factory," *California Management Review* 43 (3) (Spring 2001): 64–84; and Richard Florida, "Lean and Green: The Move to Environmentally-Conscious Manufacturing," *California Management Review* 39 (1) (Fall 1996): 80–105.

34. Field research visit and personal interviews by author.

35. Zuboff, *In the Age of the Smart Machine*; also see Joanne Gordon, "The Hands-on, Logged-on Worker," *Forbes*, October 30, 2000, pp. 136–142.

Notes to Chapter Three

1. See Daniel Bell, *The Coming of Post-Industrial Society* (New York: Basic Books, 1973); Peter Drucker, *The Age of Discontinuity* (New York: HarperCollins, 1969) and *Post-Capitalist Society* (New York: Harper Business, 1995); Fritz Machlup, *The Production and Distribution of Knowledge in the United States* (Princeton: Princeton University Press, 1962); Erik Olin Wright, *Classes* (London: Verso, 1990), *Class Counts* (Cambridge, England: Cambridge University Press, 1996), and *Class Crisis and the State* (London: Verso, paperback reissue, 1996).

2. Robert Reich, *The Work of Nations* (New York: Alfred A. Knopf, 1991).

3. Paul Fussell, *Class: A Guide Through the American Status System* (New York: Summit, 1983).

4. Steven Barley, *The New World of Work* (London: British North American Committee, 1996), p. 7.

5. Steven Brint, "Professionals and the Knowledge Economy: Rethinking the Theory of the Postindustrial Society," *Current Sociology* 49 (1) (July 2001): 101–132.

6. David Brooks, *Bobos in Paradise: The New Upper Class and How They Got There* (New York: Simon and Schuster, 2000).

7. As quoted in Steve Shuklian, "Marx, Dewey, and the Instrumentalist Approach to Political Economy," *Journal of Economic Issues* (September 1995): 781–805.

8. Barley, *The New World of Work*.

9. Edward L. Glaeser, "Review of Richard Florida's The Rise of the Creative Class," *Regional Science and Urban Economics* 35 (5) (2005): 593–596.

10. The correlation is substantial, .77, as per analysis by Charlotta Mellander.

11. Kevin Stolarick and Elizabeth Currid-Halkett, "Creativity and the Crisis: The Impact of Creative Workers on Regional Unemployment," *Cities: The International Journal of Urban Policy and Planning*, forthcoming 2012.

12. Ken Robinson, *The Element* (London: Penguin Books, 2009).

13. Richard Florida, Charlotta Mellander, and Kevin Stolarick, "Inside the Black Box of Regional Development—Human Capital, the Creative Class and Tolerance," *Journal of Economic Geography* 8 (5) (2008): 615–649.

14. Todd Gabe, "The Value of Creativity," in David Emanuel Andersson, Åke Emanuel Andersson, and Charlotta Mellander, eds., *Handbook of Creative Cities* (Cheltenham, UK: Edward Elgar, 2011), pp. 128–145.

15. David McGranahan and Timothy Wojan, "Recasting the Creative Class to Examine Growth Processes in Rural and Urban Counties," *Regional Studies* 41 (2) (2007): 197–216.

16. With the extremely significant caveat that they excluded health, education, and to a certain extent law from their measure, reducing the size of the Creative Class by some 40 percent.

17. Matthew Crawford, *Shop Class as Soulcraft: An Inquiry into the Value of Work* (New York: Penguin, 2009), p. 51.

18. See Kristina Bartsch, "The Employment Projections for 2008–2018," *Monthly Labor Review* (November 2009): 3–10. 2012 projections for "The 30 Occupations with the Fastest Projected Employment Growth 2010–2020" at www.bls.gov/news.release/ecopro.t07.htm.

19. Barbara Ehrenreich, *Nickel and Dimed: On Not Getting By in America* (New York: Henry Holt, 2001, 2011).

20. Service Class workers averaged $30,597 in salary and wages in 2010, 41 percent of Creative Class wages and salaries.

21. See Hanna Rosin, "The End of Men," *Atlantic* (July–August 2010), and online at www.theatlantic.com/magazine/archive/2010/07/the-end-of-men/8135/; and Catherine Rampell, "The Mancession," *New York Times*, Economix Blog, August 10, 2009, and online at http://economix.blogs.nytimes.com/2009/08/10/the-mancession/.

22. See Todd Gabe, Richard Florida, and Charlotta Mellander, "The Creative Class and the Crisis," Martin Prosperity Institute Research Paper, September 2011.

23. Stolarick and Currid-Halkett, "Creativity and the Crisis."

24. Scott Timberg, "The Creative Class Is a Lie," *Salon*, at http://entertainment.salon.com/2011/10/01/creative_class_is_a_lie/?source=newsletter.

25. See Richard Florida, Charlotta Mellander, and Karen King, "The Rise of Women in the Creative Class," University of Toronto, Martin Prosperity Institute Research Report, October 2011, online at www.martinprosperity.org/research-and-publications/publication/women-in-the-creative-class. Also, "The Gender Wage Gap: 2009," Institute for Women's Policy Research, 2009, online at www.iwpr.org/pdf/C350.pdf.

26. The gap is the smallest for Education ($8,700), Arts, Design, Media, Entertainment, and Sports ($9,400), and Life, Physical, and Social Science ($9,800), and the biggest for Management ($23,400), Law ($24,300), and Health Care ($26,600), the latter a sector where 75 percent of the employees are women.

27. See Ronald Inglehart, "Globalization and Postmodern Values," *Washington Quarterly* 23 (1) (Winter 2000): 215–228; *The Silent Revolution: Changing Values and Political Styles in Advanced Industrial Society* (Princeton: Princeton University Press, 1977);

Culture Shift in Advanced Industrial Society (Princeton: Princeton University Press, 1990); *Modernization and Postmodernization: Cultural, Economic and Political Change in Forty-Three Societies* (Princeton: Princeton University Press, 1997); and "Culture and Democracy," in Lawrence Harrison and Samuel Huntington, eds., *Culture Matters: How Values Shape Human Progress* (New York: Basic Books, 2000), pp. 80–97.

28. I discuss this in my book, *The Flight of the Creative Class* (New York: Harper, 2007).

29. See, Charlotta Mellander, Richard Florida, and Jason Rentfrow, "The Creative Class, Post-Industrialism and the Happiness of Nations," *Cambridge Journal of Regions, Economy and Society* (April 2011), and online at http://cjres.oxfordjournals.org/content/early/2011/04/05/cjres.rsr006.abstract.

30. Inglehart, "Globalization and Postmodern Values," p. 225.

31. Inglehart, "Culture and Democracy," p. 84.

Notes to Chapter Four

1. Todd Gabe, "The Value of Creativity," in David Emanuel Andersson, Åke Emanuel Andersson, and Charlotta Mellander, eds., *Handbook of Creative Cities* (Cheltenham, UK: Edward Elgar, 2011), pp. 128–145.

2. Noreen Malone, "The Kids Are Actually Sort of All Right," *New York,* October 16, 2011.

3. William C. Taylor, "Eric Raymond on Work," *Fast Company* (November 1999), p. 200. Also see Eric Raymond, *The Cathedral and the Bazaar: Musings on Linux and Open Source by an Accidental Revolutionary* (Sebastopol, CA: O'Reilly and Associates, 1999).

4. Peter Drucker, "Beyond the Information Revolution," *Atlantic Monthly* 284, October 4, 1999, pp. 47–57, quote from p. 57.

5. *Information Week,* Annual Salary Survey, 2000 and 2001.

6. Personal interview by author, summer 2000.

7. Personal interview by author, winter 2000.

8. Personal interview by author, spring 2000.

9. See Richard Lloyd, *Neo-Bohemia: Art and Commerce in the Postindustrial City* (New York: Routledge, 2006).

10. Laurie Levesque, "Creating New Roles: Understanding Employee Behavior in High Tech Start-Ups," Academy of Management, Washington, DC, August 2001; and "A Qualitative Study of Organizational Roles in High Tech Start-Up Firms," Academy of Management, Toronto, 2000.

11. See Robert Merton, "Priorities in Scientific Discovery: A Chapter in the Sociology of Science," *American Sociological Review* 22 (6) (1957): 635–659; and *The Sociology of Science* (Chicago: University of Chicago Press, 1973).

12. See Partha Dasgupta and Paul David, "Information Disclosure and the Economics of Science and Technology," in G. Feiwel, ed., *Arrow and the Ascent of Modern Economic Theory* (New York: New York University Press, 1987); and "Toward a New Economics of Science," *Research Policy* 23 (3) (May 1994): 487–521. Also see Paula Stephan, "The Economics of Science," *Journal of Economic Literature* 34 (1996): 1199–1235.

13. Scott Stern, "Do Scientists Pay to Be Scientists?" *Management Science* 50 (6) (June 2004): 835–853.

14. Raymond, *The Cathedral and the Bazaar.*

15. Mihaly Csikszentmihalyi, *Flow: The Psychology of Optimal Experience* (New York: Harper, 1990).

16. Nick Paumgarten, "There and Back Again," *New Yorker,* April 16, 2007.

17. Tom Rath and Jim Harter, *Wellbeing: The Five Essential Elements* (Washington, DC: Gallup, 2010).

18. Published results of *Information Week* salary survey for insurance professionals can be found here: www.4shared.com/get/i685EGSa/Information_Week_2010_Salary_S.html.

19. Robert Fogel, *The Fourth Great Awakening and the Future of Egalitarianism* (Chicago: University of Chicago Press, 2000).

Notes to Chapter Five

1. Personal interviews and communication by author, 2000–2001.

2. Richard Florida and Martin Kenney, *The Breakthrough Illusion* (New York: Basic Books, 1990).

3. US Department of Labor, Bureau of Labor Statistics, *Employee Tenure 2010*, September 14, 2010, available online at www.bls.gov/news.release/tenure.nr0.htm.

4. "The End of the Job," *Fortune* (cover story), September 19, 1994.

5. Alan Burton-Jones, *Knowledge Capitalism: Business, Work and Learning in the New Economy* (Oxford: Oxford University Press, 1999), p. 48.

6. Daniel Pink, *Free Agent Nation: How America's New Independent Workers Are Transforming the Way We Live* (New York: Warner Books, 2001).

7. Sara Horowitz, "The Freelance Surge Is the Industrial Revolution of Our Time," *Atlantic Online,* September 1, 2001, at www.theatlantic.com/business/archive/2011/09/the-freelance-surge-is-the-industrial-revolution-of-our-time/244229/.

8. Mickey Butts, "Let Freedom Ring," review of Dan Pink's *Free Agent Nation: The Industry Standard,* April 30, 2001, p. 77.

9. See Helen Jarvis and Andy C. Pratt, "Bringing It All Back Home: The Extensification and 'Overflowing' of Work: The Case of San Francisco's New Media Households," *Geoforum* 37: 331–339.

10. Ross Perlin, *Intern Nation: How to Earn Nothing and Learn Little in the New Economy* (London: Verso, 2011).

11. William H. Whyte Jr., *The Organization Man* (New York: Simon and Schuster, 1956).

12. Denise Rousseau, "The Idiosyncratic Deal: Flexibility Versus Fairness?" *Organizational Dynamics* 29 (4) (Spring 2001): 260–273; "The Boundaryless Human Resource Function: Building Agency and Community in the New Economic Era," *Organizational Dynamics* 27 (4) (Spring 1999): 6–18; and *Idiosyncratic Employment Arrangements: When Workers Bargain for Themselves* (Armonk, NY: W. E. Sharpe, 2002).

13. Rosemary Batt, Susan Christopherson, Ned Rightor, and Danielle Van Jaarsveld, *Net Working: Work Patterns and Workforce Policies for the New Media Industry* (Washington, DC: Economic Policy Institute, 2001).

14. Jeffrey Pfeffer, as cited in a review of Pink's book, "Not Holding a Job Is the New Work System," *New York Times,* May 27, 2001. Also see Pfeffer, "Fighting the War for Talent Is Hazardous to Your Organization's Health," *Organizational Dynamics* 29 (4) (Spring 2001): 248–259.

15. Jeremy Rifkin, *The End of Work: The Decline of the Global Labor Force and the Dawn of the Post-Market Era* (New York: Putnam, 1995); Stanley Aronowitz and Wil DeFazio, *The Jobless Future: Sci-Tech and the Dogma of Work* (Minneapolis: University of Minnesota Press, 1994). *The Jobless Future* was updated and reissued by the University of Minnesota Press in 2010.

16. Jill Andresky Fraser, *White-Collar Sweatshop: The Deterioration of Work and Its Rewards in Corporate America* (New York: W. W. Norton, 2001).

17. Richard Sennett, *The Corrosion of Character: The Personal Consequences of Work in the New Capitalism* (New York: W. W. Norton, 1998).

18. Gideon Kunda, Stephen R. Barley, and James A. Evans, "Why Do Contractors Contract? The Experience of Highly Skilled Technical Professionals in a Contingent Labor Market," *Industrial and Labor Relations Review*, 2001.

19. Stephen Barley, *The New World of Work* (London: British North American Committee, 1996). Lawrence Friedman argues that virtually all major economic and social institutions are moving to a horizontal structure; see his *The Horizontal Society* (New Haven: Yale University Press, 1999).

20. Joanne Ciulla, *The Working Life: The Promise and Betrayal of Modern Work* (New York: Times Books, 2000), p. 230.

21. Batt et al., *Net Working*.

22. Job Satisfaction Survey, conducted by Lucent Technologies, February 2001, on p. 262 "network professionals," at www.lucentservices.com/knowledge/surveys/01jobs/.

23. Barbara Ehrenreich, *Bait and Switch: The (Futile) Pursuit of the American Dream* (New York: Holt, 2005).

24. Sara Horowitz, *Atlantic Online*, September 1, 2001, "The Freelance Surge Is the Industrial Revolution of Our Time," at www.theatlantic.com/business/archive/2011/09/the-freelance-surge-is-the-industrial-revolution-of-our-time/244229/.

Notes to Chapter Six

1. "Geek Chic," *Wall Street Journal*, September 7, 2000.

2. See, for example, Scott Omellanuk, "Survival Strategies for the Casual Office," *Wall Street Journal*, June 23, 2000.

3. Stephanie Armour, "Companies Rethink Casual Clothes," *USA Today*, June 27, 2000.

4. Personal communication, winter 2001.

5. These figures are drawn from Lonnie Golden, "Flexible Work Schedules: What Are We Trading Off to Get Them?" *Monthly Labor Review* (March 2001): 50–67.

6. Terrence McMenamin, "A Time to Work: Recent Trends in Shift Work and Flexible Schedules," *Monthly Labor Review* (December 2007): 3–15, at www.bls.gov/opub/mlr/2007/12/art1full.pdf.

7. See Phillip Rones, Randy Ilg, and Jennifer Gardner, "Trends in Hours of Work Since the Mid-1970s," *Monthly Labor Review* (April 1997): 3–14.

8. Allison Arieff, "It's Not About the Furniture: Cubicles, Continued," *New York Times*, Opinionator Blog, August 22, 2011, at http://opinionator.blogs.nytimes.com/2011/08/22/its-not-about-the-furniture-cubicles-continued/.

9. Deborah Schoeneman, "Can Google Come Out to Play?" *New York Times*, December 31, 2006.

10. See Jane Jacobs, *The Death and Life of Great American Cities* (New York: Random House, 1961); quote is from the Modern Library Edition, p. 245.

11. Thomas Allen, *Managing the Flow of Technology* (Cambridge: MIT Press, 1977).

12. See Claudia Deutsch, "New Economy: IBM and Steelcase Lay Out Their Vision of the Office of the Future," *New York Times*, January 14, 2001.

13. See Malcolm Gladwell, "Designs for Working: Why Your Bosses Want to Turn Your Office into Greenwich Village," *New Yorker*, December 8, 2000, pp. 60–70; quotes

are from pp. 62, 64–65. Also see Jeffrey Huang, "Future Space: A New Blueprint for Business Architecture," *Harvard Business Review* (April 2001): 149–157.

14. "John Seely Brown Interview," by Michael Schrage, *Wired,* August 2000. Also see John Seely Brown and Paul Duguid, *The Social Life of Information* (Boston: Harvard Business School Press, 2001).

15. William H. Whyte Jr., *The Organization Man* (New York: Simon and Schuster, 1956), p. 446.

16. See Richard Florida, "Science, Reputation and Organization," Carnegie Mellon University, Pittsburgh, PA, unpublished working paper, January 2000. Scott Stern, "Do Scientists Pay to Be Scientists?" *Management Science* 50 (6) (June 2004): 835–853; Michelle Gittelman and Bruce Kogut, "Does Good Science Lead to Valuable Knowledge? Biotechnology Firms and the Evolutionary Logic of Citation Patterns," *Management Science* 49 (4) (2003): 366–382.

17. Richard Lloyd, *Neo-Bohemia: Art and Commerce in the Postindustrial City* (New York: Routledge, 2006).

18. Arlie Russell Hochschild, *The Time Bind: When Work Becomes Home and Home Becomes Work* (New York: Henry Holt, 2000).

19. Lydia Saad, "American Workers Generally Satisfied, but Indicate Their Jobs Leave Much to Be Desired," *Gallup News Service,* September 3, 1999, at www.gallup.com/poll /releases/pr990903.asp.

20. *The Towers Perrin Talent Report: New Realities in Today's Workplace.* New York: Towers Perrin, 2001.

21. See Peter Drucker, "Management's New Paradigm," *Forbes* 7, October 5, 1998, pp. 152–177.

22. Michelle Conlin, "Job Security, No. Tall Latte, Yes," *Business Week,* April 2, 2001, p. 63.

23. See Rick Levine, Christopher Locke, Doc Searls, and David Weinberger, *The Cluetrain Manifesto: The End of Business as Usual* (Cambridge: Perseus Books, 2000).

24. As quoted in Christine Canabou, "The Sun Sets on the Bohemian Workplace," *Fast Company,* August 2001, at www.fastcompany.com/learning/bookshelf/ross.html, p. 3.

25. Personal interviews by and communication with the author, 1999–2000.

26. Quote from "Danger: Toxic Company," *Fast Company,* November 19, 1998, p. 152; but also see Jeffrey Pfeffer, *The Human Equation: Building Profits by Putting People First* (Boston: Harvard Business School Press, 1998).

27. Teresa Amabile and Steven Kramer, "Do Happier People Work Harder?" *New York Times,* September 3, 2011.

Notes to Chapter Seven

1. The classic statements are E. P. Thompson, "Time, Work-Discipline, and Industrial Capitalism," *Past and Present* 88 (1967); David Landes, *Revolution in Time: Clocks and the Making of the Modern World* (Cambridge: Harvard University Press, 1983); Sebastian De Grazia, *Of Time, Work and Leisure* (New York: Twentieth Century Fund, 1962). Also see Stephen Jay Gould, *Time's Arrow, Time's Cycle: Myth and Metaphor in the Discovery of Geological Time* (Cambridge: Harvard University Press, 1987); Stephen Hawking, *A Brief History of Time: From the Big Bang to Black Holes* (New York: Bantam Books, 1988); Robert Levine, *A Geography of Time* (New York: Basic Books, 1997); J. David Lewis and Andrew Wiegert, "The Structure and Meanings of Social Time," *Social Forces* 60 (2) (De-

cember 1981); Frank Dubinskas, ed., *Making Time: Ethnographies of High-Tech Organizations* (Philadelphia: Temple University Press, 1988). Joanne Ciulla, *The Working Life: The Promise and Betrayal of Modern Work* (New York: Times Books, 2000), provides a very good overview of these concepts.

2. John Robinson and Geoffrey Godbey, *Time for Life: The Surprising Ways Americans Use Their Time,* 2nd ed. (University Park: Pennsylvania State University Press), 1997.

3. Ibid., chap. 16, "Perceptions of Time Pressure," pp. 229–240.

4. Ibid., p. xvi.

5. July 20, 2011, "In US, 3 in 10 Working Adults Are Strapped for Time," at www .gallup.com/poll/148583/Working-Adults-Strapped-Time.aspx?utm_source=alert &utm_medium=email&utm_campaign=syndication&utm_content=morelink&utm_term =Wellbeing.

6. Paul Romer, "Time: It Really Is Money," *Information Week,* September 11, 2001; found at www.informationweek.com/803/romer.htm, May 2001. The classic economic perspective on time is Gary Becker, "A Theory of the Allocation of Time," *Economic Journal* (75) (1965): 493–517. Also see Stephan Linder, *The Harried Leisure Class* (New York: Columbia University Press, 1970).

7. US Census Bureau, "Median Age at First Marriage, 1890–2010," at www.infoplease .com/ipa/A0005061.html.

8. "Barely Half of US Adults Are Married—a Record Trend," Pew Research Center, Social and Demographic Trends, December 12, 2011, www.pewsocialtrends.org/files /2011/12/marriage-decline-final.pdf.

9. Robinson and Godbey, *Time for Life,* p. 44.

Notes to Chapter Eight

1. Janelle Brown, "A Poster Child for Internet Idiocy," Salon.com, August 1, 2001, at www.salon.com/tech/feature/2000/08/01/dotcomguy/print.html.

2. Joseph Pine III and James H. Gilmore, *The Experience Economy: Work Is Theatre and Every Business a Stage* (Boston: Harvard Business School Press, 1999), pp. 2, 11.

3. Carl Rogers, "Toward a Theory of Creativity," in *On Becoming a Person: A Therapist's View of Psychotherapy* (Boston: Houghton Mifflin, 1961), pp. 352–354.

4. Andy Sheehan, *Chasing the Hawk* (New York: Delacorte, 2001).

5. Cited in Joan Raymond, "Happy Trails: America's Affinity for the Great Outdoors," *American Demographics* (August 2000): 1–4.

6. US Bureau of Economic Analysis, National Income and Product Accounts, at www.bea.gov/national/nipaweb/TableView.asp?SelectedTable=74&Freq=Year&FirstYear =2009&LastYear=2010.

7. Bear Stearns, *America at Leisure,* p. 33; 2009 statistic from IHRSA Press Release, at www.prnewswire.com/news-releases/us-health-club-industry-records-solid-performance -in-2009–89599167.html.

8. Kris Hudson, "Gyms Working Out for Landlords," *Wall Street Journal,* September 7, 2011.

9. John Robinson and Geoffrey Godbey, *Time for Life: The Surprising Ways Americans Use Time,* 2nd ed. (University Park: Pennsylvania State University Press, 1999).

10. *The Lifestyle Market Analyst* is compiled by Equifax and based on the responses to 15.3 million consumer-information questionnaires that are weighted and stratified, based on demographic information from the US Census and Claritas. It rates activities for various

demographic and income groups, as well as geographic regions, based on a Lifestyle Index: an index value of 100 is the national average, thus an index value over 100 exceeds the national average, whereas a value less than 100 is below the national average.

11. Bureau of Labor Statistics, Spotlight on Statistics: Sports and Exercise, May 2008, at www.bls.gov/spotlight/2008/sports/.

12. Personal interviews by author, winter 2000.

13. Personal interview by author, spring 2000.

14. Paul Fussell, *Class: A Guide Through the American Status System* (New York: Summit, 1983, p. 115).

15. The American Fitness Index was developed by the American College of Sports Medicine to gauge the relative fitness of America's fifty largest metros, based on data from the US Census, US Centers for Disease Control and Prevention's Behavioral Risk Factor Surveillance System (BRFSS), and The Trust for Public Land City Park Facts, among other sources. The AFI takes both personal health indicators (statistics on specific diseases, obesity, smoking levels, etc.) and community and environmental factors (health care access, community resources that promote fitness, etc.) into account. "The American Fitness Index, 2011," at www.americanfitnessindex.org/docs/reports/2011_afi_report _final.pdf.

16. Mark Banks, "Fit and Working Again? The Instrumental Leisure of the Creative Class," *Journal of Environment and Planning* (2009), p. 668–681. Also see Richard Lloyd, *Neo-Bohemia: Art and Commerce in the Postindustrial City* (New York: Routledge, 2006).

17. Shirley S. Wang, "Coffee Break? Walk in the Park? Why Unwinding Is Hard," *Wall Street Journal,* August 31, 2011.

18. David Byrne, *Bicycle Diaries* (New York: Viking, 2009), p. 2.

19. There is a large literature on street scenes, but see, for example, Nicholas Fyfe, ed., *Images of the Street: Planning, Identity and Control in Public Space* (New York: Routledge, 1998); Tracy Skelton and Gil Valentine, eds., *Cool Spaces: Geographies of Youth Cultures* (New York: Routledge, 1998). Also see Janine Lopiano-Misdom and Joanne De Luca, *Street Trends: How Today's Alternative Youth Cultures Are Creating Tomorrow's Mainstream Markets* (New York: HarperBusiness, 1997).

20. Ben Malbon, *Clubbing: Dancing, Ecstasy, Vitality (Critical Geographies)* (New York: Routledge, 1999), p. 174.

21. Joseph Yi and Daniel Silver, "God, Yoga and Karate: Local Amenities and Pathways to Diversity," University of Toronto, Rotman School of Management, *Martin Prosperity Institute Working Paper Series,* 2011. Available at: http://research.martinprosperity.org /2012/01/god-yoga-and-karate/.

22. See Thomas Frank, *One Market Under God: Extreme Capitalism, Market Populism, and the End of Economic Development* (New York: Doubleday, 2001); and *The Conquest of Cool: Business Culture, Counterculture, and the Rise of Hip Consumerism* (Chicago: University of Chicago Press, 1997).

23. Malbon, *Clubbing,* p. 55.

24. Kara Swisher, "How Kitchen Fixes Can Add Up Fast," *Wall Street Journal,* August 7, 2001.

Notes to Chapter Nine

1. Max Weber, *The Protestant Ethic and the Spirit of Capitalism* (London: Routledge, 1992 [orig. 1921]).

2. See, for instance, Romans 13: "Let every person be subject to the governing authorities; for there is no authority except from God, and those authorities that exist have been instituted by God," etc.; or Titus 2 and 3, in which slaves must give their masters "satisfaction in every respect" and "show complete and perfect fidelity," while all are "subject to rulers" and "ready for every good work." Quotes from the Holy Bible, New Revised Standard Version (Nashville: Thomas Nelson, 1990), New Testament, pp. 162, 214–215.

3. Cesar Graña, *Bohemian Versus Bourgeois* (New York: Basic Books, 1964), also expanded and reissued as *Modernity and Its Discontents: French Society and the French Man of Letters in the Nineteenth Century* (New York: Harper Torchbooks, 1967).

4. Georg Lukács, *History and Class Consciousness,* trans. Rodney Livingstone (Cambridge: MIT Press, 1971); Antonio Gramsci, *Prison Notebooks: Selections,* ed. and trans. Quintin Hoare (New York: Geoffrey N. Smith International Publishers Company, 1971).

5. Graña, *Modernity and Its Discontents,* p. 169.

6. Graña, of course, has Paris covered. On Greenwich Village, see Carolyn Ware's classic study, *Greenwich Village, 1920–1930* (Berkeley: University of California Press, 1963 [orig. 1935]).

7. Graña, *Modernity and Its Discontents,* p. 208.

8. Daniel Bell, *The Coming of Post-Industrial Society* (New York: Basic Books, 1973).

9. Ibid., p. 13.

10. The classic source work on narcissism in our society remains Christopher Lasch, *The Culture of Narcissism: American Life in an Age of Diminishing Expectations* (New York: W. W. Norton, 1979).

11. Bell, *The Cultural Contradictions of Capitalism* (New York: Basic Books, 1976), pp. xxiv–xxv. Italics in the original.

12. Ibid., pp. 21–22.

13. David Brooks, *Bobos in Paradise: The New Upper Class and How They Got There* (New York: Simon and Schuster, 2001).

14. Quote is from the dust jacket of *Bobos in Paradise.*

15. David Brooks, "The Organization Kid," *Atlantic* 287 (4) (April 2001): 40–54.

16. Ibid., p. 54.

17. For a full-scale conservative appraisal of the sixties, see Roger Kimball, *The Long March: How the Culture Revolution Changed America* (San Francisco: Encounter Books, 2000).

18. There is a huge literature on subcultures; see, for instance, Dick Hebidge, *Subculture: The Meaning of Style* (London: Methuen, 1979); Ken Gelder and Sarah Thornton, eds., *The Subcultures Reader* (London: Routledge, 1997).

19. Thomas Frank, *One Market Under God: Extreme Capitalism, Market Populism, and the End of Economic Development* (New York: Doubleday, 2001); and *The Conquest of Cool: Business Culture, Counterculture, and the Rise of Hip Consumerism* (Chicago: University of Chicago Press, 1997). Also see Kalle Lasn, *Culture Jam: The Uncooling of America* (New York: Eagle Brook/William and Morrow, 1999).

20. See Greil Marcus, *Mystery Train: Images of America in Rock 'n' Roll Music* (New York: Penguin, 1975); *Lipstick Traces; A Secret History of the Twentieth Century* (Cambridge: Harvard University Press, 1989); and *Double Trouble: Bill Clinton and Elvis Presley in a Land of No Alternatives* (New York: Henry Holt, 2000).

21. John Seabrook, *Nobrow: The Culture of Marketing, the Marketing of Culture* (New York: Alfred Knopf, 2000).

22. On the Homebrew Club, see Paul Freiberger and Michael Swaine, *Fire in the Valley: The Making of the Personal Computer* (Berkeley: Osborne/McGraw Hill, 1984). Also see

John Markoff, "A Strange Brew's Buzz Lingers in Silicon Valley," *New York Times,* March 26, 2000.

23. Personal interview by author and Martin Kenney, March 1987.

24. See Kevin Gray, "Paul Allen: Revenge of the Nerd," *Details* (October 2000): 256–263; Sam Howe Verhovek, "He's Turning Seattle into His Kind of Town," *New York Times* (online version), May 17, 2000; Neil Strauss, "Making a Museum out of Music," *New York Times,* June 26, 2000.

25. From the Jimi Hendrix song "If 6 Was 9," 1967.

26. See Harvey Blume, "Geek Studies," *Atlantic Unbound,* July 13, 2000, and "Two Geeks on Their Way to Byzantium: An Interview with Richard Powers," *Atlantic Unbound,* June 28, 2000; Scott Stossel, "Soul of the New Economy," *Atlantic Unbound,* June 8, 2000. All available at www.theatlantic.com.

27. Jon Katz, *Geeks: How Two Lost Boys Rode the Internet out of Idaho* (New York: Villard, 2000).

28. Visit and personal interview by author, fall 2001.

Notes to Chapter Ten

1. Adjusted for the costs of living differences, the average salary for an IT worker in Austin was $65,310, compared to $47,173 in San Francisco in 2001 (based on salary data from the Information Week Salary Survey).

2. See Thomas Friedman, *The World Is Flat* (New York: Farrar, Straus and Giroux, 2005). Also see Edward E. Leamer, "A Flat World, a Level Playing Field, a Small World After All or None of the Above? Review of Thomas L. Friedman, *The World Is Flat,*" *Journal of Economic Literature* 45 (1) (2007): 83–126.

3. The original article is Frances Cairncross, "The Death of Distance," *Economist 336* (7934), September 30, 1995. She later published an influential book by the same title, *The Death of Distance* (Boston: Harvard Business School Press, 2001 [first ed., 1997]). Also see her "Conquest of Location," *Economist,* October 7, 1999.

4. Richard Florida, "The World Is Spiky," *Atlantic* (October 2005), and *Who's Your City? How the Creative Economy Is Making Where to Live the Most Important Decision of Your Life* (New York: Basic Books, 2008).

5. "Q&A with Michael Porter," *Business Week,* August 21, 2006, at www.businessweek.com/magazine/content/06_34/b3998460.htm.

6. Some classic statements include: Robert Park, E. Burgess, and R. McKenzie, *The City* (Chicago: University of Chicago Press, 1925); Jane Jacobs, *The Death and Life of Great American Cities* (New York: Random House, 1961), *The Economy of Cities* (New York: Random House, 1969), and *Cities and the Wealth of Nations* (New York: Random House, 1984); Wilbur Thompson, *A Preface to Urban Economics* (Baltimore: The Johns Hopkins University Press, 1965); Edwin Ullman, "Regional Development and the Geography of Concentration," Papers and Proceedings of the Regional Science Association 4 (1958): 179–198.

7. Alfred Marshall, *Principles of Economics* (New York: Cosimo Classics, 2006 [original ed. 1890]).

8. The literature on agglomeration economies is vast, for a recent review see Maryann Feldman, "Location and Innovation: The New Economic Geography of Innovation, Spillovers, and Agglomeration," in Gordon Clark, Meric Gertler, and Maryann Feldman, eds., *The Oxford Handbook of Economic Geography* (New York: Oxford University Press,

2003), pp. 373–394; Adam Jaffe, "Real Effects of Academic Research," *American Economic Review* 79 (5) (1989): 957–970; David Audretsch and Maryann Feldman, "R&D Spillovers and the Geography of Innovation and Production," *American Economic Review* 86 (3) (1996): 630–640; David Audretsch, "Agglomeration and the Location of Innovative Activity," *Oxford Review of Economic Policy* 14 (2) (1998): 18–30.

9. Adam Smith, *The Wealth of Nations* (New York: Bantam, 2003 [first ed., 1776]); David Ricardo, *Principles of Political Economy and Taxation* (New York: Cosimo Classics, 2006 [first ed., 1817]).

10. Jacobs, *The Economy of Cities,* and *Cities and the Wealth of Nations.*

11. As quoted in Bill Steigerwald, "City Views: Urban Studies Legend Jane Jacobs on Gentrification, the New Urbanism, and Her Legacy," *Reason* (June 2001). Retrieved January 9, 2012, from http://reason.com/archives/2001/06/01/city-views/singlepage.

12. Robert Lucas Jr., "On the Mechanics of Economic Development," *Journal of Monetary Economics* 22 (1988): 38–39.

13. Richard Florida and Scott Jackson, "Sonic City: The Evolving Economic Geography of the Music Industry," *Journal of Planning Education and Research* 29 (3) (2010): 310–321; Richard Florida, Charlotta Mellander, and Kevin Stolarick, "From Music Scenes to Music Clusters: The Economic Geography of Music in the U.S., 1970–2000," *Environment and Planning* A 42 (4) (2010): 785–804; Richard Florida, Charlotta Mellander, and Kevin Stolarick, "Geographies of Scope: An Empirical Analysis of Entertainment, 1970–2000," *Journal of Economic Geography* 1 (2011): 1–22.

14. Edward Glaeser, *Triumph of the City* (New York: Penguin 2011).

15. See Robert Barro, "Economic Growth in a Cross Section of Countries," *Quarterly Journal of Economics* 106 (2) (1991): 407–443; and *Determinants of Economic Growth: A Cross-Country Empirical Study* (Cambridge: MIT Press, 1997). See Edward Glaeser, "Are Cities Dying?" *Journal of Economic Perspectives* 12 (1998): 139–160. The human capital literature has grown large; other important contributions include: Glaeser, "The New Economics of Urban and Regional Growth," in Clark, Gertler, and Feldman, eds., *The Oxford Handbook of Economic Geography,* pp. 83–98; James E. Rauch, "Productivity Gains from Geographic Concentrations of Human Capital: Evidence from Cities," *Journal of Urban Economics* 34 (1993): 380–400; Curtis Simon, "Human Capital and Metropolitan Employment Growth," *Journal of Urban Economics* 43 (1998): 223–243; Curtis Simon and Clark Nardinelli, "The Talk of the Town: Human Capital, Information and the Growth of English Cities, 1861–1961," *Explorations in Economic History* 33 (3) (1996): 384–413. A comprehensive review is provided by Vijay K. Mathur, "Human Capital-Based Strategy for Regional Economic Development," *Economic Development Quarterly* 13 (3) (1999): 203–216.

16. Spencer Glendon, "Urban Life Cycles," unpublished working paper, Department of Economics, Harvard University, November 1998.

17. Geoffrey West, Luis Bettencourt, Jose Lobo, Dirk Helbing, and Christian Kuehnert, "Growth, Innovation, Scaling and the Pace of Life in Cities," *Proceedings of the National Academy of Sciences* 104 (17), April 24, 2007, pp. 7301–7306.

18. George Zipf, *Human Behavior and the Principle of Least Effort* (New York: Addison–Wesley, 1949). Later, the Nobel Prize–winner Herbert Simon elaborated on Zipf's early findings; see Herbert Simon, "On a Class of Skew Distribution Functions," *Biometrika* 42 (1955): 425–440.

19. Masahisa Fujita, Paul Krugman, and Anthony J. Venables, *The Spatial Economy: Cities, Regions and International Trade* (Cambridge: MIT Press, 1999), pp. 216–225.

20. Robert Axtell and Richard Florida, "Emergent Cities: A Microeconomic Explanation," Brookings Institution, Washington, DC, April 2001.

21. Åke Andersson, "Creative People Need Creative Cities," in David Emanuel Andersson, Åke Emanuel Andersson, and Charlotta Mellander, eds., *Handbook of Creative Cities* (Cheltenham, UK: Edward Elgar, 2011), pp. 14–55. Also see Peter Hall, *Cities in Civilization* (New York: Pantheon, 1998). Charles Landry, *The Creative City: A Toolkit for Urban Innovators* (London: Earthscan, 2000).

22. See, for example, Peter J. Richerson, Peter J. Boyd, and Robert. L. Bettinger, "Cultural Innovations and Demographic Change," *Human Biology* 81 (2–3) (2009): 211–235; Stephen Shennan, "Evolutionary Demography and the Population History of the European Early Neolithic," *Human Biology* 81 (2–3) (2009): 339–355.

23. Robert Park, E. Burgess, and R. McKenzie, *The City* (Chicago: University of Chicago Press, 1925). Quotes are from p. 40.

24. Carolyn Ware, *Greenwich Village, 1920–1930* (Berkeley: University of California Press, 1963 [orig. 1935]). Quotes are from pp. 5 and 37.

25. Dean Keith Simonton, "Big-C Creativity in the Big City," in Andersson, Andersson, and Mellander, eds., *Handbook of Creative Cities*, pp. 72–84.

Notes to Chapter Eleven

1. The correlations are as follows: Economic output per capita is positively associated with business professionals (.61), technology and science (.56), and artistic occupations (.53), but negatively associated with meds and eds (–.31). Wages are similarly positively associated with professionals (.64), science and technology (.53), and especially artistic occupations (.71), but negatively associated with meds and eds (–.12). The pattern holds as well for income: it is similarly positively associated with professionals (.59), science and technology (.54), and artistic occupations (.53), and negatively with meds and eds (–.28). See Richard Florida, Charlotta Mellander, and Kevin Stolarick, "Inside the Black Box of Regional Development," *Journal of Economic Geography* 8 (2008): 615–649.

2. Todd Gabe and Jason Abel, "Agglomeration of Knowledge," *Urban Studies* 48 (7) (2011): 1353–1371.

3. Todd Gabe, "The Value of Creativity," in David Emanuel Andersson, Åke Emanuel Andersson, and Charlotta Mellander, eds., *Handbook of Creative Cities* (Cheltenham, UK: Edward Elgar, 2011), pp.128–145.

4. Available at www.onetonline.org/.

5. See, for example, Peter Drucker, *Post-Capitalist Society* (New York: HarperCollins, 1993); Daniel Bell, *The Coming of Post-Industrial Society: A Venture in Social Forecasting* (New York: Basic Books, 1973); Richard Herrnstein and Charles Murray, *The Bell Curve: Intelligence and Class Structure in American Life* (New York: Free Press, 1994); Robert Reich, *The Work of Nations: Preparing Ourselves for 21st Century Capitalism* (New York: Alfred A. Knopf, 1992).

6. I summarize this line of research in: "Where the Skills Are," *Atlantic* (October 2011), at www.theatlantic.com/magazine/archive/2011/10/where-the-skills-are/8628/, and "Rise of the Social City," TheAtlanticCities.com, September 15, 2011, at www.the atlanticcities.com/jobs-and-economy/2011/09/rise-social-city/140/. See also Marigee Bacolod, Bernardo Blum, and William Strange, "Skills in the City," *Journal of Urban*

Economics 65 (2009): 136–153; Allen J. Scott, "Human Capital Resources and Requirements Across the Metropolitan Hierarchy'of the USA," *Journal of Economic Geography* 9 (2009): 207–226; Richard Florida, Charlotta Mellander, Kevin Stolarick, Adrienne Ross, "Cities, Skills, and Wages," *Journal of Economic Geography* (May 2011), at http://joeg.oxfordjournals.org/content/early/2011/07/13/jeg.lbr017.short?rss=1&ssource=mfr.

7. The correlation coefficient between Creative Class and Working Class metros was –0.52 in the original edition. It increased to –.59 in 2010.

Notes to Chapter Twelve

1. See Joseph Schumpeter, "The Process of Creative Destruction," chap. 7 in *Capitalism, Socialism and Democracy* (New York: Harper and Brothers, 1942), pp. 81–86. Schumpeter, *The Theory of Economic Development,* trans. R. Opie (Cambridge: Harvard University Press, 1934); Robert Solow, "A Contribution to the Theory of Economic Growth," *Quarterly Journal of Economics* 70 (1956): 65–94.

2. The correlations for the Creative Class are as follows: Tech-Pole (.46), patents per capita (.56), patent growth (.35), and the overall Technology Index (.65); for the Working Class they are: Tech-Pole (–.23), patents per capita (–.26), patent growth (–.22), and the overall Technology Index (–.36).

3. See Richard Florida, "The New Geography of American Innovation," TheAtlantic .com, July 16, 2009, at www.theatlantic.com/national/archive/2009/07/the-new-geography -of-american-innovation/20574/.   .

4. John M. Quigley, "Urban Diversity and Economic Growth," *Journal of Economic Perspectives* 12 (2) (Spring 1998): 127–138.

5. See Jane Jacobs, *The Death and Life of Great American Cities* (New York: Random House, 1961), *The Economy of Cities* (New York: Random House, 1969), and *Cities and the Wealth of Nations* (New York: Random House, 1984). Also see Åke Andersson, "Creativity and Regional Development," *Papers of the Regional Science Association* 56 (1985): 5–20; Pierre Desrochers, "Local Diversity, Human Creativity, and Technological Innovation," *Growth and Change* 32 (2001): 369–394.

6. See Ronald Inglehart, *Culture Shifts in Advanced Industrial Society* (Princeton: Princeton University Press, 1989) and *Modernization and Post-Modernization* (Princeton: Princeton University Press, 1997). Inglehart and Wayne Baker, "Modernization, Cultural Change and the Persistence of Traditional Values," *American Sociological Review* 65 (2000): 19–51. Inglehart and Pippa Norris, *Rising Tide: Gender Equality and Cultural Change Around the World* (New York and Cambridge: Cambridge University Press, 2003). Inglehart and Christian Welzel, *Modernization, Cultural Change and Democracy: The Human Development Sequence* (New York and Cambridge: Cambridge University Press, 2005).

7. Scott Page, *The Difference: How the Power of Diversity Creates Better Groups, Firms, Schools, and Societies* (Princeton: Princeton University Press, 2007).

8. Matthew Hall, Audrey Singer, Gordon F. De Jong, and Deborah Roempke Graefe, "The Geography of Immigrant Skills," Brookings Institution, June 2011.

9. Giovanni Peri, "Immigration and Cities," *Vox.eu,* November 20, 2007, at http://www.voxeu.org/index.php?q=node/734. Also Gianmarco Ottaviano and Giovanni Peri, "The Effects of Immigration on U.S. Wages and Rents: A General Equilibrium Approach," CEPR Discussion Paper No. 6551, 2007; "The Economic Value of Cultural Diversity: Evidence from U.S. Cities," *Journal of Economic Geography* 6 (1) (2006): 9–44; and "Cities and Cultures," *Journal of Urban Economics* 58 (2) (2005): 304–307.

10. Daniel Black, Gary Gates, Seth Sanders, and Lowell Taylor, "Demographics of the Gay and Lesbian Population in the United States: Evidence from Available Systematic Data Sources," *Demography* 37 (2) (May 2000): 139–154.

11. The data measure only individuals in same-sex unmarried partner relationships and do not include those not in such partnerships. In addition, Black et al. note that the 1990 data captured just 35 percent of all gay and lesbian partnerships. See ibid.

12. The Pearson correlation between the 1990 Gay Index and the High-Tech Index was 0.57, and 0.48 using the 2000 Gay Index. Both are significant at the 0.001 level. The Pearson correlation between the 1990 Gay Index and technological growth was 0.17, and .16 with the 2000 Gay Index. Again, both are significant at the 0.001 level.

13. The growth index measures change in high-tech output within metropolitan areas from 1990 to 1998, relative to national change in output during the same period.

14. The correlation between the Gay Index and Creative Class regions was 0.40 in 1990 and 0.27 in 2000 (both significant), whereas the correlation between Working Class centers and the Gay Index was–0.30 in 1990 and–0.26 in 2000.

15. Bill Bishop, "Technology and Tolerance: Austin Hallmarks," *Austin American-Statesman,* June 25, 2000.

16. Terry Clark, "Urban Amenities: Lakes, Opera and Juice Bars: Do They Drive Development?" in *The City as an Entertainment Machine,* vol. 9 of *Research in Urban Policy* (Oxford: Elsevier, 2003), pp. 103–140.

17. Paul Gottlieb, "Amenity-Oriented Firm Location," unpublished doctoral dissertation, Princeton University, The Woodrow Wilson School, January 1994; "Residential Amenities, Firm Location and Economic Development," *Urban Studies* 32 (1995), pp. 1413–1436.

18. Dora Costa and Matthew E. Kahn, "Power Couples: Changes in the Locational Choice of the College Educated, 1940–1990," *Quarterly Journal of Economics* 115 (4) (2000): 1287–1315.

19. Edward L. Glaeser, Jed Kolko, and Albert Saiz, "Consumer City," *Journal of Economic Geography* 1 (2001): 27–50.

20. "The Geography of Cool," *Economist,* April 15, 2000.

21. The correlations for the Bohemian Index are as follows: high-tech industry (0.38), with population growth (0.28) and with employment growth (0.23). All are significant at the 0.001 level.

22. Alone, the Bohemian Index explained nearly 38 percent of the variation in high-tech concentration. Together, the Bohemian Index and the Talent Index account for nearly 60 percent of the high-tech concentration measure.

23. Richard Florida and Charlotta Mellander, "There Goes the Metro: How and Why Artists, Bohemians and Gays Affect Housing Values," *Journal of Economic Geography* 10 (2) (2010): 167–188.

24. Jennifer Roback, "Wages, Rents, and the Quality of Life," *Journal of Political Economy* 90 (6) (1982): 1257–1278.

25. See Glaeser, Kolko, and Saiz, "Consumer City," pp. 27–50.

26. Maya Roney, "Bohemian Today, High Rent Tomorrow," *Business Week,* February 26, 2007, at www.businessweek.com/bwdaily/dnflash/content/feb2007/db20070226 _149427.htm.

27. Florida and Mellander, "There Goes the Metro," pp. 167–188.

28. One question raised by this strong connection between gays and high technology is the extent to which gays and lesbians are overrepresented in the industry. If gays and lesbians make up large fractions of this industry, then it could be that the location of high-

technology firms brings about a larger concentration of gays in a region. To look at this, Gates analyzed 1990 census data to assess the extent to which gays and lesbians are over-represented in some high-technology fields and industries. Gay men were about 1.3 times more likely to be scientists and engineers than the population in general. Lesbians were as likely as the rest of the population to be in these occupations. Gay men and lesbians together were 1.2 times more likely than the population to be scientists and engineers. Although some of the correlation between gays and high technology might result from their overrepresentation in the industry, it seems difficult to explain how their overrepresentation would predict growth. To do so would be to suggest that gays and lesbians are somehow on the average more productive or entrepreneurial than their heterosexual counterparts.

29. The correlation coefficient between CDI and high-tech industry was 0.475. The Spearman rank order correlation between the Milken Tech-Pole and CDI was 0.63.

30. See Meric Gertler, Richard Florida, Gary Gates, and Tara Vinodrai, "Competing on Creativity," Report for the Ontario Ministry of Enterprise, Opportunity and Innovation, November 2002.

31. The correlations for the 2010 Tolerance Index are as follows: Tech-Pole (.48), patents per capital (.31), the Creative Class (.42), income (.45), housing values (.62), and happiness (.36). Conversely, it is negatively associated with the Working Class (−.46).

32. Jason Rentfrow, "The Open City," in David Emanuel Andersson, Åke Emanuel Andersson, and Charlotta Mellander, eds., Handbook of Creative Cities (Cheltenham, UK: Edward Elgar, 2011), pp. 117–127.

33. Openness to experience was positively associated with the Creative Class (.20), human capital (.29), the Bohemian Index (.25), high-tech industry (.31), immigrants (.43), and the Gay Index (.58), and negatively with the Working Class (−.31).

34. Rentfrow found openness to experience to be positively associated with college grads (.29), post-college grads (.32), high-tech industry (.46), average income (.34), the Bohemian Index (.27), percent foreign born (.43), and the Gay Index (.69). When he ran partial correlations controlling for human capital, the correlations to high-tech industry (.36), percent foreign born (.39), and the Gay Index (.65) remained positive and significant.

35. See Robert Cushing, "Creative Capital, Diversity and Urban Growth," unpublished manuscript, Austin, Texas, December 2001. My team and I collaborated a bit with Cushing on subsequent projects in the early 2000s.

36. Steven Malanga, "The Curse of the Creative Class," City Journal (Winter 2004), at www.city-journal.org/html/14_1_the_curse.html.

37. See Richard Florida, "The Great Creative Class Debate," Next American City 5 (July 2004) and Flight of the Creative Class (New York: HarperCollins, 2005).

38. On sun, skills, and sprawl, see Christopher Shea, "Road to Riches," Boston Globe, March 1, 2004. On temperature, see Glaeser, "Revenge of the Rustbelt," New York Times, Economix blog, February 3, 2009, at http://economix.blogs.nytimes.com/2009/02/03/revenge-of-the-rust-belt/. But in a 2007 study he concludes differently noting that "it seems that the growth of the Sunbelt has little to do with the sun." Glaeser and Kristina Tobio, "The Rise of the Sunbelt," NBER Working Paper No. 13071, 2007, at www.nber.org/papers/w13071.pdf.

39. Paul Gottlieb, Growth Without Growth: An Alternative Economic Development Goal for Metropolitan Areas (Washington, DC: Brookings Institution, February 2002), at www.brookings.edu/reports/2002/02useconomics_gottlieb.aspx.

40. Richard Florida, "The Metro Story: Growth Without Growth," TheAtlantic.com, April 5, 2011, at www.theatlantic.com/business/archive/2011/04/the-metro-story-growth-without-growth/73368/, and "The State Story: Growth Without Growth," TheAtlantic .com, April 4, 2011, at www.theatlantic.com/business/archive/2011/04/the-state-story-growth-without-growth/73367/.

41. See Richard Florida, "The Metro-covery and the Limits of Growth Without Growth," TheAtlanticCities.com, September 20, 2011, at www.theatlanticcities.com/jobs-and-economy/2011/09/metro-covery-and-limits-growth-without-growth/168/.

42. David McGranahan and Timothy Wojan, "Recasting the Creative Class to Examine Growth Processes in Rural and Urban Counties," *Regional Studies* 41 (April 2007): 197–216. They used O*NET data to reestimate the Creative Class and came up with a slightly narrower definition, but as they note, it still remains quite highly correlated with my original definition.

43. Gerard Marlet and Clemens van Woerkens, "Skills and Creativity in a Cross-Section of Dutch Cities," Utrecht School of Economics, Tjalling C. Koopmans Research Institute, Discussion Paper Series 04–29, October 2004; published as, "The Dutch Creative Class and How It Fosters Urban Employment Growth," *Urban Studies* 44 (13) (December 2007): 2605–2626.

Notes to Chapter Thirteen

1. Richard Florida, *Flight of the Creative Class* (New York: HarperCollins, 2005); Richard Florida and Irene Tinagli, *Europe in the Creative Age* (London: Demos, 2004), at www.demos.co.uk/publications/creativeeurope.

2. See Richard Florida, Charlotta Mellander, and Kevin Stolarick, "The 2011 Global Creativity Index," University of Toronto, Rotman School of Management, Martin Prosperity Institute, October 2011.

3. See the European Science Foundation project, "Technology, Talent and Tolerance in European Cities: A Comparative Analysis." The project was carried out over a three-year period, 2004–2006, and was coordinated by Björn T. Asheim, Lund University, Sweden, and supervised by Meric Gertler, University of Toronto (and also affiliated with the University of Oslo). The national project leaders were Ron Boschma, Utrecht University, the Netherlands; Phil Cooke, University of Cardiff, Wales; Michael Fritsch, Technical University Freiberg (now affiliated with Friedrich-Schiller University, Jena), Germany; Arne Isaksen, University of Agder, Norway; Mark Lorenzen, Copenhagen Business School, Denmark; and Markku Sotarauta, University of Tampere, Finland. Available online at: www.esf.org/activities/eurocores/running-programmes/ecrp /ecrp-scheme-2001–2004.html. Also, see the special section in *Economic Geography* 85 (4) (October 2009): 355–442. Data for French metros provided by Sébastien Chantelot of ESC Bretagne Brest University.

4. See Daniel Senor and Saul Singer, *Start-Up Nation: The Story of Israel's Economic Miracle* (New York: Twelve, 2009).

5. See Richard Florida and Gary Gates, "Technology and Tolerance," *Brookings Review* 20 (1) (2002): 32–36; Marcus Noland, "Popular Attitudes, Globalization and Risk," *International Finance* 8 (2) (2005): 199–229.

6. The GCI correlations are as follows: GDP per capita (.84), global competitiveness (.79), global entrepreneurship (.81), happiness (.74), and inequality (−.43).

Notes to Chapter Fourteen

1. Robert Putnam, *Bowling Alone: The Collapse and Revival of American Community* (New York: Simon and Schuster, 2000). Also see Putnam, "The Prosperous Community: Social Capital and Public Life," *American Prospect* (Spring 1993): 35–42, and "The Strange Disappearance of Civic America," *American Prospect* (Winter 1996): 34–38.

2. See Mark Granovetter, *Getting a Job: A Study of Contacts and Careers* (Cambridge: Harvard University Press, 1974); "Economic Action and Social Structure: The Problem of Embeddedness," *American Journal of Sociology* 91 (3) (November 1985): 481–510; "The Nature of Economic Relationships," in Richard Swedberg, ed., *Explorations in Economic Sociology* (New York: Russell Sage Foundation, 1993), pp. 3–41; "A Theoretical Agenda for Economic Sociology," in Mauro Guillen, Randall Collins, Paula England, and Marshall Meyer, eds., *New Directions in Sociology* (New York: Russell Sage Foundation, 2002). Also see Peter Marsden and Karen Campbell, "Measuring Tie Strength," *Social Forces* 63 (2) (December 1984): 482–501.

3. See Brian Uzzi, "Social Structure and Competition in Interfirm Networks: The Paradox of Embeddedness," *Administrative Science Quarterly* 42 (1997): 35–67, for an exposition of the ways that social ties affect innovation and risk taking.

4. Their contributions are succinctly outlined in the classic article by Louis Wirth, "Urbanism as a Way of Life," *American Journal of Sociology* 44 (July 1, 1938): 1–24.

5. Walter Benjamin, *The Arcades Project,* trans. Howard Eiland and Kevin McLaughlin (Cambridge: Harvard University Press, 2000).

6. Cesar Graña, *Bohemian and Bourgeois* (New York: Basic Books, 1964), pp. 135–136; also expanded and reissued as *Modernity and Its Discontents: French Society and the French Man of Letters in the Nineteenth Century* (New York: Harper Torchbooks, 1967).

7. Ibid., p. 237.

8. Carol Coletta and Joe Cortright, "The Young and the Restless in a Knowledge Economy," CEOs for Cities, 2005 and 2011 update. Available online at www.ceosforcities.org/work/young_and_the_restless.

9. See Richard Lloyd and Terry Nichols Clark, "The City as an Entertainment Machine," in Kevin Fox Gotham, ed., *Critical Perspectives on Urban Redevelopment: Research in Urban Sociology,* vol. 6 (Oxford: JAI Press/Elsevier, 2001), pp. 357–378.

10. Erica Coslor, "Work Hard, Play Hard: The Role of Nightlife in Creating Dynamic Cities," unpublished paper, Heinz School of Public Policy and Management, Carnegie Mellon University, Pittsburgh, December 2001.

11. Miller McPherson, Lynn Smith-Lovin, and Matthew E. Brashears, "Social Isolation in America: Changes in Core Discussion Networks over Two Decades," *American Sociological Review* 71 (3) (June 2006): 353–375.

12. Ethan Watters, *Urban Tribes: Are Friends the New Family?* (New York: Bloomsbury USA, 2004).

13. Ray Oldenburg, *The Great Good Place: Cafes, Coffee Shops, Bars, Hair Salons and Other Hangouts at the Heart of a Community* (New York: Marlowe and Company, 1989).

14. Richard Florida, "The Fourth Place," *Daily Beast,* July 6, 2010, at www.thedailybeast.com/articles/2010/07/06/starbucks-offers-free-wi-fi-and-the-fourth-place-for-work.html.

15. "The Singles Map," *National Geographic,* February 2007.

16. Personal interview by author, spring 2001.

17. Bonnie Menes Kahn, *Cosmopolitan Culture: The Gilt-Edged Dream of a Tolerant City* (New York: Simon and Schuster, 1987).

18. Personal interview by author, winter 2001.

19. I am indebted to Lenn Kano, a former Carnegie Mellon student for this term.

20. Simon Frith, *Performing Rites: On the Value of Popular Music* (Oxford: Oxford University Press, 1996), p. 273, italics in original.

21. Richard Caves, *Creative Industries: Contracts Between Art and Commerce* (Cambridge: Harvard University Press, 2002). See also Elizabeth Currid, *The Warhol Economy* (Princeton: Princeton University Press, 2007).

22. See Terry Nichols Clark, "Making Culture into Magic: How Can It Bring Tourists and Residents?" *International Review of Public Administration* 12 (January 2007): 13–25. Also see Terry Nichols Clark, Lawrence Rothfield, and Daniel Silver, eds., *Scenes* (Chicago: University of Chicago, 2007). Also see Richard Lloyd and Terry Nichols Clark, "The City as an Entertainment Machine," *Research in Urban Sociology: Critical Perspectives on Urban Redevelopment* 6 (2001): 357–378.

23. Daniel Silver, Terry Nichols Clark, and Christopher Graziul, "Scenes, Innovation, and Urban Development," in David Emanuel Andersson, Åke Emanuel Andersson, and Charlotta Mellander, eds., *Handbook of Creative Cities* (Cheltenham, UK: Edward Elgar, 2011), pp. 229–258.

24. Manuel Castells, *The Power of Identity: The Information Age: Economy, Society, and Culture,* vol. 1 (Oxford: Blackwell Publishers, 1997).

25. Daniel Gilbert, *Stumbling on Happiness* (New York: Knopf, 2006).

26. See the Knight Foundation's "Soul of the Community" study, at http://www .soulofthecommunity.org/.

27. "What Attaches People to Their Communities?" Gallup Organization and Knight Foundation, at www.soulofthecommunity.org/. Also see Richard Florida, Charlotta Mellander, and Kevin Stolarick, "Beautiful Places, The Role of Perceived Aesthetic Beauty in Community Satisfaction," *Regional Studies* 45 (1) (2011): 33–48; and Richard Florida, Charlotta Mellander, and Kevin Stolarick, "Here to Stay: The Effects of Community Satisfaction on the Decision to Stay," *Spatial Economic Analysis* 6 (1) (2011): 5–24.

28. See Daniel Hamermesh, *Beauty Pays: Why Attractive People Are More Successful* (Princeton: Princeton University Press, 2011); also Daniel Hamermesh and Jeff Biddle, "Beauty and the Labor Market," *American Economic Review* 84 (5): 1174–1194.

Notes to Chapter Fifteen

1. Peter Loftus, "Location, Location, Location," *Wall Street Journal,* October 15, 2001.

2. Joseph Cortright and Carol Coletta, *The Young and the Restless in a Knowledge Economy,* CEOsforCities.com, 2005 and 2011 Update. Available online at www.ceosfor cities.org/work/young_and_the_restless.

3. Sam Roberts, "In Surge in Manhattan Toddlers, Rich White Families Lead Way," *New York Times,* March 23, 2007.

4. The Segmentation Company, a division of Yankelovich, "Attracting the Young College-Educated to Cities," CEOs for Cities, May 11, 2006, at www.ceosforcities.org /rethink/research/files/CEOsforCitiesAttractingYoungEducatedPres2006.pdf.

5. Gary Gates, "How Many People Are Lesbian, Gay, Bisexual and Transgender?" UCLA Williams Institute, April 2011, at williamsinstitute.law.ucla.edu/research/census-lgbt -demographics-studies/how-many-people-are-lesbian-gay-bisexual-and-transgender/.

6. See Richard Florida, "The Role of the University: Leveraging Talent, Not Technology," *Issues in Science and Technology* (Summer 1999), at www.issues.org/15.4/florida.htm. Also, Richard Florida, Brian Knudsen, and Kevin Stolarick, "Education in the Creative Economy: Knowledge and Learning in the Age of Innovation," in Daniel Araya, ed., *The University and the Creative Economy* (New York: Peter Lang, 2010), pp. 45–76.

7. See John Siegfried and Andrew Zimbalist, "The Economics of Sports Facilities and Their Communities," *Journal of Economic Perspectives* 14 (3) (Summer 2000): 95–114.

8. Mancur Olson, *The Rise and Decline of Nations: Economic Growth, Stagflation, and Social Rigidities* (New Haven: Yale University Press, 1986); *The Logic of Collective Action: Public Goods and the Theory of Groups* (Cambridge: Harvard University Press, 1971); "Big Bills Left on the Sidewalk: Why Some Nations Are Rich, and Others Poor," *Journal of Economic Perspectives* 10 (2) (1996): 2–24; also see Jonathan Rauch, *Demosclerosis: The Silent Killer of American Government* (New York: Crown Publishing Group, 1994).

9. From his forward to the Australian edition of this book.

10. Paul Graham, "Why Startup Hubs Work," October 2011, at http://paulgraham.com/hubs.html.

11. Steven Malanga, "The Curse of the Creative Class," *City Journal* (Winter 2004).

12. Jamie Peck, "Struggling with the Creative Class," *International Journal of Urban and Regional Research* 29 (4) (December 2005): 740–770.

13. Alec MacGillis, "The Ruse of the Creative Class," *American Prospect* (January 2010), at http://prospect.org/cs/articles?article=the_ruse_of_the_creative_class.

14. Richard Florida, "How the Crash Will Reshape America," *Atlantic* (March 2009), at www.theatlantic.com/magazine/archive/2009/03/how-the-crash-will-reshape-america/7293/.

15. Ryan Avent, "More on the Urban Economy," *Bellows*, January 6, 2010. Available online at www.ryanavent.com/blog/?p=2270.

16. Aaron Renn, Review: The Great Reset by Richard Florida, urbanophile.com, May 9, 2010, at www.urbanophile.com/2010/05/09/review-the-great-reset-by-richard-florida/.

17. MacGillis, "Ruse of the Creative Class."

18. Ryan Avent, "Understanding the Rise and Fall of Urban Economies," *Seeking Alpha*, December 31, 2009, at http://seekingalpha.com/article/180466-understanding-the-rise-and-fall-of-urban-economies.

19. *The State of the Cities 2000* (Washington, DC: US Department of Housing and Urban Development, June 2000).

20. Paul Sommers and Daniel Carlson, "The New Society in Metropolitan Seattle: High Tech Firm Location Decisions Within the Metropolitan Landscape," Brookings Institution, Washington, DC, May 2000.

21. As quoted in Scott Kirsner, "Seattle Reboots Its Future," *Fast Company* (May 2001), p. 44.

22. Rebecca R. Sohmer and Robert E. Lang, "Downtown Rebound," Fannie Mae Foundation and Brookings Institution Center on Urban and Metropolitan Policy Center Note, Washington, DC, May 2001.

23. The Sohmer and Lang data set covers only a small sample of cities, and Gates and I could only match twenty-one cities to our data. We ran the analyses for two measures of downtown growth: percent change in downtown population and change in percent of the population living downtown. The correlation between the CDI and percent downtown population is 0.52 and for change in downtown share is 0.46. The Gay Index is correlated with percent downtown population at 0.48 and change in downtown share at

0.39. The Bohemian Index is correlated with percent downtown at 0.54 and change in downtown share at 0.35. The Milken High-Tech Index is correlated with percent downtown at 0.50 and downtown share at 0.30. All are statistically significant.

24. Willam Frey, "Texas Gains, Suburbs Lose in 2010 Census Preview," Brookings Institution, June 25, 2010, at www.brookings.edu/opinions/2010/0625_population_frey.aspx.

25. Ania Wieckowski, "Back to the City," *Harvard Business Review* 88 (5): 23–25. Retrieved January 9, 2012, from http://hbr.org/2010/05/back-to-the-city/ar/1.

26. Paul Graham, "How to Be Silicon Valley," May 26, 2006, at www.paulgraham.com/siliconvalley.html.

27. Dominic Basulto, "Out of the Valley and Into the Alley," *Washington Post* "Ideas @Innovations," September 21, 2011, at www.washingtonpost.com/blogs/innovations/post/out-of-the-valley-and-into-the-alley/2010/12/20/gIQAxusnjK_blog.html.

28. Emily Laremer, "New York Replaces Beantown as No. 2 Tech Hub," *Crain's New York*, July 20, 2011, at www.crainsnewyork.com/article/20110720/FREE/110729992.

29. Al Barbarino, "Sizing Up That Dream to Surpass Silicon Valley," *Crain's New York Business*, January 1, 2012, available at www.crainsnewyork.com/article/20120101/TECHNOLOGY/301019974.

30. Kyle Alspach, "Behind the City of Boston's US Surge: 25 Notable Deals," *Boston Business Journal*, January 24, 2012, www.bizjournals.com/boston/blog/startups/2012/01/boston-venture-capital-startups-funding.html?ara=twt.

31. Carlo Coletta and Joe Cortright, "The Young and the Restless in a Knowledge Economy," CEOs for Cities, 2001 Update, at www.ceosforcities.org/pagefiles/Young_and_Restless_2011.pdf.

32. Richard Florida, "Why Crime Is Down in America's Cities," TheAtlantic.com, July 2, 2010, at www.theatlantic.com/national/archive/2011/07/why-crime-is-down-in-americas-cities/240781/. Also see Elizabeth Kneebone and Steven Raphael, "City and Suburban Crime Trends in Metropolitan America," Brookings Institution, May 26, 2011, at www.brookings.edu/papers/2011/0526_metropolitan_crime_kneebone_raphael.aspx.

33. David Owen, *Green Metropolis: Why Living Smaller, Living Closer, and Driving Less are the Keys to Sustainability* (New York: Riverhead, 2009).

34. Edward Glaeser, "How Skyscrapers Can Save the City, *Atlantic* (March 2011), at www.theatlantic.com/magazine/archive/2011/03/how-skyscrapers-can-save-the-city/8387/1/.

35. Peter Gordon and Sanford Ikeda, "Does Density Matter?" in David Emanuel Andersson, Åke Emanuel Andersson, and Charlotta Mellander, eds. *Handbook of Creative Cities* (Cheltenham, UK: Edward Elgar, 2011), pp. 435–455.

36. Jane Jacobs, *The Death and Life of Great American Cities* (New York: Random House, 1989), p. 209.

37. Christopher Leinberger, "Footloose and Fancy Free: A Field Survey of Walkable Urban Places in the Top 30 U.S. Metropolitan Areas," The Brookings Institution, December 4, 2007, at www.brookings.edu/papers/2007/1128_walkableurbanism_leinberger.aspx.

38. Joe Cortright, "Walking the Walk: How Walkability Raises Housing Values in U.S. Cities," CEOs for Cities, August 2009, at www.ceosforcities.org/work/walkingthewalk.

39. The correlations based on Walkscore.com's Walkability Index are as follows: Creative Class (.5), Working Class (−.46), human capital (.44), high-tech industry (.57), average income (.66), Bohemian Index (.54), Gay Index (.51), housing prices (.63), and rents (.56).

40. "Americans' Attitudes Toward Walking and Creating Better Walking Communities," Belden, Russonello, and Stewart, Research and Communications, April 2003, at www.transact.org/library/reports_pdfs/pedpoll.pdf.

41. Elizabeth Kneebone and Emily Garr, "The Suburbanization of Poverty: Trends in Metropolitan America, 2000 to 2008," Brookings Institution, January 20, 2010, at www.brookings.edu/papers/2010/0120_poverty_kneebone.aspx.

42. Diana Olick, "Are Bulldozers Now the Best Neighbor?" CNBC.com, May 5, 2009, at www.cnbc.com/id/30580830/Are_Bulldozers_Now_The_Best_Neighbor.

43. David McGranahan and Timothy Wojan, "Recasting the Creative Class to Examine Growth Processes in Rural and Urban Countries, *Regional Studies* 41 (2) (2007): 197–216.

44. Ellen Dunham-Jones and June Williamson, *Retrofitting Suburbia, updated edition: Urban Design Solutions for Redesigning Suburbs* (Hoboken, NJ: Wiley, 2011).

45. "Greyfield Regional Mall Study," PWC Global Strategic Real Estate Group for the Congress of New Urbanism, January 2001, at www.cnu.org/sites/www.cnu.org/files /Greyfield_Feb_01.pdf.

46. Paul Taylor and Rich Morin, "For Nearly Half of Americans, Grass Is Greener Somewhere Else," Pew Research Center, January 29, 2009, at http://pewsocialtrends.org /files/2010/10/Community-Satisfaction.pdf.

47. Bruce Katz and Jennifer Bradley, "A Small-Town or Metro Nation?" October 2, 2008, Brookings Institution, at www.brookings.edu/articles/2008/1008_smalltowns _katz.aspx.

48. Audrey Singer, Susan W. Hardwick, and Caroline B. Brettell, "Twenty-first Century Gateways: Immigrants in Suburban America," Immigration Policy Institute, at www .migrationinformation.org/Feature/print.cfm?ID=680.

49. Richard Florida, Tim Gulden, and Charlotta Mellander, "The Rise of the Mega-Region," *Cambridge Journal of Regions Economy and Society* 1 (3) (2008): 459–476, at http://cjres.oxfordjournals.org/content/1/3/459.abstract.

50. This section draws from personal interviews conducted by the author between 1992 and 2001, particularly ongoing conversations with Mayor Kirk Watson and reporter Bill Bishop of the *Austin American-Statesman*. See Bob Walker's story in the October 2000 issue of *Money Magazine*, pp. 109–114; and the insightful reporting of Bishop and his colleagues: Dylan Rivera and Bill Bishop, "High-Tech Companies Leading the Charge Downtown," *Austin American-Statesman*, March 3, 2000; Bishop, "What Is Austin Becoming?" *Austin American–Statesman*, May 9, 2000; Bishop, "Austin Wants to Be Austin: Austin Doesn't Want to Be Silicon Valley," *Austin American-Statesmen*, February 26, 2000.

51. Kirk Ladendorf and Leah Quinn, "Vignette Seeks New Digs Because It Digs Downtown," *Austin American-Statesman*, August 29, 2000.

52. Available at www.jamesmcmurtry.com/blog.html.

53. My discussion of Ireland draws heavily from conversations with Anita Sands, a former Carnegie Mellon graduate student who is now my colleague in the Software Center. See Anita Sands, "Ireland and the 3Ts: Technology, Talent and Tolerance," unpublished paper, December 2001, Carnegie Mellon, Heinz School of Public Policy and Management, Pittsburgh. Also see "From Backwater to Boomtown: Dublin Is a Magnet for Technology and Young People," *New York Times*, October 31, 2000.

54. Florence Williams, "Dublin: Now Fair and Worldly." *New York Times*, October 12, 2000.

55. Paraphrase of Bono's remarks comes from the evening panel discussion with Enda Kenny, Eamon Gilmore, Bill Clinton, Loretta Brennan Glucksman, Declan Kelly, and

Willie Walsh, at www.rte.ie/news/economicforum/video.html.

56. Leigh Gallagher, "Tony Hsieh's New $350 Million Startup," *Fortune*, January 23, 2012.

57. Venkatesh Rao, "Zappos and the Rise of Corporate Neo-Urbanism," *Forbes*, October 26, 2011, at www.forbes.com/sites/venkateshrao/2011/10/26/zappos-and-the-rise-of -corporate-neo-urbanism/.

58. In March 2011, I was part of a team from the Creative Class Group that met with Hsieh, Zappos management and employees, and Las Vegas government and business people to discuss strategies for urban revitalization. Other leading urbanists and urban designers are also participating in this ambitious project.

59. Chris Briem, "Educational Attainment in the Pittsburgh Regional Workforce," *Pittsburgh Economic Quarterly* (March 2010), at www.ucsur.pitt.edu/files/peq/peq_2010-03.pdf.

60. Howard Fineman, "What Pittsburgh (Don't Laugh) Can Teach Obama," *Newsweek*, June 6, 2009.

61. William Frey, "The New Metro Minority Map: Regional Shifts in Hispanics, Asians, and Blacks from Census 2010," Brookings Institution, August 2011, at www.brookings.edu /papers/2011/0831_census_race_frey.aspx.

62. Bill Toland. "Watch Out Portland, Pittsburgh's Lookin' Hip," *Pittsburgh Post Gazette*, January 15, 2012. www.post-gazette.com/pg/12015/1203716-455.stm.

Notes to Chapter Sixteen

1. Evelyn Nieves, "Many in Silicon Valley Cannot Afford Housing Even at $50,000 a Year," *New York Times*, February 20, 2000. Also see John Ritter, "Priced Out of Silicon Valley," *USA Today*, May 18, 2000; "The California Housing Market: Squeezed Out," *Economist*, July 22, 2000.

2. Nieves, "Many in Silicon Valley."

3. Rebecca Solnit and Susan Schwartzenberg, *Hollow City: The Siege of San Francisco and the Crisis of American Urbanism* (New York: Verso, 2000). On San Francisco's history, also see Richard Walker, "Landscape and City Life: Four Ecologies of Residence in the San Francisco Bay Area," *Ecumene* 2 (1) (1995): 33–64.

4. Alan Berube and Thatcher Tiffany, "The Shape of the Curve: Household Income Distribution in U.S. Cities, 1979–1999," Brookings Institution, August 2004.

5. Richard Florida, "Where the Brains Are," *Atlantic* (October 2006), at www.the atlantic.com/magazine/archive/2006/10/where-the-brains-are/5202/.

6. Christopher Berry and Edward Glaeser, "The Divergence of Human Capital Levels Across Cities," *Papers in Regional Science* 84 (3) (2005): 407–444.

7. Joseph Stiglitz, "Of the 1%, by the 1%, for the 1%," *Vanity Fair* (May 2011), at www .vanityfair.com/society/features/2011/05/top-one-percent-201105?currentPage =all&wpisrc=nl_wonk.

8. Remarks by the president on the economy, at Osawatomie, Kansas, December 6, 2011, available at www.whitehouse.gov/the-press-office/2011/12/06/remarks-president -economy-osawatomie-kansas.

9. The Metro Wage Inequality is based on a statistical technique called the Theil Index.

10. The correlation between average overall wage and the average Creative Class wage across US metros is a whopping .94, an almost perfect relationship. The correlations between the average Creative Class wage and Working and Service Class wages are .6 and .8, respectively.

11. See Bennett Harrison and Barry Bluestone, *The Great U-Turn: Corporate Restructuring and the Polarizing of America* (New York: Basic Books, 1981).

12. See William Julius Wilson, *The Truly Disadvantaged: The Inner City, the Underclass, and Public Policy* (Chicago: University of Chicago Press, 1990).

13. See Bill Bishop, *The Big Sort: Why the Clustering of Like-Minded America Is Tearing Us Apart* (Boston: Houghton-Mifflin, 2008); Dante Chinni and James Gimpel, *Patchwork Nation: The Surprising Truth About the "Real America"* (New York: Gotham, 2010).

14. Nathaniel Baum-Snow and Ronni Pavan, "Inequality and City Size," April 2010, available at www.econ.brown.edu/fac/nathaniel_baum-snow/ineq_citysize.pdf.

15. See Richard Florida, "The Geography of Inequality," TheAtlanticCities.com, 2012; Richard Florida, "What's Behind the Geography of Inequality," TheAtlanticCities.com, 2011; Richard Florida and Charlotta Mellender, "The Inequality of Cities: Difference and Determinants of Wage and Income Inequality Across US Metros," University of Toronto, Martin Prosperity Institute, January 2012.

16. The correlations are as follows: human capital (.61), Creative Class (.68), analytical skills (.44), social skills (.55), high-tech concentration (.74).

17. The correlations are as follows: income (.46), wages (.56), economic output per capita (.48), population size (.48), population density (.38), housing costs as a share of income (.19).

18. The correlations are as follows: human capital (.3), Creative Class (.2), social skills (.24).

19. The correlation between income inequality and unionization is –.3, more than double the correlation between unions and wage inequality.

20. The correlation between income inequality and percent black is .3 percent. In contrast, there is almost no correlation between race and wage inequality.

21. The correlation between poverty and income inequality is .5, one of the highest of our analysis; there is no correlation whatsoever between poverty and wage inequality, by the way.

Notes to Chapter Seventeen

1. Herbert Muschamp, "Art, Architecture, the Year in Review," *New York Times*, December 29, 2002.

2. Robert Nisbet, "The Decline and Fall of Social Class," *Pacific Sociological Review* 2 (1) (Spring 1959): 11–17.

3. Daniel Bell, *The End of Ideology* (New York: Free Press 1960).

4. Paul Kingston, *The Classless Society* (Stanford: Stanford University Press, 2000). For a review of the concept of class, see Annette Lareau and Dalton Conley, *Social Class* (New York: Russell Sage Foundation, 2010).

5. See Antonio Gramsci, *Selections from the Prison Notebooks,* eds. Quintin Hoare and Geoffrey Nowell-Smith (London: International Publishers, 1971), p. 276. Also, David Forgacs, ed., *The Antonio Gramsci Reader: Selected Writings, 1916–1935* (New York: New York University Press, 2000).

6. Andrew Gelman, *Red State, Blue State, Rich State, Poor State: Why Americans Vote the Way They Do* (Princeton: Princeton University Press, 2009).

7. Gallup Organization, "State of the States" poll, at www.gallup.com/poll/125066 /State-States.aspx.

8. On gentrification, see Neil Smith, *The New Urban Frontier: Gentrification and the Revanchist City* (London: Routledge, 1996).

9. See Bill Hayes, "Artists vs. Dotcoms: Fighting San Francisco's Gold Rush," *New York Times,* December 14, 2000. Also see the detailed coverage in the *San Francisco Gate* at www.sfgate.com.

10. Richard Easterlin, "Does Money Buy Happiness?" *Public Interest* 30 (1973): 3–10; Easterlin, "Does Economic Growth Improve the Human Lot? Some Empirical Evidence," in P. A. David and M. W. Reder, eds., *Nations and Households in Economic Growth: Essays in Honor of Moses Abramowitz* (New York: Academic Press, 1974); Easterlin, "Will Raising the Income of All Increase the Happiness of All?" *Journal of Economic Behavior and Organization* 27 (1995): 35–47.

11. US City Well-Being Tracking, Gallup Organization, March 15, 2011, at www .gallup.com/poll/145913/City-Wellbeing-Tracking.aspx.

12. Richard Florida, Charlotta Mellander, and Jason Rentfrow, "The Happiness of Cities," *Regional Studies* (2011), at http://rsa.informaworld.com/srsa/section?content =a940484338&fulltext=713240928.

13. See Richard Florida, "America's Healthiest Metros," TheAtlanticCities.com, January 4, 2010, available at www.theatlanticcities.com/arts-and-lifestyle/2012/01/healthiest -metros/367/; Richard Florida, "Why Some Cities Are Healthier than Others," The AtlanticCities.com, January 5, 2012, available at: www.theatlanticcities.com/arts-and -lifestyle/2012/01/why-some-cities-are-healthier-others/365/. The correlations with happiness are as follows: wages (.41), income (.38), economic output per capita (.38), human capital (.69), Creative Class (.5), Working Class (.4).

14. Centers for Disease Control, Behavioral Risk Factor Surveillance System, at www .cdc.gov/brfss/.

15. The correlation is .55.

16. Richard Florida and Charlotta Mellander, "The Economic Geography of Smoking and Obesity," Martin Prosperity Institute Working Paper, University of Toronto, Rotman School of Management, September 2011, at http://research.martinprosperity.org/2011/09 /smoking-and-obesity/.

17. See again "The American Fitness Index, 2011" at www.americanfitness index.org/docs/reports/2011_afi_report_final.pdf.

18. The correlations for fitness are as follows: Creative Class (.58), Working Class (–.56), human capital (.64), high-tech industry (.42), innovation (.48), warm temperature (–.49), wages (.56), average income (.47), and happiness (.71).

19. Richard Florida, "The Geography of How We Get to Work," TheAtlantic.com, July 13, 2011, at www.theatlantic.com/national/archive/2011/07/the-geography-of-how-we -get-to-work/240258/. Also, Richard Florida, "America's Top Cities for Bike Commuting, Happier Too," TheAtlantic.com, June 22, 2011, at www.theatlantic.com/life/archive /2011/06/americas-top-cities-for-bike-commuting-happier-too/240265/.

20. Deaths from firearms are positively correlated with the Working Class (.55), poverty (.59), and McCain voters (.66), and negatively associated with the Creative Class (–.52), college grads (–.64), immigrants (–.34), and Obama voters (–.66).

21. Gallup press release, September 10, 2011, at www.gallup.com/poll/149504 /residents-mass-connecticut-lead-nation-dentist-visits.aspx. Data collected from Gallup Healthways Well-Being Index, available at www.well-beingindex.com/.

22. Dentist visits were positively correlated with the Creative Class (.31), college grads (.65), Obama voters (.38), and happiness (.57), and negatively associated with the Working Class (–.28), McCain voters (–.42), smoking (–.55), and obesity (–.6).

23. June Thomas, "The American Way of Dentistry," *Slate,* September 29, 2009, at

www.slate.com/articles/life/the_american_way_of_dentistry/2009/09/the_american_way
_of_dentistry_2.htm.

24. Ylajali Hansen, "Spooky Tooth: Dental Health and Social Determinism," March 23, 2011, Generation Bubble, www.generationbubble.com/2011/03/23/spooky-tooth -dental-health-and-social-determinism/.

Notes to Chapter Eighteen

1. Robert L. Smith, "Greater Cleveland Manufacturers Testing New Strategies to Fight Skills Gap," January 28, 2012, at www.cleveland.com/business/index/ssf/2012/01/take_this.

2. See, for example, Scott Page, *The Difference: How the Power of Diversity Creates Better Groups, Firms, Schools and Societies* (Princeton: Princeton University Press, 2007).

3. Available at www.zdnet.com/videos/green/john-doerr-how-obama-can-kick-start -green-innovation/247002.

4. Ken Robinson and Lou Aronica, *The Element: How Finding Your Passion Changes Everything* (New York: Viking, 2009).

5. "Fertile Minds Need Feeding," *Guardian,* February 9, 2009, available at www .guardian.co.uk/education/2009/feb/10/teaching-sats.

6. Raj Chetty, John N. Friedman, and Jonah E. Rockoff, *The Long-Term Impact of Teachers: Teacher Value-Added and Student Outcomes in Adulthood* (Cambridge, MA: National Bureau of Economic Research, NBER Working Paper No. 1769, December 2011). Also, Annie Lowery, "Big Study Links Good Teachers to Lasting Gain," *New York Times,* January 6, 2012, available at www.nytimes.com/2012/01/06/education/big-study -links-good-teachers-to-lasting-gain.html?_r=1&pagewanted=all.

7. See Sara Horowitz, *The Atlantic* (online), September 1, 2001, "The Freelance Surge Is the Industrial Revolution of Our Time," available at www.theatlantic.com/business/ archive/2011/09/the-freelance-surge-is-the-industrial-revolution-of-our-time/244229/.

8. See Alice Rivlin, *Reviving the American Dream: The Economy, the States and the Federal Government* (Washington, DC: Brookings Institution, 1992).

9. As quoted in Amity Shlaes, "America's Obsession with Housing Hobbles Growth," Bloomberg, August 20, 2009.

10. "Report by the Commission on the Measurement of Economic Performance and Social Progress," available at www.stiglitz-sen-fitoussi.fr/documents/rapport_anglais.pdf.

11. Kenneth Rogoff, "Rethinking the Growth Imperative," *Project Syndicate,* January 2, 2012, available at www.project-syndicate.org/commentary/rogoff88/English.

12. Raghu Rajan, "Faultlines Blog," January 2, 2012, available at http://forums.chicago booth.edu/faultlines?entry=45.

13. Andrew Whitehead, "Eric Hobsbawm on 2011: 'It Reminds Me of 1848 . . . ,'" BBC World Service News, December 22, 2011, available at www.bbc.co.uk/news/magazine -16217726.

Notes to Appendix

1. Pascal K. Whelpton, "Occupational Groups in the United States, 1820–1920," *Journal of the American Statistical Association* 21 (155) (September 1926): 335–343, available at www.jstor.org/stable/2277062. Susan B. Carter, "The Labor Force, by Industry: 1800–

1960," in Susan B. Carter, Scott Sigmund Gartner, Michael R. Haines, Alan L. Olmstead, Richard Sutch, and Gavin Wright, eds., *Historical Statistics of the United States, Earliest Times to the Present: Millennial Edition* (New York: Cambridge University Press, 2006), Table Ba814–830. Available online at http://dx.doi.org/10.1017/ISBN-9780511132971 .Ba652–1032. Matthew Sobek, "Major Occupational Groups: All Persons: 1860–1990," in Susan B. Carter, Scott Sigmund Gartner, Michael R. Haines, Alan L. Olmstead, Richard Sutch, and Gavin Wright, eds., *Historical Statistics of the United States, Earliest Times to the Present: Millennial Edition* (New York: Cambridge University Press, 2006), Table Ba1159–1395. Available online at http://hsus.cambridge.org/HSUSWeb/toc/table Toc.do?id=Ba1159–1395. Matthew Sobek, "Major Occupational Groups: All Persons: 1860–1990," in Susan B. Carter, Scott Sigmund Gartner, Michael R. Haines, Alan L. Olmstead, Richard Sutch, and Gavin Wright, eds., *Historical Statistics of the United States, Earliest Times to the Present: Millennial Edition* (New York: Cambridge University Press, 2006), Table Ba1033–1046. Available online at http://hsus.cambridge.org/HSUSWeb/toc /tableToc.do?id=Ba1033–1046.

2. Ross DeVol, "America's High Tech Economy: Growth, Development and Risks for Metropolitan Areas," Milken Institute, July 1999.

3. See Daniel Black, Gary Gates, Seth Sanders, and Lowell Taylor, "Demographics of the Gay and Lesbian Population in the United States: Evidence from Available Systematic Data Sources," *Demography* 37 (2) (May 2000): 139–154.

ACKNOWLEDGMENTS

Creativity is a team effort; both the original edition of this book and this updated one benefit from an incredible team of colleagues and collaborators. The contributions of four people stand out. First and foremost is Kevin Stolarick, who developed much of the data for both editions as my colleague at the University of Toronto's Martin Prosperity Institute (MPI), where we both are based, and earlier at Carnegie Mellon. Charlotta Mellander of the Jönköping International Business School and Martin Prosperity Institute also developed many of the key indicators and collaborated on many of the statistical studies reported here. Bill Frucht, my editor on the original edition of this book, worked closely with me on its core ideas as well as its scope, structure, and presentation. Arthur Goldwag deftly edited my writing for this revised edition.

Jim Levine, my literary agent, encouraged me to undertake this new edition, and John Sherer, publisher of Basic Books, graciously supported it. Patrick Adler, Todd Gabe, Brian Hracs, José Lobo, Jason Rentfrow, and Daniel Silver provided helpful ideas, comments, and/or data. Zara Matheson developed all the maps and assisted with data. Marisol D'Andrea assisted with overall project management, as well as fact-checking and editing. Kim Silk, our data librarian, helped track down sources and assisted with fact-checking, copyediting, and bibliographic details of the manuscript. Taylor Brydges helped with proofing the copyedited draft, checking references, fact-checking, and organizing the art files, tables, and figures. Michelle Hopgood developed several of the figures and graphics.

I have the support of great colleagues and the staff of a fantastic institute, the MPI in the Rotman School of Management at the University of Toronto. I am grateful to them, and also for the generosity of our funders, Joe and Sandy Rotman, the Province of Ontario, and the Royal Bank of Canada. My colleagues at *The Atlantic* help ground my ideas in day-to-day reality, as well as provide a supportive home for my writing. Our team at the Creative Class Group (CCG), especially Reham Alexander and Steven Pedigo, provides an exceptional level of support for my speaking, travel, and writing. I am especially grateful to the many communities, organizations, and individuals that have embraced these ideas and invited me to visit and speak to them over the years. My thinking and ideas benefit immensely from being exposed to and immersed in the real world of economic transformation and community building. I would like to express my personal gratitude to every single person who took time from his or her busy schedule to participate in field research, personal interviews, and focus groups.

Of the many people who contributed to the original edition of this book, several stand out. Gary Gates, Elizabeth Currid-Halkett, and Brian Knudsen made important contributions to the research. Bill Bishop, Don Carter, and Terry Clark provided helpful ideas and comments. Campos Research Associates conducted some of the early focus groups. Bob Evans and the team at *Information Week* provided access to their Salary Survey data. Susan Schulman, my literary agent at the time, worked diligently to find the right editor and publisher. The work for the initial edition of this book was carried out when I was a faculty member at Carnegie Mellon's Heinz School and was supported by grants from the Alfred P. Sloan Foundation, Heinz Endowments, and Richard King Mellon Foundation.

I am fortunate to have a large extended family that is the source of great comfort and joy: my brother, Robert, his wife, Ginny, and my nieces Sophia and Tessa and nephew Luca; the Kozouz clan: Ruth, Reham; my bros Markis and Adiev Alexander; Dean and Ruba Alexander; Leena, Adam, Christian, Melia, and Sophia Hosler; Tarig, Anastasia, Zackary, and Zaiden; Ramiz and Christina; and my DeCicco cousins, too numerous to mention.

This book gave me the greatest gift of all. Not long after it was published, I was invited by then governor Jennifer Granholm to speak to a conference on creative cities in Lansing, Michigan. That was the day I met my wife, Rana. We've been together ever since. She is my partner in everything I do. She helps focus and sharpen my ideas, edits what I write, and sweats the details large and small, so that I can think and write. I cannot thank her enough for everything she does. She's the love of my life and fills every day with fun, passion, and boundless energy.

INDEX